OCEAN

30°E   60°   90°   120°   150°   180°

Svalbard
(NORWAY)

NORWAY
SWEDEN FINLAND

EST.
LATVIA
LITH.

DENMARK

NETH.
BELG. GERMANY POLAND BELARUS

EUROPE UKRAINE

FRANCE SWITZ. ROM. MOLDOVA

ITALY SERBIA BULGARIA
ALB. MACED.
GREECE TURKEY

MALTA
TUNISIA CYPRUS LEB.
ISRAEL SYRIA
JORDAN IRAQ IRAN

RUSSIA

KAZAKHSTAN

ASIA

MONGOLIA

UZBEKISTAN KYRGYZSTAN

GEORGIA
ARM. AZERB.

TURKMENISTAN TAJIKISTAN

AFGHANISTAN

CHINA

NORTH
KOREA

SOUTH
KOREA

JAPAN

KUWAIT

ERIA LIBYA EGYPT

NIGER CHAD

AFRICA SUDAN

NIGERIA CENT. AFRICAN
REPUBLIC

BEN TOGO

CAMEROON

EQ. GUINEA

SAO TOME
& PRINCIPE GABON CONGO

DEMOCRATIC
REPUBLIC OF
THE CONGO

UGANDA KENYA

RWANDA
BURUNDI

TANZANIA

ANGOLA

ZAMBIA

NAMIBIA ZIMBABWE

BOTSWANA

SOUTH AFRICA SWAZILAND
LESOTHO

BAHRAIN
QATAR
SAUDI U.A.E.
ARABIA OMAN

YEMEN

ERITREA
DJIBOUTI

ETHIOPIA

SOMALIA

PAKISTAN

NEPAL BHUTAN

INDIA
BANGLADESH

MYANMAR

THAILAND VIETNAM

CAMBODIA

SRI LANKA

MALDIVES

SEYCHELLES

COMOROS

INDIAN OCEAN

MADAGASCAR
MAURITIUS

LAOS

PHILIPPINES

MALAYSIA

SINGAPORE

BRUNEI

INDONESIA

PACIFIC OCEAN

Northern
Mariana
Islands
(U.S.)

PALAU FEDERATED STATES OF MICRONESIA

MARSHALL
ISLANDS

NAURU KIRIBATI

PAPUA
NEW GUINEA

TIMOR-LESTE

SOLOMON
ISLANDS

TUVALU

VANUATU

FIJI
ISLANDS

New Caledonia
(FR.)

AUSTRALIA

0   2,000 miles
0   2,000 kilometers
SCALE AT THE EQUATOR
Winkel Tripel Projection, Central Meridian 0°

Kerguelen Islands
(FR.)

NEW ZEALAND

ANTARCTICA

SACRED PLACES
of a
LIFETIME

500
of the World's Most Peaceful and Powerful Destinations

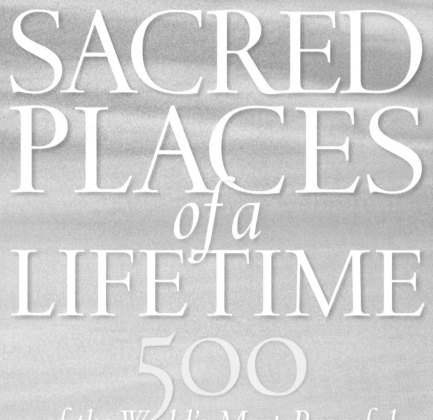

SACRED
PLACES
of a
LIFETIME

500
of the World's Most Peaceful and Powerful Destinations

INTRODUCTION BY KEITH BELLOWS
EDITOR-IN-CHIEF, NATIONAL GEOGRAPHIC TRAVELER MAGAZINE

NATIONAL GEOGRAPHIC
WASHINGTON, D.C.

CONTENTS

Previous pages: Although its exact purpose remains an enigma, prehistoric Stonehenge has long been one of the most important sacred places in the British Isles, closely associated with the celebration of the summer and winter solstices. Opposite: South Koreans carry colorful lanterns as they celebrate the forthcoming birthday of the Buddha in their capital, Seoul.

TRAVEL THAT'S GOOD FOR THE SOUL

I am in southern India, sitting before a wizened man who cannot be younger than 80. He has spent an hour examining my eyes, my feet, my hands, my breath, and, as he says, my spirit. "You need work to balance your body and your mind—and your intentions." This happened six years ago. I didn't understand what he was talking about. I do now. Our world is so busy and full of duty. So full of commitments, to-do lists, traffic jams, lost time, and the endless cycle of balancing home, work, and self. Yet as life's pace has quickened and become more complex, we yearn for something deeper, more transformative, more reflective. Something that slo-o-o-ows us down. Gives us pause. Allows us to collect our thoughts so the body and mind can catch up. Our essential spirit drives us to tap the sacred—the forces, symbols, icons, and beliefs that have touched and guided humankind for centuries. You could say that the goal is inner peace—a talisman against the complexity of modern times.

Sacred Places of a Lifetime brings together the ideas of the mind and the ground beneath your feet. It's a book not about spirituality or religion, but about those places that channel the wisdom of the ages, of far-flung cultures, and unique perspectives. This book explores the new magic—magnetic destinations that have the power to change and move you. To alter your view of the world and your life. To empower you to commune with the forces of nature and the rhythms of the body. Travel is more than a journey of paces and spaces. It should also move your spirit. As I reflect back on my visit to India, I realize my journey has just begun. You can start yours here.

Keith Bellows
Editor-in-Chief, National Geographic Traveler magazine

Opposite: A Shiite woman touches the door leading into the inner sanctuary of the Shrine of Imam Husayn in the Iraqi holy city of Karbala'.

1
SACRED
LANDSCAPES

Since humankind began, we have looked to the landscapes we live in to give us stories about ourselves and our origins, about the deities we worship, the myths we dream about, and the mysteries we cannot explain. The journeys on the following pages take travelers—of any faith or none—to inspiring, electrifying places that not only are wild and glorious in their own right, but which also truly touch the soul. Sail across the waters of Bolivia's Lake Titicaca to the islands that the Aymara, an ancient Inca people, knew as the birthplaces of the sun and the moon. On the rough coast of Northern Ireland's County Antrim, walk the strange basalt columns of the Giant's Causeway to trace the steps of the superhero of Celtic mythology, Finn McCool. In Arizona, visit the billion-year-old rock formations of Sedona—sacred to the Navajo, Apache, Hopi, and other southwestern peoples—which glow like rainbows in the changing light.

The serene surface of Crater Lake, Oregon, surrounded by the rim of a long-dead volcano, is pierced by the cone-shaped Wizard Island. The local Klamath people have held both sacred for the last 10,000 years.

LAKE OF THE WOODS

This vast body of water has been revered since the ancestors of the Ojibwe people settled here about 8,000 years ago.

NORTH AMERICA

According to Ojibwe legend, the traditional song that has been passed down through the generations was originally a gift from the Lake of the Woods. The lake has nourished the local Ojibwe people in so many ways—from its fish, to its islands' blueberries, to its traditional remedies, such as white cedar for coughs and snakeroot for general health—that it has become part of who they are. Its shoreline includes boreal forest, where the moose roams.; other areas have sandy beaches and such colorful fall trees as maple, birch, and willow. Eagles, loons, and pelicans etch the sky; below your boat on this 1,727-square-mile (4,473 square kilometer) lake straddling Minnesota and Canada—are sturgeon, those evolutionary slouches, and oversized muskies. But it's the granite rock faces around the lake that are the main lure, for they have stories to tell: they are the canvas on which the Ojibwe painted pictographs offering teachings and guidance. The Ojibwe put tobacco in the water as a gift to the spirits of both the lake and the pictures. As you haul your boat ashore, the lake will cling to it. Say not "goodbye," for that's too final a word for the Ojibwe. Bid it "*Gigaa-waabamin*—I'll see you again."

When to Go In September, water temperatures start to cool but mosquitoes are less bothersome. It's also the month of the Wild Rice Moon, the Ojibwe's harvest of *manoomin*, the food that grows upon the water.

Planning While there are many Lake of the Woods resorts catering to anglers, a wilderness camping experience is the truest way to enjoy the area's solitude and power. Allow at least four nights, as it takes time to paddle between islands. You will need detailed maps of the area, camping gear, food, a water purifier, a canoe (which can be rented at area outfitters), paddles (including an extra one), and personal flotation devices. Take care not to point your finger at people or islands as the Ojibwe take this gesture as a challenge. As you navigate, suggest the direction with your head and lips instead.

Websites fishingmn.com/lakewcamp.html (entering from Minnesota), www.lakeofthewoods.com (entering from Canada)

HIGHLIGHTS

■ Explore some of the **15,000 islands** in the Lake of the Woods. The Minnesota portion of the lake is virtually all water, while the Canadian side is dotted with numerous small islands and a few sizable ones.

■ On a clear, dark night in any season—though spring and fall are best—stay up to watch for the **aurora borealis**, or what the Ojibwe call "dancing ghosts."

■ Try interpreting the images in the Ojibwe **pictographs**. A cross or plus sign symbolizes a star; an upraised arm represents either a dance or prayer posture; horns indicate an intellectual and spiritual life; wavy lines express communication, generally between spirits.

The unbroken surface of the Lake of the Woods at twilight engenders a feeling of great calm.

The afternoon sun falls across the face of Devils Tower, emphasizing the deep gouges in the rock.

WYOMING

DEVILS TOWER

Rising from the plains of northeastern Wyoming, this otherworldly monolith still acts as a spiritual beacon for Native Americans.

Coming into view at least 10 miles (16 kilometers) away, this magnificent column of igneous rock looks like a scene from *Close Encounters of the Third Kind*. Drawing closer, you realize it actually was. In 1906, Theodore Roosevelt declared Devils Tower America's first national monument. But more than 20 Native American tribes have regarded it as a sacred dwelling place for far longer. They still perform sun dances, vision quests, and worship ceremonies here. The 867-foot (264 meter) pillar has existed for nearly 50 million years—formed by lava that pushed up through the sedimentary rock layers and then became exposed as the stone around it eroded away. More romantically, Crow legend tells how two girls were climbing a rock to escape a bear. To save them, the Great Spirit caused the peak to rise up from the ground. The bear tried to climb up to catch the girls but slipped, and his claws scored the stone, gouging out the rib marks that are visible today. Every year, Devils Tower attracts hundreds of thousands of visitors, lured by its daunting size, timelessness, and beauty. In the morning light, it appears grayish-green. Toward sunset it glows like a candle, changing from gold to orange to pink to rust. Beneath the starry sky, when the coyotes howl, the silhouette of the tower stands eerie, yet comforting.

When to Go May through September. The monument is open 24 hours a day, seven days a week. The visitor center is open early April through late November.

Planning Allow a whole day here. Bring cool clothing and plenty of water. Summer temperatures often exceed 80ºF (27ºC), but the heat can jump to more than 100ºF (38ºC). Take binoculars to watch rock climbers (an activity considered sacrilegious to Native Americans), and look out for bald eagles, prairie falcons, and turkey vultures. The area has many camping and hiking possibilities. For a panoramic view, drive outside the park to Devils Tower golf course and sit on its veranda to see the tower from afar.

Website www.nps.gov

HIGHLIGHTS

■ Hike the 1.3-mile (2 km) **Tower Trail** encircling the base, which takes 45 minutes to an hour. You can see a boulder field, where large rocks have sheered off the face.

■ Spot black-tailed **prairie dogs**. There is a 40-acre (16 hectare) Prairie Dog Town within the park bordered by Devils Tower and Belle Fourche River. These relatives of the squirrel family live in community burrows. You can walk through their "town," but do not feed them.

■ Listen to legends told by a local Native American during one of the **cultural nights** at the visitor center. Call ahead to find out when these events take place.

NORTH AMERICA

ARIZONA

SEDONA

The spiritually minded have long sought the shimmering peaks and towers of Sedona, also known as Red Rock Country, in search of energy fields.

The rock formations glow coral, flamingo pink, tawny gold, dusty violet, and maroon, depending on the time of day. The striking colors of Red Rock Country are due to iron in the sandstone and limestone. Early Native American nomads felt a spiritual tie with these peaks, and especially to Boynton Canyon, which is sacred to the Navajo, Yavapai, Apache, and Hopi. Lying between dry southern Arizona and the mountains of Flagstaff, Sedona has attracted spiritual seekers throughout its history. Who does not feel awe driving out of a spring blizzard on U.S. Highway 89A to meet 1.8 billion years of erosion? At the end of Oak Creek Canyon, a panorama of red buttes, sheer cliffs, and pinnacles opens up like a diorama of the Earth's naked past. The vision reminds you just how potent are the forces of nature—so potent that some claim certain locations, such as Bell Rock, Cathedral Rock, and Airport Mesa, conduct and amplify energy from inside the Earth. Native Americans see these places as portals to the spirit world. The term "vortex" was coined by New Agers for these areas said to be conducive to prayer, meditation, and healing. Discover one of these energy fields and you may sense a welling of emotion, euphoria, and melancholy, followed by a sense of peace and clarity. Is it real? The test is whether you return to Sedona.

When to Go October, when the cottonwoods are golden.

Planning Allow three days. Drive in via Highway 179 and see Bell Rock, or via the scenic highway through Oak Creek Canyon. There are plenty of places to pull over and take photographs. Sedona has a huge variety of accommodations, from campgrounds to country inns and luxury hotels. Activities in the area include hiking, riding, and golf. There is no shortage of shamans, psychics, and spiritual guides offering tarot card and aura readings, and some even claim to be able to cleanse your karma or take you back to a former life. Get referrals for retreats and decide how much you want to spend on spiritual activities before you go. Monday prayer service at the Chapel of the Holy Cross is at 5 p.m.

Websites www.visitsedona.com, www.gatewaytosedona.com, www.sedonaprivateguides.com

NORTH AMERICA

HIGHLIGHTS

■ **Enchantment Resort** and **Mii Amo Spa** in Boynton Canyon are said to lie at a spiritual crossroads. The Yavapai-Apache Indians consider this to be their place of origin. New Agers place an energy vortex outside Mii Amo's backdoor. The resort offers an authentic Native American cultural program.

■ The **Chapel of the Holy Cross**, a 250-ft (76 m) concrete monolith jutting out of a towering red rock wall, looks like something that could beam you up to space. The view alone is transporting—and according to some, the chapel happens to sit on a vortex.

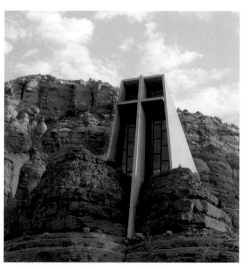

Opposite: Even storm clouds gathering over Cathedral Rock cannot dim the glowing colors of the cliffs, reflected in the waters of Oak Creek. Above left: A New-Age medicine wheel has been laid out for use in rituals and meditation. Above right: The Chapel of the Holy Cross is built into the sandstone formations of Sedona.

SAN FRANCISCO PEAKS

For Native Americans, the gods inhabit this shimmering volcanic chain; for city-dwellers, it presents a cool, benevolent sanctuary.

During a fall dusk, sunbeams kiss the tops of the five San Francisco Peaks in northern Arizona, and the air is thick with gold from the pulsating glow of the aspens. The Navajo have long called this effect *doko'oo'sliid*, or "shining on top," believing the soil came from a previous world and grew into the peaks, their life force. More than 13 Native American tribes see this holy sanctuary, part of the Coconino National Forest, as the dwelling place of their gods. On any given day, tribespeople roam the peaks as they make personal pilgrimages and meditate in front of cherished shrines. Medicine men scour the hills collecting branches, leaves, and berries for salves and ointments. Rising 12,643 feet (3,854 meters) from the expansive Colorado Plateau, Humphreys Peak is the chain's tallest summit and Arizona's highest pinnacle. In order to protect the area as much as possible, no paved road leads to the top. This wilderness is one of the most diverse terrains anywhere, with a series of ecosystems ranging from desert at the base to tundra in the upper elevations. Snow melts into the peaks' Inner Basin aquifer, providing water for the nearby city of Flagstaff and connecting the sacred mountain to the people below.

When to Go You can enjoy the peaks in different ways at different seasons. September, October, and early November are ideal times to photograph fall foliage. The hiking season runs from late June to September. In winter you can ski at the Snowbowl resort, which maintains four lifts.

Planning One day is enough for a hike or drive around the base of the peaks, but you can also camp here, May through September. As the base is 7,500 ft (2,286 m) above sea level, be alert to signs of altitude sickness, such as headaches or nausea. When hiking, be prepared for sudden changes in temperature, and wear layers. It gets windy at the top. Use sunscreen, lip balm, and sturdy hiking boots as most of the trails are steep and rocky. Bring plenty of water, as there are no streams or lakes. The volcanic peaks soak up any rainfall like a sponge.

Website www.fs.fed.us/r3/coconino

HIGHLIGHTS

■ Look out for the rare **San Francisco groundsel**, found nowhere else in the world. Resembling a miniature sunflower, the plant is protected by the U.S. Forest Service.

■ **Indigenous wildlife** includes the rare Mexican spotted owl, black bear, goshawks, deer, elk, prairie dogs, and peregrine falcons.

■ Observe the aspens in all their finery in **fall**. From a distance, the trees seem to form a golden necklace encircling the peaks.

■ The 9-mile (14.5 km) **Humphreys Peak Trail** is a strenuous round-trip. Start early as the climb to the top takes a minimum of three hours. From the summit, you can see the rim of the Grand Canyon.

A sprinkling of snow gives the San Francisco Peaks a magical appearance.

LANDSCAPES

MEGALITHS & MYSTERIES CRADLES OF FAITH MAJESTIC RUINS DAILY DEVOTION SHRINES THE PILGRIM'S WAY CEREMONIES & FESTIVALS IN REMEMBRANCE RETREATS

Big Sur has many fine secluded beaches.

CALIFORNIA

BIG SUR

The craggy coast south of San Francisco has long been a place of contemplation and pilgrimage.

There is something quintessentially Californian about soaking in a hot tub beneath towering coastal redwood trees, reflecting on the state of the universe as waves crash onto the nearby shore—and there is no more appropriate place to do this than at Big Sur. Dominated by sheer mountains that plunge straight into the Pacific, the largely inaccessible shore has long lured hermits and artists, drawn by the region's untamed beauty and moody environment. Author Henry Miller called Big Sur "the California that men dreamed of years ago . . . the face of the earth as the Creator intended it to look." Native American peoples sought healing in the area's many hot springs. The Esalen Institute, a world-renowned center for spiritual studies, grew up around one of these springs, attracting New-Age pilgrims such as Carlos Castenada and The Beatles. A Benedictine hermitage and a modern Zen retreat round out the region's spiritual offerings. But for many who frequent this coast, combing Big Sur's secluded beaches is a cathartic experience in itself.

When to Go Fall, when the Indian summer ushers in blue skies and warm temperatures, is the best time to visit. Spring can be a little wet, summer foggy, and winter windy and cold.

Planning Two or three days is enough to sample the essence of Big Sur. Carmel, its northernmost point, is 130 miles (210 km) south of San Francisco. Whatever season you visit, pack a windbreaker, a sweater, and a good pair of walking shoes. The beaches may look inviting, but the prevailing current flows down from Alaska and the sea is too cold to test without a wetsuit. Most of the state parks have campsites, and there are smart indoor digs overlooking the Pacific.

Websites www.bigsurcalifornia.org, parks.ca.gov, www.postranchinn.com, www.henrymiller.org

HIGHLIGHTS

■ Pfeiffer State Parks are wonderful to visit. **Pfeiffer Big Sur** protects towering redwoods and wildlife habitats along the Big Sur River. **Julia Pfeiffer Burns State Park** embraces an area of rugged coast, where waterfalls plunge into the sea and gray whales frolic offshore.

■ Henry Miller, author of *Tropic of Cancer* and other classics, lived in Big Sur between 1944 and 1962. His friend Emil White created the **Henry Miller Memorial Library** in his own house, and it is now a lively cultural center with an ongoing slate of film shows, poetry readings, writers' workshops, and concerts.

■ Still one of the wildest parts of California, the 160,000-acre (64,750 hectare) nature reserve of **Ventana Wilderness** sprawls across the jagged mountains behind the coast. Much of it is only accessible by foot along more than 400 miles (645 km) of trails.

■ Founded in 1962, the **Esalen Institute**, a nonprofit center of alternative thought, offers more than 500 workshops, classes, seminars, and retreats each year in a wide variety of disciplines from yoga and meditation to science and art.

NORTH AMERICA

ALASKA

DENALI NATIONAL PARK

Six million acres of pristine subarctic wilderness, craggy mountain peaks, and mammoth glaciers surround cloud-shrouded Denali, sacred to native Alaskans.

Few places on Earth offer vistas so immense that they test the human eye. Beyond the shores of crystal-clear Wonder Lake, the tundra wilderness of Denali National Park blankets an immense valley that stretches to the distant base of the Alaska Range. Towering above the other peaks, the rugged ridges of snowcapped Mount McKinley, North America's tallest mountain, are visible in the crisp, clear mountain air. Known as Denali, the Great One, by the early Athabaskan people who lived seasonally in its shadow, the mountain and surrounding land have been sacred to many native groups. These include the Tena, who believed it to be the source of all creation. Grizzly bears and Dall sheep thrive in these mountains, and caribou and moose roam freely across the land. In fall the giant bull moose roar and spar, and the resounding crash of antlers thunders across the brilliantly hued tundra, resplendent with cloudberries, blueberries, and cranberries. Join a small-plane tour to soar above Denali's idyllic valleys and towering peaks, where mountain goats perch on narrow ledges, and broad glaciers slide down to the tundra. Landing on one such glacier, you'll enter a white-and-blue world of snow, ice, and mist bounded only by rocky ridges and the vast Alaskan sky. Pause to savor the feeling of a time long past, when all humans lived in an infinite wilderness.

When to Go The Park Road into the wilderness is open from June to mid-September, which offers the best weather and ranger-led activities. Denali National Park is open year-round for those who want to ski or travel by dog sled.

Planning Denali National Park is in south-central Alaska, and you can reach it as part of a tour, by taking the spectacular Alaska Railroad, or driving the Alaska Scenic Highway. Allow for a stay of at least three days. Bring binoculars, a camera, sunscreen, hiking and rain gear, and plenty of layers of warm clothing. Advance reservations are necessary for the lodges in and near the park. There are numerous guided tours and activity packages; schedule a flightseeing trip and sign up for a Discovery Tour as soon as you arrive. The early morning tour buses travel farthest into the wilderness, where you will find the best viewpoints for Mount McKinley.

Website www.nps.gov/dena

NORTH AMERICA

HIGHLIGHTS

■ Fly over **glaciated landscape**, see **moose** and **bear** along the Tokositna River, circle Mount McKinley and view the famous **North Face** and **Wickersham Wall** before landing on a massive glacier.

■ Take the **wilderness bus tour** into the heart of Denali National Park toward Wonder Lake for prime wildlife viewing and spectacular vistas of the Alaska Range and Mount McKinley.

■ Join a **ranger-led hike** and learn about Denali's natural and cultural history while exploring tundra, oxbow lakes, and mountain slopes.

■ Put on hiking boots, load a day pack with food, water, and rain gear, and take a **Discovery Hike** into the stunning backcountry of Denali, where no trails exist.

■ Hike the Rock Creek Trail or take the shuttle to watch the **Sled Dog Demonstration** and tour the **Alaskan Huskies Kennel**.

Opposite: Denali National Park is a wonderland of mountain peaks and clear lakes. Moose are one of the most popular residents and can sometimes be spotted wading into the water to feed on aquatic plants. Above: Husky power is an exhilarating way to get around the pristine wilderness.

TEN SACRED TREES

Many religions and cultures worship trees and forests. This selection includes some of the most ancient trees on the planet.

❶ Kasugayama Primeval Forest, Japan

Since antiquity Shintoists have regarded the Kasugayama Primeval Forest outside the city of Nara as a home to their gods. For the last 1,200 years it has also been protected from hunting and tree-felling. Access is restricted, but the public can hike up the Kasuga Okuyama Trail that skirts the forest for 5.5 miles (9 km). Open all year, the trail provides panoramic views of the forest and rare species of plants and animals.

Planning The Kasuga Okuyama Trail begins near the Kasuga Taisha shrine in Nara Park. It is also accessible from the Kasuga Okuyama Driveway, a 15-minute drive from central Nara. www.pref.nara.jp

❷ Sacred Bo-Tree, Sri Lanka

Buddhist monks keep vigil over the Sacred Bo-Tree (Sri Maha Bodhi) in Anuradhapura, as prayer flags flutter in the breeze and offerings surround the tree's base. Birdsong and monkey chatter accompany pilgrims in worship and meditation under its outstretched arms. The tree dates back to 245 B.C., coinciding with the arrival of Buddhism in Sri Lanka, and is revered as a cutting from the Buddha's Tree of Enlightenment in Bodhgaya, India.

Planning The tree lies at the crossroads of Mihindu Mawatha Road and Kurunegala Road in Anuradhapura. Security is tight and armed soldiers are present. www.responsibletravel.com

❸ Cedars of God, Lebanon

The centuries gradually fall away as you stride along the gravel pathways between these ancient cedars in a forest that took root before biblical times. With 103 mentions in the Bible, the Arz el Rab, or Cedars of God, are among the few remaining pockets of these historic trees, which once blanketed most of Lebanon. Around 300 trees remain, some over 1,000 years old.

Planning The trees are in the Ehden Nature Reserve on the northwestern flank of Mount Makmel, 19 miles (30 km) southeast of Tripoli by road. You will need an authorized guide to escort you through the forest. www.destinationlebanon.gov.lb/eng/QadishaCedars.asp, www.wata.net

❹ Stelmužė Oak, Lithuania

Western Lithuania is home to the 1,500–2,000-year-old Stelmužė tree, one of Europe's oldest oaks. Its knobbled trunk has a 42-ft (13 m) girth. Just the side branches remain alive, supported by props. The tree is dedicated to the sky deity Perkūnas, god of fertility and guardian of law and order, once revered by people in the Baltic region for his powers of thunder and lightning. Witness to prayer, celebration, healing, and sacrifice, the ancient oak stands proud, enclosed by more juvenile forest.

Planning The tree is in the village of Stelmužė, in Lithuania's Zarasai region. www.visiteurope.com/ccm/experience/detail/?nav_ca

❺ Forêt de Nevet, France

Walk through the Forêt de Nevet in Brittany, under a canopy of beech, oak, and chestnut, in the footsteps of St. Ronan. This 6th-century Irish bishop established a hermitage in the forest, which had long been sacred to the Celts and Druids.

Planning Locronan, near Quimper in western Brittany, is a good base for exploring the forest. www.francethisway.com

❻ Chêne-Chapelle (Chapel Oak), France

In Allouville-Bellefosse stands a 1,000-year-old oak tree—France's oldest and largest—and in its huge, hollow trunk two chapels have been built, one above the other. The lower chapel is dedicated to the Virgin Mary and dates from 1669. The upper chapel, reached by a wooden staircase that spirals around the great trunk, was built later as a hermitage.

Planning Allouville-Bellfosse is on the D33 near Rouen. Mass is celebated at the tree each year on July 2. www.tourisme.fr

❼ Allée des Baobabs, Madagascar

Rows of baobabs fringe the dusty road east of Morondava. The tall, straight trunks barely taper as they reach high into an umbrella of short, twisting branches. Considered sacred by many Malagasy tribes, these giants have trunks that are 12-20 ft (3.6-6 m) in diameter.

Planning The alley is 30 miles (48 km) east of Morondava. www.cactus-madagascar.com

❽ Oreteti, Tanzania

According to Masai mythology, the supreme god Ngai entrusted his cattle to the tribe, passing them down to Earth through the *oreteti*, or wild fig tree, the only link between the sky and Earth. Cattle are sacred to the Masai, and the oreteti remains a focus for worship, ritual, and sacrifice.

Planning: Search out the oreteti on a safari to Ol Doinyo Lengai, the volcano sacred to the Masai. www.serengetisafaris.com

❾ Marambatemwa, Zimbabwe

The sacred forest of Rambakurimwa at Domboshawa is a typical *Marambatemwa*, or "place that resists cutting." The Shona people revere these ancient forests as places where the human, natural, and spiritual worlds intertwine.

Planning You can visit the forest on a day trip from Harare. The Domboshawa caves and rock paintings are also worth visiting. www.jambosafari.co.za

❿ Osun-Osogbo Sacred Grove, Nigeria

Thought to be the last remaining virgin high forest in southern Nigeria, this dense forest is dedicated to Oso-Igbo, the Yoruba godess of fertility, protection, and blessings. A World Heritage site, it is one of the few Yoruba sacred groves still in existence.

Planning The annual Osun-Osogbo Festival takes place at Osogbo in the first week of August. www.westafricasafari.com

The "upside-down" baobab got its name from the legend that said the gods uprooted the tree and replanted it upside down because it complained that it did not have fruit and colorful flowers.

OREGON

CRATER LAKE

Raised to the heavens like a giant chalice of pristine water,
this volcanic lake in Oregon touches all who gaze upon it.

A s they ascend the steep slopes leading up to the rim of Crater Lake, visitors imagine the scene ahead. Yet when they reach the top, their response is often one of hushed amazement—for here is a vista that defies all expectations. Hundreds of feet below, a huge lake of outrageous sapphire blue lies encircled by a ring of jagged rock 26 miles (42 kilometers) in circumference. The only feature to pierce the surface is the near-perfect volcanic cone of Wizard Island—a crater within a crater forged in the catastrophic eruption of Mount Mazama some 7,000 years ago. It is no surprise that the local Klamath people, whose ancestors have lived in the region for 12,000 years, hold the lake sacred and have woven many legends around it. One tells how the crater was formed by a cosmic battle between Llao, evil lord of the underworld, and his cohorts of demons and crayfish, and Skell, lord of the world above ground. Skell triumphed and fed Llao's butchered body to the unsuspecting crustaceans until they saw his head, which became Wizard Island. For the Klamath, Crater Lake was always a place of startling power, where giant crayfish might jump up and snatch unwary visitors. They came here on vision quests to test their spiritual potency and to undergo rites of passage in the lake's seemingly unfathomable waters.

When to Go Crater Lake National Park is open all year round. From July to early September is the best time to visit. Snow can be a hazard in winter. The Steel Visitor Center is open from April to November, the Rim Visitor Center from June to September.

Planning Crater Lake lies almost equidistant from San Francisco and Seattle, both around 430 miles (690 km) away. The nearest airport is at Klamath Falls, 60 miles (97 km) south. Well-maintained roads lead to the crater rim.

Website www.nps.gov/crla

HIGHLIGHTS

■ The astonishing **blueness of the water** is the result of the lake's immense depth: up to 1,949 ft (594 m).

■ Gaze at the **views** outward from the rim over the landscape far below. The highest point rises to about 8,000 ft (2,438 m) above sea level.

■ Follow paths that lead down the wooded slopes inside the crater to the water's edge, where visitors can take **boat trips**, **swim**, **go fishing**, and even **scuba dive**.

■ Catch a **summer thunderstorm**. This brings a different kind of drama to the crater, which fizzes with bolts of lightning while high winds whip up the lake.

An icy stillness hangs over Crater Lake in winter.

The Spanish built 14 monasteries on the slopes of Popocatépetl.

LANDSCAPES

MEGALITHS & MYSTERIES   CRADLES OF FAITH   MAJESTIC RUINS   DAILY DEVOTION   SHRINES   THE PILGRIM'S WAY   CEREMONIES & FESTIVALS   IN REMEMBRANCE   RETREATS

HIGHLIGHTS

■ Any **clear view** of Popocatépetl is rewarding; unfortunately pollution has made this increasingly rare from Mexico City.

■ Popocatépetl falls within the **Izta-Popo Zoquiapan National Park**, an area of great natural beauty with plenty of opportunities for hiking and climbing.

■ Spanish missionaries built **14 monasteries** on the slopes of Popocatépetl during the 16th century. UNESCO has declared these collectively a World Heritage site.

MEXICO

POPOCATÉPETL

The beauty and power of this irascible volcano have fostered not only myths but a whole outlook on the world.

When this volcano erupted in 1345, the Aztecs, who had recently begun to dominate Mesoamerica, named it Popocatépetl—"smoking mountain." For centuries, its irregular bouts of colossal bad temper had been shaping the cosmic vision of all within its range. The Aztecs linked Popocatépetl with their earth and water gods, Tlaltecuhtli and Tlaloc. And together with its sister mountain, Iztaccíhuatl, it also inspired enduring Nahua legends about star-crossed lovers whom the gods turned into the twin peaks. After the Spanish conquest in 1519-21, ancient Aztec gods became bonded with Catholic saints, and intertwined rites persist today among the Nahua of the area. To them, Popocatépetl ("El Popo") is alive: it breathes and has its own character. They also call it "Don Goyo" (short for Don Gregorio), after the local village's patron saint. Meanwhile, shamans "speak" to El Popo and make offerings to obtain good harvests, as well as to assuage its anger.

When to Go Any time of year, weather permitting. Climbers visiting the Izta-Popo Zoquiapan National Park prefer the dry season, from late November to early March. A visit to the park requires at least a day. Trekking and climbing expeditions require several days.

Planning Popocatépetl is 45 miles (72 km) southeast of Mexico City and 25 miles (40 km) west of Puebla. The town of Amecameca lies at the foot of the two mountains. Trekkers and climbers usually go to the higher settlement of Tlamacas (altitude 12,960 ft/3,950 m) to prepare and acclimatize. Since Popocatépetl's most recent bout of activity, which began in 1994, no one can climb the volcano, but you can get close on the Paso de Cortés, the high saddle that joins Popocatépetl to Iztaccíhuatl.

Website iztapopo.conanp.gob.mx

A fisherman works from a dugout canoe on Lake Atitlán, a scene that has been repeated for millennia.

GUATEMALA

LAKE ATITLÁN

Cradled within a high volcanic basin, this eerie yet beautiful lake continues to nurture Maya culture and belief.

All is still and calm. Noise and movement seem quieted and slowed by the vast expanse of shimmering water that is Lake Atitlán, sacred to the Maya people who live around its shore in a dozen scattered villages. Here the people have retained their traditional languages—Tzutujil and Kaqchikel—and colorful dress. Three volcanoes flank the south side of the lake and slope gently down to the water, which reflects their sculpted cones. Wild spring onions, strawberries, and coffee grow on the lush, steep hillsides, and their scent lingers in the air. A light haze hovers midway up Volcán Atitlán, and a small wooden boat bobs gently on the water, the fisherman waiting for bass. This vast caldera was formed about 84,000 years ago by a volcanic eruption, which itself must have been of terrifying proportions. The freshwater lake lies 5,118 feet (1,560 meters) above sea level; it has never been fully sounded but is estimated to be 1,115 feet (340 meters) deep. It has no visible outlets, and water is thought to flow out of deep fissures formed by the explosion. On a boat trip, with cliffs pushing up from the watery depths, the lake is, as writer Aldous Huxley said, "really too much of a good thing."

When to Go November to April to avoid the rainy season (May–October), although even then the temperature is reasonably consistent, and the sun breaks through most days.

Planning Allow at least four days to explore the lake and villages, with time to swim and relax. Frequent buses make the two- to three-hour run from Guatemala City and Antigua Guatemala (the former capital) to Panajachel on the lakeshore. There are idyllic places to stay, from exclusive boutique hotels, such as Casa Palopó, to rustic accommodation in the Arca de Noé hotel. A boat shuttle service collects you and your luggage from the jetty at Panajachel and drops you at your destination. Take a boat trip in the morning, when the water is calm. The afternoon brings a strong wind, the *xocomil*, making the lake very choppy.

Websites www.atitlan.com, www.casapalopo.com

HIGHLIGHTS

■ The **Nature Reserve of San Buenaventura** near Panajachel includes nature trails, a Butterfly Preserve, and a Bird Refuge.

■ Hunt out excellent weaving and local produce at the busy **Friday morning market** in the small village of **Sololá**. Run by the local Cakchiquel people, it is less touristy than nearby Chichicastenango and is one of the few places where the men still wear colorful traditional Maya dress.

■ The lively town of **San Pedro de la Luna**, 30-50 minutes by boat from Panajachel, has an interesting church and wonderful views.

NORTH AMERICA

BOLIVIA

Islands of the Sun and Moon

Enter the world of the ancient Aymara as you watch dawn break over these two islands at the top of the world.

At 12,500 feet (3,810 meters), you are more than 2 miles (3 kilometers) closer to the sun than you would be at sea level. The thin air will feel bitingly cold as you are ferried the 7.5 miles (12 kilometers) from Copacabana across the deep, azure waters of Lake Titicaca to the Isla del Sol (Island of the Sun). This is the largest and culturally most important of the 41 islands scattered over the lake's 3,200-square-mile (8,288 square kilometer) expanse. The island's arid soil supports only the hardiest vegetation, but the colors are dazzling, ranging from the vibrant greens of the trees to the vivid reds, yellows, and greens of the *cantutas* flowers. Something else thrives here, too— the culture of the Aymara, who have lived in this part of the Andes since pre-Inca times. The ancient Aymara believed that the sun was a god, whom they named Inti, and that he was born on the Isla del Sol. They also believed that the moon was born nearby, on the smaller Isla de la Luna, also known as Coati, or "island queen," because to the Aymara the moon was the female counterpart of the sun. To wander through the many ruins of the Aymara shrines and temples draws you into the heart of their religion and culture.

When to Go Late July, when the indigenous priests, known as *yatiris*, lead the celebration of the Aymara new year on the Isla del Sol.

Planning You can see both islands on a day trip from Copacabana, but to get a real sense of the life of the Aymara, it is best to stay overnight and set out to explore the sites at dawn. Rustic hotels and hostels are available on the Isla del Sol, but there are no accommodations on Isla de la Luna. Be prepared for substandard electricity and plumbing. A good way to see the islands is on foot; a four-hour trek will take you around most of the sights on the Isla del Sol. At this altitude the sun's heat offers some relief from the cold mountain air, but you will need sunblock and a hat. You will also need sturdy walking shoes and warm clothing.

Websites ioa.ucla.edu/staff/stanish/islands, www.enjoybolivia.com

HIGHLIGHTS

■ On the Isla del Sol, Challapampa was the site of a huge stone complex of mazes, the **Chinkana** (labyrinth), thought to have been a training center for Inca priests.

■ Seek out the **Fountain of Youth** at the top of the 206-step Inca stairway at Yumani, the main town on Isla del Sol.

■ The top of the lighthouse on Isla del Sol provides a good viewpoint for watching the **sunset** as the rays of the dying sun illuminate the lake and surrounding mountains.

■ The well-preserved temple complex of **Iñak Uyu** (the Court of Women) on Isla de la Luna was dedicated by the Aymara for the worship of the moon.

The Aymara believed that Isla del Sol was the birthplace of their sun-god.

Ten Wells and Springs

Wells and springs have long been associated with healing—as well as sacrifice.

❶ Chichen Itza, Mexico

Keep well back from the mouth of the sacred *cenote*, or sacrificial well, at Chichen Itza. The Itzas, a Maya tribe, viewed this 197-ft (60 m) diameter sinkhole as a door to the underworld, casting golden treasures—and humans—into it as sacrifices to Chaac, their god of rain and lightning.

Planning Arrive at 8 a.m. to beat the heat and crowds. You can swim at another sinkhole, Cenote Ik Kil, nearby. www.mesoweb.com/chichen

❷ Air Panas, Bali

The sulfur springs of Air Panas, close to Lovina, flow through the gaping jaws of carved stone *nagas*—representations of Hindu gods associated with rivers and springs. The bathing pools—in which the Balinese purify their spirits—resemble natural waterfalls within the artfully planned setting of stone terraces and tropical plants.

Planning The springs are 2 miles (3 km) from Bali's only Buddhist monastery, Brahma Vihara Arama. Hire an *ojek* (motorcycle) to travel between the two. www.indo.com, www.baliguide.com

❸ Tjuwaliyn Hot Springs Park, Australia

This site in the Northern Territory is sacred to women of the Wagiman group of aboriginal Australians. The hot springs feed pools that are luxuriant oases among the dry vegetation and driftwood of the Douglas River region.

Planning Water in the pools can be so hot that parents should test the temperature before allowing children to enter. The park sometimes closes for religious ceremonies. www.nt.gov.au/nreta

❹ Hermit's Cave, Rila, Bulgaria

In the tenth century, Ivan of Rila, a religious anchorite, settled in a mountain cave, from which he was said to have performed miracles of healing. Today, you can visit the grotto with Ivan's sacred cave, as well as a holy stream and a chapel containing his relics.

Planning Rila is a two-hour bus ride from Sofia. You can stay at Rila Monastery or in a mountain hut—but reserve well in advance. www.bulgarianmonastery.com

❺ Sacred Wells, Sardinia, Italy

Sardinia has more than 40 cut-stone wells, most built by the Nuragic culture between 1800 and 1200 B.C. All have an atrium or vestibule and steep stone stairways descending seemingly to the navel of the Earth. At the base of the stairway, a *tholos*, or beehive tomb, protects the sacred water itself.

Planning Santa Cristina, the best preserved sacred well, is in the small town of Paulilatino, about 62 miles (100 km) northwest of Cagliari. www.sardegnaturismo.it

❻ The Ebbing and Flowing Well, England

The water of the mysterious well at the foot of Giggleswick Scar in the Yorkshire Dales used to ebb and flow many times a day. Alas, it no longer does so quite so dramatically, except after heavy rains, since some local people dug up the well to uncover its secrets. Local legend says that the pulsing waters are the panting breaths of a nymph who raced with all her might to flee a lustful satyr.

Planning The well is near the market town of Settle. Visit the church of St. Alkelda, Giggleswick, with its interesting stained-glass windows. Water for baptism used to be taken from the well. www.outofoblivion.org.uk; www.yorkshiredales.org

❼ St. Winefride's Well, Holywell, Wales

Famed for healing, this holy well is said to have arisen in the seventh century after the decapitation of St. Winefride. The gothic, star-shaped spring basin was built around 1500 under the patronage of Margaret of Beaufort, King Henry VII's mother.

Planning Services take place at the well throughout the pilgrimage season (Pentecost to the last Sunday in September) on Sunday at 2:30 p.m. and other days at 11:30 a.m. www.saintwinefrideswell.com

❽ Carreg Cennen, Wales

The 13th-century castle ruins of Carreg Cennen teeter on an isolated crag 300 ft (90 m) above the River Cerran. Here, a vaulted passage leads to a grotto and a well fed by a freshwater spring. The well has a wishing tradition and people used to cast bent pins as offerings to the well gods; women, so they say, also braved the passageway to wish for handsome husbands.

Planning Take a flashlight to light your way down to the spring. The castle is in the scenic Brecon Beacons National Park. www.castlewales.com/carreg

❾ St. Brigid's Well, Kildare, Ireland

St. Brigid was both a pagan goddess and Christian saint, and her well—with its standing stones, small arched bridge, and a single clootie, or prayer rag, tree—suggests a gentle melding of pagan and Christian traditions.

Planning Visit on February 1 to join an evening procession to the well. www.kildare.ie

❿ Ambohimanga Springs, Madagascar

The Merina clan, who ruled Madagascar in the 19th century, practiced elaborate rituals related to ancestor worship. These included the ceremony of Fandroana, or the yearly royal bath, symbolizing purification not only of the king or queen, but society itself. Modern visitors can view the baths hollowed from limestone, as well as the holy lake of Amparihy and the sacred stream that saw royal rites.

Planning Visit during the Malagasy New Year (March) to see Fandroana rituals. www.unesco.org/en/list/950

The green water of the Air Panas springs in Bali flows over three terraces then gushes out through carved stone monsters onto the heads of bathers.

THE LAKE OF HEAVEN

Mingle with the nomadic peoples of the Tibetan
plateau in a world that appears untouched by time.

A long the *kora* (sacred circuit) around the lakeshore, the silence and stillness—enhanced by the thin air and endless blue sky—is broken only by the shuffle of pilgrims negotiating the rocky path and the occasional jangle of yak bells. The Sacred Lakes region of Tibet, about a day's drive northeast of Lhasa, is one of the most secluded corners of Central Asia. With more than 40 lakes and half that many rivers, the countryside unfolds as an earthen quilt of blues, browns, and snow-white peaks. Most revered of the lakes is Namtso Chukmo (Lake of Heaven). At 15,479 feet (4,718 meters), this is the world's highest saltwater lake. Steeped in the rites and customs of Bon, the ancient pre-Buddhist faith of Tibet, the lake and its surroundings are thought to be the dwelling place of protective deities and other gods. During summer, nomads graze their animals on the grasslands lining the shore, while pilgrims flock to waterfront shrines, such as the Tashidor Gompa (Auspicious Rock). Some pilgrims undertake an arduous three-week circuit of the entire lake, tracing the shore in a counterclockwise direction according to ancient Bon tradition and stopping to worship at the many shrines along the way.

When to Go May to September. At other times heavy snow and freezing temperatures make travel uncomfortable and often impossible.

Planning You can take guided trips to the region from Lhasa. Three days is the minimum time needed for a visit, which will involve hikes at altitudes of up to 17,000 ft (5,182 m). It is essential to allow yourself time to acclimatize to the high altitude. People who normally live at sea level may experience headaches and shortness of breath, even on brief walks. Warm clothing is essential, even in summer. Night temperatures in July often plunge below freezing. During periods of unrest Tibet's borders may be closed.

Websites www.responsibletravel.com, www.mtsobek.com

HIGHLIGHTS

■ The **Namtso Chukmo temple** lies on a promontory on the south shore of the lake. The limestone grottos have attracted hermits since the eighth century, when the legendary Tantric Buddhist guru, Rinpoche, is said to have spent time here.

■ In summer, migratory birds, such as the black-necked crane, gather at the **bird sanctuary** in a bay to the west of Tashidor Gompa to breed and rear their young.

■ Catch a rare glimpse into the **nomadic life** of central Tibet's *drokpas* (wanderers) as they summer at Namtso Chukmo. You can watch them weave cloth, tan hides, tend their stock, and prepare traditional foods, such as *tsampa*, a paste made from yak butter and barley flour.

Prayer flags overlook the Lake of Heaven.

Pilgrims climb the Stairway to Heaven toward the Gateway to Heaven Temple, on their way to the summit of Tai Shan.

CHINA

TAI SHAN

Follow in the footsteps of Confucius by paying homage to Yu Ti, the Taoist king of heaven, at his mountain home.

Of the five sacred Taoist mountains—known as the Wu-Yueh—Tai Shan is the most revered. Its craggy, 5,069-foot (1,545 meter) profile towers above the North China Plain, close to Tai'an in Shandong Province. Taoists believe that all the Wu-Yueh peaks possess spiritual energy and are home to immortal beings. The main god of Tai Shan is Yu Ti (the Jade Emperor), the ruler of heaven and the spirit from which all life flows. Local legend states that anyone who climbs to the top of Tai Shan—Yu Ti's home—will live to be 100. The emperors of ancient China believed that the mountain itself was a god and that their authority to rule was granted by its powers. Records tell of the enormous retinues that once accompanied imperial pilgrimages to Tai Shan. Confucius also climbed the mountain to pay his respects. Every year, hordes of visitors follow in their footsteps, as well as in those of ancient Chinese monks, poets, and scholars, by climbing the 6,000-odd stone steps and pathways that lead to the summit. This tradition has bequeathed an array of temples, pavilions, and stone carvings perched on ledges or in the forest glades that straddle the route. On a clear day, it is possible to see as far as the Yellow Sea, some 125 miles (200 kilometers) to the east.

When to Go Mid-April to mid-June and September to October are best. Rain is common at any time of year, but mainly in summer; winter months are very cold, but usually clear and dry. Weekends and Chinese holidays, most notably the week around May Day and National Day (October 1), can be crowded.

Planning Tai Shan is 40 miles (64 km) south of Jinan; the nearest airport is Beijing. Numerous tours visit the site, where clearly marked stone paths and steps lead to the summit. There are food stalls, teahouses, and hotels along the route. The reasonably fit can walk to the peak and back in a day, but an overnight stay near the summit, to witness the sunrise, is recommended. Another option is to take a minibus to the Midway Gate to Heaven, just a few minutes' walk from a cable car to the summit.

Websites www.mount-tai.com.cn/en, www.sacredpeaks.net

HIGHLIGHTS

■ At the foot of Tai Shan, high walls and 2,000-year-old cypress trees surround the **Dai Miao (Dai Temple) complex**. Enter through the Yao-tsun Gate and follow the ancient stone path to the 11th-century, red-walled Tian Zhu (Heavenly Blessings) Palace.

■ Built in 1009, the **Bixia Si (Azure Cloud) Temple** is dedicated to the Princess of the Azure Clouds, daughter of the Jade Emperor Yu Ti and protector deity of peasant women.

■ Stay overnight at the summit and rise early to watch the **dawn**. Ancient Chinese belief held that Tai Shan was the home of the sun, which rose out of the mountain every morning and returned there at night.

ASIA

The sharp point of Adam's Peak towers over the surrounding hills.

SRI LANKA

ADAM'S PEAK

Get a little closer to heaven on Earth by following the
pilgrim trail to the summit of this sacred mountain.

Weather-beaten prayer flags quiver in the breeze as dawn breaks over the jungle-clad foothills of Adam's Peak in southwestern Sri Lanka. A crescendo of voices, accompanied by traditional drums and flutes, greets the new day with cries of "*S'dhu, s'dhu, sa*—It is good," as pilgrims of many faiths watch the sunrise. For a moment, a giant shadow cast by the peak falls across the dense layer of morning mist that blankets the lush valleys below. Buddhists, Hindus, Christians, and Muslims all consider this 7,362-foot (2,243 meter) mountain—also known as Sri Pada and Samanalakanda—sacred. Each faith has its own belief as to the origin of the ancient impression of a giant footprint visible in the rock close to the summit. The illuminated pathway that winds up to the summit from Dalhousie comes into view from afar, ascending almost vertically in places. Pilgrims climbing the 5,000 narrow steps exchange greetings of "*Karunava*—Compassion to you," and traditional chants fill the air. The trek is punctuated by rest stops where weary climbers are greeted by the wafting steam of brewing tea and the tantalizing aroma of frying chickpeas, rotis, and a host of sweet treats on sale at local food stalls.

When to Go The best time is December to April, before the monsoon season. Avoid full moons and weekends, as the peak can be overcrowded. Check the weather before going to ensure a fairly clear day.

Planning Aim to be at the peak for sunrise. Most people begin the climb at about 2 a.m., but you can walk up the previous afternoon and stay overnight in a basic shelter at the summit. The easiest route is from Dalhousie and takes about four hours, the descent three to four hours. A tougher route starts from Ratnapura and takes up to seven hours, the descent about five hours. As there are few food stalls along the Ratnapura route, take food and drinking water. You can hire trained guides in Dalhousie.

Websites www.srilankainstyle.com, www.teatrails.com, www.srilankanexpeditions.com

HIGHLIGHTS

■ Look for the mass of **yellow butterflies** that gather once a year, just before the monsoons, at Adam's Peak. According to local folklore, the butterflies travel to the mountain to pay homage before dying there.

■ Follow the ritual of a *kodu karayo* (first-time pilgrim) by adding a strand of cloth to the cobweb-like tangle of threads at **Indikatu Pahana**. This rest stop is said to be where the Buddha halted to mend a tear in his robes.

■ Try the **white tea** that grows on Adam's Peak. Just 66 lb (30 kg) are produced weekly.

ASIA

INDIA

KANYAKUMARI

The southernmost tip of India, where three oceans unite,
is an important Hindu site for pilgrimage and prayer.

ASIA

Poets reminisce about the beautiful full moon over Kanyakumari in April, when Hindus celebrate the festival of Chitra Purnima. Onlookers can marvel at the simultaneously setting sun and rising moon over the clear blue waters that lap against the shoreline. The much-visited town of Kanyakumari, in the state of Tamil Nadu, is at the tip of southern India, where the Indian Ocean, the Arabian Sea, and the Bay of Bengal converge. Inland are the majestic, blue hills of the Western Ghats. The town is home to the 1,000-year-old Kumari Amman Temple of the deity Kanya Devi. Legend has it that she was due to wed Lord Shiva, the destroyer in the Hindu trinity, but that he failed to appear for the wedding, and so she became known as the virgin goddess. She is said to bless all who visit her shrine. Locals sell visitors handfuls of colored stones, resembling grains of rice, to scatter over the multicolored sands of Kanyakumari's mineral-rich beaches in remembrance of the food that was never cooked for Kanya Devi's wedding. A 100-year-old lighthouse and many ancient temples pepper the coastline. In the mornings, you can see devotees bathing in the sacred waters and offering prayers and flowers to the deities of the various temples.

When to Go The best time to see the simultaneous sunset and moonrise is on a day when there will be a full moon (especially in April).

Planning Trivandrum, about 55 miles (90 km) away, is the closest airport. Kanyakumari has a good choice of clean but basic hotels. A minimum of two to three days is ideal. Some temples close to the public on Mondays. At the Kumari Amman Temple, there are unspecified times when non-Hindus may not enter the innermost shrine; men must always remove their shirts before entry. Carry plenty of change, as most temples and other attractions levy a nominal entrance charge, plus a photography fee.

Websites www.kanyakumari.nic.in, www.ruinsofkumari.com, www.saviontravel.com

HIGHLIGHTS

■ The **Sri Padaparai rock**, to the southeast of the Kumari Amman Temple, is the site of the footprints in stone said to have been made by the virgin goddess, Kanya Devi, when she came down from the heavens to make a home there.

■ Take a ferry to see the **statue of Thiruvalluvar**, the Tamil poet born around 30 B.C. The statue—also referred to as India's Statue of Liberty—stands atop a tiny island.

■ Visit the **Gandhi Memorial**, where Gandhi's ashes went on public display before being cast into the sea. The memorial has been designed so that on his birthday, October 2, the sun's rays fall on the exact spot where his ashes lay.

Waves crash near the statue of Thiruvalluvar.

INDIA

SACRED GANGES

Devout Hindus travel from all over the world to bathe at the meeting place of three rivers–the Ganges, the Yamuna, and the mythical Saraswati.

You may wonder what all the fuss is about as you travel east from Allahabad in Uttar Pradesh, along the straight, dusty road and over barren plains crisscrossed by power lines. You may be puzzled that your destination appears to be nothing more than a huge, sluggish river spanned by occasional bridges. A gull or two may circle overhead, and the odd devotee may be at the water's edge, making an offering to the river gods. On most days, there is little to suggest that this is one of Hinduism's holiest places. But go when there is a full or new moon, or during a *mela* (festival), and you will find the shoreline crammed with thousands of pilgrims. Dotted among the throng, priests in vibrantly colored robes perch on small wooden platforms, assisting the devout with their ablutions. For this is the Triveni Sangam, or "three-braided meeting point," where three of Hinduism's most sacred rivers meet. Hindus consider the broad, brown Ganges to be the manifestation of the life-giving mother goddess Ganga. They associate the swifter, greenish Yamuna with Yama, god of death. And it is here, Hindus believe, that these two are joined by the mythical, underground Saraswati—the "river of enlightenment." The Triveni Sangam is also one of the four places where legend states that drops of divine nectar fell from heaven, and so it is one of four rotating locations for the Kumbha Mela, India's largest religious gathering— when the riverbanks become a temporary home to around 70 million people.

When to Go January or February is best–these are the months when the melas take place. Avoid the ferocious heat of summer. One day, even during a festival, should be enough for a non-Hindu visitor.

Planning Varanasi airport is 91 miles (146 km) from Allahabad, Lucknow airport 130 miles (210 km). Highway and rail links connect both to Allahabad. The Sangam lies about 7.5 miles (12 km) east of Allahabad, and buses and taxis are readily available. Ideally, schedule your trip to coincide with a mela. The Magha Mela takes place every year. The Ardh (half) Kumbha Mela takes place here every 12 years, most recently in 2007. The next full Kumbha Mela (which also takes place here every 12 years) is in 2013.

Website www.tourindia.com

HIGHLIGHTS

■ Cruise the sacred waters on a **boat trip**, which you can take from the quay just to the east of the majestic Mogul fort, built by Emperor Akbar in 1583.

■ On the east side of the fort is the underground **Patalpuri Temple**, believed to have been visited by Lord Rama, and a sacred Akshaya Vat, or "immortal" banyan tree.

■ Several **ancient shrines** are dotted around the Triveni Sangam. The one close to the fort is devoted to Hanuman, the monkey god.

■ Look out for the spot where the **distinctly colored waters** of the Ganges and Yamuna rivers meet and mingle.

Opposite: Pilgrims at the Ardh Khumba Mela bathe in the Ganges before dawn. For Hindus, this ceremonial bathing cleanses both body and soul. Above left: Pilgrims buy wreaths of marigolds and lotus blossom and throw them as offerings into the river. Above right: A pilgrim prays in the Ganges waters.

AUSTRALIA

The Olgas

Step into the "dreamtime" world of Australia's aboriginal peoples amid the brilliant colors of the outback.

AUSTRALIA AND OCEANIA

A flock of budgerigars turns in unison, the sun on their wings, casting a brilliant flash of olive-yellow across the massive, burnished-orange rock domes of Kata Tjuta, or the Olgas. Covering 11 square miles (28 square kilometers) of Uluru-Kata Tjuta National Park in the Northern Territory, the 500-million-year-old geological oddities are part of the indigenous culture. To the Anangu, the aboriginal keepers of this place, each of the 36 rock formations represents a totemic animal, person, or foodstuff that emerged from the earth during *alcheringa* (dreamtime), the time of creation. Anangu storytellers speak of Wanampi, the ancestral snake that lives on the 3,507-foot (1,069 meter) peak of Mount Olga, the tallest monolith in the group; of Liru, venonous snake-men; of Malu, a kangaroo-man; and his sister Mulumura, a lizard-woman. Hikers can see many of these formations from the Karu and Karingana lookouts along the Valley of the Winds trail zigzagging around several of the rocks. The Walpa Gorge trail, the only other access for non-aborigines, twists along a creek bed between two of the taller domes to a grove of *urtjanpa* (spearwood bush), which the Anangu use to make traditional spears.

When to Go Anytime, although temperatures in winter (June–August) are more comfortable for hiking.

Planning If you do not have a vehicle, organized tours to Kata Tjuta depart daily from Ayers Rock Resort, near Uluru. Make sure you have sturdy footwear, a wide-brimmed hat, sunscreen, adequate water for the hike ahead, and a fly-net hat to deter the bush flies that plague the Olgas and Uluru on hot days in summer. Allow three to four hours to walk the 4.6-mile (7.4 km) Valley of the Winds trail to reach the Karu and Karingana lookouts, which offer panoramic views of Kata Tjuta's central valley. Add another hour to complete the 1.6-mile (2.6 km) round trip through Walpa Gorge. When temperatures above 97°F (36°C) are forecast, the park restricts access to the Valley of the Winds trail past the Karu lookout after 11 a.m.

Websites www.environment.gov.au/parks/uluru, www.australia.com, www.phs.com.au

HIGHLIGHTS

■ Explore **Walpa Gorge** to view ancient petroglyphs, unique desert fauna, and rare plants, some found nowhere else on Earth.

■ **Watch the sun set** on Kata Tjuta, changing the color of the rock from orange to blood-red and mauve, before fading to a deep purple.

■ Take a **helicopter tour** of the Olgas and Uluru to appreciate the sheer size of these rock formations and the beauty of the desert.

The fiery rounded peaks of the Olgas play an important part in aboriginal "dreamtime" culture.

LANDSCAPES

MEGALITHS & MYSTERIES CRADLES OF FAITH MAJESTIC RUINS DAILY DEVOTION SHRINES THE PILGRIM'S WAY CEREMONIES & FESTIVALS IN REMEMBRANCE RETREATS

In spring, wildflowers come into bloom in the orange dunes below Uluru.

AUSTRALIA

ULURU

Sit beneath prehistoric cave paintings at the base of this giant rock and listen to ancient tales about the culture of the Anangu.

The red rock of Uluru, reaching as high as the Empire State Building (1,142 feet/348 meters), towers over the desert sands of central Australia. Formerly known as Ayers Rock—and now protected within the confines of Uluru-Kata Tjuta National Park—this massive sandstone outcrop is believed to be between 300 and 400 million years old. Aboriginal peoples have lived around the base of Uluru for more than 10,000 years, and their descendants, the Anangu, consider it to be an integral part of their heritage. According to Tjukurpa, the complex system of beliefs that governs the Anangu way of life, Uluru was fashioned by creator-beings, who transformed the Earth from a featureless place into the landscapes we know today. Many spirits are associated with Uluru, such as the python-woman Kuniya, who it is believed once lived in its caves and canyons and engaged in mortal combat with a poisonous snake-man called Liru. The massive striations visible on the mountain's sides are said to be the result of their titanic struggle.

HIGHLIGHTS

■ The aboriginal-owned Anangu Tours organizes **guided hikes**, **camel treks**, and, after dark, **astronomy lessons** under the brilliant desert stars.

■ At the **Uluru-Kata Tjuta Cultural Centre** near Uluru, you can watch aboriginal artisans at work and learn about Tjukurpa (the foundation of Anangu culture), bush tucker (food), and the area's history and natural features.

AUSTRALIA AND OCEANIA

When to Go Summer (December–February) at Uluru is blisteringly hot, with daytime temperatures often in excess of 100°F (38°C). Winter days (June–August) are pleasant, but desert nights can be very cold, sometimes with temperatures below freezing. Spring (September–November) sees a profusion of wildflowers strewn across the orange dunes. But no matter what time of year you visit, sunrise and sunset are the best times to catch Uluru in all its multicolored glory.

Planning You can race around the park in a single morning or afternoon, but at least two days are recommended to explore both Uluru and Kata Tjuta properly. Accommodations are available in Yulara, just outside the park. Sunscreen and some sort of head protection are essential, as is drinking water, even on organized tours. Don't strike off into the desert on your own. Those who ignore the wishes of the local Anangu people and decide to climb Uluru should know that footing on the rock can be treacherous.

Websites www.environment.gov.au/parks/uluru, www.ananguwaai.com.au, www.longitude131.com.au

LANDSCAPES

MEGALITHS & MYSTERIES   CRADLES OF FAITH   MAJESTIC RUINS   DAILY DEVOTION   SHRINES   THE PILGRIM'S WAY   CEREMONIES & FESTIVALS   IN REMEMBRANCE   RETREATS

NEW ZEALAND

ROTORUA

A landscape revered by the Maori, the most active geothermal area in New Zealand steams, hisses, and bubbles in a multicolored frenzy.

The town of Rotorua lies at the heart of a fermenting volcanic landscape of craters, mountains, and lakes. Scalding geysers spurt high in the sky, mud boils and bubbles, and steaming pools seethe in fantastic hues of green, pink, and blue. Everywhere, the stench of sulfur pervades the air. When the Maori first gazed on this intense thermal activity, they created legends to explain it. One tells how an ancient high priest, Ngatorioirangi, freezing on a mountaintop, pleaded with the gods of the mythical Maori homeland of Hawaiki for warmth. They answered him by sending fire deep underground. By the 19th century, Rotorua's pink-and-white terraces, formed over centuries by silica deposits, were deemed the eighth wonder of the world and had become a tourist attraction for Europeans, including celebrities of the day. But in 1886, the sacred Mount Tarawera to the south of Rotorua erupted, destroying the terraces, and engulfing the surrounding villages in a flaming river. Even this event did not deter visitors, who continued to tour the thermal reserves and take the treatments. Today you can still visit quieter areas such as Wai-o-tapu, or Sacred Waters, 17 miles (27 kilometers) south of Rotorua, and see and feel the restless spirit of the Earth at work in all its neon-colored glory. You may even think that possibly, somewhere deep in that molten core way below your feet, there really is a god-given inferno.

When to Go Rotorua's geothermal activity is lively all year round. Most of the reserves are open during the day, seven days a week.

Planning Rotorua receives daily domestic flights from Auckland, Wellington, Christchurch, and Queenstown. You can also reach it by a three-hour drive from Auckland, though there are numerous tours of the area for visitors without a car. There is a wide range of accommodations, allowing you to make the most of the sights, walk, relax, or take part in activities for a couple of days or more.

Website www.rotorua.nz.com

AUSTRALIA AND OCEANIA

HIGHLIGHTS

■ The region is rich in **Maori culture**. Guides can tell you about the landscape and the ever-changing moods of the geysers and pools. You can see Maori arts, crafts, and cultural performances, and take part in a *hangi*–a traditional meal.

■ A tour of the **Waimangu Valley** reveals the effects of the eruption of Mount Tarawera. It includes a visit to Lake Tarawera and the rock paintings there, as well as a boat trip to the village of Te Wairoa, buried in the eruption and now partly excavated.

■ This is the land of **spa treatments**. Try Polynesian Spa, on the shores of Lake Rotorua. The healing properties of its waters were first promoted in 1878, when a priest named Father Mahoney dug a pool here and found that bathing in it relieved his arthritis.

■ Kayaking, jet-skiing, fishing, and other **outdoor pursuits** are all available in the area.

Opposite: Minerals in the water create a swirling array of colors in the Artist's Palette, a pool in the Wai-o-tapu Thermal Reserve. Above left: Lady Knox Geyser is named after the daughter of a governor of New Zealand. Soap is dropped into the geyser to make it spout regularly. Above right: Steam rises constantly from Champagne Pool at Wai-o-tapu.

Ushguli has more than 20 stone tower houses. This one dates from the 12th century and protects a church.

GEORGIA

UPPER SVANETI

A remote region on the southern slopes of the Caucasus mountains has been a potent source of mythology since ancient times.

The ancient Greeks knew Georgia as Colchis. It was here that Jason is said to have come with the Argonauts to wrest the Golden Fleece from King Aeëtes. The origin of the myth may lie in the age-old practice of laying sheep fleeces in the mountain streams of Upper Svaneti to collect flecks of gold. The area's inhabitants, the Svans, are ostensibly Christian, but they still cling to pagan traditions and myths. Mount Ushba holds a special place in their culture: it was the haunt of Dali, the golden-haired goddess of nature and hunting. Hunters would observe her taboos, or she would transform into an animal of prey and lead them to their death. Some of the highest peaks of the Caucasus girdle Upper Svaneti and the region still feels remote, accessed only by poor roads. The majestic beauty of the unspoiled mountain landscapes, sparsely dotted with medieval villages, ensures its timeless quality. Rural churches and chapels contain superb frescoes and icons dating from the eighth to the 14th centuries. An unusual feature of the villages, the clusters of stone tower houses once protected families from marauding invaders and from neighboring clans during blood feuds.

When to Go Summer (May–September). Heavy winter snowfall cuts Upper Svaneti off from the rest of Georgia and blocks the road connecting Mestia (the tiny regional capital) to the tower houses of Ushguli.

Planning Most visitors fly into Tbilisi (Georgia's capital) and then take the road to Zugdidi before heading up to Mestia, a total distance of 300 miles (480 km) that takes about eight-ten hours. Buses and minibuses also connect Zugdidi to Mestia. Organized tours run trips out of Tbilisi lasting a week and cover the highlights of Upper Svaneti in about three days. Upper Svaneti has not entirely lost its reputation for lawlessness. Visitors should take care not to travel alone, and should observe the advice of trustworthy local agents, guides, and hotel-keepers. Tourists may first be greeted with suspicion, but once accepted as a guest, they should enjoy the protective shield of traditional hospitality.

Website www.caucasustravel.com

HIGHLIGHTS

■ One of the most distinctive of the Caucasus, the horn-like double peak of **Mount Ushba** (15,387 ft/ 4,690 m) lures climbers and trekkers to the region.

■ **Chazhashi** (or Chajashi) is the most famous tower-house village. It is one of a group of four villages known collectively as Ushguli, which have more than 20 towers altogether.

■ Isolated by mountains, Upper Svaneti resisted conquest in the Middle Ages and became a safe house for **church treasures**, such as gold crosses and painted icons. There is a fine collection at the **Mestia Museum of History and Ethnography**.

ASIA

ISRAEL

SEA OF GALILEE

Look across the shimmering waters of the Sea of Galilee, and walk in the footsteps of Jesus and his disciples.

ASIA

Few places have as much resonance for Christians as the Sea of Galilee. This vast freshwater lake, 62 square miles (160 square kilometers) in area, is closely identified with Jesus' ministry. Here he chose his fishermen apostles Simon Peter, Andrew, John, and James and, according to the New Testament, performed several miracles, such as the Feeding of the Five Thousand. For two millennia, therefore, the lake has been an important pilgrimage site for Christians, but it also has great significance for Jews, who know it as Lake Tiberias. The town of Tiberias was a center of rabbinical teaching from the second century to the Middle Ages and gave rise to the first Talmud, compiled over the third and fourth centuries. More recently, in 1909, the lakeshore became the setting for the Zionists' first kibbutz, following their concept of communal farming and living. Pilgrims, of course, mean tourism: today Galilee is popular for its beaches, spa resorts, and tranquil atmosphere, as well as its religious sites. As in Jesus' day, the area's main activity is fishing. The sights and sounds of fishermen bringing in their catch at sunset induce a mood of contemplation and peace, as if nothing has changed for millennia. But the most evocative way to experience the ambience is by floating in a simple wooden boat and letting your fingertips trail in some of the most hallowed waves on Earth.

When to Go Summer can be extremely hot (up to 100°F/38°C); spring and fall are the best times to visit. Avoid the Jewish Shabbat (Friday evening through Saturday evening), when most businesses, including restaurants, will be closed.

Planning You can completely cover the region by car in one day, but if you want to stay a little longer, Tiberias has the best accommodation options. While spring and fall are the best times to visit, the region can be prone to rain showers, so make sure you have an umbrella and waterproof clothing. Modest dress is required for visiting most religious sites—no shorts, short skirts, or sleeveless tops.

Website www.mfa.gov.il

HIGHLIGHTS

■ Visit the Byzantine-style **Church of the Multiplication of the Loaves and the Fishes** in Tabgha with its mosaic of bread and fish. Nearby is the **Shrine of the Beatitudes** commemorating the Sermon on the Mount.

■ **Capernaum**, Jesus' town of residence during his ministry, has churches, a synagogue, and an archaeological museum.

■ A **wooden fishing boat**, dug from the lake in the 1980s and displayed at the Yigol Allon Center in Kibbutz Ginosar, is thought to date from Jesus' time.

■ Visit the ruins of **Magdala**, near modern-day Migdal, the traditional birthplace of Mary Magdalene.

■ Dine locally on freshly caught **tilapia**, nicknamed "St. Peter's fish."

Aside from its religious significance to Christians and Jews, the Sea of Galilee draws many for its tranquil atmosphere.

YAZILIKAYA

A sacred spring in a massive outcrop of limestone
became a precious sanctuary for the Hittite kings.

In ancient times, in the fierce, dry heat of central Turkey, springs were interpreted as divine blessings. Where fresh water tumbled forth at Yazılıkaya, it was shaded and protected by high rock faces and trees that thrived in the damp soil. Two natural galleries set among the rocks around the spring provided the perfect setting for open-air shrines and may have been used for worship as early as 1900 B.C. Yazılıkaya took on greater significance when the Bronze-Age city of Hattusha developed nearby. Founded around 1500 B.C., Hattusha became the thriving capital of the Hittite empire, and Yazılıkaya became a royal sanctuary. The rock faces were inscribed with relief sculptures depicting Hittite gods and deified kings (Yazılıkaya means "inscribed rock"). In the smaller chamber, which may have been used for royal funeral rites, a superb frieze depicts a closely packed row of gods in conical hats, bearing curved swords or sickles. Look for King Tudhaliya (wearing a skullcap) in the embrace of Sharruma, god of birth, death, and rebirth. In the larger chamber, a line of goddesses in long pleated dresses marches toward a line of gods. They converge on images of the great weather god, Teshub, and his consort, the Earth goddess Hepat, parents of Sharruma. Pictured larger than all of the gods is King Tudhaliya IV, the last known Hittite king, who reigned in the late 13th century B.C.

When to Go Spring (April to mid-June) is best, although April can be wet. Fall (late September-October) is the next best time. Summer can be very hot and winter surprisingly cold.

Planning Yazılıkaya and Hattusha, near the town of Boğazkale, are about 125 miles (200 km) east of Ankara. Most visitors join a tour from Ankara, which takes about 11 hours. Yazılıkaya lies about 2 miles (3 km) from the main ruins of Hattusha. Light and shade move across the site throughout the day, and many tours start at Yazılıkaya at around noon so that visitors can see the friezes in maximum sunlight.

Website www.hattuscha.de

HIGHLIGHTS

■ In the small gallery is the so-called "**sword god**," with a human head and four lions for a body, all standing on a downward-pointing sword. This may represent Nergal, the Hittite god of the underworld.

■ You can identify gods, goddesses, and royalty by their **symbols**, such as the kings' curling scepters (resembling monkey tails). The number of "horns" on the gods' conical hats represents seniority. Many of the gods have animal attributes. Pictograms provide the names of the kings.

■ The ruins of **Hattusha** are close by. This was once a teeming city enclosed by 4 miles (6.5 km) of walls.

A bas-relief of 12 Hittite gods decorates the walls of the smaller gallery at Yazılıkaya.

LANDSCAPES

MEGALITHS & MYSTERIES CRADLES OF FAITH MAJESTIC RUINS DAILY DEVOTION SHRINES THE PILGRIM'S WAY CEREMONIES & FESTIVALS IN REMEMBRANCE RETREATS

A shepherd drives his flock past Mount Ararat, its peak shrouded in clouds.

TURKEY

Mount Ararat

Perpetually covered in snow and ice, Ararat's sprawling summit may hold the answer to an ancient mystery.

Massive, intimidating, and mysterious, the snowcapped cone of Turkey's highest mountain broods over the arid, near-treeless plateau country of northeastern Anatolia. From the dusty village of Doğubeyazıt near Turkey's frontier with Iran and Armenia, Ararat dominates the entire horizon. The main summit, Great Ararat, reaches 16,854 feet (5,137 meters) above sea level and surmounts a forbidding landscape of glaciers, barren black rock—some slabs the size of cottages—and frost-cracked lava. To the ancient Armenians the mountain was a place of awe and dread, where ice and fire met, for Ararat—Ağrı Dağı in Turkish, meaning "mountain of pain"—was once an active volcano. It is no surprise that the Armenians regarded Ararat as the home of their gods. For many visitors today, it is the biblical connection that makes it so fascinating. According to the Book of Genesis, it was on Ararat's slopes that Noah's ark landed as the waters of the Great Flood subsided, and it was from here that Noah and his progeny began to rebuild the world. Although some climbers have reported seeing the ark's remains lodged in a crevice or buried under a glacier near the summit, no actual evidence has surfaced.

When to Go July to mid September. Best in late summer.

Planning Van is the nearest airport to Ararat. Turkish Airlines flies from Ankara to Van several times a week. Doğubeyazıt and Van have accommodations ranging from very basic guesthouses to three-star hotels. However, it is cheaper, easier, and safer to use a specialized tour operator than to travel independently. Anyone wanting to climb Mount Ararat will need an official permit from the Turkish Ministry of Tourism. This is hard for an individual traveler to obtain, but several trekking companies organize climbs to the summit and can arrange the permit for you.

Website www.terra-anatolia.com

HIGHLIGHTS

■ The **Ishak Pasha Palace** in Doğubeyazıt, now a World Heritage site, is a ghostly, atmospheric complex of ruins that is more recent than it looks. Built by a local warlord in 1789, the courtyards, harem, and mosque are a unique blend of Anatolian, Armenian, Ottoman, and European architectural styles.

■ Four islands on the vast inland sea of Lake Van hold the ruins of ancient **Armenian monasteries**. The oldest are believed to date from the seventh century, long before the Turkish conquest of the region. You can visit them by boat—enquire in Van.

ASIA

TEN SACRED MOUNTAINS

Since ancient times, mountains have been sacred to many religions, although actually climbing them can be sacrilege.

❶ The Black Hills, South Dakota

These fabled mountains are the site of five national parks. With its impossibly narrow tunnels and "pigtail" bridges, driving in Custer State Park is an adventure in itself. From the vantage point of Harney Peak (altitude 7,242 ft/2,207 m), the pine-encrusted hills—sacred to the Sioux—do indeed look black.

Planning Some regard the carved faces of Mount Rushmore and Crazy Horse as tourist traps, but don't overlook their emotional power. www.travelsd.com

❷ Mount Shasta, California

The appeal of Mount Shasta in the Cascade chain lies in its solitude. In many Native American legends, it was the center of creation. Experienced climbers can scale the summit, but you can also admire its glacier-honed beauty from the trailheads around Bunny Flat, the Circle of Mount Shasta bike trail, or the Modoc Volcanic Scenic Byway.

Planning Visit May to August for hiking and climbing. www.visitsiskiyou.org

❸ Mount Fuji, Japan

Sacred in both Shintoism and Buddhism, this snowcapped mountain is an icon of Japanese art and culture. Soaring to 12,338 ft (3,760 m), the graceful peak is visible from Tokyo on clear days. During July and August, you can join the 200,000 people who hike to the top. Or simply admire the view from the town of Hakone or any of the five lakes in Fuji-Hakone-Izu National Park.

Planning Take the express bus from Shinjuku, Tokyo. The ascent takes five to eight hours; the descent three to four. www.env.go.jp

❹ Mount Agung, Bali

The center of the world to the Balinese, Mount Agung is an active volcano both revered and feared. Bali's holiest Hindu temple, Pura Besakih, sits partway up the 10,300-ft (3,140 m) slope and survived a 1963 eruption. The taxing 3-mile (5 km) climb needs no special gear, just a local guide.

Planning Visit April to October, but climbing is restricted during April, when religious festivals take place. www.indonesia-tourism.com

❺ Mauao, New Zealand

This small, extinct volcano sits like a green finial at the end of a peninsula in the Bay of Plenty. Maori believe it sacred and prize it for its natural defenses. It was terraced to create a village and fortress that were inhabited until the early 1800s.

Planning You can walk the base track in 45 minutes; the summit (offering glorious panoramic views) is a two-hour round trip. www.bayofplentynz.com, www.mountmaunganui.co.nz

❻ Mount Everest, Nepal/China border

The people of Tibet call it Goddess Mother of the Universe, the Nepalese Goddess of the Sky. Travelers looking to experience it without a death-defying climb can use Lhasa, Tibet, or Lukla, Nepal, as a starting point to trek among colorful villages and monasteries with million-dollar views.

Planning The Rongbuk Monastery, on the north side of the Himalaya in Tibetan China, holds Everest in plain sight. Once there, Base Camp is a day's hike. www.nationalgeographic.com/everest

❼ Mount Kailash, China/Tibet

Not one but four religions consider this the Earth's most sacred place. Thousands of Hindu, Buddhist, Jain, and Bönpo pilgrims crowd the remote Himalayan town of Darchen each year, not to scale the sky-scraping peak (setting foot on it is sacrilege) but to make one or more *koras*, or ritual circuits, around its base. It's a tough trek, but ponder the payoff: the faithful believe one 32-mile (52 km) kora erases a lifetime of sins.

Planning This remote mountain takes many days to reach—from any direction. Some pilgrims cover the kora in one (arduous) day; most take three. www.summitpost.org

❽ Mount Nebo, Jordan

This windy peak is said to be where the prophet Moses looked out over the Promised Land and later died. The church at the summit has a wonderful collection of early mosaics. On clear days you can see the Dead Sea, the River Jordan, Jericho, the Mount of Olives, and the rooftops of Jerusalem and Bethlehem.

Planning Take a taxi from Madaba to Mount Nebo, about 6 miles (10 km) away, or join one of the numerous organized tours. na.visitjordan.com

❾ Mount Olympus, Greece

You can't help but feel humbled by the 9,576-ft (2,919 m) high peak that was legendary home to the Greek gods. The two-to-three-day climb affords a close-up look at the mountain's diverse flora—roughly 1,700 species in all. Then visit Dion, a holy site in the northern foothills, for its mesmeric views and archaeological riches.

Planning The town of Litochoro, on the Aegean coast south of Katerini, is the starting point for anyone climbing the mount. www.oreivatein.com

❿ Mount Kilimanjaro, Tanzania

Rising to 19,336 ft (5,894 m) above the Great Rift Valley, this flat-topped volcano, sacred to local Masai, is often visible on the horizon as far as 125 miles (200 km) away. Gaze on Kilimanjaro from the Arusha National Park, or book a five-to-seven-day climb with a guide. The tough-but-doable ascent winds through farmland, forest, desert, and, finally, ice at Uhuru Peak.

Planning For the most clement weather, climb in January–March or September–October. www.tanzaniaparks.com

On a clear day Mount Fuji's perfect outline is sharply silhouetted against the sky. The mountain is regarded as the incarnation of a deity in both Shinto and Buddhist beliefs.

The monastery of St.-Martin du Canigou is an unusual mixed community of monks and nuns.

FRANCE

Mount Canigou

The sacred mountain of the Catalan people is a focal point for festivities at the summer solstice.

At 9,137 feet (2,785 meters), the Pic du Canigou (Pic del Canigó in Catalan) is the highest point of the Massif du Canigou, soaring above the Pyrenean foothills of Roussillon in southern France, near the Spanish frontier. Pagan customs still flourish in Christian guise in Catalonia, and if you visit the Pic in midsummer you will encounter one of the most striking of these throwbacks to an earlier age. The Festa de Sant Joan, which takes place every June, ostensibly commemorates a Christian saint, but it has all the characteristics of a much older summer-solstice fire festival. Younger Catalans also like to hike to the peak at less busy times of the year as an affirmation of love for their homeland, and the *calvaire* (cross) marking the top is permanently adorned with dozens of flags and pennants in the red-and-yellow colors of Catalonia.

When to Go Easter to September, but beware of possible very cold and wet conditions in winter and spring and huge crowds during the Festa de Sant Joan.

Planning Pic du Canigou is about 6 miles (10 km) south of Prades. The easiest ascent to the summit is from the Chalet des Cortalets, a mountain refuge operated by the Club Alpin Français. The trail is clearly marked, but stout walking boots, a water bottle and water purifying tablets, a hat, sunglasses, sunscreen, and waterproof outer clothing are essential. Allow four to six hours for the hike up and down. Jeep taxis operate from Prades and Vernet-les-Bains to the chalet, which offers dormitory bunks, basic twin rooms, and a simple bar-restaurant. Camping is available at the lake nearby and at Camping St.-Martin just outside Vernet.

Websites www.prades-tourisme.com, www.francethisway.com

HIGHLIGHTS

■ Though it is often referred to as a midsummer festival, the **Festa de Sant Joan** takes place on June 23–24, two days after Midsummer's Eve. Thousands of Catalans from both sides of the border gather to make merry around a huge bonfire that is visible from miles away. Smaller bonfires spring up in villages all over the region.

■ The monastery of **St.-Martin du Canigou** was founded in 1001 and restored in the 20th century. Guided tours, conducted in French, take place several times a week between February and September.

EUROPE

NORTHERN IRELAND

GIANT'S CAUSEWAY

Walk in the footsteps of a mythical hero across
a strange rock landscape that leads into the ocean.

Set in a spectacular coastline of rugged cliffs, treacherous headlands, and hidden bays on County Antrim's northern coast, the Giant's Causeway is a collection of some 40,000 tightly packed basalt columns jutting out of the water, forming an undulating walkway into the waves. Stepping from pillar to pillar, with the Atlantic on three sides, you feel the full force of the ocean. Limestone cliffs stretch away on either side, broken up by steep fields and the towering columns of dark basalt. The ocean has eroded the cliffs above the causeway into striking forms reflected in their names: Chimney Stacks, Giant's Harp, Organ Pipes, and Camel's Hump. According to Irish legend, the hero Finn McCool (Fionn mac Cumhail) created the causeway to provide a landbridge to Scotland, so that he could do battle with a Scottish giant called Benandonner, who had challenged his fighting prowess. However, McCool fell asleep and the giant came looking for him. When Benandonner saw Finn he panicked and fled back to Scotland, destroying most of the causeway, so that only the steps into the sea remained. The truth behind the causeway's formation is less poetic, but just as dramatic. Around 60 million years ago, lava bubbled up through fissures in the overlying rock. The lava contracted as it cooled and vertical cracks opened up, forming the columns, which then eroded under the constant battering of the waves.

When to Go The causeway is accessible all year round, and is busiest in summer. If you want the place to yourself, visit early in the morning in December or January.

Planning The Giant's Causeway Visitor Centre is 2 miles (3 km) north of Bushmills. The causeway is a 0.5-mile (0.8 km) walk from the center; bus service from the center operates in summer. Allow at least a couple of hours to soak up the atmosphere. Wear shoes with good grip as the rocks can be slippery. If you are planning to stay for a few hours, take food and drinks as there is no café on site.

Website www.giantscausewayofficialguide.com

EUROPE

HIGHLIGHTS

■ Watch the **evening sun** sink into the ocean, and imagine yourself back in a time of ancient legends.

■ Take one of the many **cliff hikes** in the area. Along the way, you can see **Giant's Eyes**—reddish, oval-shaped sockets where basalt boulders have fallen out of the cliffs.

■ Look out for **seabirds**. Fulmars and cormorants are present all year round. In summer, razorbills, guillemots, and shags are also common.

■ Toast Ireland's legendary hero on a tour of the **Old Bushmills whiskey distillery**, which received its license in 1608.

Rockpools among the strange rock shapes of the Giant's Causeway reflect the dying light of the sun over the ocean.

MEGALITHS & MYSTERIES

Stone circles and alignments, cryptic earthworks on a massive scale, pillared gateways into the afterlife, temples and palaces sculpted out of mountainsides, giant statues of forgotten gods, sacred narratives inscribed on living rock—all these are messages from our remotest ancestors, striving to make contact with eternity. To encounter them, wherever in the world they lie, is to take part in a conversation with the infinite. Some of the following destinations have fascinated generations of visitors, such as England's Stonehenge, the great solar and lunar temples of Mexico's Teotihuacan, and the exquisitely sculpted maidens of the Parthenon in Athens. Others will lure travelers to remote landscapes, such as the megalithic tombs in the Western Caucasus or the stone circles of Calanais in the Outer Hebrides. In certain locations, the chain of belief and ceremony remains unbroken, such as the Bighorn Medicine Wheel in Wyoming. The purpose of others, such as the Nasca Lines in Peru, remains a mystery.

The remote plateaus of northern Laos are home to groups of giant, jarlike containers that were hewn out of rock and now lie abandoned. No one is sure what their purpose was or even how old they are.

BIGHORN MEDICINE WHEEL

A stone circle at the top of Medicine Mountain
marks the position of the sun at the summer solstice.

O n a remote Wyoming mountaintop in Bighorn National Forest stands one of the
largest and most important medicine wheels in North America. Native Americans
made these constructions, which had astronomical and ceremonial significance,
by laying out stones on the ground in a wheel-like pattern. The 1.5-mile (2.4 kilometer)
hike to the Bighorn Wheel is rewarded by the circle's simple beauty and serenity. Gentle
breezes stir the brightly colored prayer-offerings of cloth and feathers that adorn a simple
wood fence around the stones. The profound stillness makes it easy to imagine the great
ceremonies, songs, chants, and dances that this site may have witnessed over many
hundreds of years. The circle is 80 feet (24 meters) in diameter, enclosing 28 radial rock
lines emanating from a central cairn. The wheel's longest spoke terminates with a cairn
that is perfectly aligned with the rising sun on the summer solstice. The circle is believed
to have been constructed by the Plains Indians several hundred years ago. Members of
around 70 tribes, including the Cheyenne, Crow, Shoshoni, Cree, and Blackfeet still gather
here, and in nearby locations on Medicine Mountain, to perform ceremonies that honor
their traditions and beliefs.

When to Go Any time between mid-June and mid-September. The greatest profusion of wildflowers is
during June and July.

Planning Allow at least a half-day for the 45-minute drive from Burgess Junction to the mountain, scenic
viewpoints along the way, and time to observe the Medicine Wheel and savor the views from Medicine
Mountain. Take your own refreshments as there are no public buildings at the site. Contact the Bighorn
National Forest visitor center in Burgess Junction in advance to check that no native ceremonies are
scheduled, as tribes occasionally conduct private religious ceremonies in the medicine wheel during the
summer and people may not visit during those times.

Websites www.fs.fed.us/r2/bighorn/contact, www.wyomingtourism.org

NORTH
AMERICA

HIGHLIGHTS

■ A dazzling profusion of spring
and summer **wildflowers** fill the
meadows beside Medicine Wheel
Passage (Scenic Byway 14A) as the
road passes through the sagebrush
and grasslands of Big Horn Basin.
Spectacular **mountain vistas** appear
as the road twists and turns up
Medicine Mountain.

■ It is traditional to walk in a
clockwise direction around the
medicine wheel. (Visitors are not
allowed within the fence, but may
circle the site outside it.)

■ Take a blanket and picnic lunch
and stop on your return to Burgess
Junction to **dine under the sky** and
enjoy the limitless views.

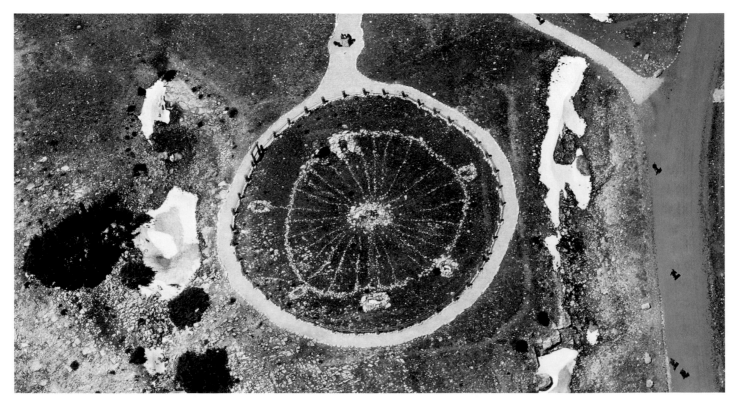

Made up of carefully aligned stones radiating out in lines from a central cairn, Bighorn Medicine Wheel is still used for Native American ceremonies.

In the high desert, the temperature drops in winter and snow sometimes blankets the canyon.

NEW MEXICO

Chaco Canyon

The largest ruins of pre-Columbian North America remain sacred to the modern descendants of their builders.

Along the dusty floor of Chaco Canyon, in northwestern New Mexico, lies a cluster of ruined pueblos (villages). Most are laid out in a D-shape, with buildings—some four stories high—constructed from sandstone blocks, mud mortar, and tree trunks that were carried in from forests 70 miles (115 kilometers) away. The timbers have provided precise dating: the pueblos were built over some 250 years, from around A.D. 900 to 1150. Constructed to preconceived plans in short bursts of collective energy, they were the work of the Anasazi (Navajo for "alien ancient ones"). A feature of the villages are the circular rooms, called *kivas*—ceremonial chambers entered from above. The number and scale of pueblos and kivas suggest that Chaco Canyon was a ceremonial and trading center for the entire Anasazi culture, which spread across the Four Corners region where New Mexico, Arizona, Utah, and Colorado meet. The canyon was abandoned in the 12th century, when a prolonged drought, probably coupled with overpopulation, shattered a fragile agricultural system dependent on rainwater for irrigation. The Anasazi migrated to neighboring regions. Modern pueblo peoples, the Hopi and (to some extent) the Navajo, regard them as forebears and see Chaco Canyon as a sacred ancestral site of powerful spiritual significance.

When to Go The Chaco Culture National Historical Park is open all year, from sunrise to sunset; the visitor center is open (except on major public holidays) from 8 a.m. to 5 p.m. The camping ground is also open year-round. Winter is very cold, summer very hot. Spring and fall have moderate temperatures, but there is a greater risk of heavy rainfall.

Planning Allow a minimum of a day to drive to and from Chaco Canyon and to see the main sights on the 9-mile (14.5 km) loop road through the park. The nearest airport is at Farmington, NM, 75 miles (120 km) north of the canyon. Albuquerque is 155 miles (250 km) to the south. The recommended route comes in from the north; signs mark the way from US Route 550. There are two routes in from the south off Highway 9; both have long segments of dirt road and may be impassable in bad weather. Bring a full range of clothes to suit all weathers: temperatures can drop suddenly, even in summer.

Website www.nps.gov/chcu

HIGHLIGHTS

■ **Pueblo Bonito** occupied center stage in the canyon. Built between 919 and 1085, it contains some 650 rooms and 40 kivas and probably housed 800–1,000 people.

■ **La Rinconada** is the largest kiva in the canyon. Measuring 63 ft (19 m) in diameter, and large enough to hold around 400 people, it is 0.5 miles (800 m) from Pueblo Bonito.

■ **Rock-carvings** and **drawings** in the canyon suggest that the Anasazi people made a close study of astronomical phenomena.

■ The remoteness of Chaco Canyon provides a remarkable **night sky**. Every year some 14,000 people come to the park's observatory to partake in the Chaco Night Sky Program (April–October).

NORTH AMERICA

Carvings of plumed serpent heads, Aztec symbol of the union of heaven and earth, adorn the Temple of Quetzalcoátl.

MEXICO

TEOTIHUACAN

The ancient Mesoamerican creation myth unfolds each morning as the first rays of the sun illuminate the stone pyramids.

Little is known about the people who built the first structures at Teotihuacan around 100 B.C., but archaeologists estimate that at its height it was one of the largest (200,000 people) and most important cities in all of the Americas, a vibrant political, commercial, and religious hub whose influence extended throughout Mexico and Central America. The fact that the original population disappeared without a trace around A.D. 700 adds to its mystery. Five centuries later, the Aztecs transformed the ruins into the sacred heart of their culture. Awed by Teotihuacan's intrinsic majesty, they synthesized the ancient remains with their own belief that this was the place where the sun, moon, and humankind were created and where mortals morphed into supernatural beings. The name means Place Where Men Become Gods. Most major structures are arranged along the Avenue of the Dead, a cobblestone thoroughfare that stretches about 2 miles (3 kilometers) from north to south. Looming above everything is the 2,000-year-old Pyramid of the Sun, more than 20 stories high and built above a lava-tube cave that may have represented the womb of Mother Earth to the long-lost people who built the original city.

When to Go Winters in the central highlands of Mexico can be surprisingly brisk, while summers tend to be hot and dusty. That leaves spring and fall—seasons of blue skies and mild temperatures—as the best times to visit Teotihuacan.

Planning Teotihuacan is about an hour's drive north of Mexico City. You can breeze through the ruins in half a day, but enthusiasts should stay at least one night in a nearby hotel and experience the sunrise on the pyramids.

Websites www.go2mexicocity.com, www.destination360.com

MEXICO

TULA

The capital of the Toltec empire was guarded by massive stone warriors thought to be representations of the god Quetzalcoátl.

NORTH AMERICA

According to legend, light and darkness meet at Tula (Tollán), the capital of the Toltec empire from which the Aztecs inherited their power. The Aztec creator god, Quetzalcoátl, is represented countless times at the site and is said to have been strongly allied with a Toltec ruler who was driven from Tula by worshipers of the evil god Tezcatlipoca. The Atlantes, 15-foot (4.5 meter) high statues of warriors, each consisting of four blocks of stone, who guard the site, are the vestiges of the endless battle between good and evil. They later became unofficial symbols of the state of Hidalgo. The site is laid out on a grid plan, with a ceremonial center surrounded by three temples shaped like truncated pyramids, the largest of which was the Temple of the Morning Star, or Tlahuizcalpantecuhtli, a god who was one of the manifestations of Quetzalcoátl, and the Palacio Quemado (Burned Palace), whose facade is decorated with figures thought to be priests or rulers. The complex also features a *juego de pelota* (ball court), where warriors converged for the ball games in which how well you played determined whether you would live to play again.

When to Go The climate is mild and dry all year.

Planning Tula is 31 miles (50 km) northwest of Mexico City, with good road and air links between the two. Tula can be combined with a stay in Pachuca, the capital of Hidalgo state, whose attractions include the Ex-Convento de San Francisco. The former convent has been converted into the Centro Cultural Hidalgo, whose Museo de la Fotografía houses more than a million photographs. Visitors who want to see Tula but whose itineraries don't include a stay in Hidalgo can take a day-trip bus tour from Mexico City. One of the Atlantes is on permanent exhibition in the Sala Tolteca in Mexico City's National Museum of Anthropology.

Website www.visitmexico.com

HIGHLIGHTS

■ The platform at the top of the Temple of Tlahuizcalpantecuhtli provides **wonderful views** of the region. Along its base are **carvings** of jaguars, eagles, and skulls.

■ The **Wall of the Snakes**, on the north face of the temple dedicated to Coatepantli, has fascinating relief carvings of snakes eating humans.

■ The **Chac Mool** is a statue of a priest set at an angle. On his stomach is a bowl, where the ancient Toltecs placed offerings for the gods.

Four giant carved Toltec warriors stand guard on top of the Pyramid of Tlahuizcalpantecuhtli. At one time they may have supported a roof.

PALENQUE

On the edge of the Mexican rain forest stand the
ruins of a great Maya city of temples and tombs.

Misty air and dense jungle shroud the towering ruins at Palenque, Mexico's greatest monument to Maya achievement. Founded in around 100 B.C., Palenque had become an important center of Maya culture by A.D. 600. Following the decline of the Maya, the city's stone structures, and the records of Maya life inscribed on their walls, lay hidden from the outside world for more than 12 centuries. Only in recent decades have archaeologists begun to decipher the ancient carved characters that tell the history of the Maya people. Nowhere are the mysterious messages more prominent than in Palenque's Temple of the Inscriptions, so named for the 620 glyphs that adorn it. The seventh-century ruler, Pakal, who reigned for 68 years, was buried here; in 1952, archaeologists discovered his tomb containing an elaborately inscribed sarcophagus. With more than 200 structures at the site, it's easy to spend days wandering through Palenque. Notable buildings grouped around the ceremonial center include the Temples of the Sun and of the Cross, and the palace, which features a spiral staircase. Numerous tombs and funerary artifacts give contemporary visitors a feel for the Maya concept of death and belief in the relationship between gods and rulers.

When to Go The winter months (December–February) are the most comfortable. Summer is very hot and humid. The site is open daily from 8 a.m. to 5 p.m.

Planning The site is about 4 miles (6.5 km) from the town of Palenque in Chiapas state. The town can be reached by train or bus from most major cities in Mexico, and local buses and taxis run between the town and the ruins. If you are traveling independently, allow at least a day to see the site. Accommodations are available at Palenque and in Villahermosa, 90 miles (145 km) away. Alternatively, numerous organized tours visit the site. The climate is hot and humid, so wear light clothing. You will also need strong walking shoes, sunscreen, insect repellant, and plenty of water. International travelers who plan an extended stay in Mexico should not make Chiapas their first stop as the government requires foreign visitors who enter the country there to leave Mexico within 15 days.

Websites www.mexperience.com, www.visitmexico.com

HIGHLIGHTS

■ Climb the steps up the front of the **Temple of the Inscriptions** for a good view of the whole site.

■ Explore the **labyrinth** of rooms and passageways in the palace.

■ The **museum** provides an interesting account of the history of the site and displays numerous artifacts found there.

■ The area surrounding the ruins is ripe for **hiking** adventure. Palenque National Park's 4,200 acres (1,700 hectares) are a haven for **bird-watching**; visitors can also get a glimpse of **jaguars** and **howler monkeys** (who are sure to be heard even if not seen).

Opposite: The palace is one of several buildings arranged around the central plaza. Above left: A Maya carving of a skull. Above right: Deep within the Temple of Inscriptions is the burial chamber of the seventh-century Maya leader, Pakal. The chamber is connected to the temple at the top of the pyramid by a stone tube.

The tallest pyramids at Tikal pierce the dense jungle canopy. The tallest of all, Temple VI, is on the left.

GUATEMALA

TIKAL'S MAYA TEMPLES

Hidden among a mass of trees and lianas in the Guatemalan jungle, massive pyramids evoke memories of a vanished civilization.

In the early-morning mists, only the shriek of howler monkeys and the plaintive cry of parrots disturb the silence of the forest. Suddenly, the path bursts into the open, where a cluster of massive towers of blackened stone reaches for the sky. The Great Plaza of Tikal is pure architectural theater. Across an expanse of trim grass, the Temple of the Great Jaguar (Temple I) faces the Temple of the Masks (Temple II). Broad steps ascend their facades—so steep that visitors descend gingerly, facing inward. The summits are crowned by roof combs of inscribed stone. Inside the pyramids lie the tombs of royalty. There are six such temples at Tikal, the tallest (Temple VI) rising to 231 feet (70 meters). Once painted vivid colors, they were the centerpieces of a city numbering perhaps 100,000 inhabitants. For centuries, Tikal dominated the other city-states of the Maya civilization, which extended across Central America. The hub of political and military power, Tikal was also a religious center where deified kings, nobles, warriors, and priests would maintain their vital bond with the gods through rituals of bloodletting and sacrifice. Then, for reasons unknown, the Maya civilization collapsed. The last dated monument in Tikal was inscribed in A.D. 869, and by about 1000 the jungle had taken over.

When to Go The best time is the dry season, from December to February. March and April are hot, and the mosquito-infested rainy season lasts from July to September.

Planning It is possible to visit the highlights of Tikal on a day trip, with about four hours in the park, but the site deserves at least two days. The park is open from 6 a.m. to 6 p.m. If you enter the park after 3 p.m., your ticket entitles you to entry the following day. The closest population center is Flores, 18 miles (30 km) to the southwest. There are several hotels of all categories at the park, and a camping ground and more hotels at Flores. "Tikal Village," located at the park entrance, has eating places and souvenir shops.

Websites www.tikalpark.com, www.belizex.com/tikal.htm

HIGHLIGHTS

■ The summit of Temple II offers a **view** of the entire complex of temples, palaces, processional routes, ball courts, altars, and stelae (inscribed stone monuments).

■ The **Lost World** area of Tikal includes a true, stepped pyramid dating from about A.D. 250 and rising to 100 ft (30 m).

■ The **museum** at the visitor center has fascinating old photographs of Tikal, still smothered by jungle, taken during early archaeological work after the rediscovery of the city in the mid-19th century.

■ The ruins are the focus of **Tikal National Park**, and some 12 miles (20 km) of trails lead off from the park entrance. Only a small portion of the ancient city has been excavated, and the remainder of the park is a rich natural reserve.

NORTH AMERICA

BOLIVIA

TIWANAKU

Set high in the Andes, this city was the spiritual and ceremonial center of a civilization that dominated the region in pre-Inca times.

SOUTH AMERICA

The ancient walls have eyes at Tiwanaku, a monumental capital city whose exact purpose remains the subject of speculation. An early Andean people first occupied the site at some point before 400 B.C. By A.D. 500, construction of the city had begun. At the time, Lake Titicaca lapped against its foundations, but the lake has since receded and is now 12 miles (19 kilometers) away. The center's many pathways wind past remnants of architectural structures—a large step-pyramid known as the Akapana, temples, and palaces—embedded with carvings and sculptures of human faces. The site was known in pre-Inca times as City of the Sun or City of the Gods, names that were interchangeable to a people who believed that the sun was both a deity and their earliest ancestor. There's little vegetation, but here and there a brave patch of green grows among the stones. The unfinished Puerta del Sol (Door of the Sun), located at the entrance to the Kalasasaya Temple, commands attention for its inscribed hieroglyphics. Though they have not yet been decoded, archaeologists believe they represent an annual agricultural calendar. The temple is also dotted with 12-foot (3.6 meter) high stone columns, each carved into a human figure.

When to Go Visit during the dry season, from May to September, to avoid persistent rains.

Planning The site is located 12,611 ft (3,844 m) above sea level and 45 miles (72 km) north of La Paz. The journey takes approximately 90 minutes, and organized day tours are available. Because of the altitude, the maximum daytime temperature in summer is only 68°F (20°C), and nights are cold, so take warm clothing.

Websites www.travel-amazing-southamerica.com, www.bolivia-explorer.com

HIGHLIGHTS

■ The **Puerta del Sol** is carved from a single block of granite, and the upper part is carved with intricate designs.

■ Most contemporary **religious** and **folkloric festivals** that take place here are held on the spring equinox– September 22 or 23–when people gather at the site before dawn to see the sun's first rays pass through the Puerta del Sol.

■ The **Kalasasaya stairway** is a single massive block of sandstone with steps carved into it.

Rows of carved stone heads are set into the wall of Tiwanaku's Subterranean Temple.

TEN ROCK-ART SITES

Humankind's earliest art was painted on rocks, cliffs, and cave walls. The meaning of the art is now lost, but the mystery endures.

❶ Valley of the Chiefs, Montana

So remote that their location was unknown to the general public until a few years ago, these rocky bluffs, which are also known as Weatherman Draw, have a half-dozen, 1,000-year-old rock-art sites. The multicolored paintings of bison, bears, tepees, and shield-bearing warriors are sacred to the Crow and other Plains Indian nations as a source of spiritual power.

Planning The roads are poor, and access is by four-wheel-drive vehicle only. A visit to all the paintings requires a strenuous round-trip hike of 5 miles (8 km). Carry plenty of water. visitmt.com

❷ Sierra de San Francisco, Mexico

The valleys of the arid Sierra de San Francisco hide more than 200 rock-art sites. Local traditions have it that these brightly colored paintings of hunters and local wildlife, including puma, goats, whales, pelicans, and fish, were made by a long-vanished race of giants. The art is believed to date from A.D. 1100–1300.

Planning The sites are in the Vizcaíno Biosphere Reserve in the Baja California peninsula. Guided visits only. The sites are accessible only on foot or by mule. www.whatmexico.com

❸ Cueva de las Manos, Argentina

Home to prehistoric guanaco hunters, this rock shelter contains some of the oldest rock art in the Americas, dating back to around 7370 B.C. Situated in the Pinturas River Canyon in the Andes foothills, the Cave of the Hands gets its name from hundreds of outlines of human hands stenciled on the walls.

Planning Easily accessed using Route 40 from Baja Caracoles. www.unique-southamerica-travel-experience.com

❹ Ubirr, Northern Territory, Australia

Australia's Aborigines have the world's oldest art tradition. At Ubirr, an ancient escarpment in the Kakadu National Park, you can see the spooky Wandjinas—representations of spirit ancestors from the Dreamtime—and the unique "x-ray" paintings that show people and animals with bones and internal organs.

Planning The best time to visit is early morning. Some paintings are accessible to wheelchair users. www.environment.gov.au/parks/kakadu

❺ Bhimbetka, Madhya Pradesh, India

Concealed on a forested ridge is the largest concentration of rock art in India. Mesolithic hunter-gatherers, attracted by the area's reliable water supply and abundant game, created these multicolored paintings of Indian wildlife, hunting, ceremonies, and childbirth between 6000 and 1000 B.C.

Planning The site can be reached by taxi or bus from Bhopal, 28 miles (45 km) away. www.indialine.com

❻ Tanum, Sweden

Rocks that had been worn smooth by glaciers provided ideal surfaces for artists to create this large collection of petroglyphs during the Scandinavian Bronze Age (1800–600 B.C.). Images of many-oared warships and axe-wielding warriors, all pecked into the rock and now highlighted with red paint, show that Scandinavia's Viking tradition had deep roots.

Planning The major sites are accessible along short walking trails from paved roads. Visit the interpretative center at Tanum first (entrance fee). tre.vastsverige.com, www.rockartscandinavia.se

❼ Valcamonica, Italy

The Italian Alps are the setting for this concentration of more than 140,000 petroglyphs. Chipped into ice-smoothed rock surfaces, the petroglyphs—which depict wildlife, religious symbols, and scenes of agriculture and war—chronicle 8,000 years of history, from the end of the Ice Age to Roman times.

Planning The main entrance to the site is at Nadro. Access to the petroglyphs is by foot only, and marked trails cater for different levels of fitness. www.arterupestre.it

❽ Niaux Cave, France

An uneven, slippery path leads for nearly a mile underground to a vast chamber in the silent heart of a mountain—to view the finest Paleolithic cave-art site that is still open to the public. (Altamira and Lascaux may be finer, but you can only view replicas.) Painted 14,000 years ago, toward the end of the last Ice Age, bison, horses, ibex, and deer gallop across the limestone walls.

Planning It is essential to book in advance to get on an English-language tour. Not suitable for claustrophobics. www.ariege.com/niaux

❾ Tassili n'Ajjer, Algeria

Visit the remote Tassili Mountains to see these rock paintings from a time when the Sahara Desert was green. The oldest paintings (9000–4500 B.C.) show herds of elephants, giraffe, rhinoceros, and buffalo. Later paintings show domesticated cattle and herders (4500–2500 B.C.). Created after 2500 B.C., paintings of horses, chariots, and camels announce the spread of the desert.

Planning Fly in from Algiers, or hire a guide and four-wheel-drive vehicle to drive across the Sahara. Seek advice on the political situation in Algeria before traveling. www.fjexpeditions.com/tassili/frameset/rockart.html

❿ Tsodilo Hills, Botswana

The San (Bushmen) hunter-gatherers revere the rugged Tsodilo Hills in Botswana's Kalahari Desert as the resting place of their ancestors. For the past 5,000 years, they have made paintings of wildlife, ancestor spirits, and shamanistic rituals on rock outcrops in the hills. Many visitors claim to have felt the brooding presence of the ancient spirits.

Planning The paintings are in a remote area requiring a 2.5-hour drive by four-wheel-drive vehicle from the nearest paved road. Or you can fly by light aircraft from Maun to the local bush airstrip. www.travelafricamag.com

Ships and armed warriors are among several features of Bronze-Age life illustrated in the rock drawings at Tanum, Sweden The red paint is a later addition.

Perched high in the mountains, this complex of temples and observatories was also home to Inca royalty and nobility.

PERU

MACHU PICCHU

Follow in the footsteps of great Inca warriors through the ruins of this sacred city in the highest reaches of the Andes.

As day breaks, shafts of sunlight fall across the ruins of Machu Picchu, the lost city of the Incas perched 7,710 feet (2,350 meters) above sea level on a ridge overlooking the Urubamba Valley in southeastern Peru. Legend tells of the Incas, or "children of the sun," founding an empire that, by the 15th century, under their leader Pachacutec, was as large as the Roman Empire had ever been. But this golden age lasted less than 100 years, brought to an end by Spanish conquerors and civil war, and Machu Picchu was abandoned. When the ruins were discovered by Hiram Bingham in 1911, they lay smothered beneath layers of jungle, known only to a handful of local farmers. From the maze of temples, gateways, palaces, chambers, and squares—clinging to terraces cut from the almost vertical hillside—archaeologists have pieced together the story of a civilization that once ruled supreme in this exotic region.

When to Go Temperatures can be high during the dry season, from May to September, but you have the the best chance of clear views during this time. From October to April, rainfall can be heavy.

Planning Allow two days to explore the ruins fully. Guided tours of the site, including a trek along the Inca Trail or an alternative route, are available, but you must be fit for these and able to cope with the high altitude. Take strong shoes, a sunhat and sunscreen, and rainwear. An alternative is to take the train from Cusco to the town of Aguas Calientes, from where local buses cover the 5 miles (8 km) to the ruins in about 20 minutes. Buy your ticket in Aguas Calientes before going up to the ruins, or you will be turned away at the gate. Check the time of the last bus down from the site, unless you are prepared to walk.

Website www.machupicchu.org

HIGHLIGHTS

■ On the Sacred Square, the **Main Temple** has fine walls, ornamental niches, and priests' chambers; the **Temple of the Three Windows** is linked to Andean cosmology.

■ At the **winter solstice**, the rising sun shines directly on the altar stone in the Temple of the Sun.

■ At the eastern end of the site is the large **funerary monolith**, where noble Incas were mummified.

■ Climb the 78 steps to **Intipunko**, "the hitching post of the sun," a carved rock pillar used by the Inca to predict solstices and equinoxes in order to monitor agricultural cycles.

■ The summit of **Huayna Picchu** (an hour's climb) provides a good overview of the whole site.

SOUTH AMERICA

PERU

SACRED VALLEY OF THE INCA

The Urubamba River flows through a fertile valley filled
with the ruins of Inca fortresses and temples.

Overlooked by the nearby White Mountain, and not far from Machu Picchu, the Urubamba River cuts through the patchwork of fields that lines the valley just north of Cusco, the Inca capital. Remnants of Inca fortresses punctuate the curves of the graceful, terraced slopes, and condors circle overhead. Both the river and the valley were of great significance to the Inca, who considered them sacred. Nearly 1,968 feet (600 meters) lower than Cusco itself, the valley's warmer, temperate climate, together with its numerous rivers and streams and its rich soil, helped to make it the breadbasket of the Inca Empire. From it came an abundance of maize, potatoes, fruits, and vegetables. At the southern end of the valley, Pisac has remains of large Inca homes, terraces, and ritual buildings. A footpath leads from Pisac's plaza to the ruined fortress above the town. Above the village of Ollantaytambo, at the northern end of the valley, lie the ruins of a vast fortress whose terraces and temples cling to a steep bluff. Ollantaytambo itself was built on top of the original Inca settlement, and many of the ancient housing blocks remain largely intact.

When to Go April to May or October to November are best. In high season (June–September), the area tends to get overcrowded. Avoid the rainy season (December–March).

Planning The valley starts 15 miles (24 km) northeast of Cusco. Buses are frequent. Although many tour companies offer a day-trip to the Sacred Valley from Cusco, aim to spend at least one night in the valley itself. Hotels and hostels are fairly basic, but most are clean and warm. A Visitor's Ticket, valid for 10 days and allowing entry to many sites in Cusco and the valley, can be bought in Cusco. Nights can be very cold, so bring warm clothing.

Websites www.peru-explorer.com/valley.htm, www.andeantravelweb.com/peru/destinations/cusco

HIGHLIGHTS

■ Explore the vast **fortress** of Ollantaytambo, which includes temples of the sun and the moon and the ceremonial Princess Baths.

■ Admire superb views and the fine **stonemasonry skills** of ancient Inca craftsmen at the hilltop fortress above Pisac. The town has a Sunday **handicrafts market**.

■ In Chinchero, the small **17th-century church**, built on Inca foundations, is decorated with paintings and murals of the Cusco school.

The Inca's massive hillside fortress at Ollantaytambo included temples and other ceremonial buildings.

PERU

The Nasca Lines

In one of the driest places on Earth, a series of vast, ancient, geometric images are scratched into the parched landscape.

SOUTH AMERICA

As you fly over the high, arid plateau south of Lima and gaze down at the sunbaked desert, the strange geometric forms of a 590-foot (180 meter) long lizard, a 295-foot (90 meter) high monkey with a coiled tail, a pair of childlike hands, a killer whale, a spider, and a tree are clearly visible in the dry earth below. These intricately patterned images, known as the Nasca Lines, were created by the pre-Inca Nasca people, who flourished between 200 B.C. and A.D. 700. Seen from the ground, they look like a random network of paths. Fully visible only from the air, the images are made up of lines that ancient people etched onto the ground by scraping up the top layer of stone to reveal the lighter-hued earth beneath. Thanks to the dry, windless climate here, they have withstood the wear and tear of centuries. Theories abound as to their purpose. The German mathematician, Maria Reiche, believed that they were a form of astronomical calendar, while others have proposed that they were offerings to the gods of water or fertility. Others again have even suggested that they are extraterrestrial landing sites. Their mystery adds to their power, but viewed from the window of a tiny Cesna plane, the Nasca Lines allow visitors a brief glimpse of a lost civilization.

When to Go Any time of year, but temperatures can be high between December and March. Flights and accommodations are more expensive during the peak tourist season (June–early September).

Planning Buses from Lima take approximately six hours to reach the oasis town of Nasca; from there it is a short bus or taxi ride to the local airport. Take an early flight over the lines, if possible, to avoid the afternoon winds, which can create a bumpy ride. Flights last 30–35 minutes, but it is worth booking overnight accommodation and giving yourself two or three days to explore Nasca and the surrounding area. Guided tours from Lima, including all transport and accommodation, are available.

Website www.nazcaperu.com

HIGHLIGHTS

■ The **Antonini Museum** in Nasca houses some of the archaeological discoveries from the site of the pre-Inca city of Cahuachi nearby. Some people believe that the artifacts found there may hold the key to the meaning of the lines.

■ Drive across the scorched desert landscape to the **Cemetery of Cahuilla**, 19 miles (30 km) from Nasca, and spend a few hours among the ancient bones and mummies on display there.

The figure of a monkey, one of more than 100 designs scratched into the parched desert, is clearly recognizable from the air.

The remains of a statue lie on one of the stone platforms scattered along the shore at Taputapuatea.

HIGHLIGHTS

■ Faaroa River, French Polynesia's only navigable river, is the place where emigrants set off across the South Pacific. Guided **kayak tours** take visitors deep into the interior.

■ The cloud-covered plateau of **Mount Temehani** in the north of the island was sacred to the ancient Polynesians. They believed that this was where they ventured into the afterlife, along one of two jagged volcanic ridges, one leading upward to heaven (the clouds) and the other downward into hell (a caldera).

■ The ancient stone temple **Tainuu Marae**, on Raiatea's western shore, is near the site of the 1897 Battle of Tevaitoa, during which the French defeated Chief Teraupo and his Polynesian forces. It was one of the decisive clashes of a decade-long war that brought the island under colonial control.

AUSTRALIA AND OCEANIA

FRENCH POLYNESIA

Taputapuatea Marae

Tucked beneath coconut palms beside an aquamarine lagoon is Polynesia's most important and mysterious sacred site.

Of all the temples scattered across the South Pacific, Taputapuatea Marae, or temple, is the most sacred. The marae was built around A.D. 1600 in the Opoa Valley, on the southeast coast of Raiatea Island, home of the ruling Tamatoa family and the center of a priestly caste that ruled over most of the Society Islands until the beginning of the 19th century. The temple precinct embraces a huge stone plaza, a rectangular *ahu* (altar) surrounded by the stone backrests of the high priests and chiefs who once presided over the sacred rituals, and a large upright volcanic slab that, according to some contemporary researchers, may have been used for human sacrifices. Although originally dedicated to other deities, the marae came to be dominated by the cult of the war god, Oro, who was thought to live in the Opoa Valley. It was the custom for emigrants to take a stone slab from Taputapuatea to use as the foundation stone of the marae they would construct in the far-off islands where they would eventually settle. Likewise, the Raiatea temple became a place of pilgrimage for faithful from all around the South Pacific.

When to Go French Polynesia is tropical throughout the year. The islands are marginally warmer during the rainy season from November to April, when cyclones sometimes sweep across the South Pacific. Blue skies prevail during the dry season from May to October.

Planning Taputapuatea Marae is near Opoa. You can reach it by road, traveling south from Uturoa. Allow an hour to explore the marae, three to seven days to explore the whole island. The highlands can be explored on foot, horseback, or in four-wheel-drive vehicles with local tour companies. Many organized excursions include a stop at Taputapuatea Marae.

Website www.raiatea.com

CHILE

EASTER ISLAND

Peering inland with sightless eyes, hundreds of giant stone heads stand guard over one of the most isolated places on Earth.

Archaeologists estimate that the first settlers may have arrived on this chunk of wind-torn volcanic terrain around A.D. 318, in the final phase of a centuries-long eastward expansion across the South Pacific. As their numbers grew, they erected monuments to their ancestral gods about 0.5 miles (1 kilometer) apart along the island's rugged shores. These flat-topped mounds, or *ahu*, were surmounted by rows of huge stone heads, or *moai*, fashioned from the island's dark volcanic rock. A total of about 288 statues are believed to have stood upright on these sites. The largest is 33 feet (10 meters) tall and weighs 80 tons (73 tonnes), the smallest is 43 inches (109 centimeters) tall. Cut from quarries deep in the heart of the lush palm forests, the massive stones were transported and erected without mechanical aids—a great feat of communal effort and purpose. But when the Dutch explorer Jacob Roggeveen arrived on Easter Sunday in 1722, the island's population had shrunk to barely 3,000. Overpopulation, deforestation, famine, and civil strife had eroded an impressive civilization. Many statues had been toppled, their shell and coral eyes lost. Disease and enforced deportations in the late 19th century decimated the population still further, severing the last human link to the past and leaving behind one of the world's most tantalizing archaeological remains.

When to Go Any time of year. Summers (December–February) are pleasantly warm and winters (June–October) are cool, but not cold. Heavy rains, mist, and drizzle can occur year-round, but the winter months are generally the driest. The Tapati Rapa Nui Festival, with its traditional music, dancing, crafts, and parades takes place each summer over two weeks in January and February.

Planning Flights between Santiago, Chile, and Tahiti go via Easter Island. Most tourist facilities and accommodations are in the capital, Hanga Roa. From there, visitors can travel to the statues by bus, car, motorcycle, bicycle, or even horseback. It is considered sacrilegious to walk on the ahu (statue mounds). Allow about two days to explore the island thoroughly. Unless arriving by cruise ship, visitors have to stay at least one night on the island due to the flight schedules.

Websites www.enjoy-chile.org, www.southpacific.org

SOUTH
AMERICA

HIGHLIGHTS

■ Visit the quarry at **Rano Raraku**, where 397 statues lie in various stages of completion. One unfinished statue, measuring 72 ft (22 m) long and weighing an estimated 165 tons (150 tonnes), would have been the largest of them all.

■ Take in the stark beauty of **Ahu Tongariki**, the largest ahu with a line-up of 15 statues.

■ Enjoy the **ocean views** from the 1,062-ft (324 m) high volcanic crater of Rano Kau.

■ At Orongo are **rock-carvings** of men with birds' heads. These are the remnants of a warrior cult. Every year, selected members of the cult would dive off the cliffs here and swim to the offshore islet of Moto Nui in a race to bring back the first sooty tern egg of the year.

Opposite: Angular features and elongated ears are characteristic of many of the giant heads that stand or lie scattered across the hillsides on Easter Island. Above: Ahu Tongariki, on the island's southeast coast, has a row of 15 moai, including the largest figures on the island.

Plain of Jars

Clusters of ancient stone jars lie scattered across the plateaus
of northern Laos, their origins and purpose a mystery.

A cross the lonely plateaus of northeastern Laos, hundreds of large, jarlike stone objects lie strewn over the landscape, like leftovers from a giant's abandoned larder. Some stand upright, others lie on their sides; some are intact, others in pieces. Most are 6.5–10 feet (2–3 meters) high, and the largest weigh around 14 tons (13 tonnes). No one knows who created them or why. The most popular theory is that they were used as funerary urns, but they could have been used for storing rice or even fermenting alcohol. Some are accompanied by large, circular, carved disks that may have been lids, or they may have been merely decorative—again, no one knows. The jars are clustered in three principal sites a few miles from Phonsavan. They probably date from 500 B.C.–A.D. 500, and although they are attributed to a Mon-Khmer people who inhabited the area throughout that time, nothing is known about the culture or society of this ancient civilization. Some historians think the jars may be clustered along an ancient route used by salt traders traveling between Vietnam and northeastern India. The air of mystery is compounded by the difficulty of access. This remote area was carpet-bombed by the U.S. Air Force during the Vietnam War, and the landscape is pockmarked with bomb craters and still littered with unexploded ordnance.

HIGHLIGHTS

■ Site 1, just 9 miles (15 km) southwest of Phonsavan, features the **largest number of relics**, with more than 250 jars. It also contains the single largest jar.

■ Site 2 has the most **picturesque setting**, with about 90 jars spread across two wooded hillsides.

■ Site 3, with some 150 jars, is set on a hillside with fine **views** of the region.

When to Go November to January, when the weather is cool and dry and the landscape is still green after the summer rains. Aim to visit early in the morning or late in the afternoon, when the light is at its best.

Planning The three sites can be reached from Phonsavan, which has a small airport with flights from Laos's capital city of Vientiane. Allow at least two nights in Phonsavan to see all three. Site 1 can be reached by trishaw from the town; sites 2 and 3 are usually accessed by four-wheel-drive. NEVER stray off the main paths as unexploded ordnance is everywhere and every year injures or kills dozens of local people. You will need a visa to enter Laos.

Website www.responsibletravel.com/TripSearch/Asia/Country100141.htm

The early dawn light adds to the sense of mystery surrounding the giant, ancient jars.

The megalithic dolmens were skillfully constructed and had small openings for placing the remains of the dead inside.

RUSSIA

ZHANE RIVER DOLMENS

Groups of Bronze-Age megalithic tombs are scattered across this beautiful region in the western Caucasus.

Modern pilgrims flock to the dolmens of the Zhane River, near Russia's Black Sea coast. Some walk the woodland paths to perform arcane rituals and lay offerings before these strange structures, others just take solace from being in their presence. There are three main groups of dolmens in the Zhane River Valley, totaling 18 dolmens altogether. Some have been excavated and reconstructed, and there is a plan to create a park here to protect the site. Visitors are free to interpret the dolmens in any way they wish since so little is known about their original function. Dating from around 3000–1800 B.C., they were built of huge stones dressed with admirable precision using primitive tools. Some have rectangular plans, others circular. Most curious are the round portals, or entrance holes, many crowned by simple carved motifs, such as zigzags. These provided access to the tiny chamber within, although stone plugs were used to close them off. In front of each was a small courtyard; it seems that funeral rites and burials took place in the courtyard and that later the bones of the dead were deposited inside the chamber. The chambers also suggest a womblike symbolism, so perhaps dolmens also denoted fertility—a physical representation of the life-and-death cycle.

When to Go Summers are very warm, with temperatures around 75–95°F (24–35°C). Winters are mild but wet.

Planning The Zhane River dolmens can be visited in a few hours. They are 3 miles (5 km) inland from the Black Sea coast. Many visitors take day-trip excursions from the Black Sea resorts, such as Gelendzhik (the nearest), Anapa, and Tuapse. The nearest airports (linked to Moscow) are at Gelendzhik and Krasnodar.

Websites www.unexpo.org, www.kubkurort.ru

HIGHLIGHTS

■ The most impressive set of **dolmens**, beside the Zhane River near Gelendzhik, consists of a rectangular dolmen flanked by two circular ones. With round entrance holes and walled courtyards, they represent perfect examples of their kind.

■ The woodland and rolling hills in the region provide an attractive and atmospheric **backdrop**.

■ A **river trip** along the beautiful Ashe Valley near Tuapse includes caves, waterfalls, and local villages.

EUROPE

The cliffs at Myra are pockmarked with house-tombs.

TURKEY

Lycian Rock Tombs

The ancient Lycians honeycombed the cliffs along their rugged coastline with ranks of magnificent tombs.

In ancient times the Lycians were admired and feared across the eastern Mediterranean. Their homeland in southwest Anatolia was protected by high, forested mountains and a rocky coastline fretted with countless coves and inlets. Here, from about 1500 B.C., a set of some 40 prosperous city-states evolved, peaceable among themselves, warlike to the outside world. Their coast was also notorious as a haunt of pirates. One feature of their distinctive culture was obsessive tomb-building. There are more than 1,000 rock tombs, many of them within the cities so that the dead were kept close to the living. Citizens would commission their own tombs in advance, expressing their status through the tomb's scale and sophistication. The grandest were styled like classical temples, with facades and chambers carved out of the soft limestone of cliffs and rock outcrops. Others resembled Lycian houses, carefully reproduced, including finely detailed ceiling beams. The less well-to-do created "pigeon-hole" tombs—small rectangular cavities that pockmark the cliff faces. The Lycians worshiped a number of gods, some borrowed from a series of invaders—including the ancient Greeks. First among these was the mother-goddess Leto and her twin children (by Zeus), Apollo and Artemis. But the veneration of ancestors was the main driving force behind the creation of the tombs.

When to Go Spring (mid-April to May) is the most agreeable season; temperatures are moderate and the mountains may still be dusted with snow. Summers can be very hot, although alleviated by coastal breezes.

Planning It takes only an hour or so to visit each of the main sites, but there are at least five of these scattered across the region, so you would need several days to see them all. Lycia occupies the mountainous region between the Gulf of Fethiye and the Gulf of Antalya, which are about 100 miles (160 km) apart. The area is served by airports at Dalaman and Antalya. There are a number of popular resorts along this coast, such as Dalyan, Kas, and Kalkan; excursions from these resorts include the ancient Lycian cities.

Website www.lycianturkey.com

HIGHLIGHTS

■ The most impressive collection of **temple-tombs** was carved in a cliff at Caunos. This was actually a part of the neighboring state of Caria, but the Lycian influence is obvious.

■ Fethiye has the fourth-century-B.C. **Tomb of Amyntas**, one of the finest temple-tombs.

■ Myra has the best **house-tombs** (fourth century B.C.). Myra was also the home of **St. Nicholas** (died A.D. 343), the original Santa Claus. His tomb and church, built in the sixth century, were a focus of Christian pilgrimage for many centuries.

■ Monolithic **pillar-tombs**, with the tomb chamber at the top, can be seen at Xanthos, the ancient capital of Lycia.

ASIA

LEBANON

BAALBECK

The extensive ruins of this ancient site pose one
of the great engineering mysteries of the ancient world.

For much of its 5,000-year history, Baalbeck was a thriving center of worship devoted to a succession of gods. In Phoenician times, from about 2000 B.C., this was Baal, god of the sky and lord of heaven and earth. But, like Lebanon itself, Baalbeck has always been at a strategic crossroads where competing empires vied for power. The Egyptians, Assyrians, and Babylonians came and conquered, followed in 333 B.C. by Alexander the Great. In the wake of Alexander, Baalbeck was hellenized to become Heliopolis (City of the Sun). Then, in 63 B.C., the Romans arrived and replaced Baal with their sky god, Jupiter. Heliopolis became famous for its oracle, consulted by successive emperors. The largest-ever temple in the Roman Empire was erected here, dedicated to Jupiter-Baal, together with temples to Bacchus and Venus. In the 4th century A.D., Rome became a Christian state and pagan Heliopolis was abandoned. Now all that remains are the ruins—and a mystery. Lining the podium of the Temple of Jupiter are at least 24 huge blocks of dressed limestone and three colossal megaliths—known as the Trilithon—that weigh around 1,000 tons (907 tonnes) each. Erosion suggests that these megaliths predate Greek and Roman times, but how they were transported and positioned baffles archaeologists and engineers to this day.

When to Go Spring (March-May) provides ideal temperatures as winters in Lebanon can be very cold and summers uncomfortably hot. July and August offer the added attraction of the prestigious Baalbeck International Festival of music, dance, and drama, which is set among the ruins.

Planning Baalbek is 53 miles (85 km) from Beirut, in the high, fertile Bekaa Valley, which is reached by a drive up from the coast through spectacular mountain scenery. Allow at least two to three hours to view the entire site. Guided tours from Beirut are available. In politically unsettled times, access to the Bekaa Valley may be restricted or forbidden.

Website www.middleeast.com/baalbek.htm

HIGHLIGHTS

■ In the Great Court leading to the Temple of Jupiter stand six 66-ft (20 m) tall **columns**, among the largest in the Roman world. Made of rose-pink granite, they were quarried in Aswan, Egypt.

■ Take in the wealth of architectural detail found in the remains of the **Temple of Bacchus**, one of the best-preserved Roman temples in the world, dating from about A.D. 150.

■ In the quarry is the **world's largest carved monolith**, measuring 69 ft (21 m) by 16 ft (4.9 m) by 13 ft 10 in (4.2 m) and weighing about 1,200 tons (1,089 tonnes).

The last remaining columns of the Temple of Jupiter complex tower over the monolithic building blocks of a much earlier temple.

JORDAN

PETRA

The ruins of an ancient city of temples and tombs lie hidden in the sandstone hills bordering the Jordanian desert.

Tall mountains loom on either side as you slowly thread your way through the long, narrow gorge known as the Siq in southern Jordan. Suddenly, like a dazzling mirage in the desert, the passageway ends to reveal Petra, a city carved entirely out of a sheer, rose-colored sandstone canyon. Built 2,000 years ago by the Nabataeans, ancient nomadic traders who settled here, the once-thriving city served as a crossroads for the trade in foreign spices and exotic wares between the Far East and the Mediterranean region. Eventually, major changes in trade routes led to Petra's decline. Through the centuries, the metropolis also served as home to Romans, Christians of the Byzantine Empire, and Crusaders before it was abandoned in the 13th century. Emerging from the Siq, you come to the monumental Treasury (*Khazneh*) with its multistoried, pink facade flanked by carved columns stretching skyward. From here you can follow winding pathways through the canyon past the ruins of this ancient city to find elaborate tombs, banqueting halls, and streets flanked by intricately carved Colonnades. At every turn, imposing structures appear, including the massive temple of Al-Deir (also sometimes known as the Monastery), dedicated to Dushara, the Nabataean god of heaven. As the day progresses, Petra's monuments turn from pale-hued pink to a deeper rose, and finally to a vivid rust as the sun sets.

When to Go Spring and fall are best. The early morning and late afternoon light reveals the spectacular colors of the rocks.

Planning Petra is 163 miles (262 km) south of Amman. The roads are good, and you can rent a car, or catch a bus or taxi, in Amman. The journey will take about two hours. Allow two to three days to see the main sights or a week to explore this vast city in depth. Accommodations are available in the nearby village of Wadi Musa. Comfortable walking or hiking shoes are a must. Bring a hat, sunglasses, and drinking water to this desert destination.

Website www.na.visitjordan.com

ASIA

HIGHLIGHTS

■ Don't miss the 7,000-seat **amphitheater**, originally built by the Nabataeans and later expanded by the Romans. It's well worth the climb up the steep stairway to see the entire theater and enjoy the view of the surrounding area.

■ Explore the **Royal Tombs** with their richly carved facades, including the two-storied Palace Tomb, projecting from the side of a canyon at the edge of the city.

■ A huge fountain, the **Nymphaeum**, was dedicated to water nymphs. It shows the engineering aptitude of the Nabataeans, who had running water in the middle of the desert.

Opposite: As visitors emerge from the Siq they get their first view of the Treasury. Despite its name, the building was originally created as a tomb and may also have been used as a temple. Above left: A Byzantine floor mosaic in a Christian church. Above right: The Treasury by candlelight is a dramatic sight.

PARTHENON

The greatest temple of ancient Greece was a monument
to wisdom, technological innovation, and imperial might.

The Parthenon, built in the fifth century B.C., looms over modern-day Athens from its hilltop site on the Acropolis. Erected to house a lavish gold-and-ivory statue of Athena—the city's guardian deity and goddess of wisdom, justice, and the arts—the entire temple, from its grand scale to the intricacy of its elegant marble friezes, was an unprecedented feat of architectural creativity and skill. Many of the sculptures and other artifacts once housed in the temple are now displayed in Athens's museums. However, the sacred intentions of the site and its significance to ancient Athenians still shine through—despite the multilingual babble of tourists and the clicking of camera shutters that are likely to accompany most visits today. Looking up at the imperious colonnades, particularly when they are floodlit at night, it is possible to understand how adored and worshiped a deity Athena once was. Her temple epitomizes all the ideals and achievements of the ancient Hellenic world. Its detail and the harmony of its forms served to demonstrate the superiority of the Athenian state to the barbarian tribes that roamed the lands beyond the city's walls.

When to Go Spring or fall, as summers are usually extremely hot and winter can be very cold.

Planning Early morning or dusk are good times to visit as the site is less crowded then. Allow a full day if you want to walk up the Acropolis to the Parthenon and tour the museums there. The climb is steep, so wear comfortable, sturdy shoes. The entrance ticket for the Parthenon covers several other ancient sights in Athens as well, so hang on to it.

Websites www.gnto.gr, www.greece-athens.com, www.athensguide.com

HIGHLIGHTS

■ The **view of Athens** from the steps of the Parthenon provides a good perspective on this bustling, crowded, modern city.

■ The **New Acropolis Museum** near the foot of the Acropolis houses many of the Parthenon's treasures, including the original marble friezes, which are displayed against the backdrop of the Parthenon visible through extensive windows.

■ Plaster replicas of six **caryatids** support the porch of the Erechtheion Temple near the Parthenon. Five of the originals are in the New Acropolis Museum and demonstrate the supreme skill of the stonemasons of ancient Athens.

The Parthenon, built with several other temples on top of the Acropolis, or Sacred Hill, towers over modern Athens.

The ruined Temple of Apollo has a dramatic location on the slopes of Mount Parnassos.

GREECE

TEMPLE OF APOLLO

Trace the path taken by centuries of
pilgrims seeking the wisdom of the sun god.

Travelers arriving at Delphi, at the foot of Mount Parnassos, enter by the route that has been used by pilgrims for the past 2,400 years. The stone-paved road leads up the rocky hillside, first to the Sanctuary of Athena, site of the circular Tholos Temple, then to the focal point of the Delphic ruins—the Sanctuary of Apollo. The sanctuary's builders believed that their construction housed the center of the world, where legend states that two eagles sent out by Zeus to find the navel of the world finally met: a spot now marked by a large stone. Passing through the sanctuary, visitors then walk along the Sacred Way leading to the Temple of Apollo, whose remarkable polygonal walls protect the sun god's sanctuary. This is where Apollo's oracle, known as the Pythia, once dispensed divine prophecies to the faithful. For hundreds of years, rich and poor traveled here to consult the Pythia, who was chosen from the local village women, as she sat in her cell. Lavish marble and bronze monuments, many adorned with precious metals, were erected at the base of the temple and along the Sacred Way by the grateful mortals who received good news.

When to Go The site is open all year, but late summer or early fall are good times to visit as the weather is warm but not too hot. The site closes by mid-afternoon on weekends and some public holidays.

Planning Delphi is 90 miles (145 km) northwest of Athens, with good public transportation links. It is also included on many organized tours. A couple of hours should be sufficient to explore the site, although enthusiasts may want to spend a whole day. You can pick up a map at the ticket office. The Archaeological Museum, which houses many of the best-preserved artifacts, is also well worth a visit.

Websites odysseus.culture.gr, www.greecetravel.com

HIGHLIGHTS

■ The tiny, circular **Sanctuary of Athena** has been adopted as an unofficial symbol of Delphi. Close by is the **Castalian spring**, where the Pythia, her priests, and pilgrims visiting Apollo's shrine were once obliged to bathe in order to purify themselves.

■ The **Treasury of the Athenians** is the most complete structure at Delphi. It was erected in 490 B.C. to house offerings from the grateful city of Athens after the Pythia's advice led to victory over Persian invaders.

■ The **amphitheater**, which seated up to 5,000 people, is one of the best preserved in Greece. During the sixth century B.C., the games at Delphi, which included music and poetry competitions as well as athletic events and chariot racing, rivaled those held at Olympia.

EUROPE

The chambers of Ggantija's temples may have been used for ritual sacrifices to the Earth Mother goddess.

MALTA

GGANTIJA

Take a walk into prehistory on the tiny Mediterranean island of Gozo through the remains of its ancient temples and caves.

R ising from a rocky plateau close to the village of Xaghra in northeastern Gozo, the massive coralline limestone blocks of the two neolithic temples of Ggantija ("belonging to giants") blend with the dun-colored earth. The trefoil-shape of each temple's floor plan, modified by the addition of pairs of side apses, is often likened to the pendulant breasts and broad hips of a fecund woman, supporting the theory that the temples were the focus of a fertility cult. The complex includes the oldest freestanding structures in the world. Dating from 3600–3200 B.C., the megaliths, some nearly 20 feet (6 meters) tall and weighing 50 tons (45 tonnes) each, account for the local legend that giants constructed the temples. In a single day, the mythical giantess, Sansuna, is said to have transported the massive stones from Ta' Cenc, near Sannat on Gozo's southern coast, balancing them on her head as she cradled her infant.

When to Go April to June and September to October are best, when the heat is less fierce than at the height of summer. Fall can be subject to strong *xlokk* (sirocco) winds.

Planning Gozo is an island in the Maltese archipelago and part of Malta. It can be reached by ferry from Malta, and Ggantija is easy to get to by road. There is a bus service from Victoria to Xaghra, but it sometimes runs infrequently, especially later in the day. Allow two to three hours to visit the temples and at least another two hours if you want to explore Xaghra. Purchase a combination ticket for Ggantija and the museum in the Ta' Kola Windmill in Xaghra for a discount on same-day admission to both sites.

Websites www.visitmalta.com, www.xaghra.com, www.heritagemalta.org

HIGHLIGHTS

■ Explore the medieval streets and alleyways of the nearby village of **Xaghra**, which has ancient churches and a folklore museum housed in the 300-year-old Ta' Kola Windmill.

■ In the cliffs to the northeast of Xaghra are the **alabaster caves**, overlooking the Bay of Ir-Ramla. These include the L-Ghar ta' Kalipso (Calypso Cave) where, according to Homer's epic poem, the beautiful sea nymph Calypso kept Odysseus captive for seven years.

■ Visit the **Archaeology Museum** of Gozo in the island's capital, Victoria (known locally as Rabat), about 3 miles (5 km) from Xaghra. The finely worked artifacts include two carved female heads from Ggantija's original excavation in 1827.

EUROPE

MALTA

HAGAR QIM AND MNAJDRA

Though partially reconstructed, a group of ancient temples are a testament to the skills and vision of Malta's Stone-Age craftsmen.

The ruins of the neolithic temples of Hagar Qim ("standing stones") and Mnajdra are situated on Malta's rocky southern coast. The irregular slabs of limestone that form their outer walls and chambers appear to lock together seamlessly, an enduring testament to the engineering genius of Malta's ancient inhabitants. Hagar Qim, which consists of six large, circular rooms arranged along a central corridor, was built between 3600 and 3200 B.C. as a place of worship. One of the mammoth stones weighs 40 tons (36 tonnes) and is believed to be the largest single block used in any megalithic temple on Earth. About 1,600 feet (500 meters) away are the remains of the three temples of Mnajdra. Their thick stone walls and pillars are decorated with curious spiral carvings. The purpose of the temples is unknown, although their ingenious celestial alignment, particularly of the lower temple, suggests that they were used for astronomical observation and for ceremonies to mark the solstices and equinoxes. Excavations in the mid-19th century added to the puzzle, with discoveries of sacrificial altars and full-figured female statues—including the Venus of Malta at Hagar Qim—that are consistent with the worship of a fertility cult.

When to Go April to June. Summers can be very hot and winters rainy. Fall is prone to *xlokk* (sirocco) winds.

Planning The site, close to the village of Qrendi, is open all year except on Christmas and New Year. Equinox and solstice days are good times to visit as the gates open to the public at sunrise. Arrive early to watch the sun's rays enter the lower Mnajdra temple and flood into the inner chambers, finally illuminating the altar stone. Allow three to five hours to explore both sites. Wear sturdy walking shoes, as a visit involves a considerable amount of walking, often over rough ground. Boat trips to the Blue Grotto leave from Wied iz-Zurrieq, southeast of Qrendi.

Websites www.visitmalta.com, www.heritagemalta.org

EUROPE

HIGHLIGHTS

■ Admire the **precision engineering** and **intricate stonemasonry** of the neolithic builders in the jumble of courtyards, corridors, and chambers.

■ Take a boat trip to the **Blue Grotto**, a cave carved by the sea where the water and the multicolored minerals in the rock sparkle in the sun.

■ The National Museum of Archaeology in Valletta houses many statues, including the **Venus of Malta**, and a decorated pillar altar, all excavated at the temples.

The curving walls of the temple of Hagar Qim were constructed with vast blocks of stone.

ITALY

VALLEY OF THE TEMPLES

Stand among the ruined columns and statues high above the sun-drenched shores of southern Sicily and sense the might of ancient Greece.

Centuries before the rise of imperial Rome, the seafaring Greeks commandeered much of the eastern Mediterranean, establishing settlements right across southern Italy and the island of Sicily. At Agrigento (then known as Akragas) on Sicily's southwestern shores, the remains of sacred temples still loom imposingly from their hilltop site, with the crystal-blue sea in the distance. The temples, which were built in a line along the top of a ridge, all face east and were aligned so that the rising sun struck the statue of the god housed in each one. The names Zeus, Heracles, and Demeter may be the stuff of legend now, but enter the tranquil setting of these shrines erected in their names—filled in spring with the heady aroma of wildflowers blanketing the surrounding hills—and the powers that these deities exerted over their devout followers is everywhere in evidence. The architectural skill and painstaking devotion of the Greek stonemasons who, during the fifth and sixth centuries B.C., carved the elaborate Doric columns and giant statues as embodiments of their all-powerful divinities—shines out. An intricate labyrinth of catacombs links the site to early Christianity. Restoration by archaeologists in the 19th and early 20th centuries has helped to preserve this place of quiet contemplation, where the reverberations of ancient prayers still seem to fill the air.

When to Go Spring and fall are best, when the weather is warm but not too hot.

Planning Agrigento has good road and rail connections to Sicily's other main towns. You can reach the site itself by bus or car. If you are traveling independently, you can book a guided tour at the ticket office. The scrub landscape requires comfortable shoes, preferably with some ankle protection. Half a day is sufficient to see the temples, but allow a full day if you want to make the most of the museum as well. Visit the museum first, in the morning, as it is closed most afternoons.

Websites www.valleyofthetemples.com, www.sicily-tour.com

EUROPE

HIGHLIGHTS

■ The **Temple of Concorde** is one of the finest surviving Greek temples in the Mediterranean region, thanks in part to its conversion into a Christian church in A.D. 597. The Christian catacombs, hewn out of the rocky cliffs, are close by.

■ The fifth-century-B.C. **Temple of Hera** is largely intact and has commanding views over the Mediterranean.

■ The **Temple of Olympian Zeus**, built to commemorate a victory at the Battle of Himera in 480 B.C., is believed to have been the largest Doric-style temple in the world.

■ The **Archaeological Museum**, just north of the temple complex, has numerous artifacts from the temples, along with Roman finds dating from around the second century A.D.

■ At the end of a day's exploration, in the gathering twilight, gaze back at the **floodlit temples** nestling in the gathering darkness.

Opposite: The towering remnants of the Temple of Castor and Pollux, built during the 5th century B.C., catches the evening sun. Above: The beautifully proportioned Temple of Concorde, built around 430 B.C., is one of the best-preserved Doric temples in the world.

The majestic Temple of Apollo is the most complete of the three temples at Paestum.

ITALY

PAESTUM

Soak up the glory of the ancient Greeks on Italy's Amalfi coast, where monumental temples were built to honor the Olympian deities.

I n the 19th century, three Greek temples that had been neglected for many centuries were uncovered close to the ruins of the classical city of Paestum, south of Naples. The towering columns and intricately worked stones of these architectural masterpieces, combined with their isolated position high above the coast, demonstrate the extent to which the lives of the ancient Greeks were ruled by their devotion to their gods and goddesses. The Temple of Hera, the oldest temple at the site, dates from the sixth century B.C. Its early construction and dedication to the goddess of fertility imply that the area around the site was seen as a place of settlement. Built around 450 B.C., the nearby Temple of Apollo (which is also sometimes attributed to Neptune or Hera II), is the most beautiful and best-preserved temple at the site. The Temple of Athena, set apart from the others on the opposite side of the space that was occupied by the forum, and still sometimes known as the Temple of Ceres, has three medieval tombs set into the floor, indicating that the building was also used as a Christian church at one time.

When to Go Spring or fall, when it is neither too hot nor too cold, although the site is open all year. The museum is closed on some Mondays.

Planning Paestum lies on the Piana del Sele coastline, 52 miles (84 km) south of Naples, and can be reached by train or car. Allow half a day for the temples alone, or a full day to take in the museum as well. Ideally, stay overnight, visiting the museum in the morning and the ruins in the late afternoon, when it is likely to be cooler. A combined ticket for the temples and the museum is cheaper than buying separate tickets. In hot weather make sure you have bottled water and the protection of a sunhat, and avoid walking around the temples during the midday heat.

Websites www.turismoregionecampania.it, www.paestum.de

HIGHLIGHTS

■ The **museum** houses a large collection of finds excavated from the site. Most fascinating are the tomb frescoes, especially those from the so-called **Tomb of the Diver**, as they are the only examples of tomb frescoes from ancient Greece to survive.

■ Explore the foundations of **Roman houses and public buildings** around the forum.

■ Stay overnight in Agropoli, 6 miles (10 km) away, and enjoy the deserted ruins at **sunset**.

EUROPE

GERMANY

EXTERNSTEINE

A group of rock towers in Germany's ancient northern forest have been a place of worship and pilgrimage since prehistoric times.

Hidden deep in the Teutoburger Forest, an expanse of ancient woodland in the North Rhine-Westphalia region in northwestern Germany, is a line of five gigantic, ragged limestone columns. It is little wonder that ancient local tribes may have attributed supernatural powers to these natural wonders, known as the Externsteine ("stones of the Egge hills"). Legend has it that the columns were a focus of pagan worship and possibly even the site of the Saxons' sacred Irminsul, the "tree of life." The early German hero, Arminius (or Hermann), Chieftain of the Cherusci, is said to have made sacrifices to the gods here after his great victory over the Romans in A.D. 9. When the Emperor Charlemagne conquered the Germanic tribes in 772 and imposed Christianity in the region, the Externsteine became a place of retreat for Christian hermits, who settled in caves at the base of the rocks and chiseled out staircases and tombs inside them. Close to the summit of the tallest columns the hermits created an open-air chapel with a round window that faces the sunrise on the midsummer solstice, one of many features at the site that blends Christian with pagan tradition.

When to Go Any time of year. The surrounding woods are particularly beautiful in fall, while in winter, snow on the rocks can make them appear sharper and more mystical. Informal pagan festivals are celebrated at the site on Walpurgis Nacht (April 30/May 1) and the summer solstice (June 21).

Planning The Externsteine are near the hamlet of Holzhausen-Externsteine, 7.5 miles (12 km) south of the city of Detmold, and are signposted off the B1 and B239 roads. Parking is available close by. The nearest local bus and rail connections are at Horn-Bad Meinberg, 1.5 miles (2 km) west of the Externsteine. Allow about two hours for a visit, or longer if you also plan to follow the Hermannsweg path to the huge 19th-century statue of Arminius (Hermann) in Detmold.

Website www.nrw-tourism.com

HIGHLIGHTS

■ An **iron bridge** between two columns gives access to the chapel constructed close to the summit of the tallest rock (124 ft/37.8 m).

■ The staircases inside the rock columns provide access to **viewing platforms** where you can take in the panorama across the rolling forest landscape.

■ At the base of one of the rocks is a 12th-century **relief sculpture** depicting Jesus' descent from the cross. Near the foot of the cross is a symbol resembling a bent tree, thought to represent the pagan Irminsul bowing in service to Christ.

The Externsteine is riddled with passageways and tombs. The chapel at the top of the highest tower (far right) may also have been used as an observatory.

CALANAIS

For more than 4,000 years, an extraordinary group of megaliths has dominated the island of Lewis on Europe's northwestern fringes.

EUROPE

Visitors can only speculate about the beliefs that inspired the long-vanished people who erected these stones on the Isle of Lewis, off Scotland's west coast. But even though vast stretches of time and the relentless Atlantic winds have eradicated all clues to the world-view behind it, Calanais (or Callanish) is a place where the sense of something sacred still survives. At its center, a circle of 13 stones, some 11 feet (3.5 meters) tall, surrounds an imposing slablike central monolith 15.5 feet (4.75 meters) high. Rows and avenues of stones radiate out from this ring, compared by observers to the shape of a Celtic cross. A small chambered burial cairn, or tomb, holding a few charred fragments of human bone lies at the heart of the circle, but it is believed to be of slightly later origin than the stone circle itself. The stones are local gneiss and may have come from a ridge just a few miles away. It is estimated that each stone required a team of 20 men to haul it to the site. The stones were not erected on wasteland; recent archaeological excavations have revealed that this was once cultivated ground, worked by the communities whose homes and farmsteads are gradually being excavated and explored.

When to Go The climate on Lewis is cool and changeable, but May through September offers long hours of daylight and generally the best chance of dry weather.

Planning The Isle of Lewis can be reached by a 2.5-hour ferry ride from Ullapool, on the Scottish mainland, or by air. Plan to stay at least one night to visit—and perhaps revisit—the Calanais stones and other archaeological sites. The highly informative visitor center at Calanais is not open on Sundays, but the stones are accessible at all times. In the Outer Hebrides place names now appear in their Gaelic versions, and the Gaelic "Calanais" is increasingly favored over the anglicized but previously more common "Callanish."

Websites www.isle-of-lewis.com, www.scotland-inverness.co.uk

HIGHLIGHTS

■ Smaller sites nearby include Calanais II and Calanais III. Less frequented by tourists than the main set of stones, **Calanais III** in particular is very atmospheric.

■ A few miles north of Calanais on the A858 is **Carloway Broch**, an Iron-Age fortification set on top of a cliff. Visitors can explore the broch and its spectacular views over the sea. The visitor center includes a reconstruction of the interior of the broch.

The stones at Calanais have several astronomical alignments and may have been used for tracking the movement of the sun, moon, and planets in relation to Earth.

The massive stones, arranged as a horseshoe within a circle, form an observatory for tracking the movements of the sun.

ENGLAND

STONEHENGE

One of the most sacred sites in Europe remains an enigma, its past shrouded in mystery.

Erected in stages between around 3000 and 1600 B.C., Stonehenge was the site of rituals that we can only guess at. Was it designed as a temple for sun worship, or was it part of an oversized astronomical calendar? Why did its builders expend so much effort, over so many years, to create it? Despite all the questions, one fact is known: the stones are aligned to coincide with the rising sun and the passing seasons, leaving little doubt that its builders possessed a sophisticated understanding of both arithmetic and astronomy. This is evident in all phases of construction, from the outer ditch and bank, the oldest feature, to the construction of the linteled sarsen-stone (sandstone) megaliths and bluestones that were arranged during the final phase into a horseshoe and circle formation in the center. While Stonehenge's purpose and uses still elude us and may have changed over the centuries, this site was the central focus of people's lives. Latter-day druids still gather at this sacred temple to celebrate the winter and summer solstices, when sunlight streams through gaps between the sarsen stones. The Heel Stone, outside the ditch on the northeast side, marks the spot where the summer-solstice sun rises, casting a long shadow toward the heart of the circle.

When to Go Stonehenge is open all year, but sunrise during the summer solstice is particularly spectacular, if crowded with worshipers and visitors.

Planning Stonehenge is at the intersection of the A303 to the south and the A344 to the north and is easy to reach by car or bus. The nearby towns of Salisbury and Amesbury make excellent bases for visiting Stonehenge and exploring the surrounding countryside. Allow two hours to explore the site. During regular opening hours, visitors are prohibited from entering the center circle. An after-hours Stone Circle Access pass is available from English Heritage.

Websites www.stonehenge.co.uk, www.english-heritage.org.uk

HIGHLIGHTS

■ In the middle of the stone circle is the **bluestone horseshoe**, a U-shaped ring of smaller stones from the Preseli Mountains in Wales that turn blue when wet.

■ Excavations have revealed cremated human bones in some of the chalk filling in the **Aubrey Holes** on the outer circumference of the site.

■ From Amesbury, follow an 8.5-mile (13.7 km) **round-trip hike** through a landscape of fields and woodland, taking in prehistoric monuments, Bronze-Age burial mounds, Woodhenge, and Stonehenge.

EUROPE

Ten Mighty Sculptures

Since ancient times, monumental sculptures have held the power to fire the imagination and awaken the soul.

❶ Olmec Heads, La Venta Park, Mexico

Follow the lush archaeological trail through La Venta Park and you will encounter some of the oldest known monuments in Mexico. Carved by the Olmecs, an ancient civilization predating the Maya, these magnificent colossal heads are thought to portray their mighty rulers. The heads are arranged in the same order in which they were found at their original site 80 miles (129 km) away at La Venta. The largest of them is 8 ft (2.4 m) high and weighs 24 tons (22 tonnes).

Planning La Venta is in the state of Tabasco. Visit the park after dark for the impressive sound and light show. www.tourbymexico.com

❷ La Virgen Maria del Panecillo, Ecuador

Towering over the city of Quito, the winged 148-ft (45 m) tall aluminum Virgin stands at the top of Panecillo Hill, named by the Spanish for its resemblance to *pan*, the small bread roll. The hill, a sacred site since the days of the Inca, is 9,840 ft (3,000 m) above sea level, and a trip to the top offers spectacular views. The majestic Virgin stands on top of a globe with her feet on a snake—the brave can climb up to a balcony in the plinth.

Planning For the best viewing, get there early in the morning before the clouds settle. Take a taxi to the top and have the driver wait while visiting the area. A half-hour is sufficient to take in the sights. www.in-quito.com

❸ Christ the Redeemer, Brazil

An enduring symbol of Rio, the statue of Christ the Redeemer seems to receive visitors with open arms. Located on the peak of the 3,000-ft (914 m) Corcovado Mountain, the art-deco-style 125-ft (38 m) statue is constructed from reinforced concrete and weighs 700 tons (635 tonnes). The chapel, in the base of the statue, is large enough for 150 worshipers, and the site has been formally declared a Roman Catholic sanctuary.

Planning For the ultimate experience, take the Corcovado Rack Railway on the 20-minute journey through the awe-inspiring Tijuca National Forest. This is the same train that carried the parts of the statue to the top of the mountain. www.corcovado.com.br, www.rio.rj.gov.br/riotur/en

❹ Buddha Vairocana, Todai-ji Temple, Japan

Japan's enormous gilded bronze Buddha is housed in what is considered to be the largest wooden building in the world, the Todai-ji Temple. Legend has it that nearly 2.6 million people helped construct the Buddha, which was finally completed in A.D. 752. Today, the temple and its peaceful surroundings serve as the headquarters of the Kegon school of Buddhism.

Planning Nara Park is located on the eastern side of the city of Nara. www.jnto.go.jp/eng

❺ Amida Buddha, Kamakura, Japan

Originally housed inside a wooden temple, the Kamakura Buddha has been in the open air for more than 700 years. At nearly 44 ft (over 13 m) high, and set against a breathtaking backdrop of wooded hills, it is one of the great icons of Japan.

Planning Kamakura is located 30 miles (48 km) from Tokyo; the Buddha is a short walk from the train station. For a small fee, visitors can go inside the statue, which is hollow. www.kamakuratoday.com/e

❻ Giant Buddha, Leshan, China

At 233 ft (71 m) tall, this is the largest Buddha in the world. Carved into the cliff face of Lingyun Mountain, the smiling statue faces Mount Emei, where Buddhism was first established in China. The Buddha was placed at the spot where three rivers meet in the hope of helping to calm the turbulent waters. Visitors can gather at his instep or climb into one of his ears for an impressive up-close view.

Planning The statue is east of Leshan City. Arrive at the site by ferry for an awe-inspiring first impression. www.travelchinaguide.com

❼ Gomateshwara, Shravanabelagola, India

This granite statue was erected to honor Lord Gomateshwara, the Jain saint who, according to legend, gave up his kingdom for meditation. Every 12 years, priests bathe the statue with milk, honey, curd, rice, sugar, almonds, saffron, dates, and bananas in a special ceremony—the next will be held in 2018.

Planning Shravanabelagola is 8 miles (13 km) from Channaravapatna, and buses run between the two locations. www.hoysalatourism.com

❽ Aukana Buddha, Sri Lanka

Aukana means "sun-eating," and today monks still gather flowers at dawn and offer them in front of the 50-ft (15 m) tall, fifth-century-A.D. Buddha statue as the first rays of the sun inch down its form. On most days there are few visitors.

Planning The Buddha is 31 miles (50 km) southeast of Anuradhapura. Visitors are advised to dress modestly. www.travelsrilanka.com

❾ The Great Sphinx, Egypt

The megalithic statue of the Sphinx beside the pyramids at Giza has the head of a god and the body of a lion. At 185 ft (56.4 m) long and 65 ft (20 m) high, it is believed to be the largest stone statue ever created.

Planning Giza is a few miles outside Cairo and is open to the public from 7 a.m. to 5:30 p.m. daily. www.touregypt.net

❿ Temple Expiatori del Sagrat Cor, Spain

This monumental temple, crowned by a giant bronze statue of Christ, sits at the peak of Tibidabo Mountain, 1,886 ft (575 m) up. A trip to the top of the temple affords panoramic views over Barcelona and the surrounding coastline.

Planning The Blue Tram takes visitors to the foot of the funicular railway. From there, board the Tibidabo Funicular up the mountain to the temple. www.bcn.es

The great bronze statue of the Amida Buddha in Kamakura was cast in 1252. Located on the grounds of the Kotokuin Temple, the statue is so tall that it towers above the treetops.

THE MEGALITHS OF CARNAC

On the coast of Celtic Brittany, a 5,000-year-old
stone army marches out of the mist.

O f all the megalithic sites in Europe, none can compare for sheer quantity and precise alignment to the lines of standing stones at Carnac. More than 3,000 march across 2 miles (3 kilometers) of Breton moorland. In the sea-scoured light of this Atlantic coastline they take on lives of their own, sculpted over the millennia by wind and weather into a procession of fantastical shapes: hooded figures, hunched forest creatures, jabbing spearpoints of rock, walking warriors, prisms, and footstools. It is small wonder that old Breton folklore identified the stones as the remains of a pagan army from the dawn of Christian times that pursued a local saint across the countryside with murder on their minds. Cornered, the holy man saved himself by miraculously turning his enemies to stone. But 19th-century antiquarians and 20th-century archaeologists have proved these megaliths to be much older. The stones, hauled from some distance away on giant rollers, were most likely deposited here in several stages, probably during the fourth millennium B.C. Their purpose is unknown, but they may be markers for communal worship, gifts to the gods, memorials to the human dead, or calendrical devices to mark harvests, holy days, and the turning of the year.

When to Go The Carnac area, with its sunny beaches, is a popular tourist destination, and during July and August access to some parts of the archaeological sites may be restricted to protect the stones. Guided tours in English are available. October–early April can provide the most atmospheric experience.

Planning Allow at least three days, but up to a week if prehistoric archaeology is your passion. A car and a comprehensive map of the area are essential. The most significant sites are well marked, with accessible parking areas. Bring comfortable walking shoes or boots, since some of the most fascinating and quieter sites are only accessible by walking through forest or across rough ground. Take a flashlight as the interiors of the dolmens are dimly lit. For an overview, you can start at the Prehistory Museum in Carnac.

Websites www.ot-carnac.fr, www.stations-bretagne.com

HIGHLIGHTS

■ The landscape is dotted with individual **stone circles** and **dolmens**—the remnants of chambered tombs, some shaped like open gateways into the afterlife, others like giant tortoises or sacrificial altars.

■ Explore the maze of footpaths that penetrate the forest of **Petit Ménec**, which has smaller alignments of moss-covered stones, some resembling petrified woodland creatures, that seem to grow out of the forest floor.

The Carnac area is dotted with passage graves. This one at Gavrinis is filled with ornately carved, patterned stones.

The menhirs at Almendres Cromlech have stood here for 6,000 years.

PORTUGAL

ALMENDRES CROMLECH

With its minimal tourist fanfare, this impressive
stone circle retains a strong spirit of place.

There are about 95 megaliths in the Almendres Cromlech in central Portugal. These closely spaced, giant, rounded stones arranged in two interlocking rings came to public notice only in the mid-1960s, in the wake of new theories about the astronomical implications of Stonehenge. The circle of smaller stones on lower ground may have been the first installation, dating back perhaps to 4000 B.C. It may originally have been horseshoe-shaped, like other megalithic enclosures in the region, with the open side facing the eastern horizon and the rising sun. Uphill, larger stones form an elliptical ring. The orientation of the stones may relate to astronomical observations. In particular, a pair of large menhirs at each end of the ellipse forms an axis that points to sunset and sunrise at the equinox. But there are so many stones here that any number of other astronomical positions could also be indicated. A clue may lie in the symbols engraved in shallow relief on a number of the stones: circles, lines, crozier shapes, and sets of holes. But for now the mystery of the cromlech's function persists.

When to Go The Almendres Cromlech is accessible all year. Spring (April–early May) is particularly beautiful: the climate is mild and the slopes are carpeted with wildflowers. July is the hottest month.

Planning The site is close to the village of Guadalupe, 3 miles (5 km) from the city of Évora and about 95 miles (153 km) east of Lisbon. Access is free. The stones are on private land, but signposts lead to the site along roads and dirt tracks. Some bus tours include Almendres on their itinerary; otherwise, visitors can reach the site by car or bicycle.

Website www.crookscape.org/textjan2005/text_eng.html

HIGHLIGHTS

■ A single standing stone known as the **Almendres menhir**, dating from 4000-5000 B.C., can be reached via a 0.5-mile (1 km) walk from the main site with fine views of the rural landscape and, in summer, an array of wildflowers.

■ The **setting** of the Almendres Cromlech is beguiling: the lichen-spattered stones stand on open ground on a gentle east-facing slope, rimmed by a grove of cork trees.

■ **Views** from the cromlech look out over the rural landscape and to the historic city of Évora.

■ Spend some time in nearby Évora. The ruins of the Roman **Temple of Diana** date from A.D. 100-200. The walls and ceiling of the 16th-century **Chapel of Bones** (Capela dos Ossos) is lined with approximately 5,000 human skulls and bones.

EUROPE

MEROE'S ANCIENT PYRAMIDS

Sandy paths weave around the truncated columns
and royal burial chambers of this once-noble city.

AFRICA

The warm desert wind whips up a fine layer of dust that hugs the earth, almost covering the faint tracks that lead to the ancient pyramids of the kingdom of Kush in northern Sudan. Built between 300 B.C. and A.D. 300, these steep-sided, weathered structures—more than 200, arranged in three groups—are all that remain of the burial chambers of generations of kings and queens, hinting at the past importance of the ancient royal city of Meroe, around which they stand. Just 3 miles (5 kilometers) from the fertile banks of the Nile, the ruins of this once-vibrant city and its procession of pyramids are now banked up with fine sand. Each pyramid has an imposing colonnaded entrance. Frescoes and hieroglyphs half-hidden under a gritty, golden veil are etched into the vast stone blocks of the burial chambers. Although they are not yet fully understood, the frescoes tell stories of gods and other immortal beings and of the monarch buried within each tomb. Inside the huge, stone-walled enclosure of the city itself are the remains of a royal palace, several small temples, and a *nymphaeum*, or Roman bath.

When to Go November through February, when temperatures are at their coolest. Avoid May and June, when high temperatures average around 120°F (49°C) and are accompanied by frequent dust storms.

Planning Meroe is about a three-hour drive north from Khartoum and 4 miles (6.4 km) northeast of Kabushiya train station, near Shendi, where taxis and buses are available. Allow at least a day to wander among the pyramids and visit the ancient city. Simple accommodations are available in the village of Bagrawiyah, next to the site. Bring your own food and water, and a sleeping bag if you plan an overnight stay. Protection against dehydration and the fierce desert sun are essential. The gatekeeper may charge a negotiable entrance fee. Barter if you want a camel ride. You may need a permit to take photographs—check with a travel company or local tourist adviser before setting out.

Websites www.numibia.net/nubia/meroe.htm, www.imagineafrica.co.uk

HIGHLIGHTS

■ Take a **camel tour** of the pyramids.

■ Where permitted, run your fingers over the ancient **hieroglyphs** carved in the stone.

■ Look for the **tomb of Queen Amanishakheto**, which was partly destroyed in 1834 after the discovery of her gold jewelry hidden in a chamber at the top of her pyramid.

■ Spend a **night in the desert** at the Meroe Tented Camp, about 2 miles (3 km) from the pyramids.

■ Visit the remains of the **temple devoted to Amun**, located between the railway line and the Nile River.

The Kushite people, who originally came from Egypt, continued the custom of erecting pyramids within which to bury their dead.

The stones at Wassu, like those at the other sites in the Senegambia region, were skilfully cut and shaped with iron tools.

GAMBIA/SENEGAL

STONE CIRCLES

Scattered along the valley of the Gambia River is the most concentrated collection of stone circles in the world.

In an area 62 miles (100 kilometers) long and 217 miles (350 kilometers) wide, between the Saloum River in Senegal and the Gambia River, pillars of pitted and weathered laterite (a type of sandstone) handcrafted by a forgotten civilization encircle the burial mounds of nameless kings and chiefs dating back at least 1,200 years. More than 1,000 stone circles, together with tumuli and burial mounds, are grouped in four concentrations, at Sine Ngayène and Wanar in Senegal, and Wassu and Ker Batch in the Gambia. Each circle consists of 10–20 stones of various shapes and sizes, from flat-topped columns to square or tapering stones. Several explanations have been proposed for the arrangement of the stones, including the theories that a large stone next to a small stone represents parents buried with their child and that V-shaped stones indicate two close relatives who died at the same time and were buried together. Recent excavations suggest that bodies were not buried intact, but that different bones were given ceremonial burials at different times. Clay pots and rudimentary tools have been found in the mounds and may have been placed there in the belief that they would aid the monarch's journey into the afterlife.

When to Go In the dry season (mid-October–April).

Planning Wassu is 12.5 miles (20 km) northwest of Janjanbureh (Georgetown) on the Gambia River. You can reach it by bush taxi from the north bank of the river. Ker Batch is on the north bank near Nyanga Bantang. You will need to rent a jeep to visit Ker Batch and the Senegal sites, which are in the Kaolock region, near Ngayène, about 110 miles (177 km) southeast of Dakar. Allow about seven days to see all the sites, depending on road conditions. Travel by river wherever possible as the roads are in a bad state of repair. Take malaria pills as malaria is present in the Gambia River area.

Websites www.gambia.co.uk, www.adventurecenter.com, www.accessgambia.com/information/index.html

HIGHLIGHTS

■ **Djalloumbéré**, near Ngayène in Senegal, has the largest concentration of stone circles in the area–52, made up of a total of 1,000 stones.

■ The **Wassu Museum** explores the history and culture surrounding the creation of the sites, which are now a World Heritage site.

■ The **largest stones** are at N'jai Kunda, near Ker Batch. They were transported down a steep hill to be placed in position.

■ The Bird Safari Camp in Janjanbureh in the Gambia River is a great spot for **birdwatching.**

AFRICA

CRADLES OF FAITH

Every religion has its own sacred geography—the places where the founders of the great faiths were born or buried, sites of purported revelations, vital landmarks on personal and collective journeys, shrines where holy texts and images have been created or preserved. While sacred to their followers, many of these places also offer inspiration and insight to travelers of any faith, or none. For example, the temple complex of Qufu in China is not only the place where Confucius expounded the philosophy that inspired two millennia of Chinese civilization, but also the family home of his modern descendants. And in Istanbul, Hagia Sophia is a glorious 1,500-year-old example of the architecture of awe, a great monument to Byzantine Christianity and its art. Some, such as Mount Sinai, are rich in meaning for Jews and Christians alike. Others are specific in their significance; Hill Cumorah in New York State, for example, marks the site of Mormon prophet Joseph Smith's reported encounter with an angel.

As dusk falls in Old Jerusalem, floodlights pick out the ancient Western (or Wailing) Wall and the beautiful Dome of the Rock on the Temple Mount beyond it, holy places for followers of the Jewish, Islamic, and Christian faiths.

PALMYRA

Follow the path of the visions and purported miracles
that led to the founding of a major new faith.

The pastoral tranquility of Hill Cumorah, a small mound nestled in the rolling farmland close to Palmyra in western New York State, belies the importance of this site as the birthplace of one of the younger offshoots of Christianty. Every summer, more than 100,000 visitors arrive here to witness a dazzling theatrical pageant, re-creating the astonishing events that led to the founding of the Church of Jesus Christ of Latter Day Saints, or Mormonism as it is more commonly known. Believers and the curious gather to follow a path leading up to the summit of Hill Cumorah and a monument to the angel Moroni, a Mormon prophet believed to have been reincarnated as an angel. It was on this spot, according to Mormon teachings, that young Joseph Smith received guidance and wisdom from the angel in preparation for the unearthing of the sacred golden plates inscribed with the text that Joseph translated into the Book of Mormon. Close by is the woodland clearing—now known as the Sacred Grove—where, in 1820, the 14-year-old Joseph is said to have received his first vision. Believers and nonbelievers alike cannot fail to sense the deep peace that pervades this spot.

When to Go Visitors are welcome at any time of the year, but the best time is mid-July, when the Hill Cumorah Pageant is performed.

Planning The Hill Cumorah Pageant is free but very popular. Limited seating is available only on a first-come basis, so arrive well before the performance begins. Advance reservations for accommodations are essential during the pageant, and advisable at any time of the year, as there are few hotels or guesthouses in this rural area. The Hill Cumorah Visitor Center sells maps of the historic sites nearby, while films and exhibits recount the history of the area. Allow at least one day to tour the sites in the Palmyra area.

Website www.hillcumorah.org

HIGHLIGHTS

■ Soak up the excitement that builds as the cast of richly costumed performers moves through the crowd of spectators and onto the stage during the grand opening procession of the annual **Hill Cumorah Pageant**.

■ Tour the **Grandin Print Shop**, and visit the room where the first copies of the Book of Mormon were printed in 1830.

■ At Whitmer Farm in nearby Waterloo is a reconstruction of the modest 20x30-ft (6x9 m) **log cabin** in which Joseph Smith lived while he transcribed the Book of Mormon.

Each year, more than 600 performers take part in the Hill Cumorah Pageant, which tells the story of the Book of Mormon.

The Amida-do hall is one of Enryaku-ji's many temples scattered through the woodlands on Mount Hiei.

JAPAN

ENRYAKU-JI TEMPLE COMPLEX

The flame of Tendai Buddhism has been burning
on Mount Hiei, above Kyoto, for 1,200 years.

The 2,782-foot (848 meter) peak of Mount Hiei, between Kyoto and Lake Biwa, is a place of great natural beauty and repose, where in A.D. 804 the Buddhist monk Saicho, who introduced Tiantai, or Tendai, Buddhism to Japan, established a monastic community. Colorful pavilions, temples, and courtyards are spread over an area of some 5,000 acres (2,025 hectares) on the mountain's higher slopes, linked by stone paths and stairways through the trees. Daily rituals, accompanied by chanting, bells, candlelight, and incense are performed in the temples. The complex is divided into three areas. Todo (the East Precinct), which is always thronged with pilgrims, monks, and tourists, has the most buildings, including the largest and most sacred: the Kompon Chu-do (central hall), built on the site of Saicho's original hermitage. Saito (the West Precinct) is 20-minutes' walk from Todo and includes the mausoleum housing Saicho's remains. The more remote Yokawa has several small halls and shrines.

When to Go Enryaku-ji is open all year. In winter the mountain may be covered in snow, while views may be closed off by fog at any time of year.

Planning One day is enough to visit the sites and to appreciate the natural beauty of the location. Cable cars and ropeway gondolas take visitors close to the top of Mount Hiei. There are two routes: the Eizan cable car and ropeway is accessible by train from Kyoto; the Sakamoto cable car reaches the summit (in 11 minutes) from the Lake Biwa side. Both services depart regularly throughout the day. It is also possible (but slower) to reach the summit by bus.

Websites www.hieizan.or.jp/enryakuji/econt/index.html, www.japan-guide.com

HIGHLIGHTS

■ The **Kompon Chu-do** has a sunken floor, which makes the altar in the center appear to float at eye level in a chasm of darkness. The altar shelters a lamp that has been kept alight for 1,200 years.

■ The Kokuhoden in the Todo area houses many **statues**, including a beautiful 9th-century statue of a **Senju, or 1,000-armed, Kannon** (god).

■ The **museum** houses an excellent collection of Buddhist sculpture, calligraphy, paintings, and other religious artifacts.

■ The **Tenporin-do** (central hall) in Saito is the oldest temple at Enryakuji. Originally built at the foot of the mountain, it was moved here in 1596.

ASIA

TEN SACRED TEXTS

Beautifully illustrated and produced texts attest to the strength of the faith of past peoples and their love of beauty.

❶ Prayer Book of Anne de Bretagne, New York

This prayer book was commissioned by Anne, the "twice-crowned queen" of France, to teach her only son to read—before he died at the age of three. Illuminated by Jean Poyet of Tours in 1492-95, page borders are illustrated with the letters ANE, spelling Anne's name, and interlaced cordeliers, or ropes, alluding to Francis of Assisi, one of Anne's patron saints.

Planning Pierpont Morgan Library, New York. www.morganlibrary.org

❷ Nany's Scroll, New York

The Book of the Dead is the collective name for the illustrated scrolls that accompanied ancient Egyptians to their graves. The scroll in New York was produced around 1040–945 B.C. for Nany, a ritual singer, and shows the prototypical scene in the Hall of Judgment presided over by Osiris, where Nany's heart is weighed in the scales of Maat, the goddess of truth.

Planning Metropolitan Museum of Art, New York. www.metmuseum.org

❸ Gutenberg Bible, Austin, Texas

Printed in 1454-5, the Gutenberg Bible was the first substantial book printed with movable type. Each of the 48 Gutenberg Bibles that survive today was decorated and bound according to the buyer's taste. Texas's copy has 14th-century textual annotations on many of its pages, more than 40 illuminated initial letters, and paper watermarks of a grape cluster and a bull's head.

Planning The Texas copy of the Bible is in the collection of the Harry Ransom Center, located on the campus of the University of Texas at Austin. www.hrc.utexas.edu

❹ Othman Koran, Tashkent, Uzbekistan

Completed in A.D. 651, the world's oldest Koran was compiled in Medina by the third caliph, Othman ibn Affan. This manuscript copy is inscribed on deerskin. Caliph Othman was murdered while reading his Koran, and a dark stain on the pages is said to be his blood.

Planning Library of the Telyashayakh Mosque. news.bbc.co.uk/2/hi/asia-pacific/4581684.stm

❺ Ostromir Gospels, St. Petersburg, Russia

Dating from 1056-7, the Ostromir Gospels make up the oldest dated East Slavic sacred book in existence. They contain feast-day readings inscribed on vellum and decorated with gold leaf and ornate paintings of the disciples. Taken from the Novgorod monasteries, the book was lost for 85 years and surfaced in 1805 in the personal effects of Catherine II.

Planning National Library of Russia, St. Petersburg. www.nlr.ru

❻ Sarajevo Haggadah, Bosnia-Herzegovina

Created in 1350 in Barcelona, the world's oldest Sephardic Haggadah—the part of the Talmud that is recited at the ceremonial meal, or Seder, at Passover—survived several wars as it was spirited across Europe over the centuries. Gold and copper leaf and pigments made from semiprecious minerals endow its 34 full-page miniatures with vivid color. Wine stains speak to its presence at long-ago seders.

Planning The National Museum of Bosnia and Herzegovina, in central Sarajevo. www.zemaljskimuzej.ba

❼ Dead Sea Scrolls, Jerusalem, Israel

In 1947, a Bedouin boy discovered a cave in which there were more than 900 scroll fragments; some, like the great Isaiah Scroll, have been carbon-dated to 335–122 B.C. Written in Hebrew dialects and in Aramaic, the scrolls include the earliest extant copies of biblical scriptures and other texts. The Copper Scroll gives sites of buried treasure, and calendar scrolls deal with lunar timekeeping and horoscopes.

Planning The scrolls can be seen in the Shrine of the Book at the Israel Museum, Jerusalem. www.imj.org.il

❽ Diamond Sutra, London, England

Discovered in a cave in the Chinese Silk Road town of Dunhuang in 1907, the Buddhist text known as the *Diamond Sutra* is inscribed with a date corresponding to May 11, A.D. 868, making it the world's oldest example of a dated, printed book. Woodblock-printed onto a scroll, the *Diamond Sutra* is named from a passage stating that it will "cut like a diamond" through the world's illusions.

Planning The book is kept at the British Library, London. www.bl.uk, www.silkroadfoundation.org/toc/index.html

❾ Luttrell Psalter, London, England

This 14th-century copy of the Psalms has more than 200 pages of illustrations detailing the minutiae of medieval life with an impish sense of humor. Plowing, reaping, dinner at table with friars in attendance, a woman combing her hair, a cook hacking at carcasses on a chopping block—the psalter celebrates the sacred by its delight in the everyday.

Planning The *Psalter* is in the British Library, London. www.bl.uk

❿ Book of Kells, Dublin, Ireland

Books and Christianity were new when Irish monks produced the *Book of Kells* in the late eighth century. The text includes gospels, prefaces, and summaries. The intensity of color and dense, passionate interweaving of decorative motifs from various cultures show the excitement that the monks must have felt at this new religion and their desire to produce a book as ornate as any jewel.

Planning The *Book of Kells* is in Trinity College Library, Dublin. www.tcd.ie/Library

The use of bright colors and telling details by the illustrators of the *Book of Kells* produced a work of great character and charm. In this scene the devil is tempting Christ to throw himself from the temple.

QUFU

Chinese visitors come to worship virtue and academic
achievement at the spot where Confucius lived and is buried.

ASIA

The second-largest temple complex in China is in Qufu (the largest being Beijing's Forbidden City). From its crenellated main Star Gate to the south, once only opened for visits by the emperor himself, a path leads past twisted pines and cypresses through courtyards containing huge stone *bixi*—tortoise-like statues with stelae on their backs—to the grand Confucius Temple, or Kong Miao. Here arched marble bridges span a dried-up moat, and great sweeps of yellow-tiled roofs top vast, crimson halls. The Xingtan Pavilion, or Apricot Altar, marks the site where Confucius taught, and behind it the Hall of Great Achievements, mounted on a double terrace, forms a vivid centerpiece. The hall's front pillars are single blocks of stone, carved in relief with writhing dragons, clouds, and pearls. The magnificently dilapidated buildings of the Kong mansion, Confucius' family home, lie to the east and date from 1038 onward. Visitors can peer through the windows at dark furniture, ornate screens, and a grandfather clock—all left as they were when the last descendant fled in 1940. The Confucius Forest, about 20-minutes' walk north, is a shady combination of clan cemetery and sculpture park. Various halls used for sacrifices dwarf the plain burial mounds of Confucius, his son, and grandson.

When to Go April to May and September to October are the best months, with dry, comfortably warm weather. July and August are the wettest and hottest months, and January is the coldest.

Planning Qufu is around 300 miles (483 km) from Beijing and has a station on one of the Beijing-to-Shanghai train lines, although Yanzhou, 10 miles (16 km) away by bus or taxi, has more services. The best prices for accommodations in the area are obtained by booking not in advance but when you arrive. Allow a full day to explore the complex, and avoid the first few days of May and the first week of October, which are national holidays.

Websites www.sanyachinatravel.com, www.travelchinaguide.com

HIGHLIGHTS

■ The magnificent three-story **Pavilion for Worshiping Literature**, dating from 1018, has triple layers of eaves supported by a mesh of decorative beams and brackets.

■ The **Hall of Great Achievements' pillars** were finer than anything that was owned by the emperors, so they were covered in yellow silk during imperial visits.

■ Qufu restaurants offer **banquets** of dozens of exotic courses based on those served to the Yansheng Dukes, the last descendants of Confucius.

The Hall of Great Achievements, which houses a statue of Confucius, was used for ceremonies to celebrate the sage.

A boat-ride on the Yamuna River in Mathura provides an excellent view of the colorful temples and shrines that line the bank.

INDIA

KRISHNA JANMABHOOMI

At the heart of the ancient city of Mathura is the birthplace of Krishna, one of Hinduism's most colorful deities.

Krishna was born more than 5,000 years ago in Mathura on the Yamuna River in northern India. According to Hindu legend, his parents had been imprisoned by his uncle, Kamsa, ruler of Mathura, and in order to protect Krishna, the baby was spirited away and raised in the idyllic world of the *gopis* (cowherd girls) in nearby Vrindavan. Both Mathura and Vrindavan are now filled with shrines and temples celebrating this story—all are the focus of pilgrimage and devotion to Krishna, thought to be an avatar, or incarnation, of the god Vishnu. Chief among the sites is the Krishna Janmabhoomi, or "birthplace of Krishna" (also known as the Sri Krishna Janmasthan)—a large complex of temples, shrines, and gardens centered on the supposed site of the prison cell. In the 1660s, the Muslim Mogul emperor Aurangzeb destroyed the original Hindu temple on the site and built the Katra Masjid (mosque) in its place. The new Krishna Janmabhoomi complex grew up next door; the current temple was opened to the public in 1984.

When to Go October to March is best, although the winter months can be cold and foggy. Summer is very hot (up to 113°F/45°C). The monsoon rains fall between July and September. The Janmashtami Festival marking Krishna's birthday is held in August or September, the Holi Festival in February/March.

Planning Mathura is in Uttar Pradesh, in central-north India. The nearest airport is at Agra, 40 miles (64 km) to the southeast. Delhi is 90 miles (145 km) to the north. There are good road connections to Mathura. The main railway station, Mathura Junction, is centrally located. Vrindavan is 10 miles (16 km) north of Mathura. Allow a couple of hours to visit the Krishna Janmabhoomi (open daily 5 a.m.-12 p.m. and 4-9 p.m.). Bag checks and other security at the entrance of the Krishna Janmabhoomi can cause long delays: be patient. Cameras and mobile phones are not permitted inside the complex.

Website india.journeymart.com/mathura

HIGHLIGHTS

■ The **Keshava Deo Temple** is said to mark the site of the original prison cell where Krishna was born. The atmosphere is intense as devotees line up to pay their respects.

■ The temple complex's modern **gateway**, flanked by security staff, consists of an arch surmounted by a painted statue of Krishna riding his horse-drawn chariot.

■ The **Gita Mandir** (temple) is decorated with vivid wall-paintings illustrating scenes from the *Bhagavad Gita* (Song of God), a section of the Mahabharata that consists of Krishna's advice to Arjuna.

ASIA

CHINA/TIBET

JOKHANG TEMPLE

The most sacred temple in Tibetan Buddhism
houses a rare and precious statue of the Buddha.

The heart and soul of Tibetan Buddhism, Jokhang Temple attracts several hundred pilgrims each day. Many trek for hundreds of miles to this temple in the old section of Lhasa, the Tibetan capital. Some even make the journey by prostrating themselves each step of the way. The original parts of the temple were built by the Tibetan king, Songtsen Gampo, in the seventh century to house images of the Buddha that his wives brought to Tibet from China as part of their dowries. The temple was later expanded several times to reach its current, massive, four-story proportions. At the entrance a crowd of devotees rises and falls in grand prostrations; so many pilgrims have performed this ritual over the centuries that the paving stones have been worn smooth. Red-robed Tibetan lamas mingle with the faithful, whose small prayer wheels whir as they walk in a clockwise direction around the holy building in order to earn karmic merit. Inside the temple, butter lamps flicker in the dim light, casting a soft yellow glow on walls filled with ornate paintings, carved columns, deep red fabrics, and a wealth of statues of merciful or wrathful Tibetan deities. The hum of devotees murmuring their heartfelt prayers blends with the hypnotic sound of lamas chanting, all set against a background of clashing cymbals and the blaring of sacred trumpets.

When to Go April through October is best. The winter months (December–February) are very cold.

Planning The temple opens at 8 a.m. to pilgrims; tourists cannot enter until the afternoon. You need both a visa to visit China and a Tibet travel permit. Your travel agent can help in arranging these. During periods of unrest, Tibet's borders may be closed. Lhasa is at an altitude of 12,000 ft (3,660 m). To avoid altitude sickness, rest for a few days when you arrive and drink plenty of water.

Websites www.visittibet.com, www.cnto.org, www.travelchinaguide.com

ASIA

HIGHLIGHTS

■ Don't miss the statue of the **Jowo Buddha**, located on the temple's ground floor. This magnificent gilded and jeweled image of the Buddha as a 12-year-old was brought to Songsten Gampo by his wife, Wencheng.

■ Explore the **temple roof**, with its sculpture of two gilded deer flanking the Dharma Wheel (wheel of teaching), unparalleled views of the Potala Palace, former home of the Dalai Lamas, and the Tibetan mountains in the distance.

■ Wander around the **Barkhor** surrounding the temple. This **sacred path** is used by pilgrims to circumambulate the temple, and it also serves as a marketplace where stalls sell wares such as yak butter, for making offerings, and turquoise and amber jewelry.

Opposite: The temple rooftop has four finely decorated bell towers. Above left: The Jowo Buddha is the most revered object in Tibetan Buddhism. Above right: The ornate roof is covered in gilded bronze tiles and carved with Buddha figures and dragons' heads.

Colorful prayer flags flutter under a sal tree in the Sacred Garden, marking the place where the Buddha was born.

NEPAL

LUMBINI

The birthplace of the Buddha is one of Buddhism's most sacred sites and an international pilgrimage center.

Lumbini is in the foothills of the Himalaya, in southern Nepal, close to the Indian border. Massive mountains loom in the distance and soaring temple spires reach to the sky. Known as the birthplace of Gautama Buddha, the area has always been legendary for its lush gardens and limpid ponds. In the center of the Sacred Garden of ancient monuments is the restored Maya Devi Temple, complete with a Marker Stone claiming to show the exact spot where the Buddha was born around 563 B.C. The current temple was built on the foundations of an earlier one erected in the third century B.C. Next to the temple is the sacred pond known as Puskarni, surrounded by ancient stupas. Maya Devi, the Buddha's mother, was said to have bathed in this lotus-filled pond before giving birth under the branches of a sal tree, a native tree of southern Asia. Nearby is a pillar erected in the third century B.C. by the Buddhist emperor, Asoka; it is one of a series he erected throughout Nepal and northern India. Lumbini is also home to a fast-growing international Buddhist center, known as the Monastic Zone, where a number of countries have built monasteries, temples, and shrines in a range of styles filled with colorful frescoes and Buddhist statues glimmering in the tranquil surroundings.

When to Go The best times are October through March. Avoid the hot season from April to July and the monsoons from July through September.

Planning Lumbini is about six hours from Kathmandu by bus or car. You will need a visa to enter Nepal. The New Lumbini Village has lodges, restaurants, and other tourist facilities. Because of sporadic outbreaks of violence in parts of the country, including the south, travel warnings are sometimes issued. Check for updated information before your trip.

Websites www.nepalhomepage.com, www.infohub.com

HIGHLIGHTS

■ The elegant, pagoda-style **Maya Devi Temple** houses a bas-relief image of the Buddha's mother.

■ In the Monastic Zone, explore the shimmering, gold-and-white **Myanmar Temple** and the Chinese **Zhong Hua Buddhist Monastery** with its golden Buddha statues and manicured garden.

■ Meditate at the **Japan Peace Stupa**, dedicated to uniting people from around the world in their search for peace.

ASIA

PAKISTAN

NANKANA SAHIB

The birthplace of the founder of Sikhism is
filled with elegant temples built in his honor.

With its domes, arches, soft amber colors, lawns, and pools, the Gurdwara Janam Asthan expresses with suitable dignity the honor of standing on this most sacred Sikh site. The temple marks the birthplace of Guru Nanak Dev, the founder of Sikhism. Born in 1469, Guru Nanak Dev spent his childhood and young adulthood in Nankana Sahib, where nine *gurdwaras*, or places of worship, of varying size have been built, each recalling a different incident from his childhood. They have become objects of devotion for Sikhs all over the world. The Gurdwara Mall Ji Sahib marks the place where Rai Bular Bhatti, ruler of Talwindi, came upon a cobra using its hood to shield the face of a sleeping boy from the sun. The boy was Guru Nanak Dev, and this incident convinced Rai Bular of the child's divinity. The Gurdwara Patti Sahib stands on the site of Guru Nanak Dev's first school, where he demonstrated his unusual wisdom at an early age. Since the partition of India in 1947, Nankana Sahib has become a Muslim town, with only about 30 Sikh families remaining, but every year some 25,000 Sikhs come here to pay their respects, gathering especially for the festival that celebrates Guru Nanak Dev's birthday.

When to Go The climate is best from October through March, but the gurdwaras really come alive during the three main Sikh festivals: Vaisakhi (April); the commemoration of the death of the Sikh Maharaja Ranjit Singh (the Lion of the Punjab), who ruled the region in the early 19th century (June); and the birthday of Guru Nanak Dev (November).

Planning Nankana Sahib is 48 miles (77 km) west of Lahore and is well connected to the city by road and rail. Check for travel restrictions that may be in force before setting out. The gurdwaras are open to all comers, from any religion, although most visitors are Sikhs. Allow at least a day to see all the sites.

Website www.nankana.com

ASIA

HIGHLIGHTS

■ **Gurdwara Janam Asthan** contains a shrine representing Guru Nanak Dev's parental home.

■ **Gurdwara Kiara Sahib** marks the place where Guru Nanek Dev, as a boy, allowed cattle to stray into a neighbor's field while he was in a meditative trance. According to legend, he miraculously repaired the damage to the field with just a glance.

Sikh pilgrims pay homage to Guru Nanak Dev during the festival to mark his birthday.

CRADLES OF FAITH | 95

TRINITY MONASTERY

The spiritual home of the Russian Orthodox Church is a glittering fortified monastery founded by one of its most beloved saints.

EUROPE

From the approaches to the monastery along the streets of Sergiyev Posad, the Troitse-Sergiyeva Lavra looms like a giant fairy-tale jewelry box, its gleaming domes of gold and sapphire piled up behind neat white walls. The monastery is a place of pilgrimage visited by thousands every year from all reaches of the Russian Orthodox Church. The monastery was founded in 1345 as a small wooden chapel, dedicated to the Trinity, by St. Sergius (Sergiyev), a hermit of noble origin. Sergius attracted a band of faithful followers and devised a charter for their communal life that became the basis of monastic life in the Russian Orthodox Church. After his death and the destruction of the wooden church by Tatar raiders in 1408, his successor, St. Nikon, constructed a stone church on the site, the gold-domed Trinity Cathedral, where Sergius's remains were reburied. Over the centuries, the cathedral was joined by a dozen more churches, including the very striking Cathedral of the Assumption, its blue domes decorated with a star-spangled pattern. The monastery was fortified in the 1550s by massive walls and towers, and its heroic resistance against a Polish siege in 1608–10 reinforced its reputation as a sacred and inviolable symbol of Russian national pride.

When to Go The monastery is open from 8 a.m. to 6 p.m. throughout the year. The churches are not generally open to tourists on weekends, when the complex is, in any case, often very crowded with pilgrims. Winter temperatures (November–March) can hover around 12ºF (-11ºC).

Planning Five of the 13 churches and numerous other buildings are open to the public. Most foreign visitors come to Sergiyev Posad on a day trip from Moscow, 46 miles (74 km) to the southwest. Trains run every half-hour or so from Moscow's Yaroslavsky Station. At Sergiyev Posad, the station is about a ten-minute walk from the monastery. Road connections to Moscow are reasonably good. Women are expected to cover their head with a scarf when entering the churches.

Website www.stsl.ru

HIGHLIGHTS

■ The **Cathedral of the Holy Trinity** contains works by the greatest Russian icon painter of the medieval period, Andrei Rublev.

■ The interior of the **Cathedral of the Assumption** is richly decorated with frescoes painted in 1684.

■ The **Chapel-at-the-Well** was built over the sacred spring of St. Sergius. The waters (accessible at a fountain under a 19th-century canopy) are believed to effect cures.

■ The **Refectory of St. Sergius** and the **Palace of the Patriarchs** were both built in Baroque style in the 17th century, the era of ornate and lavish building at the monastery.

Thirteen churches, all richly decorated inside and out, cluster within the fortified walls of the Trinity Monastery.

Carved images of St. Trdat (on the left) and St. Gregory the Illuminator greet visitors at the gateway to St. Etchmiadzin.

ARMENIA

St. Etchmiadzin

Set in the heart of the Caucasus Mountains, one of the world's oldest surviving cathedrals houses several early Christian relics.

The imposing but plain gateway is a sharp contrast to the riches to be found within St. Etchmiadzin—the "Vatican" of the Armenian Apostolic Church. The cathedral building may resemble other Armenian churches from afar, but its history and treasures make it special. The cathedral stands on the spot where St. Gregory the Illuminator, patron saint of the Armenian Church, claimed he was instructed by Jesus in a dream to build a church. That first church, built in the fourth century, was replaced in the fifth–seventh centuries by the edifice that still stands today. Pause at the main door to take in the fine detail of the intricate stone carving. Once inside, look up at the 18th-century murals that adorn the ceiling, from which the eyes of painted angels appear to follow you as you cross the ancient paving stones or fix on you if you pause in contemplation. To the right of the altar is the entrance to the cathedral museum, which houses a vast and dazzling display of artworks and sacred relics. The presiding clergy can point out items that the Armenian Church identifies as fragments from the cross on which Christ died and from his crown of thorns.

When to Go The cathedral and compound are open from the beginning of April to the end of October, Tuesday to Sunday, from 7:30 a.m. to 8 p.m.

Planning There is no tourist information at St. Etchmiadzin, so it is advisable to book a private or group tour of the site. Guided tours depart regularly from Yerevan, the Armenian capital, about 12 miles (20 km) away. In addition to travel time, you need approximately half a day to see St. Etchmiadzin properly. Visitors can attend the main service at the cathedral, held on Sundays at 11 a.m. (10:30 a.m. on special occasions). The service lasts about two hours; be prepared to stand as there are no seats. Women are expected to cover their heads. The cathedral museum is closed during the service.

Websites www.etchmiadzin.com, www.armeniainfo.am

HIGHLIGHTS

■ The many **khachkars** (cross-stones) scattered around the cathedral compound commemorate significant events in Armenia's turbulent history.

■ Enjoy the view of the often snow-covered **Caucasus Mountains**, including Mount Ararat, where, according to the Bible, Noah's Ark landed after the flood.

■ The seventh-century church of **St. Hripsimé** in Etchmiadzin houses St. Hripsimé's tomb. She was killed by the pagan king of Armenia, Trdat, who subsequently converted to Christianity under the guidance of St. Gregory.

ASIA

TEN SACRED SOUNDS

From hymns to rhythmic drumbeats, somber chants or stirring exaltations, music has the power to uplift the mind and stir the soul.

❶ Harlem Gospel Choir, New York

Every Sunday the Harlem Gospel Choir, the most famous of its kind in the U.S., sings in Times Square. You won't be able to resist clapping your hands and tapping your feet, so go along to enjoy the music and all-you-can-eat free buffet.

Planning The Gospel Brunch is at the BB King Blues Club every Sunday. Doors open at 12:30 p.m. www.harlemgospelchoir.com, www.bbkingblues.com

❷ Taiko Drummers, Japan

For the last thousand years, the thundering sound of the Japanese taiko drum has seen off evil spirits, signaled the start of war, and celebrated festivals. Once believed to have been inhabited by gods, the drum soon found its place in religion, and its sound can be heard at Shinto shrines and temples.

Planning Kyoto's Yasaka-jinja Shrine is the scene of many taiko events held as part of its annual Gion Matsuri Festival in July. www.kyoto.travel, www.taiko.com

❸ The Monks' Choir, Kiev, Ukraine

The solemn yet beautiful voices of the choir soar above the golden domes of the Kiev-Pechersk Lavra Monastery. This complex of churches, museums, and caves dates back almost a thousand years, and its renowned cathedral choir has long attracted pilgrims and visitors alike.

Planning The monastery is open to the public and is a short trolley ride from the center of Kiev. www.miysvit.com, www.lavra.kiev.ua

❹ Don Cossack Choir, Germany

The Don Cossack Choir is proof that beauty can emerge from the ravages of war. Founded in 1921 by a group of Russian refugees interned in a prison camp, the original choir sang folk, opera, and religious songs a cappella. Subsequent Don Cossack Choirs continue to perform to this day.

Planning The current German Don Cossak Choir Wanja Hlibka was formed by a member of the original lineup. www.don-kosaken-solisten.de

❺ Bach Festival, Leipzig, Germany

Johann Sebastian Bach lived in Leipzig for 27 years until he died in 1750. He worked as director of music at St. Thomas Church, and every June, his adopted city celebrates his music with a festival of concerts and cultural events.

Planning Top-class musicians from across the globe perform in venues throughout the city. It is advisable to book well in advance. www.bach-leipzig.de

❻ Vienna Boys' Choir, Austria

The Austrian composers, Bruckner, Haydn, Mozart, and Schubert, give their names to the four Vienna Boys' Choirs in the city today. With their angelic voices and sailor-suit outfits, the boys travel the world, performing about 300 concerts every year to audiences totaling half a million.

Planning The four choirs tour extensively around Europe, Asia, Australia, and the Americas and give regular concerts in Vienna. www.wsk.at

❼ The Monks' Choir, St. Wandrille, France

The order of Benedictine monks at St. Wandrille Abbey are famous for their Gregorian chants. Every day, ringing bells announce the start of morning Mass and the monks congregate in the chapter to sing. Visitors are welcome to join them in the church afterward for the service.

Planning The monastery welcomes overnight visitors and has guest-quarters on the grounds. Booking is essential. www.st-wandrille.com

❽ Monks of Santo Domingo de Silos, Spain

The Benedictine Monks of Santo Domingo de Silos enjoyed unexpected, chart-topping success in 1994 when their album of Gregorian chants, aptly titled *Chant*, was released. The modest CD soon became a bestseller, and the monks followed it up with a second album. They still celebrate the Gregorian Mass at their monastery, a masterpiece of Romanesque architecture in northern Spain.

Planning The monks sing Gregorian chants at their services six times daily, seven times on Sundays and holidays. www.spain.info, www.angelrecords.com

❾ King's College Choir, Cambridge, England

The choristers of King's College sing Evensong daily during term-time, but the highlight of their year is the Festival of Nine Lessons and Carols. Broadcast by the BBC to families across the world, the festival marks the beginning of Christmas. The chapel that the choir calls home is an ornate gem; it took more than a century to build and was completed in 1547.

Planning Evensong is celebrated at 5:30 p.m., Mondays to Saturdays. The carol service begins at 3 p.m. on Christmas Eve, but be warned– you'll almost certainly have to start lining up at 9 a.m. www.kings.cam.ac.uk

❿ Fès Festival, Fès, Morocco

Each June, the ancient walled city of Fès celebrates its heritage with a week-long festival of sacred music. Sufi musicians, Sami folk singers, Celts, Tuareg, and Berbers come together from all corners of the globe to bridge their differences under the Moroccan sky–be it beneath an oak tree or in the courtyard of a palace.

Planning Many hotels in Fès's modern section, the Ville Nouvelle, offer a shuttle-bus service to and from the festival. www.fesfestival.com, www.spiritoffes.com

A drummer in traditional dress beats the large taiko drum during a Shinto ceremony at the Yasaka Shrine, Kyoto. The ornate drum is supported on an elaborately carved stand.

A series of terraced gardens surrounds the golden-domed Shrine of the Báb.

ISRAEL

Shrine of the Báb

One of the holiest sites of the Bahai faith, the shrine gleams like a jewel in its setting on the slopes of Mount Carmel.

D odging the traffic on Ben Gurion Boulevard to see the ornate mausoleum and golden-tiled roof of the Shrine of the Báb is not the safest way to see Haifa's showpiece, but it provides the most impressive view, especially at night, when the shrine is lit up like a beacon. Built in the early 1900s to house the remains of the Báb, regarded by Bahais as a messenger of God and forerunner of Bahá'u'lláh, the founder of the Bahai faith, the shrine is constructed from Italian cut stone. The mausoleum itself is surmounted by colonnaded tiers that support a dome covered with more than 12,000 golden tiles. The shrine, which is 130 feet (40 meters) in height overall, stands at the center of a series of terraced gardens—nine above and nine below—that extends up the slopes of Mount Carmel for half a mile (1 kilometer) to Yefe Nov Street. From here you get a panoramic view of the terraces, which cut across Haifa's bustling streets as they step down to the edge of the Mediterranean Sea.

When to Go Any time of year. The shrine is open every morning excluding Bahai holy days. The terraces are open in the mornings and afternoons every day except Wednesdays.

Planning The entrance is on Haifa's Zionut Avenue, and admission is free. The terraces can be seen only by taking a guided tour, which does not include the shrine, and advance booking is essential. Dress should be modest—no shorts, short sleeves, or anything revealing. The tour of the terraces involves a demanding 0.5-mile (1 km) climb. An alternative is to take a rental car or taxi to see the shrine from Ben Gurion Boulevard and then drive up to Yefe Nov Street, which runs across the top of the site, or Panorama Road at the top of Mount Carmel, to enjoy the view.

Websites www.inisrael.com, www.terraces.bahai.org

HIGHLIGHTS

■ Panorama Road, at the top of Mount Carmel, provides a **bird's-eye view** of the shrine, the terraces, and the Mediterranean beyond.

■ On the wall of the shrine hangs a prayer called the **Tablet of Visitation**, which is used by Bahais when they visit the shrine.

■ Near the base of the Bahai shrine is the **German Colony**, a collection of beautiful houses on Ben Gurion Boulevard built by members of the Temple Society, a faction of the Lutheran Church, who began migrating to Israel in 1868 to create communal agricultural settlements.

ASIA

CAVE OF THE NATIVITY

One of Christianity's holiest places rests
beneath the Church of the Nativity in Bethlehem.

ASIA

M ary, Joseph, and the three wise men probably wouldn't recognize the cave where Jesus is said to have been born more than 2,000 years ago. The grotto, then used as a barn, is beneath the oldest church in the Holy Land, located on Manger Square. Entering through a low, stone doorway called the Door of Humility, visitors find themselves in a cavernous, somber church. The cave entrance next to the main altar is accessed by steps descending to a slim, arched doorway, through which is the nativity scene. On the right of the entrance is the Altar of the Nativity, draped in rich fabrics. A silver star is set into the floor beneath it, marking what is thought to be Jesus' birthplace. On the left is a second altar, marking the place where Jesus lay in the manger. Centuries of faithful followers have transformed the once-simple cave. The floor that was covered with hay and dirt now consists of stone and marble. Oil lamps hang from the ceiling, and gold icons are everywhere—decorations added over the centuries by the faithful to venerate a cave considered to be one of Christianity's most holy sites. Though the cave has been transformed, faith and feelings have not. Visitors are quiet and subdued. Some pray, some kiss the marble where Mary is believed to have given birth, while others light candles to honor Joseph, Mary, and Jesus.

When to Go The cave is open all year. The area is crowded at Christmas, which is celebrated at the Church of St. Catherine, next to the Church of the Nativity, on December 24, and by followers of the Greek and Armenian Orthodox Churches on January 7. Check Israeli government websites for security warnings.

Planning Bethlehem is a ten-minute drive from Jerusalem. Allow an afternoon to see the cave and other churches nearby. Admission is free, and several services are held there daily. Wear modest clothing when entering any church or holy spot in Israel. Manger Square has a Peace Center and tourist information office where information is available on this and other nearby sites.

Websites www.goisrael.com, www.mfa.gov.il

HIGHLIGHTS

■ Almost 50 columns run in double lines along the sides of the church where archaeologists have found tiles from the **original church**, built in the fourth century by St. Helena, mother of Constantine, the first Christian Roman emperor.

■ Large crowds gather for a candlelit **carol service** in Manger Square on Christmas Eve.

■ The **souk** to the west of the church is filled with stalls selling religious objects, local crafts, and souvenirs.

A 14-pointed silver star set into marble beneath the Altar of the Nativity marks the place where Jesus is believed to have been born.

THE TEMPLE MOUNT

This most ancient of sites is central to the history
and beliefs of three of the world's major faiths.

The Temple Mount in the heart of Old Jerusalem overlooks this ancient center of religious and political power, its quiet, spacious grounds a sharp contrast to the hustle and bustle all around. Also known as Mount Moriah and, by Muslims, as the Noble Sanctuary, Temple Mount is held sacred by Jews, Christians, and Muslims. At its heart is an outcrop of jagged rock that is believed to be the spot where Abraham offered to sacrifice his son Isaac. Temple Mount is the site of the First Temple, built by Solomon to house the Ark of the Covenant. Solomon's First Temple was destroyed some time before 600 B.C. A Second Temple built in its place in 515 B.C. was destroyed by the Roman emperor Titus. The exact locations of the First and Second Temples are disputed, but some people believe that the Dome of the Tablets, a small sanctuary near the Dome of the Rock, marks the position of the "Holy of Holies," the inner sanctuary of Solomon's temple where the golden, angel-topped Ark of the Covenant was kept. Muslims believe that Temple Mount was the place where Muhammad ascended to heaven, and after the Muslim conquest of Jerusalem in A.D. 638, the ruling caliph built the Dome of the Rock, its glittering gold-leaf roof forming the city's most striking landmark. This Islamic shrine encloses the exposed rock thought to be the place of Abraham's proposed sacrifice. To the south of the Dome, its minarets towering overhead, is the Al Aqsa Mosque, which dates in its present form from 1035.

When to Go Any time of year, except on Christian, Muslim, and Jewish holidays. Non-Muslims cannot enter the Dome of the Rock or Al Aqsa Mosque during midday prayers, but the area remains open.

Planning Carve out a few hours to roam around and under the Temple Mount. Dress modestly—short sleeves, shorts, and skimpy clothes are considered offensive. The area can be accessed through more than ten gates. Check for government security warnings at www.mfa.gov.il before visiting.

Website www.goisrael.com

HIGHLIGHTS

■ Walk around the **holy rock** within the Dome of the Rock. The interior of the drum and dome are decorated with beautiful Byzantine mosaics.

■ Legend has it that in the **Well of Souls**, a cavity beneath the rock, the voices of the dead mix with the rivers of Paradise as they flow to eternity.

■ The **Islamic Museum**, located near the ticket office, has a collection of valuable Korans and Islamic artifacts.

■ The **ramparts walking tour** provides a bird's-eye view of Jerusalem's Old City and the Western (or Wailing) Wall, which is a remnant of the Second Temple.

Opposite: The gold-covered Dome of the Rock, the oldest surviving Islamic monument in the world, shimmers in the sunlight, its exterior decorated with brightly colored, intricate tile mosaics and Arabic inscriptions. Above: The cool, elegant interior of the Al Aqsa Mosque has several aisles separated by rows of beautifully carved columns.

Muslim pilgrims cluster around the entrance to the Cave of Hira.

CAVE OF HIRA

This tiny, concealed cave near Mecca is where
Muhammad is said to have first received the word of God.

The Cave of Hira (or Hera) is not an obligatory site for pilgrims on the hajj to Mecca, but it is a place of colossal significance to all Muslims. For several years Muhammad retreated to this isolated mountaintop cave during Ramadan. According to the Islamic faith, it was here that the angel Gabriel visited Muhammad one night in A.D. 610 to deliver the first five verses of his message from Allah—which would form the Koran. Today's pilgrims make the climb up a dusty, winding path to the summit of Jabal an-Nour (Mountain of Light), some 2,000 feet (610 meters) high. At the summit, the cave is nowhere to be seen. In fact, it is hidden some 65 feet (20 meters) below the ridge and can be accessed only through a narrow passage beneath some huge boulders. From here, a precipitous path leads down to a small, natural balcony. Ahead, framed by more boulders and decorated with colorful, hand-drawn inscriptions, is the cave. Measuring just 12 feet (3.7 meters) deep and 5 feet (1.5 meters) wide, it is at once humbling and sublime.

When to Go Muslims can visit the Cave of Hira during the hajj, when it is very busy, or as part of an *umrah*, or pilgrimage at other times of the year.

Planning Only Muslims can make the climb up Jabal an-Nour, which lies about 6 miles (10 km) to the northeast of Mecca. The best way to reach the starting point of the path up to the cave is to take a taxi. The climb is long and steep, and this is no place to hurry, so allow several hours and wear suitable, sturdy shoes. At the summit, the route to the cave is not clear, so follow others or ask. The summer months are searingly hot in Mecca, so wear appropriate but modest clothing and cover your head.

Website www.hajinformation.com

HIGHLIGHTS

■ Pause on the summit of Jabal an-Nour for a **view** of the bone-dry, desert hills surrounding the holy city of Mecca, a landscape that must look much the same today as it did in Muhammad's time.

■ Sit in the courtyard in front of the cave and sense the intimacy of this **sheltered space**, with views only of the clear sky above.

■ Wait for other visitors to leave the cave in order to appreciate the sense of utter **isolation** and exceptional **spiritual intensity**.

ASIA

ETHIOPIA

AKSUM

This ancient city, once the capital of a powerful empire,
contains the holiest Christian sanctuary in Ethiopia.

From about 200 B.C. to A.D. 700, Aksum was the center of the mighty Aksumite Empire that stretched across the Red Sea into the heart of Arabia. In its narrow, dusty streets, the only sound now breaking the stillness of a sultry afternoon is likely to be a procession of brightly clad priests and white-robed pilgrims of the Ethiopian Orthodox Church, shaded by red and orange parasols and accompanied by the rhythmic beat of the kebero drum and the ringing of bells. Trailing wisps of incense, they are probably making their way to the 16th-century Mariamtsion Church (Church of St. Mary of Zion). Next to the church are the foundations of the original church, which was built during the fourth century, when the Aksumite kingdom converted to Christianity. Ethiopians claim that the Chapel of the Tablet, adjacent to the present church, houses the original Ark of the Covenant, but no visitor is ever allowed to see it. A sole monk stands guard over this sacred treasure. Next to the 16th-century church is the new Church of St. Mary, founded by Emperor Haile Selassie and completed in 1964. Unlike the old church, it allows women to enter.

When to Go Go for the T'imk'et Festival on January 19 (in the Western calendar), which celebrates the baptism of Jesus by St. John the Baptist, or in late November for the Festival of Maryam Zion. Heavy rains make access difficult between June and September.

Planning Tickets to enter the ancient sites around Aksum can be bought from the tourist office next to the main post office. The price includes a guide, although a tip is expected and is best negotiated beforehand. Allow two to four days to visit all the sites. Bring a flashlight as there is no lighting in the tombs. Aksum is home to Ethiopia's most sacred Christian and Muslim locations, so dress modestly.

Websites www.rainbowtours.co.uk, www.ethiopiatravel.com

HIGHLIGHTS

■ Both the 16th-century and the new churches of St. Mary are decorated with **colorful murals**.

■ The church museum houses a dazzling display of **silver crowns** worn by the emperors of Ethiopia, which testify to the masterful skills of Aksum's ancient craftsmen.

■ In a park just north of Aksum's central square are several towering granite **obelisks** guarding the tombs of ancient Aksumite kings.

■ **Aba Pantaleon** is located on the Debre Katin Mountain just outside Aksum. Founded at the beginning of the sixth century, it is one of the oldest surviving churches in Ethiopia.

The fortress-like 16th-century Church of St. Mary was built to replace a much older church.

MOUNT SINAI

Follow in the footsteps of Moses, the
legendary prophet of the Old Testament.

The Sinai Peninsula in modern-day Egypt is thought to be the wilderness through which Moses and the Israelites are said to have wandered for more than 40 years in search of the Promised Land. According to the book of Exodus, when the landless Israelites fell into lawless ways, Moses scaled the 7,497-foot (2,285 meter) high Mount Sinai to seek the advice of God and returned with the Ten Commandments, a set of laws that has formed the basis of western society ever since. Muslims also believe that the Prophet Muhammad's horse ascended to heaven from Mount Sinai. Today, just to reach either the small chapel (which is not open to the public) or the mosque at the summit is the goal for many visitors, but others come to enjoy the silence and sense of peace that pervades the air up here. Some make the ascent in the cool of the night in time to watch the sun rise over the scorched earth below. Camel riders and the less fit jostle for space along the Siket El Bashait path, working their way around the carpet of animal droppings. Hardier travelers can take the steeper Siket Sayidna Musa (Steps of Penitence)—3,750 steps cut directly into the rock. This quicker route gives the best views and is the most popular way down.

When to Go Any time of year. The site is generally most crowded in the cooler winter months.

Planning The mountain is about a two-hour drive from the Sinai's beach resorts. Once there, allow another two to three hours for the climb to the summit via the longer, less steep camel track, or just under an hour using the Siket Sayidna Musa. Take water for the climb, as drinks sold at stops along the way are usually expensive. Nighttime temperatures can drop below freezing at the summit, so bring enough suitable clothing to deal with the wide range of temperatures you may encounter.

Websites www.egypt.travel, www.geographia.com/egypt/sinai/mtsinai.htm

HIGHLIGHTS

■ **St Catherine's Monastery** at the base of the mountain has one of the world's oldest churches, consecrated in A.D. 551.

■ Relax and recover from your exertions at the **teashop at Elijah's Hollow**, a shady clearing just beneath the summit.

■ Bring a sleeping bag and bed down in one of the walled refuges built on ledges just below the peak in order to see the **sunrise**.

The 20th-century Chapel of the Holy Trinity on the summit of Mount Sinai is said to enclose a cave where Moses waited to receive the Ten Commandments.

The disks decorated with Arabic inscriptions were added in the 19th century.

TURKEY

HAGIA SOPHIA

This awe-inspiring statement of religious faith
is testament to the genius and daring of its creators.

All the wealth, magnificence, and technical brilliance of Byzantium are showcased in the immense Church of Hagia Sophia (Divine Wisdom) in Istanbul. Commissioned by Emperor Justinian I and consecrated in A.D. 537, it was the center of the Eastern Orthodox Church for many centuries and is the greatest surviving example of Byzantine architecture. Walls and pillars are lavishly adorned with green- and violet-colored marble, while intricate mosaics embellished with gold leaf glow in the semi-darkness. A complex arrangement of arches and semi-domes leads the eye to the massive, golden central dome. Light pours in from the 40 windows around the dome's base, creating the impression that it is floating high overhead—or suspended from heaven, as the Byzantines believed, on a golden chain. When the Ottoman Turks captured Constantinople in 1453, Hagia Sophia became a mosque and many of the mosaics were plastered over. Uncovered when the building became a museum in 1934, the mosaics now dazzle visitors with their virtuosity. High in the apse is a mosaic of the Virgin and Child. The finely wrought features of Mary's face, sharp against her pale skin, gaze down, her emotions laid bare to the groups of visitors milling around far below.

When to Go Any time of year. It is best to visit early in the day during summer to avoid the crowds.

Planning Hagia Sophia is on Sultanahmet Square in the old part of the city. It is open Tuesday to Sunday, from 9 a.m. to 5 p.m. (longer in summer). The South Gallery closes earlier than the rest of the building.

Website www.istanbultravelguide.net

HIGHLIGHTS

■ The 14th-century **Deësis mosaic** (the Last Judgment) in the South Gallery is famous for the delicacy of execution and humanity expressed on the faces of Jesus, John the Baptist, and the Virgin Mary.

■ The central doorway on the west side of the nave, known as the **Imperial Gate**, was used only by the emperor and his procession. Above it is a mosaic of **Christ Pantocrator**, or Ruler of the Universe.

■ Outside the building on the southeast side are three **mausoleums** of sultans. The right-hand one belongs to Murat III, who was buried in 1599 after having sired 103 children.

ASIA

TEN MOSAIC INTERIORS

Whether made from colored stones and pebbles or pieces of glass and gold leaf, mosaic interiors were created to impress.

❶ Cathedral Basilica, St. Louis, Missouri

The vast interior of this Roman Catholic cathedral is decorated from floor to ceiling with mosaics, the last of which were installed in 1988. Stories from the Bible vie for attention with geometric patterns, forming the largest collection of mosaics in the world.

Planning The cathedral is on Lindell Boulevard in central St. Louis. www.cathedralstl.org

❷ Kariye Museum, Istanbul, Turkey

The mosaics in this former Church of the Holy Savior in Chora ("in the country") date from around 1320 and, together with the frescoes in the side chapel, form the most extensive collection of Byzantine art in the city. Thousands of tiny pieces of glass were used to produce images of great expressiveness.

Planning The museum is in Edirnekapi in the Western District of Istanbul. www.turkeytravelplanner.com

❸ The Church of the Map, Madaba, Jordan

A sixth-century mosaic map of Jerusalem and the Holy Land—thought to be the oldest surviving map of Jerusalem in the world—once formed the floor of a long-gone Byzantine church where the Church of St. George now stands. More than two million tiny pieces of stone were used to illustrate towns and topographical features in minute detail.

Planning Madaba is a 20-minute drive south from Amman along the King's Highway. www.atlastours.net/jordan/madaba.html

❹ Beth Alpha Synagogue, Hefzibah, Israel

Twenty-two different types of stone were used to produce a vividly colored floor mosaic of a zodiac and images of Abraham preparing to sacrifice Isaac. Preserved in its entirety, the mosaic is one of the finest ever discovered in Israel and is all that remains of a fifth-century synagogue.

Planning Kibbutz Hefzibah is on Route 669 in northeastern Israel. www.goisrael.com

❺ Basilica of Euphrasius, Poreč, Croatia

The apse of this ancient cathedral is decorated with glittering sixth-century mosaics, including Christ in Majesty, the Virgin and Child flanked by angels, and the Annunciation. Pieces of glass in more than 50 colors were used, together with gold leaf and marble, all cut with uneven surfaces to maximize the variations in color.

Planning The nearest airport is at Pula. Poreč can also be reached by bus from Zagreb and by ferry from Venice. www.croatiatraveller.com/Istria/Porec.htm

❻ Monastery of Hosios Loukas, Steiri, Greece

The principal church of this secluded Greek Orthodox monastery on the slopes of Mount Helicon has spectacular 11th-century mosaics illustrating scenes from Jesus' life, culminating in a portrait of Christ Pantocrator in the central dome. He appears against a background of gold leaf as if "looking down from the rim of heaven."

Planning Steiri is the nearest town. The monastery can be visited on a day trip from Athens and is included on some bus tours to Delphi. users.teledomenet.gr/pavloubetty/fullday_uk.htm

❼ Santa Maria Maggiore, Rome, Italy

Fifth-century mosaics fill the upper walls on either side of the nave of this, the largest church in Rome dedicated to the Virgin Mary. Illustrating Old Testament scenes in a style reminiscent of ancient Roman mosaics, they form the earliest known large-scale cycle of biblical scenes produced in Rome. Scenes from the life of Jesus, also dating from the fifth century, can be seen over the triumphal arch, and in the apse is a late-13th-century Coronation of the Virgin.

Planning Located on Piazza Santa Maria Maggiore, the church is open daily from 7 a.m. to 7 p.m. www.tours-italy.com/rome/mosaics.htm

❽ Mausoleum of Galla Placidia, Ravenna, Italy

Built around A.D. 430 to house the tomb of the sister of the last Roman emperor, the mausoleum is decorated with the oldest mosaics in Ravenna. Biblical scenes in brilliant blues, greens, golds, and reds adorn the walls, while the ceiling is covered in gold stars set in a deep blue sky.

Planning Ravenna can be reached by road or rail. www.tours-italy.com/ravenna-tourist-information.htm

❾ Cappella Palatina, Palermo, Sicily

The tiny chapel in Palermo's 12th-century Arab-Norman palace—which blends Arab, Norman, Byzantine, and Sicilian artistic styles—is filled with glistening mosaics illustrating stories from the Bible and scenes from Arab and Norman life. All are rendered in vivid colors and a realistic style, and the gold-backed and silver mosaic pieces and marble inlays gleam in the chapel's soft light.

Planning The chapel is in the Palazzo dei Normanni on Piazza del Parlamento. www.travelplan.it/palermo_guide.htm

❿ Vence Cathedral, France

On the wall of the baptistry is a delicately colored mosaic by the 20th-century artist Marc Chagall. Entitled "Moses in the Bullrushes," or "Moses Saved from the Nile," it shows the pharaoh's daughter leaning over to pick up Moses, surrounded by trees, flowers, and sunshine reflected in the water, in celebration of the joy of baptism.

Planning The cathedral is open daily, from 10 a.m. to 6 p.m. www.beyond.fr/villages/vence.html

Glittering mosaics set in a background of gold leaf cover every surface of the Cappella Palatina, Palermo. Here, Christ Pantocrator (or Ruler of the Universe) stares out from the cupola.

MOUNT ATHOS

By the glistening waters of the Aegean, the faithful and the curious can sample the contemplative seclusion of monastic life.

EUROPE

A salty breeze blows over the Aegean as ferries cross to a remote peninsula in northern Greece. Mount Athos looms in the distance, its snowcapped crown shrouded in mist. Steep ravines slice through rugged hills blanketed with pine trees. Perched along the peninsula are 20 Eastern Orthodox monasteries resembling ancient fortresses, dotted across the landscape of this self-governing, monastic state. Monks have led lives of work and prayer on the mountain ever since the first monastery was founded here in A.D. 963. The monasteries have a strong tradition of hospitality and welcome male pilgrims (women are not allowed) with spring water, Greek coffee, and a chewy sweet called *loukoumi*, accompanied by a glass of brandy. Each morning at 3 a.m., the unrelenting beat of a wooden mallet signals the start of a new day. Figures shuffle down dim corridors to the shared bathroom for a cold shower before dressing and dashing to the church, where candles flicker and clouds of incense fill the air. A choir intones hymns under the watchful eyes of saintly icons. Then, as the sun rises, shafts of light stream through the stained-glass windows and fill the church with splashes of dazzling color.

When to Go Visitors are welcome all year, but spring, when the weather is generally good and the landscape first flowers, is the ideal time.

Planning A ferry leaves Ouranopolis for the Mount Athos port of Dafni daily at 9:45 a.m. There is also a ferry from Ierissos during the summer. Only men may visit Mount Athos, but women can take a cruise around the island. Visitors need a permit to visit Mount Athos. Orthodox Christian visitors should contact the Pilgrim Bureau in Thessaloniki; non-Orthodox visitors should contact the Ministry of Foreign Affairs in Athens or the Ministry of Macedonia and Thrace in Thessaloniki. Arrange your trip well in advance as the number of visitors is strictly controlled. Permits allow a stay of up to three nights. Phone monasteries that you want to visit in advance. Most offer a free night's stay plus two meals, but donations are welcome.

Websites www.macedonian-heritage.gr, www.athosfriends.org

HIGHLIGHTS

■ The monasteries, especially the larger ones, such as Great Lavra, Vatopedi, and Iveron, are filled with a wealth of **treasures**, including icons, murals, and libraries of rare books and illuminated manuscripts.

■ At Vatopedi, admire the intricate detail of the **mosaics**, such as the 11th-century the "Annunciation" and "Christ Enthroned."

■ Gaze at **icons** that are said to work miracles, such as the "Axion Esti" in the Protaton church in Karyes, the "Virgin Portaitissa" at Iviron, and the "Virgin Koukouzelissa" at Great Lavra.

■ **Hike** through virgin forests, hills flecked with colorful wildflowers, and along mountain paths overlooking the Aegean Sea.

Esphigmenou is one of several monasteries on Mount Athos that perches precariously by the sea.

The dark, brooding tower of Wittenberg Church dominates the castle, which was built at the same time.

GERMANY

WITTENBERG CHURCH

For centuries, visitors have flocked to a small German town to pay homage to a man who sparked the Protestant Reformation.

No visitor to the All Saints' or Castle Church (Schlosskirche), in the medieval heart of Wittenberg could be in any doubt about the importance of the place. The tall, dark, bronze doors are inscribed from top to bottom with the Latin text of the "95 Theses" written by Martin Luther, in which he attacked the Roman Catholic church for selling "letters of indulgence" for the absolution of sins. Luther nailed his treatise to the church's original wooden door in October 1517 and, in doing so, changed the course of history. The original door and the church were damaged beyond repair during a French bombardment of the city in the mid-1700s; the grander, more majestic entrance that greets today's visitor is a 19th-century replacement. Above the door, images of Luther, holding a Bible, and his like-minded compatriot, Philip Melanchthon, on either side of Jesus on the cross gaze down on all who pass through. Luther's simple, stone tomb is sited near the altar. Stained glass, flying buttresses, pointed arches, intricate woodcarvings, and richly colored paintings of leaders of the Protestant Reformation fill the Gothic space, which was restored in the late 19th century. It also contains the curious relic collection of Friedrich the Wise, Elector of Saxony, builder of the church and protector and friend of Luther.

When to Go All year, although the weather is best from April to October.

Planning Wittenberg is 62 miles (100 km) southwest of Berlin and has good road and rail links to the city. Allow at least half a day to visit the church and other sites linked to Luther; or stay overnight in the Old Town and enjoy the medieval atmosphere. The Tourist Information Office offers guided tours.

Website http://wbinfo.de

HIGHLIGHTS

■ **Portraits** of Luther and other reformers by the German Renaissance painter, Lucas Cranach the Younger, are among many fine paintings in the church.

■ Climb the church tower to enjoy the **far-reaching view** over the surrounding countryside.

■ In the **Luther House,** a former Augustinian monastery and later Luther's family home, you can see the desk at which the reformer worked, his pulpit, and first editions of his books.

■ From May to October, on alternate Saturday evenings, visitors can attend an **English service** and sing Luther's translated hymns.

EUROPE

4 MAJESTIC RUINS

Because of antiquity, remote locations, or the savage assaults of war and weather, the following sites are all, strictly speaking, ruins. The fact that many are merely surviving fragments or the last tantalizing traces of a vanished shrine or a forgotten faith does not diminish their fascination or their ability to inspire. The elaborate architecture of Cambodia's Angkor Wat, for instance, makes this 12th-century temple complex one of the world's greatest wonders, East or West. In Khajuraho in central India, 10th-century Hindu sculptors applied their skills to represent the mingling of the very earthy and the divine, with amorous couples demonstrating positions from the *Kama Sutra*, the ancient Sanskritic manual on the art of love. In Europe, soaring arches and roofless sanctuaries at England's Rievaulx Abbey and Cluny in France testify to the brilliant efforts of medieval Christian builders to encapsulate the truths and hopes of their faith.

In the rain forest of Cambodia, temple ruins of the Khmer civilization lie half-hidden in the undergrowth. This stone head at the Ta Prohm Temple near Angkor Wat is wrapped in the roots of a kapok tree.

ANGKOR WAT

The funerary temple of an ancient Khmer king is an architectural wonder and a place of pilgrimage for Buddhists and Hindus.

As you cross the stone causeway over the moat on the way into Angkor Wat, only three of the temple's elaborately carved sandstone towers are immediately visible. Built in the 12th century by Suryavarman II and dedicated to the Hindu god Vishnu, the shrine was later taken over by Buddhist monks, who converted it into a thriving monastery and *wat* (temple). A series of three concentric rectangular walls enclose a raised central shrine symbolizing the Hindu sacred mountain, Meru. Ornate gateways lead from one enclosure to the next, and flights of narrow steps climb to the shrine entrances. Streams of visitors climb the steps or sit to admire the intricately carved details on the buildings. Exquisitely executed bas-reliefs in the galleries of the inner enclosure depict scenes from the ancient Hindu epics and from the life of Suryavarman, who is buried beneath the central *prasat* (tower). Angkor Wat is one spectacular element in the massive Khmer capital that once covered nearly 150 square miles (390 square kilometers). Lost in the rain forest for several centuries before its rediscovery in 1860, the site was impossible to visit for much of the 20th century due to war and political turmoil in Indochina.

When to Go January through April is the hottest time of year, June through September the wettest, leaving October to December as the most pleasant time. Daytime temperatures are always somewhere between 78 and 90ºF (26-32ºC).

Planning The temple can be seen in half a day, but you will need two or three full days for a thorough exploration of the other major monuments at Angkor. One-, three-, and seven-day passes are available for Angkor Wat and other monuments in the area. Since the 1990s, the city of Siem Reap has grown into a thriving tourist hub with numerous hotels at different price levels. Several airlines fly direct to Siem Reap from Bangkok, Chiang Mai, Singapore, Kuala Lumpur, and other major cities in the region.

Websites www.siemreap-town.gov.kh, www.autoriteapsara.org, www.angkornationalmuseum.com, www.tourismcambodia.com

HIGHLIGHTS

■ The gateways are decorated with 300 carved **dancing apsaras** (sacred nymphs), each unique.

■ A series of **bas-reliefs** on the inner walls of the second enclosure include the Battle of Kurukshetra from the Hindu epic tale, the *Mahabharata*; scenes from the 37 Heavens and 32 Hells of Indian tradition; and "The Churning of the Sea of Milk by Gods and Demons" from Vishnu lore.

■ Much of the nearby **Ta Prohm Temple** is wrapped in the roots of giant kapok trees. The temple has been left unrestored to show how the rain forest hid the temples.

■ The glories of the Khmer civilization unfold inside the **Angkor National Museum** in Siem Reap.

The vast rectangular temple was built on three levels. The main shrine at the heart of the temple has a large central tower and a smaller tower at each corner.

A Buddhist monk prays in Wat Si Chum before Old Sukhothai's largest statue of the Buddha.

THAILAND

OLD SUKHOTHAI

A wealth of ancient temples, carved monuments, and graceful Buddhas are gathered together in this former royal capital.

The charm of Muang Kao Sukhothai (Old Sukhothai) in north-central Thailand lies in its setting among expansive green fields shaded by leafy trees and a lotus-covered lake, as well as in its elegant assembly of regal ruins. Sukhothai (Dawn of Happiness) emerged in 1238 as the first truly unified Thai kingdom, and the old city of Sukhothai was the kingdom's most influential religious and cultural center for 200 years. In its prime this ancient royal city, protected by a series of walls, moats, and ramparts, was surrounded by 40 temple complexes. It is now designated an Historical Park, with the remains of the royal palace as the nucleus. Twenty-one *wats* (temples) are scattered across this haven of lawns and plants laced with canals and ponds, the largest and most spectacular being Wat Mahathat, which is made up of more than 200 pagodas, ten *viharas* (refuges for wandering monks), and four reflecting ponds, all encircled by a moat. Throughout the park, *prangs* (spires) and *chedis* (domed monuments) are embellished with unique Sukhothai ornamentation. Some, especially the many island-bound edifices, have obvious Khmer and Sri Lankan influences. Around 70 smaller sites and ruins dot the landscape outside the park.

When to Go Early morning and evening bring fewer buses and groups, and the site is cooler and more serene. Allow two days to explore the whole site.

Planning The Historical Park is open daily from 6 a.m. to 6 p.m. There are several guesthouses just outside the park gates, but good accommodations and services are available in New Sukhothai or Phitsanulok (where the nearest railroad station is), both a short commute away. There are several ways to get to the park, including local buses, a *samlor* (three-wheeled motorcycle taxi that will take you to and around the site), or private car. Outside the park gate are many shops that rent bicycles. They also sell the best maps. Buy plenty of water at the entrance.

Website www.tourismthailand.org

HIGHLIGHTS

■ The grounds of Wat Traphang Ngoen, on an island in the middle of Traphang Ngoen (Silver Lake), provide **extensive views** of the surrounding monuments.

■ To the north of the park, Wat Si Chum houses Sukhothai's **tallest surviving Buddha image**, a 49-ft (15 m) high seated Buddha.

■ The **Phra Attaros Buddha** sits on the hilltop ruin of Wat Saphan Hin to the west of the park. The steep, five-minute climb is well worth it to study the 39-ft (12 m) tall figure towering above the wat's remains.

■ Take a day trip to **Si Satchanalai**. The journey through sugarcane and tobacco fields, as well as the crumbling grandeur of the buildings, make the detour worthwhile.

ASIA

Statues of the Buddha line a pathway at Wat Yai Chai Mongkhon.

AYUTTHAYA

This former Thai capital is richly endowed
with temples, shrines, and Buddha statues.

At its zenith in the 15th century, Ayutthaya was a majestic city with three palaces and 400 temples, bounded by the Chao Phraya, Lop Buri, and Pa Sak rivers. A 2.5-mile (4 kilometer) wide island formed the core of the former capital, where today modern buildings and busy canalside streets are juxtaposed with elegant ruins. Visitors flock to the ancient city's remains, which are characterized by cactus-shaped *prangs* (temple towers) and massive *wats* (temples) that hint at the city's past splendor. Dotted with reclining and seated Buddhas, many draped with saffron-colored cloth, fine statues of mythical birds and sacred elephants, and bell-shaped *chedis* (monuments), Ayutthaya melds Sukhothai Buddhist influences and Hindu-inspired Khmer (or ancient Cambodian) motifs. At Wat Mahathat, one of the oldest temples here, rows of headless Buddhas surround large crumbling chedis. Wat Chai Watthanaram, west of the city-island, was conceived as a replica of Angkor Wat. Mostly intact and now restored, it provides a good idea of how a working temple might have appeared some 300 years ago.

When to Go November to March, when temperatures are pleasant with blue skies and low rainfall.

Planning Trains connect Ayutthaya with Bangkok, 40 miles (64 km) away, and other major cities. Buses from Bangkok are a slower alternative. If time is short, you can visit Ayutthaya by cruise ship on the Chao Phraya River from Bangkok. The terrain in and around Ayutthaya is flat, so renting a bicycle is a fun and convenient way to get from one site to another. Guides are a good idea as they can transform the city's remains into living history.

Website www.tourismthailand.org

HIGHLIGHTS

■ Visit Wat Mahathat to see the **Buddha head** lodged in a tree trunk.

■ See the ruins of a 262-ft (80 m) high pagoda at **Wat Yai Chai Mongkhon**—one of the largest pagodas in the city.

■ Take a stroll around the ancient city at night; the **floodlit ruins** look spectacular.

■ Every October and November, Ayutthaya lights up for **Loi Krathong** (Festival of Lights). Events include the traditional floating of banana-leaf lanterns downstream, processions of carved, brightly painted chariots, and a fireworks display.

ASIA

CHINA

Dunhuang Cave Temples

An ancient network of caves carved into a mountainside
contains thousands of Buddha statues and frescoes.

ASIA

In A.D. 366, a Buddhist monk traveling along the ancient Silk Road close to Echoing-Sand Mountain, on the edge of the Taklimakan Desert in northeastern China, reported a vision of multiple Buddhas in haloed glory and cut a cave into the mountain slope at the site of his revelation. During the next 1,000 years, many other monks sought refuge here, living in caves that they decorated with carvings and murals. Travelers praying for a safe journey would also decorate caves, or pay the monks to decorate one on their behalf, until nearly 3,000 decorated caves honeycombed the cliff. Some contain exquisitely sculpted Buddha figures, while others are decorated with detailed wall-paintings of scenes from the journeys of Silk Road merchants and envoys as they crossed the desert. The styles vary between slender Central Asian figures in the earlier murals and plumper Chinese ones in later caves, illustrating that travelers carried new ideas as well as goods along the Silk Road. Linked by rock-cut stairways that eventually collapsed, many caves became unreachable without ropes. Over the years their interiors were exposed to the elements and filled up with sand; some of the giant rock-cut Buddhas have been enclosed in new buildings to protect them. Of the remaining 492 grottoes, about 30 are open to the public.

When to Go April to early June, or September to early October are best. In winter, air pollution is at its worst and temperatures in the desert can be freezing. The summer months are very hot.

Planning The caves are 15 miles (24 km) southeast of Dunhuang. Allow one full day to see them. The most delicate and important caves require an extra payment. Rather than waiting for one of Dunhuang's many minibuses to fill up on the day you plan to visit, you can book a bus a day in advance for a specific departure time. Take a flashlight as many caves are poorly lit.

Websites www.imperialtours.net, www.greatwalltour.com, www.elong.com

HIGHLIGHTS

■ The late-fifth-century cave 101 has a **Western-style painted Buddha**.

■ The mural in cave 323 depicts the departure of China's **General Zhang Qian** into the Taklimakan Desert in 138 B.C.

■ The Tang-dynasty (seventh–tenth century) cave 96 has a giant, 111-ft (34 m) high **seated Buddha** dressed in imperial dragon robes.

■ Cave 220 is decorated in a sophisticated Tang-dynasty style, suggesting the influence of court painters, and shows **moral tales from the life of the Buddha**.

Some of the oldest caves have a central Buddha statue in terra-cotta surrounded by rows of tiny painted Buddhas on the walls.

MYANMAR

BAGAN

A complex of redbrick temples
rises, dreamlike, from the jungle.

More than two thousand temples and pagodas sprawl across the dusty plain bordering the upper valley of the Irrawaddy River, close to the ancient city of Bagan in Myanmar (Burma). Most of these sacred structures were erected between 1057 and 1287, when Bagan was capital of the kingdom of Pagan, the first Burmese Empire. At the time, Theravada Buddhism flourished in the city, attracting monks and devotees from all over southern Asia. Many temples are now in ruins, but the remaining ones have been meticulously restored, their interiors scented by joss sticks planted by pilgrims around the feet of giant, golden Buddhas. With its golden stupa, the Shwezigon Pagoda is the most elegant of Bagan's many shrines. Erected in the late 11th century to house a replica of the Relic of the Tooth (reputed to be the tooth of the Buddha) housed in the city of Kandy in Sri Lanka, the compound is now the foremost place of Buddhist worship in the area and always alive with saffron-robed monks. The Ananda Temple is the most ornate, its interior a maze of corridors filled with statues of the Buddha. Each day, a steady throng of visitors weaves around the larger monuments, but only a few stray off the beaten path. In quiet spots, people may pause to meditate and pray, surrounded by ancient walls that still exude a sense of the divine, more than 1,000 years after they were erected.

When to Go October to March is the cooler part of the year. A number of annual religious celebrations are staged at Bagan, including the Ananda Temple Festival in January or February, the three-day Thadingyut Candle Light Festival in October, and the Manuha Pagoda Festival in September or October.

Planning Bagan can be reached by daily flights from Yangon (Rangoon) (one hour) and Mandalay (20 minutes). The drive from Yangon is fascinating but takes 12 hours along two-lane highways. The luxury steamer Road to Mandalay (operated by Orient-Express) offers cruises between Mandalay and Bagan. Allow two to three days minimum to visit the main temples and a week to explore the entire ruined city. Cycling is an excellent way to explore the ruins, and bike rentals are available at many local hotels and shops. Pro-democracy campaigners ask tourists not to visit Myanmar while the military junta is in power. If you visit, try to spend money in such a way that it goes directly to the local people.

Websites www.ancientbagan.com, www.roadtomandalay.net

ASIA

HIGHLIGHTS

■ Looming more than 200 ft (61 m) above the plains, the multitiered, 12th-century **Thatbyinnyu Temple** is the tallest of Bagan's monuments and an excellent perch from which to view the rest of the city and watch the sun rise or set over the Bagan plain.

■ A glimmering golden pagoda surmounts the **Ananda Temple**, which was built sometime around A.D. 1100 and named after one of Buddha's cousins and most devoted disciples. Inside are four giant golden standing Buddhas, each 30 ft (9 m) tall.

■ Among the many treasures in the Shwezigon Pagoda are the **Jataka tablets** relating the life of Buddha, the **magic horse of King Kyanzittha**, and the **37 golden Nats** (spirits).

■ Pass an hour or so in the **Archaeological Museum**, where many of the artifacts that once graced the inside of Bagan's temples are now on display. There are far-reaching views from the roof garden.

Opposite: Bagan's temples, scattered as far as the eye can see, tower above the treetops. Above left: A large stone Buddha statue has been decorated with an offering of plants. Above right: The bell-shaped stupa of the Shwezigon Pagoda (on the left) houses relics of the Buddha.

THE SOMAPURA MAHAVIHARA

The perfect geometry and rich decoration of the Great
Monastery inspired generations of Buddhist monks.

ASIA

This perfectly proportioned structure, half-hidden underground, lay in ruins for centuries before it was discovered and excavated between 1923 and 1934. But for four centuries after it was built in the seventh century A.D., the Somapura Mahavihara, or Great Monastery, at Paharpur in northeast Bangladesh, attracted Buddhist monks from far and wide. Today, the ruins retain a certain magic; perhaps the hundreds of monks who lived, studied, and prayed in the 177 tiny cells surrounding the central stupa imbued the place with its haunting quality. Visit in the evening, as the light fades and the warm wind rises, and you can almost hear the cadences of a Buddhist hymn being chanted by a hundred voices. Like most Buddhist sacred spots, the Somapura Mahavihara is richly embellished. Terra-cotta plaques of musicians, snake charmers, animals, and human figures decorate the temple's outer walls and provide an insight into the life of those who lived in the early seventh century. The site was a major architectural influence not only on other Buddhist buildings in India but even on those as far away as Myanmar, Java, and Cambodia.

When to Go In winter (October to mid-March) temperatures are pleasant and the tumultuous monsoon-fed Padma River is under control.

Planning Paharpur is a village near the city of Rajshahi, in Naogaon District. The nearest railway station is at Jamalganj on the Khulna-Parbatipur route, connected with Paharpur by a 3-mile (5 km) paved minor road. Paharpur can also be reached from the airport at Saidpur by following a paved road via Joypurhat. To get the most out of the area, stay for two days. Dress respectfully—no shorts, and you may have to remove your shoes at some active shrines. The sun can be hot even in winter, so sunscreen and hats are recommended.

Website travel.discoverybangladesh.com

HIGHLIGHTS

■ Admire the texture and strength of the **brick walls** that have withstood the assault of centuries.

■ The beautifully proportioned stances and garments of the **carved figures** show the influences of Buddhism, Hinduism, and Christianity.

■ The small **museum** houses a representative collection of objects, including carved statues of Buddha and Vishnu.

■ Visit the **Varendra Research Museum** at Rajshahi. The antiquities on display include terra-cotta plaques, images of gods and goddesses, pottery, coins, inscriptions, and ornamental bricks.

From the top of the grassy stupa, at center, you can appreciate the site's perfect symmetry.

Sensual carvings cover the exterior of the Kandariya Mahadeo Temple, a masterpiece of Indian art.

HIGHLIGHTS

■ An 8-ft (2.4 m) high, polished **lingam**, or phallus, symbolizing Shiva's procreative power, stands in the Matangesvara Temple.

■ The exterior of the Kandariya Mahadeo Temple is decorated with panels of **erotic sculptures** on the north and south sides.

■ The carved **scenes of everyday life** at the Jain Parsavanatha Temple in the Eastern Group depict the minutiae of human existence in exquisite detail.

■ At sunset, the sandstone of the temples turns a **deep shade of red** and the sculptures appear almost to creep forward out from the shadows.

INDIA

KHAJURAHO'S HINDU TEMPLES

In a modest village in central India, crowds flock
to view the erotic carvings on "the temple of love."

ASIA

Lofty temples glow ocher and gold under a blue sky, and saris flutter as pilgrims tour the many temples here, set in a vast compound where prayers echo from morning to night. The Hindu temples of Khajuraho, in central India, were built by the Chandella dynasty, believed by the devout to be descendants of the Moon God. Hindus believe that the gods Siva and Parvati were united on this spot, and for more than 100 years, from A.D. 950, craftsmen worked to create more than 80 ornately carved temples. Twenty-two temples have survived, and almost every inch of their lofty walls is covered with intricate carvings of life at court along with erotic scenes of adventurous men and sensuous women indulging in the many acrobatic poses of the *Kama Sutra*, the ancient Sanskrit treatise on the art of lovemaking. The temples are arranged in three groups. The Western Group includes the best-known temples, such as the Kandariya Mahadeo, dedicated to Lord Siva and the largest Khajuraho temple, and Chaunsat Yogini, the oldest, dedicated to the goddess Kali.

When to Go In winter the weather is at its coolest and driest. A week-long festival is held annually at the end of February or beginning of March in celebration of the marriage of the gods Shiva and Parvati.

Planning The most convenient way to reach Khajuraho is by an Indian Airlines flight from Delhi, Agra, or Varanasi. The nearest railway stations are Jhansi or Satna; Khajuraho is a three-four-hour road journey from there. The site is spread over 8 sq miles (21 sq km), so allow a full day to see the sculptures in detail. A local guide will help you make sense of the buildings. A visit involves a fair amount of walking, so wear comfortable shoes and a hat, and carry sunscreen and plenty of drinking water.

Websites www.liveindia.com, www.khajuraho.org.uk

SANCHI

A well-preserved hilltop complex of monuments provides
a unique history of Indian Buddhist architecture.

During the full moon, or Buddha Purnima, which falls in April or May according to the lunar calendar, hundreds of Buddhists from around the world gather at Sanchi to celebrate the Buddha's birth, enlightenment, and *parinirvana* (final death). The hilltop is dotted with more than 50 ruined monasteries, pillars, and stupas, and its quiet, meditative energy is perhaps what attracted the Buddhist emperor, Asoka, to Sanchi to found a Buddhist settlement dedicated to peace shortly after the bloody Battle of Kalinga in 261 B.C. Asoka built eight stupas, and more were added in succeeding centuries, the last in the 12th century A.D. Once used as burial mounds to hold the ashes of the deceased, they provide an architectural history of Indian Buddhism in one location, from its inception to its decay. Most magnificent is the Great Stupa commissioned by Asoka, a solid stone-and-brick dome 103 feet (31 meters) in diameter and 42 feet (13 meters) high. Surrounding the Great Stupa is a railing with four carved *toranas*, or gateways, facing east, west, north, and south. The carvings on each gateway signify a different time in Buddha's life—a lotus for his birth, a tree depicting his enlightenment, a wheel representing his first sermon, and footprints to symbolize his presence.

When to Go Any time between October and March. In November, Sanchi celebrates the festival of Chethiyagiri Vihara.

Planning Sanchi is about 28 miles (45 km) north of Bhopal in the central Indian state of Madhya Pradesh and is well connected by road to all the main towns of the state. Bhopal has road, rail, and air links to major cities in India. You will walk uphill to reach the site, so wear appropriate shoes and bring water. The museum is open from 10 a.m. to 5 p.m. every day except Friday. You will need half a day to tour the ruins. You can buy a guidebook and map from the museum at the entrance.

Websites www.indyahills.com, www.tourism-of-india.com

HIGHLIGHTS

■ Stupa Number One, or the **Great Stupa**, was originally built of burnt mud bricks in the third century B.C. It was damaged during a war and rebuilt in its current form during the second century B.C.

■ The **Great Bowl**, carved out of a single giant stone block, once contained grain that was distributed to the Buddhist monks.

■ The **Archaeological Survey of India Museum** at the entrance to the site houses artifacts that were discovered during excavations at Sanchi, including four stone lions that once crowned the Asoka Pillar.

The Great Stupa at Sanchi is one of the oldest stone structures in India.

The tower of Virupaksha Temple, the oldest at Hampi, is glimpsed between giant boulders.

INDIA

HAMPI

Discover a lost civilization in a bizarre landscape
largely untouched by the passage of the centuries.

Hidden away in the badlands of the Deccan plateau in central India, a bizarre landscape of giant boulders provides the backdrop to the scattered ruins of a series of temples and palaces. For two centuries Hampi was a wealthy royal city and capital of the Vijayanagar Empire, with a royal court renowned for its indulgence and magnificence. But in the 16th century an alliance of Mogul invaders overthrew the ruling king. The city was abandoned and has been crumbling into the earth ever since. Because they are made of the same sunbaked stone as the land, some of the ruined buildings blend into their surroundings, but a number of well-preserved and exquisitely carved Hindu and Jain temples stand out. Most extravagant of all is the 15th-century Vitthala Temple, its exterior covered with sculpted figures of the king's army and dancing girls, its interior a series of ornate pillared halls. The Virupaksha Temple complex, parts of which date from the 11th century, consists of towered gateways, halls, pillared cloisters, and shrines. After the day's toil, local farmers stroll through the shaded lanes of the present-day village of Hampi Bazaar while parrots and hummingbirds flit through the hot evening air.

When to Go October to March. April and May are intensely hot, and from late May until early October the monsoon rains and accompanying high humidity make activity uncomfortable.

Planning The nearest railway station is at Hospet, 8 miles (13 km) to the east; buses and taxis are available there. Hospet is reached by an overnight train from Bangalore. Allow at least three or four days to explore the area. This gives you time to unwind, adjust to the slow pace of local life, and see all the sites. Hampi Bazaar offers good but basic accommodations.

Websites www.hampi.in, www.hampionline.com

HIGHLIGHTS

■ The Vitthala Temple's Maha-Mantapa, or great hall, contains 56 **musical pillars**—each produces a different sound when tapped. Outside the main building is a miniature shrine in the form of an ornately carved **stone chariot**.

■ Virupaksha's entrance tower has **erotic stucco figures** on the south side. The open pavilion known as the **Ranga Mantapa** includes rows of pillars shaped into mythical, lionlike creatures ridden by warriors.

■ In the Royal Enclosure, south of Matanga Hill, the **Ramachandra Temple** has fine wall-carvings and **outsized stables** that once housed the royal elephants.

ASIA

AJANTA AND ELLORA CAVES

Marvel at the creativity of the devout, who lived lives of prayer and meditation among the green hills of central India.

A small stream flows through the quiet valley of Ajanta in northwest India. Nothing would indicate to anyone stumbling on this place that some of the world's greatest art treasures rest here. But behind the unpromising cliff faces stand entire temples complete with cavernous chambers, ornate pillars, and intricately worked carvings that were cut from the hillside by Buddhist monks between the second century B.C. and the fifth century A.D. Within the temples' dark interiors, an extravagant array of fine architectural detail awaits the visitor. Mud-plastered walls are crowded with images of the life of the Buddha painted in brilliant but subtle hues. Deserted and forgotten for centuries, the 30 cave-temples of Ajanta were reclaimed from the jungle in 1819. And they are not unique, for just over an hour's drive away, in a crook of the Charanadari Hill, 34 similar structures were hewn out of the mountainside at Ellora some time between the sixth and ninth centuries A.D. by the devotees of three faiths— Buddhism, Hinduism, and Jainism. The huge Hindu Kailash Temple, measuring 164 feet (50 meters) deep and 98 feet (30 meters) high, is the largest monolithic structure in the world. During its excavation, some 200,000 tons of rock were removed, a process that took nearly 100 years to complete.

When to Go October to November, after the monsoon rains have cleared. December to March is also good, but by late March the heat begins to become unbearable.

Planning The city of Aurangabad, approximately 186 miles (300 km) northeast of Mumbai and connected with it by regular flights and trains, makes a good base for visiting Ajanta (just under two hours away by road) and Ellora (around 40 minutes away by road). Tourist buses run regularly between all three places. For more flexibility, consider hiring a taxi for a day or two. Alternatively, join a tour group from Aurangabad. The Ellora Caves are best seen in the afternoon, when the sunlight illuminates their courtyards. Each site merits at least a full day's viewing. Take a flashlight, as some caves are quite dark.

Websites ajantacaves.com, www.travelmasti.com

HIGHLIGHTS

■ The fifth-century Vihara Cave (cave 1) at Ajanta contains detailed **murals** that relate the many kind and merciful deeds performed by the Buddha on his path to enlightenment.

■ Chaitya Griha (cave 19) at Ajanta is a perfectly cut Buddhist **prayer hall.**

■ Visit Ellora's **Viswakarma Cave** (cave 10) in the middle of the afternoon, when sunlight bathes the interior. This Buddhist chapel features a large hall with stupendous carvings, including a 14.8-ft (4.4 m) tall Buddha.

■ The **exterior** of the **Kailash Temple** (cave 16) at Ellora is carved with pillars and niches, deities, and other figures. The interior has several halls on different levels.

Opposite: The monumental exterior of the Kailash Temple (cave 16) at Ellora is carved out of the cliff face. Above left: A wall-painting of a bodhisattva at Ajanta. Above right: The apse, pillars, and figures in cave 19 at Ajanta were all carved out of the rock.

TEN SACRED CAVES

Remote and secluded, caves feature in the histories of all religions—as refuges, shrines, hiding places, temples, and burial sites.

❶ Actun Tunichil Muknal, Belize

In myths, journeys to the underworld are never easy, and after visiting Actun Tunichil Muknal (Cave of the Stone Sepulchre), you may feel that you have been through your own epic test! Access to the Mayan sacrificial site within the cave involves hiking, wading, and underwater swimming, but nearly a mile underground you will reach the resting place of the "crystal maiden," a complete female skeleton that sparkles from eons of crystal calcification. The cave also contains Maya pottery shards, many showing the "kill hole" intended to allow spirits to escape.

Planning To reach the cave you must be physically fit and accompanied by a guide certified by the Belize Institute of Archaeology. www.mayabelize.ca

❷ Elephanta Caves, Gharapuri Island, India

Carved out of a hillside in the 5th century, the ecstatic faces and swaying bodies of Hindu deities in the temples of the Elephanta Caves seem to be listening to the drone of ancient Indian instruments. The sinuous curves of the Siva Nataraja, or many-armed cosmic dancer, and the three faces of the Trimurti, representing the creator, preserver, and destroyer aspects of the god Siva, are as expressive today as centuries ago.

Planning The cave temples are located on monkey-inhabited Gharapuri Island in Mumbai Harbor and can be reached via an hour-long ride on launches that depart regularly (except during monsoon season) from the Gateway of India monument. www.slstour.com/elephanta-caves.html

❸ Longmen Caves, China

Cut into the Xiangshan and Longmen Shan hillsides above the Yi River, the Longmen (or "Dragon's Gate") complex of temple grottoes is an exquisite treasury of Buddhist carvings comprising 2,345 caves and niches, 2,800 inscriptions, and 43 pagodas, the earliest dating from the Northern Wei dynasty (493 A.D.).

Planning The caves, in Henan Province, can be reached by buses departing from the Luoyang train station. Although you cannot go into them, the caves are shallow and the carvings are visible from outside. The hillsides are traversed by stairways and catwalks that afford a variety of perspectives. www.chinatour.com

❹ Dambulla Cave, Sri Lanka

This complex of five Buddhist cave shrines was commissioned by King Valagambahu in 1 B.C. and has been a pilgrimage site for 22 centuries. Exquisitely painted and gilded murals, as well as sculptures, shimmer in the caves; ceiling murals have been painted directly onto the rough contours of the rock.

Planning Dambulla is on the main road from Sigiriya to Kandy, about 11 miles (18 km) from Sigiriya. www.travelsrilanka.com

❺ Corycian Cave, Greece

In ancient Greece this vast cave on Mount Parnassus was a place of worship of the god Pan and the nymphs. A rock near the entrance may have been used as an altar.

Planning The cave is near the town of Arachova. Take a flashlight. www.travel-to-arachova.com

❻ Bronze-Age Minoan Caves, Crete, Greece

Crete has more than 3,000 caves, many associated with the gods of Greek mythology and with goddess worship practiced by the Minoans, a Bronze-Age civilization that lasted from 2600 to 1100 B.C. The Dikteon Cave is said to be where Rhea gave birth to Zeus; the Idaian Cave, where Rhea hid Zeus from his father Cronus.

Planning The Dikteon Cave is just south of Psychro; the Idaian Cave is 12 miles (19 km) south of Anogia. www.crete.tournet.gr

❼ St. Paul's Grotto, Malta

In A.D. 60, St. Paul, then a Roman prisoner, was shipwrecked on Malta and is said to have sheltered in this tiny cave. In the Bible, Acts 28 relates that Paul was treated well by the Maltese and that during his stay he performed miraculous cures and survived a viper's bite, leading the locals to view him as a god.

Planning The grotto is under the Chapel of St. Publius, next to St. Paul's Church, in the village of Rabat. www.visitmalta.com

❽ St. Michael's Shrine, Italy

Christian legend says that this cave shrine in Monte Sant'Angelo was chosen by the archangel Michael, who appeared to the Bishop of Sipontum in A.D. 490 and promised, "Where the rocks open widely, the sins of men may be pardoned." It is said that Michael left an altar, a red cloth, and his footprint in stone to mark the spot.

Planning Most visitors to the shrine stay in San Giovanni Rotondo nearby. www.itwg.com/city4122

❾ Grotte de Font-de-Gaume, France

Bison, horses, and mammoths are among the animals painted into the rough limestone walls of this cave in the Dordogne. Created at least 15,000 years ago, the paintings still have vivid colors and a sense of vitality. Their purpose may have been to do with hunting or with an attempt to represent a lunar calendar.

Planning The cave is outside the village of Les Eyzies-de-Tayac, near Sarlat. Advance booking is essential. www.showcaves.com

❿ Sof Omar Caves, Ethiopia

It is said that Allah revealed the opening to this limestone cave system to Sheikh Sof Omar in the 12th century. The sheikh and his followers used the caves as a mosque, a purpose to which the caves were well suited as they had been eroded into columns, buttresses, domes, vaults, and pillars—a natural architectural marvel still used as a gathering place by local Muslims.

Planning The caves are in Bale Mountains National Park. Take a flashlight and maps. www.tour-to-ethiopia.com, www.linkethiopia.org

A visitor contemplates a large statue of a god carved out of the rock in the Elephanta Caves on Gharapuri Island, India. Hindu worshipers have used the caves since the fifth century A.D.

This giant standing Buddha, 23 ft (7 m) tall, is part of the Gal Viharaya group of Buddha statues.

SRI LANKA

POLONNARUWA

The grandeur of the Vijayabahu dynasty
shines out from the ruins of its capital city.

After King Vijayabahu I vanquished Chola invaders and united the island of Sri Lanka under one crown in the 11th century, he founded a new capital, Polonnaruwa, to symbolize the fresh start for his country. In it he created palaces, gardens, and pilgrimage sites for Buddhists from all over Asia. Most important of these was the Relic of the Tooth, which Sri Lankan monarchs safeguarded for many centuries as a symbol of their divine right to rule. Temples and shrines were richly endowed with carvings, paintings, and sculptures to reflect the king's power and wisdom. But Polonnaruwa's golden age lasted for only 200 years, until invasion and civil war prompted most of the population to flee. Abandoned gradually, rather than sacked and destroyed in one great swoop, Polonnaruwa decayed slowly, leaving structures that still impress with their intricate craftsmanship, such as the two giant Buddha figures carved into a cliff face, and Lankathilaka, the city's most imposing temple.

When to Go Sri Lanka has a hot, tropical climate. The drier, cooler months are October through February.

Planning An overnight train covers the 134 miles (216 km) from Colombo to Kaduruwela station. From there it is a short ride by bus or taxi to Polonnaruwa. Allow a least a day, although a thorough exploration takes two to three days. There are many fine hotels in the area, most of which will arrange day trips to Polonnaruwa. The Visitor Information Centre and Museum, with its detailed scale model of the ancient city, is a good place to begin.

Websites www.srilankatourism.org, www.tourism-srilanka.com

HIGHLIGHTS

■ Four Buddha images are carved into the long granite outcrop of **Gal Viharaya.** The first figure is in meditation pose, the next is in a cave, the third is standing, the fourth reclines.

■ **Lankathilaka** has similarities to a medieval European cathedral. Its long "nave" flanked by towering stone walls culminates in an "altar" with a 59-ft (18 m) high, headless Buddha. Richly colored frescoes adorn the interior walls.

■ Enter the circular Vatadage Temple via one of its four sweeping doors, and walk up to the largely ruined, central *dagoba* (bell-shaped shrine) to gaze up at the **four seated, stone Buddhas** housed there.

■ The rust-colored shrine of **Rankot Vihara** looms 180 ft (55 m) above the surrounding plains. It was once the heart of a monastic school called the Alahana Pirivena.

ASIA

TURKEY

CHURCH OF THE HOLY CROSS

This remnant of Armenian culture on an island
in Lake Van is also a work of art set in stone.

The Church of the Holy Cross isn't famous for its size. It's just 49 feet (15 meters) long, but its setting is enough to impress. Perched on Akdamar Island off the southern shore of Lake Van in eastern Turkey, it is a testament to the human ambition to conquer the environment. Visitors arrive humbled by nature. The 20-minute boat trip to the island is an epic journey across the dazzling blue waters of the world's largest salt lake. From the middle of the lake the encircling mountains come clearly into focus, soaring 13,000 feet (3,962 meters) high, powdered with snow. Today, the tiny island is a place of ruins, serene and tranquil, but 1,100 years ago it was the center of a remote Armenian kingdom ruled by King Gagik I. In a few short years, from 915 to 921 A.D., he fortified the island and built a palace, monastery, and church. Following a recent $2-million restoration, the church's beautifully cut walls of pinkish sandstone once again sparkle in the sunlight. The exterior walls are covered in exquisite relief carvings of snakes, lions, and gazelles alongside figures from the Bible, such as Adam and Eve, and David and Goliath.

When to Go Late spring sees the island swathed in color as the trees bloom, but cold weather at this high elevation make summer and early fall the best times for a visit.

Planning The church is now a museum with exhibits explaining the building's history. Boats to the island leave from Gevas in the southeastern corner of Lake Van. They depart when there are enough people to fill them–usually a minimum of ten. The city of Van, 27 miles (44 km) away, is the best base for exploring the region. For a more rustic setting, there's a camping ground at Akdamar Camping & Restaurant, opposite the boat departure point, with superb views of the lake. You only need one full day to explore the island, but you should allow at least three days in the Van area to see the main sights and a week to truly lose yourself in the landscape.

Website www.easternturkeytour.com

HIGHLIGHTS

■ Decipher the **carvings** on the church's outer walls. On the south wall you'll find Jonah about to be swallowed by a whale; on the west wall is the founder, King Gagik, presenting a miniature of his church to Christ.

■ Take **a swim** from the small, rocky bathing spot near the landing stage, and immerse yourself in a lake that is 5,479 ft (1,670 m) above sea level. The extreme salinity of the water makes it very buoyant.

■ Climb to the top of the small island for **superb views** over the lake to the towering, snow-covered peaks of the Anti-Taurus Mountains.

Like a pink jewel, the tiny Church of the Holy Cross sits on an island in the vast, mountain-fringed Lake Van.

ROCK CHURCHES OF ANATOLIA

Hidden away in a maze of valleys are the remains of hundreds
of ancient churches carved directly out of the rock.

ASIA

C appadocia in central Turkey is a strange and haunting place. Waves of volcanic
rock undulate across the region in ever-changing patterns, interspersed with
valleys dotted with olive and apricot trees. Small houses cluster around the bases
of rock towers pockmarked with door and window openings, and scattered among
them are the remains of churches and monasteries that were carved out by the early
Christian communities who lived here. Dark entrances, some accessed by ladders, open
into rock-cut chambers complete with domes, apses, columns, barrel-vaulting, and
altars. Many interiors are covered with exceptionally vivid wall-paintings, ranging from
simple fifth-century geometric designs to colorful 10th- and 11th-century fresco cycles
of New Testament stories. The main concentration of churches is around Göreme,
home to St. Basil the Great, Bishop of Caesarea (Kayseri) in the fourth century, and a
major monastic settlement during Byzantine times. Local people have named some of
the churches after distinguishing features—the Church of the Apple for the shape of
its dome, Snake Church after the frescoes of St. George battling the dragon, and Sandal
Church after two foot-shaped imprints in the rock near the entrance.

When to Go Spring through fall. Winters can be very cold, with snow on the ground. The Göreme and
Zelve open-air museums are open daily throughout the year.

Planning Göreme is near the towns of Nevsehir, Avanos, and Urgup. The area is an hour's drive south of Kayseri,
which has daily flights from Istanbul, and offers numerous accommodation options, including boutique hotels—small
hotels decorated in the local style with cave bedrooms in the rock chimneys. Public transport is good, with dolmuses
(minibuses) operating between the main sites. There are hundreds of churches in the area, so allow a minimum of
two to three days, or longer if you want to explore the region in detail.

Websites www.turkeytravelplanner.com, www.byzastoursturkey.com, www.deepnature.com

HIGHLIGHTS

■ The Buckle Church in Göreme
has four chambers dating from
different times. The chamber
known as the **New Church** has
ornate arches and arcades along
one wall and paintings of Bible
scenes set against a bright blue
and gold background.

■ The **Pigeon House** in Cavusin,
near Göreme, is one of the few
churches inside a rock chimney.
The fifth-century **Church of St.
John the Baptist** in Cavusin is the
oldest known Christian sanctuary
in Cappadocia.

■ Other concentrations of churches
can be found in the **Zelve**, **Ihlara**,
and **Soganli** valleys a few miles
south of Göreme.

Because little natural light enters the 11th-century Dark Church in Göreme, the wall-paintings have retained their brilliant colors.

The ruined fortress on top of the Masada plateau overlooks the desert and the Dead Sea.

ISRAEL

MASADA

Positioned high above the Judaean desert, the remains of this ancient fortress have become a symbol of Jewish resistance.

The high plateau of Masada overlooking the Dead Sea is a natural fortress. In the first century B.C. King Herod, who ruled Judaea on behalf of the Romans, built a luxurious fortified citadel on the site. And in A.D. 70, during the Jewish Revolt against the Romans, a group of Jewish fighters took over the plateau and converted the buildings into a refuge for their supporters and families. In A.D. 72, Roman legionaries began a siege of the fortress. During the night before the final assault, the rebels set fire to their food stores and committed mass suicide rather than be captured. The site lay empty until the fifth century, when a group of Byzantine monks temporarily took refuge here, living in caves around the summit and building a small chapel. Today, you can wander through the remains of Roman palaces, storerooms, and bathhouses, and imagine the lavish lifestyle of Herod and his guests. The ruined synagogue built by the Jewish rebels on the remains of Herod's stable, a few of their dwellings, and the Roman siege works tell of the rebels' struggle. Looking down, you can see the remains of the Roman camp, the fortifications they built around the base of the cliff to prevent anyone escaping from the fortress above, and the large assault ramp up which the Romans heaved huge battering rams to attack the fortress walls.

When to Go The Masada plateau is in the Masada National Park, which is open all year except during Yom Kippur, a two-day religious observance that takes place in late September or early October.

Planning Masada is about 60 miles (97 km) south of Jerusalem. It can be reached from the east via Road 90. From the Visitor Center there is a cable car to the plateau that takes about two minutes. Alternatively, you can hike up the ancient Snake Route, which takes about 45–60 minutes, depending on your level of fitness. The plateau can be reached from the west via Road 3199 and an easy, 15–20 minute climb. Take water and extra layers of clothing as the wind can be very strong at the top.

Websites www.jewishvirtuallibrary.org, www.bibleplaces.com/masada.htm

HIGHLIGHTS

■ Extending over the Dead Sea Valley and Jordan, the **view** alone is well worth the visit.

■ In the **Roman bathhouse** you can see the underfloor heating system and the oven where fires heated water to create steam.

■ The restored remains of Herod's sumptuous **three-tiered villa**, constructed on the edge of the precipice, contains fragments of original frescoes.

■ A well-preserved section of beautiful **mosaic floor** has survived in the Byzantine chapel.

■ The **Masada Museum** has displays relating to the history of Masada and of rare coins, pottery shards, and textiles found at the site.

ASIA

Sataniv's cemetery has extraordinarily ornate tombstones, some of which date from the 16th century. Many are carved with animal designs.

UKRAINE

Sataniv's Ruined Synagogue

A ruined fortress synagogue evokes
bygone battles to repel invaders.

The solid ruins of a monumental synagogue loom above a clutch of simple homes and muddy lanes at the edge of the small town of Sataniv in western Ukraine. Luxuriant vines climb the pitted stone walls, and bushy saplings sprout through the row of empty loopholes that pierce the parapet beneath the ravaged roofline. Built in the late-16th or early-17th century, the synagogue is one of the oldest surviving examples of the numerous fortress synagogues in this part of eastern Europe. These buildings formed part of a town's fortifications for the defense of the Jewish population and of the town as a whole. The tall, arched windows are boarded up now, and the cavernous sanctuary is empty under a vaulted ceiling that threatens to collapse. On the eastern wall, though, a haunting reminder of the building's former beauty survives. There you can still see the stone remains of the baroque-style holy ark; elegant columns flank the empty, arched niche where the Torah was kept. Between them, against a flaking background of brilliant blue, a pair of golden griffins frame priestly hands raised in blessing. Above, two rearing lions with curling tails seem to smile as they triumphantly raise a crown atop a sculpted version of the Ten Commandments.

When to Go The synagogue and cemetery are open to the elements, so choose good weather. Summer is ideal; spring or fall are also good.

Planning Allow a full day for the trip since Sataniv is several hours' car drive from either L'viv or Chernivtsi and roads can be bad. Hire a local driver or guide who speaks Ukrainian and can read the signposts written in Cyrillic.

Websites www.inlviv.info, travel-2-ukraine.com, krylos.com, judaica.spb.ru/artcl/a6/archsyn_e.shtml,

HIGHLIGHTS

■ Try to make your way into the ruined sanctuary, or at least stand in the doorway, to see the ravaged remains of the **holy ark**, a rare example of the rich **painted and sculptural ornamentation** that once decorated the synagogue's interior.

■ The abandoned **Jewish cemetery** dates back to the 1550s. Look for the three stones bearing the rare and mysterious **"three hares" motif**—three hares chasing each other in a circle, connected by their ears.

EUROPE ▫

ITALY

ABBAZIA DI SAN GALGANO

The Gothic arches of a ruined medieval abbey
reach skyward in Tuscany's Merse Valley.

EUROPE

Set in a sunny, open valley with forests and mountains in the background, the isolated ruins of the Abbazia di San Galgano are picture-postcard perfect. About 19 miles (30 kilometers) southwest of Siena, the abbey lies in the plain below the hermitage Cappella di Monte Siepi (Chapel of Monte Siepi), built at the end of the 12th century to honor Galgano Guidotti, who was canonized in 1185. The abbey, erected to accommodate monks and pilgrims visiting the hilltop chapel, dates from 1218 and was built by French Cistercian monks. The abbey's plan resembles a Latin cross with a nave and two aisles replete with richly carved capitals, rose windows, a cloister, and a bell tower. The altar remains in position to this day. Its pure French Gothic style—which never fully caught on in Italy—is obvious in the large, high windows and delicate pointed arches. Once a powerful institution, the abbey never fully recovered after losing most of its population to bubonic plague in 1348 and was eventually deconsecrated. In the 16th century, the structure began to succumb: the roof collapsed in 1550 and the bell tower two centuries later. Careful restoration has revived the standing facade and walls.

When to Go The clear days of spring and summer are the best times to soak up the contrast between the majestic ruins, the azure sky, and the emerald carpet of grass. In July and August, the abbey plays host to concerts sponsored by Accademia Musicale Chigiana.

Planning Allow one hour. The abbey is open all the time, but the chapel is open only in the mornings. Although a bus reportedly comes here from Siena, driving is your best option. San Galgano is about an hour southwest of Siena, just outside Monticiano. A small bar at the end of the chapel driveway provides a quick snack. Bring a towel and stop by the Petriolo Hot Springs for a dip. They're only 20 minutes away on the SS 223 superstrada (highway) midway between Siena and Grosseto.

Website www.sangalgano.info

HIGHLIGHTS

■ From inside the abbey, you can see the **chapel** on the hill framed by the empty windows.

■ The small section of **cloister wall** to the left of the entrance is all that remains of a wall that enclosed the garden where the monks were allowed their daily hour of conversation.

■ The grassy surroundings make for a **perfect picnic spot.**

■ In the Cappella di Monte Siepi a real **"sword in the stone"** is preserved under glass. Legend has it that Galgano thrust his sword into a rock to indicate his renunciation of worldly life and it has been there ever since. The adjoining chapel is decorated with **frescoes** by Ambrogio Lorenzetti.

The hauntingly beautiful nave of San Galgano is all that remains of this Gothic masterpiece.

FRANCE

CLUNY ABBEY

A scattering of medieval buildings testifies to one of the greatest triumphs of Gothic architecture.

Worn yellow sandstone marks the path through the remains of the south transept of what was once the largest and possibly the most magnificent church in Christendom. The stones lead to the great bell tower, which, with the transept wall, are all that remain of the abbey church of Cluny. Here, the monks of the Cluniac Order—founded in 910 by William the Pious, Duke of Aquitaine—were engaged in *laus perennis* (perpetual prayer). There is little left to indicate the elevated status of an institution that for centuries was second in importance only to Rome as a focus of Christian worship. But step into the abbey ruins—this was the third abbey to be built on the site (therefore known as Cluny III)—or into the monastery's cavernous 12th-century flour store, and the grandiose scale of the buildings that have disappeared is immediately apparent. In the Tour des Fromages, originally one of several defensive towers that formed part of the monastery's fortifications, the monks ripened wheels of époisses cheese, a local specialty. From the tower's dizzying heights, the hills of Burgundy stretch away far below. Over the centuries, the abbey was constantly enlarged. New abbots' palaces were built in the 15th and 16th centuries, and the monastery buildings were reconstructed in the 18th century. The beauty, riches, and power of Cluny attracted both awe and envy, and in 1790, when French revolutionaries glimpsed its hoarded treasures, it was closed, later to be torn apart, leaving the shell that now remains.

When to Go Any time of year—even in winter the weather is pleasantly mild.

Planning Beaune, the nearest town, can be reached easily by the TGV train service from Paris. From there, local trains depart regularly for Cluny, but a car is essential for trips into the surrounding countryside. Allow one day for the abbey, plus two or three more to explore the region and its celebrated vineyards.

Website www.uk.cluny-tourisme.com

HIGHLIGHTS

■ The beautifully crafted **roof frame** in the monastery flour store is made from chestnut. The building houses the remains of **carved capitals** from the choir of the abbey church.

■ The **Ochier Museum** in Cluny has exhibits relating to the history of the abbey and the medieval town. It also houses a large collection of books from the abbey library.

■ Behind the abbey, **Les Haras Nationaux**, or the **National Stud Farm** of Burgundy, is open to visitors. Some of France's top racehorses are bred here.

■ The most famous **charity wine auction** in the world takes place at the Hospices de Beaune each November and sets prices for the Burgundy vintages around the world.

Opposite: The Tour de Fromages (on the left), the octagonal bell tower, and the small clock tower are all that is still standing of the original 11th-century abbey. Above left: The current cloisters are part of the 18th-century reconstruction of the monastery. Above right: Characterful stone carvings decorate the remains of the medieval abbey buildings.

Built on the site of the last refuge of the Cathars, this French fortress lies in ruins.

FRANCE

MONTSÉGUR

This craggy pinnacle of rock was the last
stronghold of a group of Catholic rebels.

One March morning in 1244, a siege in southern France brought an end to the resistance of the Cathars, a religious community that had broken with the Catholic Church, much to the anger of the pope and the French king. Montségur Castle, a fortress built at the top of a 3,900-foot (1,200 meter) craggy outcrop in the Languedoc-Roussillon region, became the Cathar headquarters and last stronghold—and home to 500-600 people. Perched on top of a sheer cliff, with sweeping views of the surrounding mountains and valleys, the site must have appeared impregnable, and when the king's forces laid siege in 1243, the Cathars resisted for ten months before surrendering. They were given a stark choice: renounce their faith or be burned alive. A procession of more than 200 men and women descended to the funeral pyre on that spring morning. Today, nothing remains of the Cathar refuge except the foundations of some dwellings outside the walls of the present castle, known as Montségur III, which was built by French forces on the site of the Cathar stronghold. Its thick, stocky walls appear to grow out of the rock, catching the intense light in this stark landscape. A footpath leads up from the village of Montségur. At the castle, you can get into the keep and walk around the walls, peering down at the rooftops of the village far below.

When to Go April through May and September through October are best, to avoid summer's intense heat.

Planning Located in the Ariège region in the eastern Pyrenees, Montségur is 12 miles (19 km) south of Lavelanet. The nearest large town is Foix, to the west of Lavelanet. The hike from the village of Montségur to the top is very steep and takes about 30-45 minutes. Guided tours are available every day in July and August and on weekends and public holidays during May, June, and September. Opening times vary.

Websites www.france-for-visitors.com, www.epyrenees.com, www.ariege.com

HIGHLIGHTS

■ A **stele** at the foot of Montségur marks the site of the funeral pyre.

■ Below the summit, on the terraced plateau called the Roc de la Tour, **missiles** that were catapulted at the castle walls by the French lie scattered across the rocky ground.

■ Just below the summit are the remains of a few **dwellings**, which were abandoned when the families fled inside the fortress walls.

■ Tools dating back to the neolithic era are displayed in the one-room **Archaeology Museum** in the village.

ENGLAND

RIEVAULX ABBEY

Tucked away in a pretty valley lie the ruins
of one of the greatest abbeys of the medieval age.

More than 800 years ago an abbot of Rievaulx Abbey wrote, "Everywhere peace, everywhere serenity, and a marvellous freedom from the tumult of the world." Today, these atmospheric stone ruins set in a wooded Yorkshire valley still inspire a profound sense of calm. Rievaulx Abbey was founded in 1132 when St. Bernard of Clairvaux sent 12 monks to England from France. The first Cistercian monastery to be built in the north of England, it became one of the wealthiest and most powerful in Europe; at its peak, Rievaulx housed 150 monks and 500 lay brothers. They passed their time not only in prayer (they prayed at least eight times each day) but also in operating a highly successful sheep-farming and wool export business. Then, in 1538, King Henry VIII ordered the dissolution of the monasteries. The abbey was closed and the buildings were handed over to the Earl of Rutland, who set about taking them apart. Today, the remains of fewer than half are left, but the abbey church is particularly well preserved and has good examples of early English flying buttresses. The foundations, and in some cases walls, of several outbuildings are easy to make out, including the warming-house, where a large fire burned from November 1 to Good Friday. Behind the tall walls and elegant lancet windows of the refectory, some visitors claim to sense the ghosts of monks who, hundreds of years later, still seem to roam this haven of tranquility.

When to Go Rievaulx Abbey is open year-round.

Planning Allow an hour to tour the ruins, plus extra time for the indoor exhibition. Rievaulx Abbey is off the B1257, about 3 miles (5 km) north of Helmsley. Parking is available for visitors arriving by car. Buses operate from Helmsley every day in summer and two days a week in winter. Opening times vary through the year.

Website www.english-heritage.org.uk

EUROPE

HIGHLIGHTS

■ **"The Work of God and Man"** indoor exhibition uses interactive displays to describe the agricultural, industrial, spiritual, and commercial aspects of Rievaulx's history.

■ Rievaulx Abbey is surrounded by hiking and cycling trails. The energetic can walk to Helmsley Castle, about 3 miles (5 km) away, via the **Cleveland Way National Trail.**

The abbey ruins, which include the majestic three-story-high church, are set in a secluded, wooded valley beside the River Rye.

DAILY DEVOTION

ouses of worship, however grand or austere, are
far more than mere buildings. They are visible
statements about tradition and belief, mapped
out in brick, wood, glass, or stone. This architecture of faith
takes many forms, from the azure splendor of Istanbul's
Blue Mosque to the gilded walls of Japan's Golden Pavilion
Temple to the modest hand-hewn wooden churches of New
England. This chapter's sanctuaries may actively welcome—or
discreetly tolerate—visitors, but to their daily users they are
not primarily tourist attractions or museums. Some are places
of great antiquity, with gripping tales to tell, such as Prague's
tiny but hugely poignant Old-New Synagogue—where Jews
have prayed since the Middle Ages—or the delicately carved
temples of China's 1,500-year-old Hanging Monastery, perched
precariously on a precipitous cliff. Others are boldly modernist:
California's 23-story Crystal Cathedral is one of the world's
largest glass buildings and the base for a weekly televised service
attracting some 20 million viewers worldwide.

Heavy with soot, a crucifix known as the Señor de Los Temblores (Lord of the
Earthquakes) hangs above a solid silver altar in Cusco Cathedral, Peru. During
Holy Week, devotees carry it in procession through the streets of the town.

Touro Synagogue gracefully blends Georgian colonial architecture and Sephardic Jewish elements.

RHODE ISLAND

TOURO SYNAGOGUE

This fine 18th-century synagogue is a symbol of
religious freedom for Jews—and Americans of all faiths.

The oldest extant Jewish temple in the U.S., Touro Synagogue in Newport, Rhode Island, is a classic example of colonial architecture. It became a national symbol of religious freedom in 1790, when George Washington wrote its congregation a letter assuring that the new nation would protect the right to worship for all faiths. The serene white chamber with its tall columns, gallery, and fine wooden detailing is a masterwork of architect Peter Harrison, who volunteered his services. Sephardic Jews fleeing the Iberian Inquisition established the congregation in 1658, seeking the liberty to worship pledged by Roger Williams, founder of the Rhode Island colony. Their descendants' spiritual leader, Isaac Touro, dedicated the group's first permanent home in 1762. When the British captured Newport in 1776, many Jews fled. The synagogue then became a British military hospital, and later a town hall, before falling into neglect. Isaac Touro's sons left bequests to fund its repair and upkeep, although it only reopened for worship in 1883, when East European émigrés boosted Newport's Jewish population.

When to Go The temple is open year-round but closed on Saturday except for services. Tour days and schedules change with the seasons. A reading of the letter from Washington takes place every August.

Planning Guided tours last 30 minutes. A fee applies, although U.S. National Park pass holders enter free. The last tour starts at 2:30 p.m. There are services each Friday night and Saturday and on Jewish holidays. Women must sit upstairs. Dress appropriately—no shorts or sleeveless shirts. The Touro Synagogue National Historic Site also includes a Jewish cemetery and a park honoring colonial Jewish leaders.

Website www.tourosynagogue.org

HIGHLIGHTS

■ Men and women worship separately in the Sephardic Orthodox tradition. The women's upstairs gallery is supported by 12 **Ionic columns**, each made from a single tree. Above these, 12 **Corinthian columns** rise to the domed ceiling.

■ Five **massive brass candelabra** hang from the ceiling.

■ Note how the building stands at a **sharp angle** from the street to allow worshipers praying before the holy ark to face east toward Jerusalem.

■ On display inside the synagogue, **Washington's letter** to the Touro congregation includes the following words: "Happily the Government of the United States, which gives to bigotry no sanction, to persecution no assistance requires only that they who live under its protection should demean themselves as good citizens in giving it on all occasions their effectual support."

NORTH AMERICA

TEXAS

MISIÓN CONCEPCIÓN

This outpost of Catholicism and Spanish imperial might takes visitors back to the earliest days of Texan Christianity.

NORTH AMERICA

Many aspects of the Misión de Nuestra Señora de la Purísima Concepción de Acuña are sublime, but the qualities of light and color are foremost. Mid-18th-century plaster frescoes of extraordinary beauty adorn the interior, and the stark sunlight of this arid region makes dramatic entrances. You can discern faint traces of paintings on the outer walls of what is one of America's oldest unrestored stone churches. You can feel the weight of the stones in vaults and domes overhead and smell the dust of bygone days wafting across sunbeams that stab through small openings and project across the sanctuary at jaunty angles. Although all of them survive, Concepción, built in 1755, is the most intact and unaltered of the five original Spanish colonial missions that established San Antonio, Texas. Founded as outposts to convert Native Americans into Catholics and loyal Spanish citizens, and to protect borders from French encroachment, the missions stretch along the San Antonio River at regular intervals. The oldest acequia, or irrigation ditch, in San Antonio runs past the mission. All the missions were built of stone quarried by local people, but of the five, Concepción achieved the highest level of completion, religious prominence, and beauty.

When to Go Avoid Texas in summer, when it is hot and arid. In April, a ten-day fiesta takes place, with pageantry, parades, and parties all over town. Catholic Sunday services and feast days are open to all.

Planning An hour's walk apart, Concepción and the three other missions composing Missions National Historic Park are open daily from 9 a.m. to 5 p.m., except Thanksgiving, December 25, and January 1. The fifth and southernmost, Espada, is a half-hour walk from neighboring mission San Juan Capistrano to the north. Bicycle paths link all five.

Websites www.nps.gov/saan, www.loscompadres.org

HIGHLIGHTS

■ Within the walls supporting the dome, four small windows point north, east, south, and west. The southern window functions as a **solar clock**, with light striking across the altar of the north alcove chapel on the winter solstice (December 21).

■ During the **Feast of the Assumption** (August 15), evening sunlight enters Concepción's small oculus west window. At about 6:30 p.m. the shaft of light strikes the center of the transept, directly beneath the dome.

■ The *convento* (priests' quarters) contains **ceiling frescoes** of remarkable quality. One very striking section in the center of a barrel vault is said to represent the eye of God.

Tourists have been coming to enjoy Concepción since the railroads arrived in the 1870s. Preservation efforts started very early in the 20th century.

Ten New England Churches

Scattered across the states of New England are some of the most historic churches in the United States.

❶ First Church of Christ, Farmington, CT

Completed in 1772, the First Church of Christ is distinguished by its elegant octagonal belfry topped by a beautiful spire. It is the third meeting house on this site.

Planning Visit the art collection at the nearby Hill-Stead Museum. www.ctfreedomtrail.com, www.firstchurch1652.org, www.hillstead.org

❷ First Church, Windsor, CT

The First Church congregation settled in Windsor in 1635 and completed the present meeting house in 1794, making it the state's oldest Congregational church. The gravestones of Palisado Cemetery next door help tell the town's history.

Planning Visit Dr. Hezekiah Chaffee's house, built in 1765; it is open from April to October. www.firstchurchinwindsor.org, www.windsorcc.org

❸ First Baptist Church, Providence, RI

The First Baptist Church, a successful blend of Georgian English and New England Meeting House design, was completed in 1775. With room for 1,200 worshipers, it was the largest building project in New England at the time. The church benefited from the expertise of carpenters and shipwrights left idle when the British closed the port of Boston after the Boston Tea Party.

Planning Walk up the hill to Brown University; the green has many fine buildings. www.fbcia.org, www.pwcvb.com, www.ppsri.org

❹ West Parish of Barnstable Congregational Church, Barnstable, MA

The current meeting house dates from 1719, making it the oldest Congregational church still in use in the world. One of the earliest bell towers in New England was added four years later, on top of which sits a gilded weather vane giving rise to the building's popular name, the Rooster Church.

Planning See the rich diversity of shore life on the 8-mile (13 km) long Sandy Neck Beach. www.westparish.org, www.town.barnstable.ma.us

❺ Old North Church, Boston, MA

Built in 1723, the Old North Church is the oldest surviving church in Boston. Its official name is Christ Church, and it played a pivotal role in the American Revolution. On the evening of April 18, 1775, Paul Revere undertook his celebrated midnight ride after Robert Newman, the church sexton, signaled to him with two lanterns from the Old North Church steeple.

Planning Explore the history of the American Revolution at the city's museums or on a tour of the Boston Freedom Trail. www.oldnorth.com, www.bostonhistory.org, www.cityofboston.gov, www.thefreedomtrail.org

❻ Seamen's Bethel, New Bedford, MA

Built in 1832 to provide religious salvation for seamen visiting the port, the Seaman's Bethel inspired the Whaleman's Chapel in Herman Melville's *Moby-Dick*. Melville visited the church in 1840 and the pew where he sat is marked with a plaque. The bow-shaped pulpit the author described was a product of his imagination, but here life imitates art as an appropriately shaped pulpit was constructed in 1961. On the walls, cenotaphs commemorating sailors and whalers who lost their lives at sea are particularly moving.

Planning You can also visit the Whaling Museum across the road. www.whalingmuseum.org, www.rixsan.com/nbvisit/guide.htm

❼ Meeting House, Greenfield, NH

New England churches doubled as meeting houses for early settlers. Built in 1795, and in continuous use ever since, Greenfield's Meeting House is the oldest such building still functioning in New Hampshire and is now listed as a New Hampshire Historical Marker.

Planning Visit in winter to take advantage of nearby ski slopes. www.greenfield-nh.gov, www.nhstateparks.com/greenfield.html

❽ Stowe Community Church, Stowe, VT

In the shadow of Mount Mansfield, Stowe is the former home of the real-life von Trapps, the Austrian family immortalized in *The Sound of Music*. The church, completed in 1863, cost $12,000 and became one of the first nondenominational churches in the U.S. when the Congregationalists, Methodists, Universalists, and Baptists of Stowe united in 1920.

Planning Visit in winter and hit the slopes at the Stowe Mountain Resort. www.stowechurch.org, www.gostowe.com

❾ St. Paul's Episcopal Church, Wells, VT

People first settled in Wells—named for Wells in Somerset, England—in 1751, and this is one of three churches built on the town green. John Henry Hopkins, the first bishop of Vermont, designed and built St. Paul's in 1841 and also carved its altar.

Planning Wells hosts various events on weekends throughout the summer, including a carnival in August. www.dioceseofvermont.org

❿ First Congregational Church, Woodstock, VT

This graceful church in the quintessential New England small town of Woodstock dates from 1806-08. Its construction was the result of a vigorous campaign by attorney Charles Marsh, who did not want to live in a town without a place of worship. In 1934, Laurance Rockefeller married Mary Billings French in this church. Ever since, the church and the town, both beautifully preserved, have benefited from Rockefeller largesse.

Planning Try to time your visit to coincide with the Vermont Wood Festival in late September. www.fccw.net, www.woodstockvt.com, www.nps.gov/mabi, www.vermontwoodfestival.org

The simple lines and tiered tower of St. Paul's Episcopal Church in Wells, Vermont, stand out against the glowing fall colors of the town green.

Often attracting celebrity guest speakers, the cathedral's Sunday services, known as the *Hour of Power*, are televised worldwide and translated into four languages on-site.

CALIFORNIA

CRYSTAL CATHEDRAL

This ultramodern glass tower makes a daring architectural statement and is a temple of televangelism, too.

Twelve stories tall with a wedge-shaped contour, the Crystal Cathedral rises like a glass galleon piercing the concrete jungle of southern California. From the air, this futuristic totem to Christ shines more brilliantly than Disneyland's Sleeping Beauty Castle, another landmark less than 3 miles (5 kilometers) away. The Crystal Cathedral is made not of crystal, but of more than 10,000 panes of silver glass attached by silicone, for earthquake flexibility, onto a white, weblike steel grid. With a length of 415 feet (126 meters) and a width of 207 feet (63 meters), it's one of the world's largest glass structures, although, lacking a bishop, it is a cathedral in name only. In the vein of movie glamour, and adding to the architectural and spiritual impact, are two 90-foot (27 meter) doors that seem to slide open magically behind the pulpit. In 1980 architect Philip Johnson completed the building, fulfilling the lifelong dream of Dr. Robert H. Schuller, who started the original, more modest structure on the site of an old drive-in cinema. The simple creed of this Protestant church is: "Find a heart and fill it; find a hurt and heal it." Yet at the same time, this 2,890-seat, 17-million-dollar megachurch scales up everything in true Hollywood style. With some 20 million viewers, its weekly *Hour of Power* service, presented by the founder's son Rev. Dr. Robert A. Schuller, is the world's most watched Christian program.

When to Go Visit at any time of year. There are gala musical performances at Christmas and Easter.

Planning An hour to 90 minutes is enough to take a tour and browse the premises. Allow two hours if you want to read the plaques; it's easy to overlook the smaller details. Take time to visit the marble Mary Hood Chapel, a 24-hour place of prayer inscribed: "My House Shall Be Called a House of Prayer for All People." There are quotations and names from the scriptures on the stone paths around the church. Find a bench for contemplation in the memorial gardens. Free guided tours run Mondays through Saturdays, 9 a.m. to 3:30 p.m., and Sundays after morning services. Group tours are available on request.

Website www.crystalcathedral.org

HIGHLIGHTS

■ Two spectacular **musicals** draw thousands annually: *The Glory of Christmas*—with flying angels and live camels—and *The Glory of Easter*, with extraordinary special effects.

■ Added In 1990, the **Crean Tower** is a shiny belfry made of stainless-steel prisms with a 52-bell carillon.

■ The **pipe organ** in the sanctuary is one of the five largest in the world. Multitiered, it sits on a chancel made of quarried marble from Spain.

■ During services, worshipers in the back can view the preacher on an **enormous indoor television screen**.

■ The grounds have **life-size bronze sculptures** of biblical figures, such as "Moses Holding up the Ten Commandments" and "Christ the Good Shepherd."

NORTH AMERICA

COLOMBIA

SALT CATHEDRAL

This magnificent subterranean temple carved out of the salt rock of the Zipaquirá Mountain can hold up to 10,000 worshipers.

SOUTH AMERICA

As you walk through the cavernous, slowly spiraling tunnel into this vast subterranean church, the sounds and colors of the outside world become muted; it's as if you're entering another world. Into the gray-black salt walls are carved the 14 stations of the cross, each in its own small chapel, and at the passage end a gallery overlooks a vast chamber. The Salt Cathedral's majestic interior contains a nave, a pulpit, and an altar, overseen by an imposing crucifix carved into the wall of rock. This still-functioning salt mine, 30 miles (48 kilometers) northwest of Bogotá, is thought to date back some 2,000 years; the first to exploit its deposits were the pre-Hispanic Muisca people. Overseen by a local architect, the project for the current cathedral began in 1991; it took miners and sculptors from the region nearly five years to complete. Every Sunday more than 3,000 visitors come to worship here.

When to Go The cave is open all year. The region's pleasant, mild weather is fairly consistent. December to February tend to be the driest months, with April to May and October to November being wetter.

Planning Take an umbrella, since you may have to wait in line outside and there is no cover. Weekends are extremely busy with local tourists; visit during the week for peace and quiet. For the best chance of capturing the light and atmosphere, avoid using the flash inside. Keep your camera steady; tripods are not allowed. There are a number of places to stay in Zipaquirá, but most people choose to stay in Bogotá and visit Zipaquirá for the day. There are frequent buses between Bogotá and Zipaquirá. From the village, a bus runs to the Salt Cathedral. On weekends and public holidays a slow steam train, complete with roving musicians, goes to Zipaquirá. Buy tickets in advance from Bogotá's Sabana Station.

Websites www.latinguides.com, www.turismocolombia.com

HIGHLIGHTS

■ Before you reach the main cathedral chamber, have a good look around some of the smaller vaults, where there are some wonderful **sculptures carved into the salt**.

■ In what were once the old salt-processing rooms, there is an excellent on-site **museum** showing the history of the mine.

■ Visit during a **religious service**. Worshipers pack the cathedral's enormous, softly lit principal chamber and fill it with the sound of prayer.

A miner prays on a kneeling platform in one of the Salt Cathedral's 14 small chapels representing the stations of the cross.

Cusco's main square contains a fine assembly of Spanish colonial buildings, including the cathedral.

PERU

Cusco Cathedral

In both its art and legends, this cathedral represents a fascinating fusion of colonial Spanish and indigenous Inca traditions.

The true beauty of Cusco Cathedral—a masterpiece of Spanish colonial architecture in the Americas—lies not in its somewhat restrained overall majesty but in the details. These reflect a remarkable fusion of Iberian and Inca cultures. Look for local touches like the animistic puma head carved into the huge main doors or the *cuyo* (guinea pig) among the dishes being served in "The Last Supper" that Marcos Zapata painted high above the nave. Begun in 1560, it took Spanish architects and Inca artisans and laborers more than a century to finish the vast edifice, built over the ruins of the Inca emperor Viracocha's palace. Much of the stone came precut—pilfered from Inca structures like Sacsayhuamán Fortress. And with these stones came myth and legend. One such story is that an Inca prince lives bricked up in one of the massive bell towers, awaiting the day when it falls and he can lead his civilization to renewed glory.

When to Go High in the Andes, Cusco enjoys a typical dry mountain climate of mostly sunny days and nights that turn surprisingly chilly. Temperatures can range anywhere from 20 to 70°F (-7 to 21°C).

Planning Even a brief tour of the cathedral merits at least an hour. You'll need half a day for a thorough browse through the nave, side chapels, and precinct. Mass is said daily in one of the side chapels. Although Christmas and Santa Semana (Easter week) are good times to visit, the year's main event is the Corpus Christi Festival, 60 days after Easter Sunday. Celebrants bear effigies of 15 saints and virgins from parish churches all over Cusco in a sacred parade around the plaza and into the cathedral for an all-night vigil.

Websites www.perutourism.com/info/cusco.htm, www.cusco-peru.org

HIGHLIGHTS

■ Supported by 14 vast pillars, the nave abuts a highly elaborate **solid silver altar** and **ten side chapels**, where most actual worship occurs.

■ A painting in the **Triunfo Chapel** portrays the 1650 earthquake that devastated Cusco. It is said that a gold-and-jewel-encrusted crucifix in the chapel of **Nuestro Señor de los Temblores** (Our Lord of Earthquakes) miraculously spared the cathedral.

■ **La Compañía de Jesús**, a Jesuit church facing the cathedral, is Iberian baroque architecture at its finest.

■ Built on the ruins of the Inca Temple of Sun Virgins, the nearby church and convent of **Santa Catalina** are good examples of the city's indigenous–colonial fusion.

■ The **Museo de Arte Religioso** displays Colonial Catholic artifacts in the old archbishop's palace, a block east of the cathedral plaza.

■ Cusco is a departure point for Peru's most visited attraction, the Inca city of **Machu Picchu**, 44 miles (71 km) to the northwest. The train ride from Cusco offers superb views of the landscape.

SOUTH AMERICA

JAPAN

KINKAKU-JI

A vision of tranquillity, the Golden Pavilion Temple
is a superb Japanese rendition of paradise on earth.

ASIA

This three-story building topped with a delicately curving roof owes its nickname Kinkaku-ji (Golden Pavilion Temple) to the fine gold leaf coating the walls and eaves of the upper two floors. Officially named Rokuon-ji (Deer Garden Temple), the pagoda sits on the edge of the tranquil Kyoko-chi (Mirror Pond) in northern Kyoto. The beauty of the gleaming Buddhist temple fringed with elegant formal gardens was said to evoke paradise on earth. In this marvelous example of Muromachi-era architecture, religious carvings and paintings fill the first two floors, while the third serves as a Buddha hall in the Chinese Chan (Zen) temple style. The present structure dates from 1955, rebuilt after a fanatical young monk burnt down the original pavilion in 1950. The temple is a copy of a structure erected in 1397 as a retirement villa for the shogun Ashikaga Yoshimitsu (1358-1408). Apparently, he lived in blatant luxury while just miles away, Kyoto residents endured famine, earthquakes, and plagues. After he died in 1408, his son altered the building, turning it into a Zen temple of the Rinzai school. Today, it serves as a *shariden*, a hall housing sacred relics of the Buddha, drawing Buddhists and nonbelievers alike.

When to Go Visit year-round. Every season has something to offer. On a clear spring or summer day, the Golden Pavilion shimmers against a blue sky, its reflection captured in the waters of the calm pond. In fall, the gardens are ablaze with orange and red maples, and in winter, the pavilion is a tranquil sight, cloaked in snowy white. Kinkaku-ji is open daily from 9 a.m. to 5 p.m. Arrive early to avoid the crowds.

Planning Allow two hours to cover the temple and gardens, and leave time to visit the teahouse for traditional *matcha* (Japanese whipped green tea). Kinkaku-ji is accessible by bus from Kyoto station. Or take the Karasuma subway line to Kitaoji station, then it is just a short bus or taxi ride to the temple.

Website www.shokoku-ji.or.jp

HIGHLIGHTS

■ Just as the pavilion rose from the ashes, a gilded finial bearing a **phoenix**—an auspicious mythical beast in China and Japan—crowns its roof.

■ The garden's 7.5-ft (2.3 m) tall **Dragon Gate Falls** (Ryumon Taki) empty into a pool dotted with stones resembling carp. An ancient myth says that when a carp swims up a waterfall it transforms into a dragon, represented here by a diagonal rock.

■ Enjoy fine twilight views from the three-mat Sekkatei (Favorable Sunset) **teahouse** beyond the Anmintaku (Tranquillity Pond) and up a steep winding path. Note the nandina-wood pillar beneath the alcove. As nandina grows very slowly, a pillar of this girth comes from a very ancient tree.

On a sunny day, the Mirror Pond shimmers with the reflection of the Golden Pavilion Temple and the formal gardens behind.

CHINA

TEMPLE OF HEAVEN

Its blue-roofed circular halls seeming to link earth to heaven,
this temple is perhaps the finest achievement of Ming architecture.

To the Chinese, curved objects denote heaven, while square ones represent earth.
So the outline of the vast walled enclosure around the Altar of Heaven is rounded
at the top and square at the bottom, symbolizing the site's role as a place of
intercession between the two. The temple with its central axis of extravagant halls—some
round and some square—and an altar was, like the Forbidden City, completed in 1420.
The perfectly circular Hall of Prayer for Good Harvests is perhaps Beijing's most beautiful
ancient building. Painted blue, green, and gold, the hall has a circle of red latticed doors
and triple-layered roofs in deep blue—reflecting a heavenly focus—topped with a large
golden knob. The triple-layered, disk-shaped altar in white stone to the south is the true
heart of the site. Sublime in its simplicity, this is where, right up until 1912, emperors
performed a complicated three-part supplication ceremony of fasting, prayer, and
elaborate sacrifices, culminating in the burning of a bullock, with the aim of ensuring
bumper crops. As ancient Chinese emperors were traditionally believed to be the sons of
heaven, it was important for them to venerate the sources of their authority.

When to Go In winter, communal heating in residential buildings, much of it from coal-fired boilers,
makes air pollution a problem. In late September and early October, winds blow away much of the
pollution. April is also nice, but beware: the spring winds can sometimes be laden with sand.

Planning Start at the new subway station on Beijing's Line 5 directly outside the east gate. You will exit
on the opposite side of the temple. From there, you can walk ten minutes west to the much less visited
Altar of Agriculture, perhaps pausing for lunch in the Tian Qiao district en route. Visit soon after 6 a.m. to
find local recreation, such as tai chi, kite flying, and opera singing in full swing, to be first when the halls
open, and to be able to try the sonic effects of the Imperial Vault of Heaven and experience the solemnity
of the altar before the tour groups arrive. Allow two to three hours for a visit, to include side halls with
exhibitions and a moated complex where the emperor spent the night before the supplication ceremony.

Websites www.tiantanpark.com, www.kinabaloo.com

HIGHLIGHTS

■ Stand at the central point of the
altar, as the emperors once did,
and survey both the site and the
Beijing skyline.

■ The **Hall of Prayer for Good
Harvests** is supported by 28 massive
pillars made from single tree trunks.

■ Test the **strange sonic effects** of
the circular enclosing wall of the
Imperial Vault of Heaven, with its
odd amplification of clapping and its
whispering gallery effect.

■ The park around the various halls is
full of local people practicing **Beijing
traditions**, including opera singers
and *erhu* (two-string fiddle) players,
kite fliers, and devotees of various
martial art exercises.

Not a single nail went into the Hall of Prayer for Good Harvests, constructed entirely of wood.

Apparently perched on stilts, the Hanging Monastery seems to cling to the side of a cliff.

CHINA

HANGING MONASTERY

Jutting improbably from a cliff, this gravity-defying site combines precarious pavilions, vertiginous views, and time-honored temples.

Tiny and delicate temples more than 1,500 years old form a real-life castle in the sky at one of China's most photogenic spiritual sites. The Hanging Monastery, or Xuankong Si, is a handful of fragile temples connected by narrow stairways and walkways glued improbably to the side of a sheer cliff, apparently supported by slender stilts. Luckily for visitors, these poles have more of a decorative than structural function; the beams on which the pavilions sit go far back into the cliff. It's an ecumenical site, with Taoism, Buddhism, and Confucianism all represented within its 40 incense-clouded halls and pavilions. Very unusually, all three faiths share a single tiny temple. One building has a Buddha whose face you can touch for luck, although the custom has not been lucky for the statue itself, now eroded by the passage of many hands. Another Buddhist chamber has a fine clay-and-wood tracery of flying and suspended figures perfectly suited to the monastery's own semblance of levitation, and one of the Taoist halls has a particularly fine set of dragons in relief. The site was elevated to avoid damage from the flood-prone river below. Now that the river is dammed, the views from the monastery are unappealing. But the journey is worthwhile to see the unlikely position of the temples, even without entering to shuffle between the minuscule chambers.

When to Go Visit year-round, but in winter, November to March, it can be bitterly cold.

Planning It's just possible to make a one-day visit by taking an overnight train from Beijing west to Datong and returning the same way. But a three-day stay is better so that you can visit other nearby sites: Datong has several particularly old temples, one of the best cave temple sites in the country is on the edge of the city at Yungang, and the oldest wooden pagoda in China is not far away. The monastery is 40 miles (65 km) southeast of Datong, and although reachable by public transport, you need to take two buses and haggle the price for both. China International Travel Service (CITS) runs a useful day tour, which also includes the Yungang Caves. You can buy tickets at its office in the railway station.

Websites www.orientalarchitecture.com, www.cnto.org

HIGHLIGHTS

■ Gaps between the boards of the creakingly cantilevered balconies give **unnerving views** straight down: this is part religious site and part circus high-wire act.

■ Whatever else you visit in China, this incredible cliff site is likely to provide the **photographs** that most surprise and impress your friends and family back home.

■ Forty tiny halls and niches contain **colorful statuary**, including a rare grouping of Laozi (founder of Taoism), Confucius, and the Sakyamuni Buddha all standing together in harmony.

ASIA

WENWU TEMPLE

Under the gaze of gods, dragons, and phoenixes, Taoists and Confucians write prayers on red cards before lighting incense coils to purify their pleas and waft them heavenward.

The chimes of hundreds of blessing wind-bells are carried on the sultry afternoon breeze, sending their prayers over the still azure waters of Sun Moon Lake and on into the haze of the encircling Chung-yang Shan mountain range. The orange-tiled, tiered roofs, protected by dragons positioned along each ridge, shelter Wenwu Temple, tucked into the shoulder of a forest-covered hill. Sacred to Taoists and Confucianists, the temple is dedicated to the philosopher Confucius and to Guan Yu (A.D. 160–219) and Yue Fei (1103–42), the only Chinese generals to be deified. Inside, fragrant tendrils of smoke from spiraling sticks of incense drift around dangling prayer cards and weave up to the high temple ceiling, which is covered with miniature gilded deities. The sound of worn divination sticks hitting the ground marks the shuffling steps of worshipers seeking to know their future, while students throng Dacheng Hall, praying for academic success before the bronze seated statue of Confucius. Under the watchful eye of a pair of phoenixes guarding the entrance to an oven, people burn *hongbao* (ghost money) and incense as offerings to the gods. Built in the palace style of northern China, Wenwu was created in 1938 from the merger of two ancient temples that were moved because construction of a hydroelectric power plant raised water levels in the lake, threatening the original sites with flooding.

When to Go The best weather is from October to January. The typhoon season lasts from June to September. Weekdays tend to be less busy. The temple is open 24 hours, but use the side entrance after 8 p.m. In September, experience the Thao Harvest Festival (New Year), see the fireworks festival on the lake, and take part in the annual cross-lake swim starting at Chaowu Wharf.

Planning One to two hours is enough to visit the temple, but allow more time to see the lake by boat; trips start from any of the lake's four wharfs. Rent a bike to explore the lakeshore road. In larger towns (especially the capital Taipei) beware of pickpockets and vehicles, that may not stop for pedestrians.

Website www.sunmoonlake.gov.tw

HIGHLIGHTS

■ Look at the cast of the **Green Dragon Moon Spear** *(qinlongyianyuedao)*. It is said to have been the weapon of Guan Yu hardened by dragon's blood.

■ On the way up to the temple of Confucius, touch the **Golden Ball of Wisdom** surrounded by gaily colored dragons playing in water. In Taoism, dragons symbolize power, wisdom, and good fortune, and they are often depicted playing with a pearl or thunderball representing the font of their wisdom.

■ Try the **fortune-telling machine** in the central Wushen Temple: a mechanical maiden emerges from the miniature temple doors with your fortune on a small scroll.

■ If you arrive by boat, you ascend to the temple from the jetty by 366 steps—one for each day of the year (and an extra for leap years)—known as the **Year of Steps**. There is a platform with a seat at the beginning of each month where you can rest on the way up. Festooned with blessing wind-bells, the vertical metal railings on either side of the staircase each denote a year in the Chinese calendar.

Opposite: The thickness of the incense coils purifying the prayer cards gives the coils the appearance of baskets. Above left: The observatory gives a fine view of the temple's orange tiled roofs and Sun Moon Lake. Above right: Brightly colored sacred dragons protect the Golden Ball of Wisdom outside Dacheng Hall, dedicated to Confucius.

Monastery of 10,000 Buddhas

This decidedly eccentric shrine houses statues of the Buddha
in an incredible range of shapes, sizes, and poses.

Hong Kong's most celebrated religious shrine hangs above the crowded high-rise suburb of Sha Tin in the New Territories and is reached by scaling 431 steps from the valley floor. But the climb amply repays both pilgrims and casual observers. At last count, the sprawling monastery and temple complex held around 13,000 images of the Buddha, large and small, no two the same. Many are surprisingly light-hearted—even comical. Although the architecture looks old, it is actually a modern creation, started in 1949 by Rev. Yuet Kai Fai Sei and completed in 1957. Formerly a philosophy teacher in Beijing, Yuet Kai renounced all his earthly possessions before crossing China on foot and settling in the lush hills over Sha Tin. Towering over everything is a nine-story pagoda painted candy-apple red with yellow trim. Its circular staircase, lined on both sides with statues of Buddhas, leads up to a panoramic view over the valley. Nearby stands the oddest of the myriad statues—a golden figure of Manjusri (whom Buddhists revere as the embodiment of transcendent wisdom) atop a huge blue lion. Around the central courtyard stand various temples and pavilions housing most of the Buddhas. Each represents a *bodhi* (fully liberated follower) who has achieved enlightenment.

When to Go Hong Kong is northerly enough to have four distinct seasons. Summer is hot and sticky, and winter colder than one might expect and often windy. Spring and fall are sunny and warm and make perfect walking weather. The Ching Ming Festival in April and the Shang Yuan Lantern Festival, the 15th and final day of the Chinese New Year festivities, are good times to visit.

Planning You need about half a day to make the round-trip between central Hong Kong and Sha Tin and explore the complex. You can get there only by foot from Sha Tin station, which you can reach by train from Kowloon station, or by bus or taxi. If you come by taxi, ask to be dropped outside Grand Central Plaza shopping mall. Across the street the first of several signs points the way to the monastery steps.

Websites www.10kbuddhas.org, www.discoverhongkong.com

HIGHLIGHTS

■ As well as numerous Buddhas, the main temple holds the **tomb of Yuet Kai**, whose mummified form is smothered in gold leaf applied by devotees since his death in 1965. His body, covered by a red silk cloak, poses serenely in a lotus position inside a glass box.

■ Life-size statues flanking the central courtyard—the **18 Arhans** ("worthy ones" in Sanskrit)—depict enlightened disciples of the Buddha who have temporarily renounced well-earned nirvana to help other people. Among south China's faithful they enjoy near-superhero status.

■ At the **Buddha Bathing Festival** marking the Buddha's birthday, monks carry out the ritual washing of the statues. They also distribute noodles. It falls on the eighth day of the fourth lunar month (usually May).

A double row of life-sized gold-painted Buddhas lines the 431 steps up to Hong Kong's best-known, and quirkiest, shrine.

The gold-plated spires of the Temple of the Emerald Buddha pierce Bangkok's skyline.

THAILAND

TEMPLE OF THE EMERALD BUDDHA

Built to shelter a diminutive statue, Thailand's most sacred site is a glittering explosion of color and light.

The Buddha is made of jade and is just 30 inches (76 centimeters) tall. Yet join the crowds at his feet and you sense this is the very soul of Thailand. Protected by a nine-tiered golden umbrella, he looks down on the sumptuous Royal Chapel, where three times a year the king comes to change his glittering robes according to season. But before you even reach the chapel, the courtyard hits you like a thunderbolt with a blast of color and light straight out of an Oriental fantasy. Its pagodas, pavilions, bell towers, spires, and overlapping roofs curling up at the edges sparkle with gold leaf and mosaics. Green-faced demons and graceful mythological creatures—half bird, half human—peer down at you. The air is fragrant with offerings of flowers and incense. Tucked into a corner of Bangkok's Grand Palace, this is Thailand's holiest spot. Discovered in the 1400s, the little jade Buddha repeatedly changed hands across borders as a coveted spoil of war before slipping back to Thailand in the 18th century. King Chakri then built the Buddha a temple: it was the first permanent structure in his new capital.

When to Go Winter promises the best climate. The temple is open daily from 8 a.m. to 4 p.m., except during special events. Visit on Chakri Day, April 6—the only date that the Royal Pantheon is open to the public—to see the life-size royal effigies.

Planning The Temple of the Emerald Buddha (Wat Phra Keo) and other main attractions are near the river. So choose a hotel nearby and you won't have to worry about traffic. To get there take a riverboat to Tha Chang Pier, which is a short walk from the temple. Dress conservatively to visit both the palace and the temple. In the chapel, you should be quiet and sit on the floor, feet away from the Buddha. Photography is forbidden inside and the rule is strictly enforced. Arrive early to avoid the crowds.

Websites www.bangkok.com, www.bangkoktourist.com

HIGHLIGHTS

■ Inside the **Royal Chapel**, listen to the constant whisper of prayers, then enjoy the view over the compound from the upper terrace. The chapel's **murals** depict the Buddha's life. Those in the cloisters show scenes from the *Ramakien*, the Thai version of the Hindu *Ramayana* epic.

■ The **statue of a hermit** near the entrance represents an anonymous Hindu man who is said to have invented yoga.

■ Spot the **sacred white elephant statues** and a **model of Angkor Wat**, commissioned by King Mongkut who reigned from 1851 to 1868. Cambodia was long a Thai vassal and the king wanted to remind his people of past imperial glories.

ASIA

Mahabalipuram Shore Temple

This masterpiece of the Dravidian architectural style
only recently emerged from beneath centuries of silt.

ASIA

In December 2004, a miracle seemingly occurred in Mahabalipuram, near the southern tip of India in Tamil Nadu. As a tsunami lashed the beachfront, tearing away at the sand, it unearthed 6-foot (1.8 meter) tall, intricately crafted, centuries-old carvings—of an elephant's head, a stallion in flight, and a lion poised to pounce. Fishermen claim that, as the Indian Ocean receded, they also saw the ruins of a lost city and its fabled Seven Pagodas, which, legend has it, once lined the shore. Mahabalipuram is a town made of legends. The Pallava kings, pioneers of the classical Dravidian style of architecture, built this port city in the seventh century, and the elaborate Hindu temples and carved stone pyramids were so magnificent that, the story goes, jealous gods unleashed a flood that swallowed most of the city. Today, the remaining structures, set among casuarina trees and palms, make up a site drawing thousands of pilgrims and tourists a year. Mahabalipuram contains nearly 40 monuments of different types, including a balancing boulder, known as Krishna's Butter Ball, and Arjuna's Penance, one of the world's largest open-air bas-reliefs, named after the hero of the Hindu epic, the *Mahabharata*. As visitors walk through the town, the music of Mahabalipuram serenades them—the breath of the surf and the tap, tap, tap of artisans' chisels as they sculpt granite into miniature temple replicas.

When to Go The best time to visit is winter, between November and March. A tour of most of the monuments takes half a day. Go between December and February for the acclaimed dance festival, which uses Arjuna's Penance as a stage backdrop.

Planning Buses are available daily from Pondicherry, Kanchipuram, Chengalpattu, and Chennai; you can also hire a taxi from Chennai, which is about a 90-minute drive away. Bring swimwear to take a dip in the ocean. Take a stone-carving class from local artisans.

Websites www.mahabalipuram.co.in, www.asi.nic.in, www.orientalarchitecture.com

HIGHLIGHTS

■ Archaeologists have yet to find conclusive evidence confirming the existence of the fabled seven pagodas. If they do exist, the **Shore Temple** is the only one that remains above water, having survived the supposed wrath of the gods. Named for its proximity to the ocean—during high tide, waves lap at the walls—it is believed to be southern India's oldest stone temple.

■ The **Pancha Rathas**, mid-seventh-century monolithic temples in the form of chariots, are each carved from a single pink granite boulder.

■ Ninety-six feet (29 meters) long and 43 feet (13 meters) high, **Arjuna's Penance**, also known as the Descent of the Ganga, comprises about 150 figures—celestial nymphs, elephants, monkeys, and other animals—observing Arjuna, the epic hero of the *Mahabharata,* in a yogic pose of penance.

Hindu with Buddhist influences, Dravidian architecture made lavish use of intricate stone carving. Here, dancing deities hover above life-size elephants hewn into the rock.

Meenakshi has 12 *gopuram*s, or towers, of solid granite beneath painted stucco figures of deities and mythical beasts.

INDIA

SRI MEENAKSHI TEMPLE

This enjoyably chaotic Hindu temple is not only
a place of worship but a hive of commerce.

Mythology, history, and commerce blend seamlessly in the temple-dominated city of Madurai that has stood since at least A.D. 550. Hindu Tamil culture still reigns here—despite the influences of the Greeks, Romans, Muslims, and British—and the temple of Siva's goddess consort has a hold over the minds of Madurai's inhabitants. And little wonder, for the temple has always been the heart of the city. Take your time to amble around the 15-acre (6 hectare) temple complex with its fortlike walls and lofty embellished towers. Near the entrance, the corridors around the Golden Lily Tank have absorbing murals with scenes from an ancient Tamil epic. Legend has it that at periodic meetings of the Tamil Sangam, or Academy of Tamil Learning, in the distant past, poets submitting their verses for assessment would have their literary outpourings thrown into the tank; only works of merit would float to the top, while the worthless would sink to the bottom. Around the temple are many smaller shrines and halls with grand pillars. A city within a city, Sri Meenakshi buzzes with every type of activity from weddings to bangle hawking and palm reading.

When to Go Winter, from December through February, is the best time to visit.

Planning Allow three hours to wander around the temple but a day or two for Madurai. The city has good air, rail, and road connections. The Golden Quadrilateral railroad and a four-lane highway connect it to Madras. You can fly in from Bangalore, Chennai, or Mumbai. The airport is 8 miles (13 km) away from the city and will soon have international flights. Traditional culture prevails: cover yours legs and arms, especially during temple visits. Leave your footwear at the temple door. Visit in early morning or late evening to avoid the crowds. Some parts of the temple are off-limits to non-Hindus.

Websites www.maduraimeenakshi.org, www.madurai.com

HIGHLIGHTS

■ The most noteworthy of the stucco figures are the varied carvings you notice as you walk through the immense **Hall of a Thousand Pillars**. Each pillar is carved intricately and differently and when struck gently will produce a different musical note.

■ Visit Madurai's only historic mosque: the **Kazimar Periya Pallivasal**, or Kazimar Big Mosque, within half a mile (1 km) of the temple. An enlightened ruler, King Ku Pandiyan constructed it in the late 12th century.

■ Madurai is famed for its jasmine trade. Visit a **jasmine farm** at the foothills of Kodaikanal near the city, and walk through a field of delicate white buds beginning to swell for picking the next day. The indigenous *Jasminum sambac* has to be plucked when the buds are the point of popping open, which usually happens in the early morning.

■ At Madurai's morning **flower market**, narrow alleys are crowded with more than 2,000 farmers selling thousands of tons of colorful and fragrant herbs and blooms.

■ The **Tirupparankundram Temple**, 5 miles (8 km) from Madurai, is built into a hill and has an inner shrine cut from solid rock.

ASIA

BADSHAHI MOSQUE

Serene and spacious in a city that is often neither, this mosque is an ambassador for Mogul architecture—and Islam.

Lahore may be overcrowded and in need of more than a lick of paint in places, but at its heart lies a lovingly tended oasis of tranquillity and serenity where it is easy to appreciate the finest aspects of Islam. Built entirely of red sandstone, Badshahi (Royal) Mosque hovers above the old city and was the largest architectural project and crowning achievement of Aurangzeb, the last great Mogul emperor, who commissioned it in 1671. Enter up a staircase through a vast gateway lined with floral frescoes. Inside, the first impression of the almost square open courtyard is of sheer space. Badshahi holds some 60,000 people and is said to have the largest outdoor worship space of any mosque in the world—530 by 527 feet (161.5 by 160.6 meters). But it is rarely busy—on most days there are more vacationing Pakistani families than worshipers. The courtyard has a 176-foot (54 meter) tall octagonal minaret at each corner and a square marble fountain in the center. At its west end, through a doorway topped with three exquisite marble onion domes, are seven prayer halls. Like much Islamic architecture, Badshahi features elaborate use of surface color to foil the often harsh midday sunlight. The floral designs incorporate almost every hue, but the overall effect, like that of the warm red sandstone, is delicate and harmonious. Perhaps the most surprising fact about Badshahi is that it was built in a mere two and a half years.

When to Go The best time to visit Lahore is winter: October to March. Summer (May-July) is very hot. From July to September, the monsoon rains give some relief from the heat. Ideally, visit in the cool of the morning, then return in the evening to enjoy the floodlit dome's luminous pink glow.

Planning Allow one to two hours for the mosque—and at least two days for Lahore. Lahore is Pakistan's most enjoyable large city, with a burst of attractions. It has good rail and air links with the rest of Pakistan. In summer, the red sandstone tiles of Badshahi Mosque can burn bare feet: wear socks. Remove shoes when entering, and pay a porter to look after them. Dress conservatively. Although Lahore is a relatively laid-back, hospitable, and safe place, check travel advisories before visiting.

Websites www.lahore.gov.pk, www.tourism.gov.pk, http://tdcp.punjab.gov.pk

HIGHLIGHTS

■ A room above the entrance gate, closed to the public, houses **relics** of the Prophet Muhammad, his daughter Fatima, and son-in-law Ali.

■ For a superb **view** of Badshahi, climb to the top of one of its minarets. Or visit **Minar-e Pakistan** in Iqbal Park facing the mosque. Built in 1960-68, the 197-ft (60 m) minaret celebrates a 1940 resolution paving the way for Pakistani nationhood.

■ **Lahore Fort**, opposite Badshahi and built at the same time, is one of the world's foremost Mogul monuments.

■ In the northwest corner of the fort, the **Shish Mahal** (Palace of Mirrors) still retains much of its original inlay and has superb fort views. Built by Shah Jahan in 1631 for the women of his court, the most intact pavilion, the **Naulakha,** is so named because it cost nine lakhs (900,000 rupees) to build.

■ Stroll, picnic, or simply laze in **Shalimar Gardens**, located 3 miles (5 km) northeast of Lahore and originally laid out for private use by Shah Jahan's family. Another fine garden, **Hazuri Bagh**, lies between Badshahi and Lahore Fort. It once housed a Mogul parade review ground and the mosque's caravansary.

Opposite: Muslims traditionally perform Eid prayers, marking the end of the fasting month of Ramadan, in large groups—and Badshahi Mosque is a perfect venue. Above left: Badshahi's cloisters offer respite from Lahore's fierce summer heat. Above right: At night, the floodlit mosque is an unmistakable landmark dominating Lahore's old city.

At sunrise, Shwedagon Pagoda shimmers in a golden hue of extraordinary intensity.

MYANMAR

SHWEDAGON PAGODA

Covered in gold and capped with jewels,
this golden dome towers over the city.

One of Asia's most remarkable sights, and perhaps its most spectacular Buddhist monument, the giant golden pagoda of Shwedagon is staggering in its beauty, size, and form, soaring high over the hazy skies of Rangoon (Yangon). A more singularly exotic structure is hard to imagine anywhere on Earth. Shwedagon is also of great, if uncertain, vintage. Legend dates its origins to some 2,500 years ago, in the Buddha's lifetime, but archaeologists reckon it to be a millennium or more younger. The sacred complex looms large in the life of Myanmar's Buddhists, and the place buzzes with activity from early morning to late evening. Although numbers have dwindled since the government's monastery crackdown of 2007, a constant stream of monks and pilgrims normally throngs the platform, circumambulating the pagoda and praying in the many side pavilions and shrines, and the air is filled with the noise of the monks' monotone chanting and clouds of pungent incense.

When to Go The best time is from November to February, which is dry and fairly cool. March to May is sweltering and June to October is oppressively humid, often with torrential rain.

Planning Allow at least three hours for a visit. The site is open from 4 a.m. (6 a.m. for foreigners) to 10 p.m. Spend a few days in Rangoon, returning to Shwedagon at different times of day to view its changing colors before leaving. This was a hub of antigovernment protests in 2007; many monks were arrested or fled. Aung San Suu Kyi, the democratically elected prime minister, has urged tourists to boycott the country and its brutal dictatorship, which tourist money helps shore up. Visitors should dress respectfully—no shorts or skimpy T-shirts. Remove shoes on entry.

Websites www.shwedagonpagoda.com, www.burmacampaign.org.uk, www.shwedagon.org

HIGHLIGHTS

■ Thousands of **solid gold bars**—more, it is said, than in the Bank of England—cover the 361-ft (110 m) pagoda. Jewels crown the spire—more than **5,000 diamonds** and **2,000 rubies and sapphires.**

■ The **Shwedagon Pagoda Festival,** on the full moon of Tabaung (March), is a superb time to visit. There is a ceremony of almsgiving to the monks, when devotees make offerings for temple upkeep. For the event, monks spruce up the complex, which looks particularly gorgeous in the candlelit evening display.

■ The wide **terrace** bounding the stupa's octagonal base is made of marble and has been worn down at the four main entrances by the feet of myriad pilgrims.

■ Visit in the cool of **early morning** to enjoy the pagoda at its most magical.

RUSSIA

KIZHI POGOST

This tiny island houses one of Russia's most spectacular religious ensembles, a glorious example of Karelian folk architecture.

EUROPE

Clustered along the shores of tiny Kizhi Island on Russia's Lake Onega, the two multiple-domed wooden churches and octagonal bell tower of Kizhi *pogost* (enclosure) are an enduring tribute to the ingenuity and remarkable construction and engineering skills of the 18th-century Karelian carpenters who built them. Completed in 1714, the 121-foot (37 meter) high Church of the Transfiguration of the Savior is the showpiece of the group. To create its pyramidal design, the builders stacked three timber octahedrons, each addition smaller than the one below. The pine logs are not held together with nails but with dovetail joints and hand-hewn wooden pegs. The curved *bochka*—or barrel—roofs are as functional as they are decorative. They support 22 domes of varying sizes, each covered with layers of thin aspen shingles, which time has weathered to a luminescent silvery color. The other temple in the ensemble is the rectangular Church of the Intercession. Built in 1764 as a winter church, it was designed to complement the larger, showier Transfiguration Church, which was too big and costly to heat in cold weather. In keeping with the Transfiguration Church's architectural style, nine domes replaced the tent roof traditional for this "octahedron on quadrangle" construction style.

When to Go The Kizhi museum-reserve is open daily, 9 a.m. to 8 p.m., from late May to mid-October. You will need three hours to tour it but almost a full day to make the round-trip by hydrofoil to the island.

Planning Make advance reservations for the hydrofoil, which departs from Petrozavodsk for the 75-minute trip to Kizhi. During New Year's week there are special tours and programs on the island, accessible by helicopter, ranging from an island tour to sampling Karelian foods and participation in folk games and Russian holiday rituals. Kizhi is fiercely cold in winter, with only about 50 permanent residents, but it fills with visitors in summer.

Website www.kizhi.karelia.ru

HIGHLIGHTS

■ Enlivening the modest interior of the Church of the Intercession is a meticulously restored, original **iconostasis**, or illustrated screen dividing the sanctuary and nave, with superb 17th- to 19th-century icons from Kizhi and other islands in the Zaonezhye Archipelago.

■ Study Kizhi Pogost's **unusual folk architecture** at the Kizhi State Open-Air Museum of History, Architecture, and Ethnography. Exhibits include Karelian houses, agricultural buildings, and Russia's oldest wooden church—all moved to the island from throughout Russian Karelia.

The wooden churches of Kizhi Pogost are a remarkable tribute to the ingenuity and skill of the 18th-century carpenters who built them.

CATHEDRAL OF THE ASSUMPTION

The Kremlin's oldest and most important church has for centuries played a central role in Russian Orthodoxy—and Russia itself.

EUROPE

The austere limestone exterior belies the lavish interior of the Cathedral of the Assumption on Cathedral Square in Moscow's Kremlin. The work of Italian architect Aristotile Fioravanti, from 1475 to 1479, the five-domed cathedral was Russia's official church for several centuries. Inside, a panoply of richly colored religious frescoes painted on gilt graces every surface, including the massive columns and interior of the main dome. Each of the centuries-old icons adorning the multitiered, 52-foot (16 meter) high iconostasis—the painted screen dividing the sanctuary and nave—tells a story. Themes include biblical events, as well as saints' and feast days, notably the Assumption of the Virgin Mary, to whom the cathedral is dedicated. Take time to see the early-12th-century works and the numerous paintings in the Muscovite mannerism style by Dionysius, a prominent late-15th-century iconographer. The cathedral's grandeur befits its ceremonial function as the site of coronations, official weddings, and burials of patriarchs and metropolitans. The tombs with their ornate caskets are works of art, as are the 16th-century stone patriarch's seat and the canopied throne of Monomakh, a beautifully carved wooden praying seat made for Ivan the Terrible, Russia's first tsar.

When to Go The Kremlin, including the Cathedral of the Assumption, is open daily, except Thursdays, from 10 a.m. to 5 p.m., although it sometimes closes for official functions.

Planning Set aside two to three hours, or a full day to include the Armory Chamber and other buildings. There are separate tickets for entry to the Kremlin grounds and the cathedrals and museums. The main ticket office is in Alexandrov Gardens on the western side of the Kremlin. If you are not on a guided tour, rent an English audio guide here. Photography is forbidden inside the cathedral.

Websites www.kremlin.ru, www.kreml.ru

HIGHLIGHTS

■ Among the cathedral's most revered **art treasures** are "The Assumption of the Holy Virgin," a fresco painted for the cathedral's consecration in 1479, and "St. George," an early-12th-century icon.

■ Gaze up to view the 12 **magnificent gilded chandeliers**, including the 46-branch Harvest Chandelier, cast from silver looted from the cathedral in 1812 by Napoleon Bonaparte and later recovered.

■ Allot time to visit **more of the Kremlin**, including its 15th-17th-century cathedrals, the 16th-century Ivan the Great Bell Tower, built as a belfry for the cathedrals, and the Armory Chamber, the repository of Russia's national treasures.

Exquisite religious frescoes fill the interior of the Cathedral of the Assumption. Throughout its history it has attracted some of Russia's finest architects and artists.

Originally a private chapel, St. George's Church probably dates back to the late 14th century.

GREECE

St. George's Church

Now undergoing restoration, the ghost town of Mystras is a monument to Byzantine architecture and spirituality.

The very name Mystras is redolent of holy mysteries. It stands high above the fertile lands of Laconia in the Greek Peloponnese, with a plethora of Orthodox churches and chapels—some half-ruined, some lovingly restored—lining its maze of overgrown alleys. Yet this Byzantine ghost city had very secular beginnings, founded in the early 13th century as one of three great fortresses guarding the Principality of the Morea. From the mid-14th century, Mystras was a haven for artists, scholars, and theologians as well as Byzantine warrior-aristocrats, who resisted Ottoman rule until 1460. It remained a thriving city until abandoned less than 200 years ago, and nowadays its only residents are a small community of Old Calendarist Greek Orthodox nuns. But many churches built during Mystras's golden age survived. Perhaps the most typical, the Church of Agios Georgios (St. George) was restored from ruins in 1953. Originally the private chapel of some long-forgotten noble family, it has an arched roof and decorative brickwork typical of the late Byzantine period. Its interior today is almost bare, though a few church tapers usually burn in front of a small modern icon of St. George. One of Greece's great hero-saints, he is usually depicted on a white charger, driving his lance into the black coils of a winged serpent. It's a place to imagine Mystras in the days of its last flickering glory.

When to Go The mildest weather is in early summer (April to May) and fall (mid-September to October).

Planning A day is enough to explore Mystras. Sparta, the nearest large town, is 3 miles (5 km) away and has frequent bus connections with Athens, three to four hours away. A taxi to Mystras from Sparta takes around ten minutes. There are plentiful hotels and guesthouses in Sparta and in the village of Neas (New) Mystras, a few minutes' walk from the historic site. Sparta has many car rental agencies. Bring sunblock and sunglasses. On May 29 a requiem is held at Mystras in honor of Constantine Palaeologus—the last Byzantine emperor and an unofficial Orthodox saint—along with various cultural events.

Websites www.laconia.org/Mystra1_intro.htm, www.gnto.gr

HIGHLIGHTS

■ **Pantanassa**, built in 1428, is the town's youngest church, serving a small convent of friendly nuns. The church's relatively well-preserved frescoes include "Descent of Christ into Hell" and the "Raising of Lazarus."

■ The 13th-century **Vrontochion**—once a rich monastery—is a prominent landmark with its many domes.

■ Currently under restoration, the shell of the vast **Palace of the Despots** is one of Greece's few remaining secular Byzantine buildings.

■ Climb to the ruined walls of the hilltop **castle** *(kastro)* above the town for an eagle's-eye view of ancient Mystras, the vale below, and the rugged slopes of the Taigetos range.

EUROPE

TURKEY

BLUE MOSQUE

Istanbul's Blue Mosque once dared to rival Islam's most sacred site and remains one of the world's greatest showcases of Islamic architecture.

Massive and magnificent, the Blue—or Sultan Ahmed—Mosque dominates Istanbul's skyline. Six minarets, shining silver in the sun, pierce the air. Built in 1609–17 by order of Sultan Ahmed I, the mosque was designed to rival the great Church of Hagia Sophia, just a stone's throw to the north. Not content with challenging one of Christendom's most sacred shrines, the Blue Mosque even vied for supremacy with Islam's holiest mosque at Mecca—then the only mosque with six minarets. To quash the scandal, the sultan funded the construction of a seventh minaret at Mecca. Alas for Ahmed I, he died, aged just 27, of typhus shortly after the Blue Mosque's opening ceremony and before its actual completion. Stroll into the Blue Mosque's vast courtyard, and arches, domes, and semidomes fill your view in every direction. Enter the hushed inner sanctum, and you'll see these architectural cascades weren't built just to impress. They have the practical purpose of creating a vast interior with giant columns, stained-glass windows, and thousands of tiles whose bluish hue gives the mosque its moniker. Throughout the upper surface, ceramic lilies, tulips, trees, and abstract patterns swirl in bright blues and greens like aquamarine dervishes.

When to Go Spring and fall have the best weather. Visit from mid-April to early June or September to October to avoid the intense summer heat and crowds.

Planning Take your time. The courtyard is a glorious place to sit and soak up the atmosphere. A nighttime visit offers a wonderfully different perspective. The mosque closes to nonworshipers for about half an hour for the five daily prayers. Lunchtime prayers on Friday, the Muslim holy day, are busiest of all, and the mosque can shut for an hour or more. Dress modestly, although you can borrow shawls at the entrance. The building is very cold in winter; wrap up warm and wear extra socks since you need to remove your shoes to go in.

Websites www.istanbul.com, www.turkeytravelplanner.com

ASIA

HIGHLIGHTS

■ Count the **tiles**. There are more than 20,000 of them—the finest money could buy from the celebrated kilns of İznik.

■ Go at night. During summer there is a free **son et lumière** performance retelling the story of the mosque's construction. It is in different languages on different evenings.

■ To appreciate the building best, walk from the west, approaching from the **hippodrome side**, slowly. Walk through the first portal and into the courtyard. The mosque's epic roof comes into sight, and your perspective of the domes cascading down changes with every step.

■ Raise your eyes to the sky. Marvel at the six slender and elegant **minarets** soaring upward.

■ The mihrab, or prayer niche indicating the direction of Mecca, contains a piece of the **sacred Black Stone** from the Kaaba in Islam's holiest city.

Opposite: The Blue Mosque takes its name from the dominant color of the hand-painted İznik tiles lining its lavishly decorated interior, even though their hue changes with the light flooding in through the building's 260 stained-glass windows. Above: Very few mosques in the world have more minarets than Istanbul's Blue Mosque.

This fresco in the dome of the Church of Panagia Forviotissa depicts Christ encircled by angels and evangelists about to judge the 12 tribes of Israel.

CYPRUS

PAINTED CHURCHES
OF TROÖDOS

The painted churches of the Troödos Mountains bear eloquent witness to the skill and devotion of the monks who adorned them.

Greek Orthodox monks retreated into the Troödos Mountains in the early Middle Ages to escape the secular world's temptations. While they might have left other earthly belongings behind, they didn't forget their palettes or paints. Over the next thousand years, they created some of the most vibrant art in the Mediterranean basin. Their implausibly detailed frescoes and lifelike icons are now among Cyprus's national treasures. From busy monasteries like Kykkos to small local chapels like Panagia Forviotissa, the paintings portray Christian saints or biblical scenes in a highly stylized Byzantine mode. They often include gold leaf delicately applied by brush. The monks rendered frescoes on plaster walls and arches, and icons on wood that they often grouped together on an elaborate iconostasis. The largest and most ornate of the Troödos monasteries, Kykkos oozes with frescoes. Founded in the 11th century, the mountaintop retreat contains a large church with a golden iconostasis and extensive monastic quarters with richly decorated cloisters. Attributed to St. Luke, its "Most Merciful Virgin" icon is claimed to work miracles.

HIGHLIGHTS

■ Kykkos houses its most prized **icons** in modern light- and temperature-controlled displays in its museum. Lookouts on the pine-covered hillside behind the monastery provide a place to see **sweeping Troödos views.**

■ The highly detailed and dynamic floor mosaics at **Kato Pafos**, near Pafos harbor, date from Roman times.

■ Panagia Forviotissa, a 12th-century stone church near Nikitari, holds many **Byzantine frescoes and icons**, including a startlingly lifelike rendering of the Last Judgment.

EUROPE

When to Go Reaching a maximum altitude of 6,400 ft (1,950 m), the Troödos Mountains have a slightly different climate from the sun-splashed Cypriot coast. Summers are relatively mild and winters, when it sometimes snows, unexpectedly brisk. Fall is a time of brilliant foliage and wine festivals.

Planning The Troödos monasteries attract not only art enthusiasts but also wine lovers. Recent excavations reveal that Cyprus has been producing the drink since at least 3500 B.C. The island is the home of Commandaria, the world's oldest appellation, in continuous production since the Crusades. Many wineries now open their doors to visitors, allowing them to taste and buy wines. Kykkos Monastery has a wine shop, as well as open-air stalls outside the walls, as does Panagia Chrysorrogiatissa on the western Troödos slopes. The resorts of Platres and Kakopetria both offer a wide range of hotels.

Websites www.visitcyprus.com, www.kykkos-museum.cy.net, www.cypruswinemuseum.com

ST. CATHERINE'S MONASTERY

One of the world's oldest monasteries marks the site where God is said to have spoken to Moses from the burning bush.

AFRICA

The bleating of camels floats on the dry desert wind reaching high over the red granite walls guarding St. Catherine's Monastery. The Byzantine emperor Justinian I ordered the monastery to be built at the base of Mount Sinai to protect the Chapel of the Burning Bush—said to stand on the original site of the burning bush from the Book of Exodus through which God instructed Moses to lead the Israelites out of Egypt. Construction lasted from A.D. 527 to 565. Untouched by invaders, the Church of Transfiguration within this Greek Orthodox monastery has a superb array of art, some at least as old as the monastery. It also has one of the world's finest illuminated manuscript collections and some of its oldest icons. The greatest treasure, however, hangs on the vault of the apse above the altar: a sixth-century mosaic depicting the Transfiguration of Christ. A skull and a left hand lying in a sarcophagus to the right of the altar are said to be relics of St. Catherine of Alexandria, but she is not the monks' only protector. A letter displayed near the monastery gate, supposedly dictated by Muhammad, is one reason the monastery still stands. When the Prophet visited, it is said, the monks treated him so well he guaranteed the monastery's protection—a vow incumbent upon all Muslims.

When to Go November-April is ideal. The monastery is open from 9 a.m. to noon (except Sundays and Fridays); you can visit only the Chapel of the Burning Bush, where monks worship on Saturday.

Planning You can combine a visit to St. Catherine's with a hike to the top of Mount Sinai. Allow a day and night for both if you want to climb Mount Sinai for sunrise. The hike takes about two to three hours. The area also has many other ancient sites, so to make the most of your trip, stay several days. Be prepared for extremes of temperature and bring a flashlight. Men—but not women—may be able to stay in the monastery. Keep your passport handy for frequent police checks when traveling in the area.

Websites www.touregypt.net, www.ecolodges.saharasafaris.org

HIGHLIGHTS

■ The **library** houses the world's largest collection of codices outside the Vatican, including 12 pages and some fragments of the fourth-century Codex Sinaiticus (the earliest extant copy of the Greek Bible) and Codex Syriacus (a fourth- to fifth-century translation of the Gospels into Syriac).

■ Grateful for Muhammad's pledge, the monks allowed a **Fatimid mosque** to be built within the monastery. It is rarely used as it does not align with Mecca.

■ On the **anniversary of St. Catherine's martyrdom** on November 25, monks carry her relics in procession around the church.

■ Listen out for the **wooden bell** that is rung daily; the metal ones chime on Sundays and holidays.

In a picturesque gorge at the base of Mount Sinai, this remote fastness has been functioning as a monastery continuously since the sixth century.

Carved wooden doors lead to the Hanging Church.

EGYPT

HANGING CHURCH

Coptic Christians have been worshiping in Egypt for more than 19 centuries, and this church has been standing for most of them.

C arved wooden double doors open through the southern tower of the Babylon Fortress in Al-Fustat (Old Cairo) from quietly busy Mari Girgis Street. Through a porch lined with mosaics of biblical scenes and carvings of feathered palms, you enter the hush of a narrow courtyard. From here, 29 steps lead up to the central wooden entrance doors of the Coptic Hanging Church, also known as the Staircase Church. This is one of Egypt's oldest churches, probably built in the seventh century. Many of its treasures are now in the nearby Coptic Museum, including the earliest relic found in the oldest section of the church—a carved wooden lintel dating from the fifth century depicting Jesus' entry into Jerusalem. The nave overhangs the gatehouse passageway leading to the 11th-century elevated marble pulpit. Murals and inlaid screens line the paneled walls and candles flicker at the eastern end of the church, where altars are dedicated to St. George, the Virgin Mary, and St. John the Baptist.

When to Go Egyptian winters are mild—visit from November to April. The church is open daily from 9 a.m. to 4 p.m., except during services. There is no entrance fee.

Planning Allow an hour or two, but take time to visit the other Coptic churches as well as the Ben Ezra Synagogue in Al-Fustat. Egypt is a predominantly Muslim society: remember to dress respectably and follow religious etiquette. Avoid shorts and cover bare arms when visiting the church.

Websites www.touregypt.net

HIGHLIGHTS

■ Look closely at the **13 columns** supporting the pulpit. One is black, representing Judas, another gray for doubting Thomas, while the other 11 white pillars represent Jesus and his devoted Apostles. This is a common feature in Coptic churches.

■ Find the intricately detailed small pine door in the southern aisle, which leads to a tiny chapel and a baptistery of red granite—the **oldest part of the church.**

■ Look for the **painting of the Virgin Mary** near the entrance of the church. Wherever you walk, her eyes will follow you.

■ Visit the adjoining **Coptic Museum**, which now holds many treasures from the Hanging Church.

■ Try some roadside **kushari**—a thick spicy mixture of lentils, rice, pasta, onions, garlic, tomatoes, and chillis.

AFRICA

POLAND

Wieliczka Salt Mine

Known as Poland's underground salt cathedral, this extraordinary maze of corridors and chambers is full of chapels hewn by miners.

The lambent glow of crystalized-salt chandeliers illuminates the Chapel of St. Kinga in the Wieliczka salt mine near Kraków, spotlighting the ornate altars, 9-foot (2.7 m) tall papal cross, and statues of saints—all carved from rock salt by miners. But the masterpieces of the 39-foot (12 meter) high, 177-foot (54 meter) long underground chapel are its biblical bas-reliefs, including a striking salt carving of Leonardo da Vinci's "Last Supper." The mine has nine levels, the lowest 1,073 feet (327 meters) below ground. Seven unbroken centuries of excavations—until a catastrophic flood in 1996 closed Wieliczka to active mining—created roughly 180 miles (290 kilometers) of corridors and countless chambers. The Wieliczka miners transformed many of these into richly decorated chapels for daily worship. St. Anthony's, the oldest surviving chapel, dates from the late 17th century. Descending 378 steps to the mine's first level, 210 feet (64 meters) below ground, visitors follow their guide through a subterranean labyrinth of passageways for more than 2 miles (3.2 kilometers), past deep saline lakes and vast caverns. The tour ends 443 feet (135 meters) below ground at the world's largest mining museum.

When to Go The salt mine is open year-round. There are English-language tours several times daily, most frequently in summer, which also is the busiest time to visit.

Planning Bring a sweater as the temperature in the mine is a constant 57°F (14°C). The tour lasts about three hours and allots time at the end to visit the underground restaurant, post office, and gift shops before taking the elevator back to the surface. Trained mine employees lead a separate geology tour, primarily of 19th-century excavation sites. The three-hour excursion demands a reasonable level of fitness—and reservation at least two weeks in advance. On New Year's Eve the mine hosts a ball.

Website www.kopalnia.pl

EUROPE

HIGHLIGHTS

■ Admire the carved-salt religious iconography, murals, and sculptures throughout the mine, including **statues of famous Poles, saints, and gnomes.** The miners believed the gnomes brought luck.

■ Attend a concert in the **Chapel of St. Kinga** or visit on a Sunday morning or during religious holidays, such as the Feast of St. Kinga (July 24) or St. Barbara (December 4) for High Mass. Sts. Kinga and Barbara are the patrons of salt and miners, respectively.

■ The **museum** has 14 galleries of historic mining equipment.

■ Let the salt air whet your appetite at the Witold Budryk Chamber **restaurant**, 410 ft (125 m) underground.

Wieliczka's ornate chapels are the result of centuries of labor.

OLD-NEW SYNAGOGUE

Home of the mythical Golem, this tiny temple has been Prague's main Jewish place of worship since around 1270 and is the oldest surviving medieval twin-nave synagogue.

Enveloped by legends and embraced by time, the Old-New Synagogue, Staronová Synagoga, or Altneuschul, in the heart of Prague is a living symbol of Jewish faith and endurance. The steep-roofed Gothic temple, with its distinctive, saw-toothed gables, is Europe's oldest active synagogue. Save for a spell under Nazi occupation from 1941 to 1945, Jews have been worshiping in this tiny, twin-naved sanctuary for more than 700 years. Inside, its focal point is the central bimah, or raised platform for the reading of services, enclosed by a late-Gothic grille set between two tall columns supporting the vaulted ceiling. In the east wall, five steps lead up to the Gothic stone ark holding the Torah. The building was erected around 1270 and—according to the most popular explanation—was originally the New Synagogue, only acquiring its strange name centuries later, when newer temples went up nearby. Always the main house of worship in Jewish Prague, it has withstood destruction and generated legions of legends. According to one, doves flapped their wings to save it from fire. In another tale, its best-known rabbi, the 16th-century Jehuda Löw ben Bezalel, created an artificial man, the Golem, to protect the Jews. When the monster ran amok, the story goes, he disabled the creature and hid its slumbering body in the synagogue's attic.

EUROPE

When to Go The synagogue is closed to tourists on Saturdays and Jewish holidays.

Planning Josefov, the Jewish quarter, is one of Prague's most popular tourist venues. Several tour agencies specialize in Jewish tours. Two of the most experienced are Wittmann Tours and Precious Legacy Tours. As the Old-New Synagogue is not part of the Jewish Museum, you must purchase separate tickets to visit it. Allow at least a full morning or afternoon to visit the synagogue and Prague's other Jewish sites; for some, a full day won't be enough. Men must cover their heads in the synagogue. Religious services take place on the Sabbath and during Jewish holidays. Men and women pray separately, with women in an annex where they can view the sanctuary only through deep, narrow openings in the thick walls. Visitors to the synagogue must go through a security check.

Websites www.synagogue.cz, www.jewishmuseum.cz, www.legacytours.net, www.wittmann-tours.com

HIGHLIGHTS

■ The 13th-century sculpted grapevines decorating the Gothic arch above the entrance and the triangular tympanum above the ark are said to symbolize the **12 tribes of Israel.**

■ The stiff, red banner above the bimah dates from 1716. A restored version of a much earlier pendant, it bears the **historic official emblems** of Prague's Jewish community—the Star of David and the pointed hat that the city's Jews once had to wear.

■ Several former synagogues in Josefov collectively house Prague's **Jewish Museum.** Known as the "precious legacy," the exhibits detail the history, legends, and traditions of Prague's Jews and form one of the world's richest collections of Judaica.

■ Be sure to visit the **old Jewish cemetery,** just a few steps away, which is also part of the Jewish Museum. Here, some 12,000 tombstones crowd together in a jagged jumble of elegantly carved ancient stone that has inspired artists and other romantics for centuries. One of the most visited tombs is Rabbi Löw's.

Opposite: Following Orthodox custom, the Old-New Synagogue's main sanctuary is for men only; women worship from a side gallery. Above left: The Star of David above the synagogue's main entrance. Above right: This decorative plaque, or *shiviti,* at the prayer lectern bears the words: "I have set the Lord always before me."

PAINTED CHURCHES OF BUCOVINA

In a remote northeastern corner of Romania, these tranquil painted monasteries are perhaps the country's greatest contribution to art.

Their exterior walls alive with scenes of biblical and historical events, the painted monastery churches of the remote Bucovina region, also known as northern Moldavia, resemble the pages of illuminated manuscripts magically enlarged in scope and form. These mostly 16th-century ecclesiastical treasures are primarily used today as convents. Of the dozen or so churches, Voroneț, known as the Sistine Chapel of the East, is perhaps the most spectacular. Blending serenely into its remote mountain setting, it marks the highest achievement of Moldavian painting and architecture. This Orthodox bastion is best known for the bright blue used in the frescoes lining its walls inside and out. Derived from lapis lazuli, the intense dye used in the frescoes gave rise to the name Voroneț blue. Stephen the Great founded the monastery in 1488 to honor a pledge to a hermit, St. Daniil of Voroneț, who promised him victory in a forthcoming battle against the Ottomans. Stephen duly won and built the religious foundation on the site of Daniil's hermitage; the hermit became its first abbot. In 1785 the Habsburgs closed the monastery, but it reopened as a nunnery in 1991.

When to Go April-October is pleasant, but the most atmospheric time to visit any of the monasteries is during a pilgrimage or feast day, or in the days before Easter. The feast day of St. George, patron of Voroneț and Humor, is April 23. Thousands attend St. Stephen the Great's feast day at Putna on July 2.

Planning Public transportation in this part of Romania is poor. If you are not on a guided tour, driving or hiking is the only way to see all the sites. Base yourself in Gura Humorului, close to Voroneț and Humor, or—for more comfort—in Suceava. Allow a half-day if you are driving or a day if hiking. The monasteries have nominal opening hours, usually 8 a.m-8 p.m., with Mass at least four times daily, but you are unlikely to be refused entry at other times. All have admission charges. Dress respectfully—no shorts. Women should cover their heads when entering the churches; scarves are usually available at the entrance.

Websites www.romanianmonasteries.org, www.turismbucovina.3x.ro, www.beyondtheforest.com

HIGHLIGHTS

■ Marvel at the vivid colors and artistry of **"The Last Judgment"** on Voroneț's west outer wall, considered the finest of the Bucovina paintings. On the north facade, "**Jesse's Tree**," outlining Jesus' genealogy, is another celebrated work.

■ **Sucevița** has a superb setting and is dramatically fortified. **Moldovița** is smaller, isolated, and beautiful, while **Humor** has a spectacular interior. Visit forested **Putna** Monastery to see St. Stephen the Great's tomb.

■ Watch out for a nun or monk beating a **wooden bell board**, or *toacă*, before the start of a service.

■ Walk through the glorious landscape of **beech woods and hills** between Humor and Sucevița monasteries, or between Sucevița and Moldovița monasteries.

A vivid Voroneț fresco shows the Last Judgment in chilling detail: an angel blows a *bucium*, a shepherd's bugle, the graves disgorge their dead, and animals devour limbs.

Hurezi Monastery was originally for monks, but since 1872 it has been a female community. Currently about 60 nuns live here in pretty cloisters lined with flower baskets.

ROMANIA

HUREZI MONASTERY

This serene nunnery in one of Romania's most unspoiled rural regions is a tribute to a national hero who died for his faith.

The onomatopoeic *huhurezi,* or eagle owls, are by some accounts behind the name of this Orthodox monastery high above the Horezu Valley in Romania's southern region of Oltenia. A story goes that from 1690 to 1697 its builders worked only at night for fear of alerting the Ottomans. Its founder, Constantin Brâncoveanu, Wallachia's great ruler, became a Romanian national hero and Orthodox saint for his efforts to resist Ottoman invasion. He intended the monastery to be not just a bulwark against invasion by the Turks but also his burial place, but neither came to be. He and his four sons were beheaded in Constantinople for refusing to convert to Islam. Still, Hurezi stands as the most complete and perfect legacy of the most distinctively Romanian architectural style, the Brâncoveanu style. It incorporates intricate stone carving and lavish frescoes, while harmoniously fusing Oriental, Renaissance, and Byzantine elements. Covering 7 acres (3 hectares), Hurezi has two precincts; the upper, inner one is entered through a vast wooden gate. Inside, buildings and neat whitewashed cloisters line three sides of a tranquil courtyard. Behind doors of thick sculpted pear wood, the main church has a superb array of original religious frescoes, icon lamps, and an iconostasis of carved lime wood coated in gold. In this blissful sylvan setting, even the least religious may feel a spirit of peace come upon them.

HIGHLIGHTS

■ **Sleep like royalty.** The monastery offers guest rooms that were good enough, on a private visit in 2005, for the Prince of Wales to stay in for three nights.

■ **Brâncoveanu's funeral monument** is inside the main church, although his actual remains lie at St. George the New Church in Bucharest.

■ The town of Horezu is one of Romania's best places to buy **ceramics.** On the first weekend of every June, Horezu hosts Romania's largest pottery fair, **Cocoşul de Horezu** (the Cock of Horezu), named for the rooster motif common in its ceramics.

■ Ideal for gentle hikes, the **Horezu Valley** has some of Romania's most unspoiled countryside and a burgeoning ecotourism industry.

EUROPE

When to Go Horezu has hot summers and cold winters. May, June, and September are the best months. You're unlikely to be turned away whatever hour you visit the convent. Easter attracts the most pilgrims.

Planning Allow Hurezi at least a couple of hours. From Bucharest, take a train or bus to Râmnicu Vâlcea, then a minibus or bus to Horezu. The monastery is 2 miles (3 km) north of Horezu, near the village of Românii de Sus. Unless you have a vehicle, you will have to walk from Horezu to the monastery. If you are driving, take the DN67 from Râmnicu Vâlcea and, just before Horezu, turn right to Românii de Sus. Horezu has a hotel and a few guesthouses. There are also plenty of houses offering bed and breakfast throughout the tranquil Horezu Valley; look for signs saying *cazare* or *camere*.

Websites www.eco-oltenia.ro, www.romaniatravel.com, www.romanianmonasteries.org, www.autogari.ro

TEN SACRED SPIRES

In religions across the ages, gods have dwelt on high and people have built towering spires to take themselves closer to heaven.

❶ Chicago Temple, Illinois

At 568 ft (173 m) and 23 stories, this home to Chicago's First United Methodist Church is the tallest church building in the U.S. Its intricately carved Gothic stone spire soars atop a skyscraper of commercial offices amid the downtown city blocks. On the church's first floor, the sanctuary seats a congregation of a thousand, who worship amid wood carvings and stained-glass windows, while the tiny Sky Chapel, just below the spire and 400 ft (122 m) up, is popular for baptisms and weddings.

Planning The temple is at 77 West Washington Street in the heart of downtown Chicago. The public is invited to join regular services from Wednesday to Sunday each week. www.chicagotemple.org

❷ Kashi Vishwanath Temple, Varanasi, India

On the west bank of the holy Ganges River stands this Hindu temple of shimmering gold. Each year millions flock here in search of *moksha*, or liberation. Dedicated to Lord Siva, the temple has stood in various forms for thousands of years. In 1839 the ruler of Punjab, Maharaja Ranji Singh, donated around a ton (1,000 kg) of gold, which was used to plate its 50-ft (15.3 m) spire.

Planning The temple is in the town of Varanasi (Banaras) in Uttar Pradesh. It is open daily. www.varanasicity.com

❸ Birla Mandir, New Delhi, India

Birla Mandir is one of the most popular Hindu temples in India's capital, New Delhi. Mahatma Gandhi inaugurated it in 1939 on condition that people of all castes, including the untouchables, could worship there. Its most prominent features are the curved, red *shikaras*, or towers, the highest of which reaches to 165 ft (50 m). Reflecting the Orissa architectural style, the shikaras bear elaborate ribbed designs.

Planning Time your visit to coincide with the Janamashtami Festival, celebrated annually at the temple during August or September. www.delhi-india.net

❹ Minaret of Jam, Afghanistan

The 213-ft (65 m) high Minaret of Jam has stood in a remote part of central Afghanistan since the 12th century. Surrounded by foreboding mountain peaks, it has withstood droughts and floods, earthquakes and wars, and the purges of Ghengis Khan. This elegant structure, built from baked brick and decorated with stucco, glazed tiles, and calligraphy and verses from the Koran, provides a poignant reminder of empires past.

Planning The Minaret of Jam is in a remote region with poor infrastructure. Independent travel is not recommended—try a group tour instead. www.greatgametravel.com, www.afghan-logistics.com

❺ Great Mosque of Samarra', Iraq

The most famous feature of the ninth-century Great Mosque of Samarra' is its spiraling brick minaret, up whose exterior staircase the mosque's founder, the Caliph Al-Mutawakkil, is said to have ridden on a white donkey.

Planning Samarra' is on the Tigris River, about 80 miles (130 km) north of Baghdad. Check the situation in Iraq before traveling. www.muslimheritage.com

❻ Borgund Stave Church, Lærdal, Norway

Of the thousands of stave churches that once flourished in Norway, only about 30 survive today. Made almost entirely from wood, their main structures are centered on huge upright staves (posts). The church at Borgund has an ornate roof and spire decorated with carved dragons' heads that hark back to Viking times.

Planning The church is open from May 18 to September 14. www.stavechurch.com

❼ Ulm Minster, Ulm, Germany

Lace up your walking shoes—there are 768 steps to the top of Ulm Minster's spire, the highest church steeple in the world. Soaring skyward to almost 530 ft (161.5 m), it promises outstanding views from the top. On fine days a vista of the Alps rewards weary climbers.

Planning Every December, the square outside the minster throngs with shoppers visiting the Christmas Market. www.tourismus.ulm.de

❽ University Church of St. Mary, Oxford, England

Of all of Oxford's "dreaming spires," this is the most striking. It's also remarkably old—the tower dates from 1280 while the intricately decorated spire, adorned with Gothic pinnacles, is a work of the 14th century. A 124-step climb to the top of this spire offers a panorama of the others.

Planning Seek out the Virgin Porch beneath the tower—it is home to a statue of the Virgin and Child that is riddled with bullet holes from Cromwell's soldiers (1642). www.university-church.ox.ac.uk

❾ Salisbury Cathedral, England

Salisbury's glorious cathedral, completed in 1258, supports the tallest masonry spire in Britain. At 404 ft (123 m), and leaning slightly, it dominates the city and was the inspiration for some of the paintings of John Constable (1776-1837).

Planning The cathedral is home to the largest cloisters in the U.K. www.salisburycathedral.org.uk

❿ Hassan II Mosque, Casablanca, Morocco

The world's tallest minaret stands at a colossal 689 ft (210 m) in Casablanca. Exquisite patterns of green, glazed ceramic tiles adorn the top and, every night, a laser points the way to Mecca.

Planning Non-Muslims may only enter the mosque with guided tours. www.visitmorocco.com

Ascended by an external staircase, the assymetrical, spiral Al-Malwiyya minaret of the Great Mosque of Samarra' is 164 ft (55 m) tall and recalls the design of an ancient Mesopotamian ziggurat.

The pagan Vikings used carved dragons' heads on their ships to ward off evil spirits, and the tradition did not die out when they started building churches.

NORWAY

LOM STAVE CHURCH

Built of sturdy Norwegian pine 850 years ago,
Lom Church blends Christian and Viking motifs.

When Norway embraced Christianity a thousand years ago, the first churches built there were called stave churches, consisting of strong, Norwegian pine frames holding together the walls and foundations. Around 30 of these stave churches survive today. In the Gudbrandsdalen Valley within the majestic Jotunheimen Mountains of central Norway, one of the largest and most beautiful of these, Lom Stave Church, still functions as a place of worship. Built in 1158, and enlarged several times in later centuries, this parish church was restored in the 20th century. In summer the deep hues of its roof, walls, and decorative dragons' heads stand out elegantly against the verdant surroundings. You enter the holy site through a doorway, framed by ornate animal carvings reminiscent of Viking art. As you explore the dim interior, you observe pale blue painted pews in the faint light cast by flickering candles, pendulous chandeliers, and three small openings under the roof. Above, curved arches loom and a carved choir houses an organ with metal pipes. Religious paintings line the walls, and rows of supporting posts stand tall; but the dominant interior feature is the stately pulpit with multiple floral carvings.

When to Go Visit from May to September as the church is closed to the public during the rest of the year.

Planning The church is closed to tourists during services. Guided tours are available if you contact the church in advance. Allow at least an hour for a visit. No photography is allowed inside the church.

Websites www.stavechurch.org, www.visitlom.com

HIGHLIGHTS

■ Along the walls of the church, look out for some **paintings** by 18th-century local artist Eggert Munch, a distant relative of the renowned Edvard Munch.

■ In Lom County, you will also find two wooden—but not stave—religious buildings: the much-later **Garmo Church**, built in the late 1800s, and **Bøverdal Church**, erected in 1864 and restored in 1951.

■ Lom is the gateway to Norway's beautiful **Jotunheimen National Park**, which contains the country's tallest mountain. The trails are challenging, but experienced hikers will marvel at the scenery.

EUROPE

HUNGARY

ESZTERGOM BASILICA

A collection of superlatives, the basilica
may not be old but it is certainly impressive.

The third-largest church building in Europe, this huge basilica is a focus of religious and national identity for Hungarians. Esztergom is the place where Prince Géza and his son Vajk brought Hungary into the Roman Catholic sphere after Pope Sylvester II granted Vajk the title of King Stephen I in 1000. Visible from miles around, the giant bulk of the Basilica of the Blessed Virgin Mary of the Assumption and St. Adalbert—a neoclassical behemoth with a vast copper-green dome—towers high on a hill above the Danubian plain of northern Hungary. Despite its preeminence in Magyar religious identity, the building is quite recent—a 19th-century construction on the site of a series of earlier churches. With massive walls that are 56 feet (17 meters) thick in places and a vast interior soaring 300 feet (90 meters) high in the dome, the cathedral was built to last. Within it is the Italianate Bakócz Chapel. Created in the 16th century by Tuscan craftsmen, this is all that remains of the previous church. Over the cathedral's high altar is the world's largest painting produced on a single piece of canvas, the Titianesque "Assumption of the Blessed Virgin Mary" by Michelangelo Grigoletti.

When to Go The best times are May to June and September to October, when Esztergom is less crowded than in high summer. Midwinter can be beautiful if there is snow on the ground, and Easter is a special time. The Esztergom International Guitar Festival–the world's oldest–takes place in early August, with classical concerts inside the cathedral.

Planning Esztergom is on the Danube around 31 miles (50 km) northwest of Budapest on the border with Slovakia. The cathedral is open to visitors daily from 6 a.m. to 6 p.m. There are entrance fees for the treasury, the crypt, and for ascending the steps into the dome–all open daily from 9 a.m. to 4:30 p.m. Allow a full day to explore the town. There are several good hotels, and staying in the town provides the opportunity to enjoy the church in peace and quiet in the early morning before tour groups arrive.

Websites www.bazilika-esztergom.hu, www.esztergom.hu/wps/portal/english

HIGHLIGHTS

■ Visit the **treasury**, which houses a dazzling array of medieval crooks, chalices, and chasubles, many of gold.

■ The crypt holds the **tomb of Cardinal József Mindszenty** (1892-1975), who led Hungarian resistance to communism. He spent 15 years in asylum at the U.S. Embassy and died in exile in Vienna. His body was returned in 1991, after communism fell.

■ Climb the 300 steps inside the dome for a **tremendous view** of the Pilis and Börzsöny hills, the pastel-hued old town below, and the majestic Danube.

■ The **Bakócz Chapel** has walls of ornately carved red marble. Built in 1506-11, it was dismantled, then reassembled, and incorporated into the south wing of the basilica in 1823.

The basilica seems to survey the Danube from its hilltop vantage.

GREAT SYNAGOGUE OF BUDAPEST

Newly restored as a glittering symbol of hope, Europe's largest synagogue lies at the heart of Budapest's old Jewish quarter.

Approach any central European synagogue and you sense ghosts of profound trauma. But here the sumptuous grandeur, the deep stillness in contrast to the hum of the city, and the velvet light hold out the comforting prospect of eternity. There were 30,000 Jews in Pest (Budapest's eastern part) in the mid-1800s, an era of optimism coinciding with their increasingly prominent role in Hungarian society. Reflecting this mood, an influential group of reformist Jews—the Neologues—built the Great (or Dohány) Synagogue in 1854–59. Its architect, Ludwig Förster, mixed Moorish and Byzantine elements into an exotic Romantic style. Its minaret-like spires, domes, and lavish gilding proved the thriving Jewish community's liberalism and modernity. But in the 1920s repression returned, first under Admiral Miklós Horthy's rightist regime, then escalating to segregation, deportation, and extermination under Nazi occupation, when the synagogue lay at the heart of the Jewish ghetto. Soviet bombardment in the liberation of Budapest caused further damage, as did vandalism during the communist period. Not until Hungary gained autonomy in 1989 did restoration begin in earnest. Now the stone-and-brick exterior once more presents a proud face to the world.

When to Go The synagogue is open to the public all year, Sundays to Thursdays and Friday mornings; check opening times. There are services open to Jews on Friday evenings and Saturday mornings.

Planning Located on Dohány utca (Tobacco Street), the synagogue is close to the center of Pest, just 1,500 ft (450 m) from Elizabeth Bridge (Erzsébet híd) and the Danube River. The nearest metro stop is Astoria, on the M2 line. Guided tours of the synagogue in English or Hebrew depart every hour during opening hours (other languages by arrangement). A visit to the synagogue takes an hour or so; also make time for the Museum of Jewish History, part of the same complex. You can combine the visit with an organized tour of Jewish Budapest lasting up to three hours.

Websites www.budapest-tourist-guide.com/budapest-great-synagogue.html, www.greatsynagogue.hu

HIGHLIGHTS

■ The **richly decorated interior** is all the more remarkable for its colossal size. Built essentially in a rectangular basilica style, it is 246 ft (75 m) long and 89 ft (27 m) wide. There are **2,964 seats:** this is Europe's largest functioning synagogue.

■ Attend one of the regular **concerts:** the acoustics are splendid. Most unusually, the synagogue has an organ, sometimes used for recitals.

■ In **Raoul Wallenberg Memorial Park** outside, there is a moving memorial to Hungarian victims of the Holocaust. The "Tree of Life" takes the form of a weeping willow in metal, each leaf inscribed with a name. As first secretary of the wartime Swedish legation in Budapest, Wallenberg saved some 15,000 Jews from Nazi death camps.

Shifting pools of colored light filtering in through stained-glass windows add to the enveloping drama of the Great Synagogue's interior.

Elegantly proportioned, this church, set in the heart of nature, is both a shrine and a place of repose.

GERMANY

CHURCH OF ST. COLOMAN

Tucked jewel-like into a pristine corner of Bavaria, this pilgrimage church still casts its spell on the faithful seeking old-world worship.

With the majestic Alps in the distance, and swathes of flowery meadows and green pasture all around, it is not hard to imagine yourself resting with St. Coloman in 11th-century Schwangau as he traveled to the Holy Land from his native Ireland. Though he never reached his destination, since he died as an innocent casualty of war, Coloman was informally canonized after a number of miracles were attributed to him after his death. The first chapel in Schwangau to be dedicated to the saint was built next to a plague pit after the Black Death had raged through Europe in the 14th century, and pilgrims flocked to invoke his protection against all pestilence. His cult expanded. The church was rebuilt with baroque flourish in 1673–78, and it has remained almost unchanged ever since. The very wood of its interior smells of centuries of history and quiet communion. While the Colomansfest—the annual gathering celebrating the saint's feast day in October—is a high point in the church's year, visit on days when Mass is said and savor the church's simple beauty in the company of a few like-minded souls.

When to Go The church is usually open daily from late May to mid-October (but check with the Schwangau Tourist Office). It is enchanting in all seasons, not least when blanketed in snow.

Planning Schwangau lies about 100 miles (160 km) southwest of Munich, and 3 miles (5 km) from Füssen, reachable by train or bus. The church lies 0.5 mile (1 km) outside the village. The church alone takes only an hour or so to visit.

Websites www.koenigswinkel.com/koenigswinkel/frame2.htm, www.schwangau.de

HIGHLIGHTS

■ The **interior** is an uplifting confection of baroque stuccowork, rose-colored marble, paintings, and sculpture.

■ The precious **St. Coloman monstrance**, kept in the church, contains a holy relic of the saint: a piece of jawbone provided by the Abbey of Melk, where the saint's body was taken after his death.

■ The **Colomansfest** is on the nearest Sunday to St. Coloman's feast day (October 13). Following ancient tradition, some 250 costumed riders on immaculately groomed horses arrive for an open-air Mass. They receive the saint's blessing by riding three times around the church, then share a feast of meat and beer. It is a serious religious event conducted with great charm and dignity.

■ A backdrop of **Alpine peaks** is a perfect foil for the white walls and onion-domed tower of the church with its tree-shaded churchyard.

EUROPE

Ten East European Synagogues

Sumptuous or ruined, grandiose or unadorned, Eastern Europe's surviving synagogues bear powerful witness to a shattered world.

❶ Zhovkva, Ukraine

Though partly destroyed by a Nazi bomb, Zhovkva's 17th-century fortress synagogue retains the somber power of its stirring past. Its thick pink walls, sculpted portals, arched windows, and crenelated roof form part of Zhovkva's Renaissance center, which was based on a model for an "ideal city" conceived in the late 16th century.

Planning The town of Zhovkva is about 25 miles (40 km) from L'viv and makes an easy day trip. www.go2kiev.com

❷ Great Synagogue, Botoşani, Romania

The understated facade belies the opulent interior of this synagogue, built in 1834. A carved, gilded, and boldly painted ark arches over the sanctuary, and touchingly naive paintings of the Ten Commandments, biblical beasts, and the 12 tribes of Israel decorate the walls and ceiling.

Planning Contact the Botoşani Jewish Community Center directly at +40 (0)231 514659, or through any Romanian consulate or national tourist office, to visit the synagogue. www.romanianjewish.org, www.romaniatourism.com/jewishher.html, www.jewishtourseurope.com

❸ Pakruojis, Lithuania

Elaborate wooden synagogues were once a common sight in East European villages. Nowadays, only a handful of the simplest survive, and Pakruojis is most likely the oldest. Built in 1801, it once shone with paintings of flowers and animals. Today, with its sagging walls and listing roof, it is a precious, if forlorn, reminder of an utterly vanished world.

Planning Lithuania is home to nearly a dozen wooden synagogues, all easiest to reach by car. www.litjews.org, www.shtetlinks.jewishgen.org, http://cja.huji.ac.il/Architecture/Wooden-synagogues-Lithuania.htm

❹ Tykocin, Poland

Tykocin's majestic baroque synagogue towers over narrow streets and low houses that retain the look of a pre-war shtetl. Built in 1642, the building once housed a school, law courts, and even a prison. Today, skillfully restored, it is a Jewish museum.

Planning The synagogue museum is open daily from 10 a.m. to 5 p.m., except Mondays and the days after public holiday. www.tykocinmolsouthernregion.org

❺ Remuh Synagogue, Kraków, Poland

Set deep within a walled, cobbled courtyard, the 16th-century Remuh Synagogue is the living heart of Kraków's old Jewish quarter, Kazimierz. Ancient prayers still fill the snug, vaulted sanctuary on the Sabbath and Jewish holidays.

Planning Time your visit to coincide with the summer Jewish Cultural Festival. www.jewishkrakow.net

❻ Trnava, Slovakia

When converting Trnava's ruined, twin-towered synagogue into a center for contemporary art, the architects deliberately retained evidence of the building's desecration. In doing so, they created a modern cultural space that is also a compelling memorial.

Planning The Ján Koniarek Gallery has a permanent exhibit on local Jewish history. www.travel.spectator.sk/ss2006/03_trnava.html

❼ Central Synagogue, Sofia, Bulgaria

With its Moorish striping and cupola-topped dome, Sofia's Central Synagogue harmonizes with other downtown landmarks, including a 16th-century mosque. Celebrating its centennial in 2009, it is the largest Sephardic synagogue in Europe, with a lavishly decorated octagonal sanctuary lit by a 2-ton (1.8 tonne) brass chandelier.

Planning The synagogue complex houses the Jewish Museum of History. www.sofiasynagogue.com

❽ New Synagogue, Szeged, Hungary

The majestic dome of the New Synagogue soars skyward above a forest of spires and smaller cupolas. But much of the beauty is in the extraordinary intricacy of the interior decoration, a fusion of many Eastern and Western styles. Inaugurated in 1903, it was the masterpiece of architect Lipót Baumhorn, who designed more than 20 synagogues. Jewish symbolism pervades each ornament and architectural detail. The result delights the eye and stirs the soul.

Planning Take a train (2.5 hours) from Budapest. www.zsinagoga.szeged.hu

❾ Mád, Hungary

Recently restored, this compact baroque synagogue rises above the wine-making village of Mád in northeastern Hungary. Pastel decorations adorn the walls, and gilded lions and griffins rear above the ark. The complex is exceptional because the religious school and rabbi's house next door have survived intact. A small exhibit in a room adjoining the sanctuary documents Mád's Jewish history.

Planning Since its award-winning restoration in 2004, the synagogue has been one of Mád's chief attractions. Visit some of the local wineries; many once supplied the kosher market. www.isjm.org/country/mad.htm

❿ Úštěk, Czech Republic

World War II and communism left Úštěk's 18th-century sandstone synagogue a ruin, but a ten-year effort, ending in 2003, restored it to its former glory and it is now the pride of the town. The uniquely shaped, tomato-red building resembles a miniature tower and hosts regular cultural events. Inside, the permanent display of local Jewish history includes a reconstructed 19th-century schoolroom.

Planning The synagogue is 44 miles (71 km) north of Prague and is open from April to October. www.mesto-ustek.cz, www.litomerice.cz

Lipót Baumhorn was modern Europe's most prolific architect of synagogues, with 22 to his name, but the exuberant New Synagogue, Szeged, was his most acclaimed work.

AACHEN CATHEDRAL

Northern Europe's oldest cathedral has impeccable imperial connections and houses the sarcophagus of Charlemagne.

EUROPE

A simple construct of marble slabs, Charlemagne's throne sits to one side of Aachen Cathedral. The 32 Holy Roman emperors crowned here would descend the throne's steps and walk out to greet their subjects beneath a cupola so soaring and graceful it's no wonder they and their subjects believed in divine right. Charlemagne, who declared himself the first Holy Roman emperor, began the cathedral's central Palatine Chapel in 786. Its architect, Odo of Metz, designed it as an homage to Ravenna's Byzantine-style Basilica of San Vitale. Aachen is northern Europe's oldest cathedral and its chapel is a masterpiece of Carolingian architecture. Yet those designations cannot capture the awesome grandeur of the 105-foot (32 meter) octagonal tower, once Europe's highest vaulted interior. The tower's elaborate gilt and mosaic ceiling is partially framed from below by Frederick Barbarossa's bronze chandelier encircling Charlemagne's sarcophagus. Pilgrims have long traveled to the cathedral because Charlemagne collected holy relics as well as territories. Some of the most cherished relics are believed to have belonged to the Virgin Mary or Jesus: Mary's cloak, the swaddling clothes of the infant Jesus, and the loincloth worn by Jesus on the Cross. Another relic is the cloth that is believed to have held John the Baptist's severed head. These lie in the Shrine of St. Mary, and for years the cathedral was known as the Royal Church of St. Mary at Aachen.

When to Go Visit at any time of year, although the Aachen Christmas Market makes for a festive trip.

Planning Between restoration, regular services, and planned pilgrimages, the various chapels and museums sometimes close to visitors. Call ahead to be sure that what you want to see will be open. Two days is ideal, allowing for considered viewing of the cathedral and its museums.

Website www.aachen.de

HIGHLIGHTS

■ From outside, Aachen Cathedral is a hodgepodge of different architectural styles wedged between city buildings. Don't judge it by its exterior; the **interior** is exquisite and extraordinary.

■ The Byzantine-inspired **mosaics** make the interior feel quite distinct from other Carolingian buildings; don't miss the sumptuous depiction of the four rivers of the world meeting at the heavenly Jerusalem.

■ The cathedral was enlarged in the 15th century because of the huge flow of pilgrims. In 1414 a two-part *cappella vitrea*, or **glass chapel**, was added and consecrated on the 600th anniversary of Charlemagne's death. Its original stained glass needed replacing after its destruction in World War II.

Sculptures on the gable of Charlemagne's sarcophagus depict him enthroned between Pope Leo III and Archbishop Turpin of Reims–both symbolically shorter.

The Basilica of San Vitale's plain exterior belies its interior, gloriously decorated with a riot of mosaics.

ITALY

BASILICA OF SAN VITALE

This sixth-century basilica has the finest collection of Byzantine mosaics anywhere outside Istanbul.

Ravenna's Basilica of San Vitale, its multileveled octagonal exterior following crisp lines and curves, is almost plain compared with the intricately crafted art within. A wealth of the world's best-preserved early Christian Byzantine mosaics graces its partly restored interior. Like the basilica itself, all are from the 6th century. One of the most notable is in the apse. There in small, colorful golden-hued tiles, Jesus Christ, beardless, short-haired, and purple-robed, bestows the crown of martydom on St. Vitalis for his faith and loyalty. On the right side of the mosaic, Bishop Ecclesius holds a model of the cathedral, which he founded. To the left, another apse mosaic commemorates the Byzantine emperor Justinian, under whose reign the cathedral was built, and his wife Theodora alongside Bishop Maximian, who consecrated it in 547. Other saints and political figures of the day adorn the apse and choir walls and spar for visual attention. Rome, whose emperors had previously considered Ravenna insignificant, claimed it only in 90 B.C. By the fifth century, however, it had become a hub of the Roman Empire, and this may be why San Vitale and other religious edifices sprouted here. According to legend, the church was erected over the spot where the Romans judged St. Vitalis of Milan a Christian—not always a popular moniker in the early centuries. They tortured and buried him alive, and he became Ravenna's first and most cherished martyr for his faith.

When to Go San Vitale is open daily from 9 a.m. to 7 p.m. The best light to catch the mosaics is generally from noon to 1 p.m.

Planning In the Emilia-Romagna region of northern Italy, Ravenna is accessible by well-maintained highways and has good railroad connections—so rent a car, catch a bus, or hop on a train. The basilica is an hour or two by train or car from Bologna airport and 1,640 ft (500 m) from Piazza del Popolo, the public square. Allow a day for San Vitale, or longer if you plan on visiting the rest of the city.

Websites www.greatbuildings.com, www.italiantourism.com

HIGHLIGHTS

■ Ravenna has impeccable literary associations. Author of *The Divine Comedy*, Dante Alighieri died in Ravenna in 1321. His **tomb** is near the Church of San Francesco (St. Francis). Later, Irish romantic William Butler Yeats found inspiration for his Byzantine poems in the basilica's **mosaics.**

■ The **Piazza del Popolo** is Ravenna's public square. Fountains, monuments, cathedrals, churches, and other buildings accent the edges of a space that is actually two half circles. Make time to sit and enjoy the view and the architecturally diverse skyline.

■ The **Archbishop's Palace** merits a visit. The **Cathedral of Sant'Orso** holds two sixth-century marble sarcophagi, and the **National Museum** covers Ravenna's history.

EUROPE

CASALE MONFERRATO SYNAGOGUE

While it may no longer have much of a congregation, this lovingly restored synagogue is a showpiece of Jewish art.

EUROPE

You enter Casale Monferrato's synagogue through the anonymous door of what looks like an ordinary building. Inside though, hidden away from prying eyes, an explosion of gilded glory celebrates the divine. "This is the gate of heaven," declares an oversized Hebrew inscription on the ceiling. Below, swaths of gilt stuccowork frame Hebrew texts on the pastel walls, and sinuous gratings screen the galleries reserved for women. A whimsical wrought-iron grille divides the majestic holy ark, built in the late 18th century, from the sanctuary. Corinthian columns support a towering tympanum alive with carvings. Corkscrew candelabra stand at its sides, and a golden crown, symbolizing the Torah, floats above. The lavish fittings all shimmer in the sunlight filtering down through 14 windows set high amid the ribs of the handsome overhead vaulting. Built in 1595, and enlarged and further embellished over the centuries, this is the most opulent of a dozen ornate synagogues in the Piedmont region. Today, just two Jewish families live in Casale Monferrato. The synagogue now forms the glistening core of a museum and cultural complex showcasing both historic and contemporary Jewish ritual art.

When to Go The synagogue complex is open year-round on Sundays, from 10 a.m. to noon and 3 to 5 p.m. Visits during the week are by appointment only: telephone +39 0142 71807.

Planning Just off the A26 motorway, Casale Monferrato is less than a 90-minute drive from Milan or Turin. Some other Piedmont synagogues, such as those in Asti, Alessandria, and Carmagnola, are also open to the public; visit them on the way. Try to give Casale Monferrato's synagogue and museums a full morning or afternoon, then browse the surrounding former Jewish quarter and visit the Jewish cemetery.

Websites www.casalebraica.org, www.initaly.com/regions/piedmont/turin.htm

HIGHLIGHTS

■ A **memorial** at the complex's entrance remembers local Jews killed in the Holocaust. Nearby, a **sculptural installation** under the central courtyard's arcade reveals the Hebrew alphabet's mystic symbolism.

■ Note two 16th-century **bas-reliefs** near the ark. One depicts Jerusalem and the Temple of King Solomon, the other ancient Hebron. Nearby, a **marble plaque** in Hebrew and Italian honors King Carlo Alberto's 1848 emancipation of Piedmont's Jews.

■ See the embroidery, silver ritual objects, Torahs, and other Judaica in the **Jewish Art and History Museum.**

■ The **Museum of Lights** shows striking Hanukkah menorahs, or candelabra, by modern artists.

The interior of Casale Monferrato Synagogue is a baroque glory suffused with Jewish symbolism.

LANDSCAPES MEGALITHS & MYSTERIES CRADLES OF FAITH MAJESTIC RUINS SHRINES THE PILGRIM'S WAY CEREMONIES & FESTIVALS IN REMEMBRANCE RETREATS

DAILY DEVOTION

Light flows in through the dome of St. Peter's.

VATICAN CITY

St. Peter's Basilica

Over the burial site of many popes, including, it is said, St. Peter, stands one of the world's richest treasuries of sacred art.

Within the world's smallest city-state—Vatican City—St. Peter's Basilica is one of the holiest Catholic sites and one of the world's largest churches. Begun in 1506, with designs and decorations by Michelangelo and other great Reniassance artists, the basilica brims with sublime sacred art. The basilica lies within St. Peter's Square, a 10-acre (4 hectare) piazza designed by Bernini, where the curved colonnade stretches like open arms to embrace visitors. Entering through one of the five bronze doorways from the square, you are in the long nave, which is decorated with intricate marble inlay. Enormous statues, soaring columns, and ornate altarpieces appear at every turn. Arnolfo di Cambio's statue of St. Peter has several toes worn down by the touch of pilgrims. Around the dome, a ring of windows lets in streams of light. Inside, mosaics depict Christ, the Virgin Mary, and God, alongside solemn saints and soaring angels. Underneath, the focus of the interior is Bernini's baldachin, or canopy, loftily sheltering the high altar. According to the Vatican—and ancient tradition—the burial place of St. Peter, the first pope, lies in a Roman necropolis directly below.

When to Go Visit St. Peter's early in the morning before the crowds assemble.

Planning Allow three hours or more. Expect to stand in line, especially on Sundays, if you're not on a guided tour. Every Sunday, throughout the day, Masses in Italian—and one in Latin—are said in the nave. Ask about free tours at the information—and post-office (open daily except Sundays) at the basilica's south side wing. A strict dress code applies: you won't get in wearing shorts, a short skirt, or a tank top. To visit the Roman necropolis, request tickets far in advance from the Vatican excavations office.

Websites www.vatican.va, www.saintpetersbasilica.org, www.vaticancitytours.com

HIGHLIGHTS

■ In the first chapel immediately right of the entrance, **Michelangelo's "Pietà"** depicts a mournful Virgin Mary cradling Jesus in her lap after his crucifixion. Naturalistic and serenely poignant, the sculpture vies with Michelangelo's "David" as a masterpiece of Renaissance art—and of technical composition.

■ A fine place for quiet contemplation, Bernini's **Blessed Sacrament Chapel** is reserved for prayer. All day long from 7 a.m., priests from around the world say Mass in various languages in chapels throughout St. Peter's.

■ Take an elevator to the roof to walk inside the dome for a **dizzying view** of the basilica. Then climb 320 steps to a lookout, where your reward is a panoramic Roman vista.

■ Every Sunday at noon (except during the Pontiff's summer holiday or when he is traveling), Catholics gather in **St. Peter's Square,** where the pope delivers the **Angelus blessing** from his balcony.

■ A guided tour of the **Roman necropolis** takes you through the excavations beneath the basilica to what Catholics believe is St. Peter's Tomb. Many scholars, however, believe that a tomb discovered in 1953 on Jerusalem's Mount of Olives is St. Peter's actual burial site.

EUROPE

TEN ARTISTS' CHAPELS

Many have found creative inspiration in religion. Here are some fine examples of chapels closely associated with artists.

❶ Beth Shalom Synagogue, Elkins Park, PA

In the 1950s, Frank Lloyd Wright planned this as the first truly American synagogue, studding its design with Jewish emblems. Its overall shape represents a mountain, as well as ancient tent tabernacles and Native American tepees. The translucent materials he used in the walls allow light to flood in during the day; at night, from outside, the building glows, in Wright's words, like "a luminous Mount Sinai."

Planning Services take place daily. Reservations are advisable for a tour of the building. www.bethshalomcongregation.org

❷ Rothko Chapel, Houston, TX

In the 1960s, John and Dominique de Menil hired abstract expressionist painter Mark Rothko to create a meditative space. The result is an octagonal room housing eight large paintings mainly in shades of black with subtle variations in dark blues, plums, and reds. Images seeming to shimmer on the walls inspire visitors to ponder the nature of reality.

Planning The chapel is open 10 a.m.-6 p.m., Saturday-Tuesday, and 10 a.m.-7 p.m., Wednesday-Friday. www.rothkochapel.org

❸ Chapel of the Tsars, Moscow, Russia

Early-16th-century frescoes once lined the walls of this small, richly adorned chapel in the Annunciation Cathedral. But the great glory is the multitiered iconostasis (screen covered with icons) by Russia's leading iconographers. It includes Theophanes's "St. John the Baptist" and "Archangel Gabriel," and Rublev's "St. Michael the Archangel;" all glow like gems.

Planning The Kremlin is closed on Thursdays. www.kremlin.ru/eng

❹ Church of St. Sebastian, Venice, Italy

Canvasses and frescoes by 16th-century Venetian Paolo Veronese cover the sacristy ceiling, the ceiling and upper walls of the nave, the organ doors, and the chancel. Colorful and alive with drama, they depict St. Sebastian's life and scenes from the Bible.

Planning The Chorus Pass covers entry to St. Sebastian and 14 other Venetian churches. Buy it at any one of them. www.chorusvenezia.org

❺ Arena Chapel, Padua, Italy

This small chapel has a marvel of Renaissance art: a series of 14th-century Giotto frescoes. The two narrative cycles—of the life of Christ and of the Virgin—fill both side-walls. The chapel is full of color, from the deep-blue ceiling and the trompe l'oeil porphyry and marble on the walls to the vibrant frescoes. The emotional realism of the figures is engaging.

Planning Reservations are required. www.cappelladegliscrovegni.it

❻ The Sistine Chapel, Vatican City

In the pope's residence, the Sistine Chapel's vast, high ceiling teems with Michelangelo's epic figures—343 in all—which he painted almost single-handedly in 1508–09 and 1511–12. Depicting Old Testament scenes, especially the story of Genesis, the images include the famed image of God giving Adam life. Above the altar is Michelangelo's thronged and terrifying vision of the Last Judgment, completed in 1541.

Planning The chapel is open Monday through Saturday and on the last Sunday of most months. www.vatican.va

❼ The Chapel of the Rosary, Vence, France

Every aspect of this tranquil chapel—the building, the stained-glass windows, the decor, and even the priest's robes—was the work of Henri Matisse. Inside, the windows cast patterns of yellow, green, and blue light—signifying the colors of God and light itself, of nature, and of the sky—across the floor and the ceramic-tile murals on the walls, bringing the natural world into the cool, white interior.

Planning The chapel is a five-to-ten minute walk from the center of Vence, near Nice. It is open on Tuesdays and Thursdays, from 10 to 11:30 a.m. and 2:30 to 5:30 p.m., longer in summer. It is closed in November. http://pagesperso-orange.fr/maison.lacordaire

❽ Chapelle St.-Pierre, Villefranche, France

Flamboyant chalk drawings tracing the life of St. Peter, patron saint of fishermen, cover the inside of this tiny, 14th-century chapel in the fishing village of Villefranche. They are the work of film director Jean Cocteau, who, in 1957, began the chapel's renovation. He modeled the murals on local people and villages.

Planning: Chapelle St.-Pierre is by the harbor entrance in Villefranche, 3 miles (5 km) east of Nice. www.villefranche-sur-mer.com

❾ San Antonio de la Florida Hermitage, Madrid, Spain

Just inside the entrance of this former royal chapel is Francisco de Goya's tomb, encircled on the upper walls by a series of Goya's own frescoes telling the story of a miracle by St. Antony. In 1928, to protect them from damage from candle smoke and incense-burning, an identical chapel was added alongside, where services take place.

Planning The chapel is on Paseo de la Florida. The nearest metro is Príncipe Pío. Opening times are Tuesday-Friday, 10 a.m.-2 p.m. and 4-8 p.m., and Saturday-Sunday, 10 a.m.-2 p.m. www.spain.info

❿ Sandham Memorial Chapel, Burghclere, England

From 1927 to 1932, British artist Stanley Spencer created 19 paintings for this chapel, all based on his life as a medical orderly in World War I. The quiet but moving images depict scenes of daily military routine, with titles such as "Scrubbing the Floor" and "Sorting and Moving Kit-Bags," culminating in the "Resurrection of the Soldiers" behind the altar.

Planning Located in Hampshire, the chapel is open from early March to late December. Opening hours vary. www.nationaltrust.org.uk

The anguish of the figures mourning the death of Jesus, while the Virgin Mary looks for signs of life, is all too palpable in this detail from Giotto's "The Lamentation" in Padua's Arena Chapel, Italy.

ITALY

DUOMO

The architectural quintessence of the Renaissance, the Duomo in Florence attracted a roll call of Italy's most illustrious artists and architects.

Dominating Florence's skyline, Santa Maria del Fiore, better known as the Duomo, is the city's majestic Roman Catholic cathedral, started in the late 13th century and not finished until the mid-15th century. Some of Italy's most talented painters, sculptors, and architects—among them Giotto, Brunelleschi, Donatello, Domenico, Ghirlandaio, Pisano, and Luca Della Robbia—contributed to its splendor. Its showpiece is the massive dome designed by Filippo Brunelleschi and built at the start of the 15th century. You can see the dome's graceful, curved lines from many parts of Florence. The Duomo's rich red, green, and white marble facade is covered with geometric designs and punctuated with florid niches displaying majestic figures of saints. Inside the magnificent cathedral, you walk across floors of inlaid marble and stand surrounded by massive columns with gilded tops, while soft light streams through soaring stained-glass windows. Stop under the exterior of the majestic dome, look upward, and you'll gaze in wonder at the awe-inspiring scenes of the frescoes of the Last Judgment, which line the huge expanses of the dome. For a close-up look at these masterpieces, climb the 463 steps to the dome's top. Then step outside, where an amazing panoramic view of Florence awaits.

When to Go Visit the Duomo in late spring, when the weather is mild and the city has fewer tourists. Avoid the crowded summer season. Except on Sundays, when opening hours are longer, it's best to come in the early afternoon if you want to catch all the buildings. The various parts of the Duomo—the cathedral, dome, belfry, and baptistery—and the museum all have different opening hours. Check the first website below for the exact times.

Planning To reach Florence, fly directly to the city's airport, or take a flight to Rome and then a train. Allow at least three hours to see all the Duomo buildings and at least three days for Florence itself. Bring an umbrella for spring showers, and dress in layers during spring and fall. Florence is a compact, walkable city. Don't rent a car here because you won't be able to park near the city's highlights.

Websites www.operaduomo.firenze.it, www.florence-accom.com, www.florence-tickets.com

EUROPE

HIGHLIGHTS

■ Just opposite the Duomo look out for the octagonal **baptistery**, with its renowned doors by Lorenzo Ghiberti, richly decorated with gilded bronze panels of biblical subjects.

■ Don't miss the Duomo's ornate Giotto-designed campanile, or **bell tower**, faced with white, red, and green marble. Here you can climb up 414 steps for another magnificent but less-crowded view of the city and also of the cathedral itself.

■ Just behind the Duomo, the wonderful **Museo dell'Opera del Duomo**—the cathedral museum—displays masterpieces formerly in the Duomo itself. These include sculptures by Donatello and the glazed terra-cotta Madonnas and singing angels of Luca Della Robbia.

■ Lovers of renaissance art may envy the monks who used to live at the **Convent of San Marco**, now a museum. The Dominicans who founded it use the word convent for communities of monks or nuns. While residing there as a friar from 1436 to 1445, the outstanding painter Fra Angelico covered much of the building, including the tiny monastic cells, with frescoes, including his celebrated "Annunciation."

Opposite: This classic view of the Duomo takes in the Brunelleschi-designed dome, the nave, and Giotto's bell tower.
Above left: The chilling frescoes in the dome of the Last Judgment were designed to put the fear of God into worshipers.
Above right: Much of the Duomo's beauty lies in the elaborate detail of the facade.

Originally monks worshiped in the choir, but now resident choristers, boys and men, sing daily services here.

ENGLAND

WESTMINSTER ABBEY

For pomp and circumstance few settings can match this ancient and distinguished parish church of England and the British nation.

Were stones to speak, Westminster Abbey would have much to tell. Burial site of 17 English, Scottish, and British monarchs and numerous important personages, and scene of royal weddings and every coronation since William I's on Christmas Day 1066, this is a church of superlatives, with England's highest Gothic vault and pageantry galore. At the heart of London, it is a royal peculiar, subject to no bishop but only to the monarch, and a focus for public ceremonies and Anglican devotion. On steps worn smooth by pilgrims, worshipers still honor the shrine of Edward the Confessor, who founded the original 11th-century abbey. Most of what we see today was built in the 13th century by Henry III, emulating French cathedrals with their rose windows, pointed arches, and ribbed vaulting. But there are English touches, too, such as single aisles, and the style of the moldings, sculptures, and marble columns. As you survey tombs and memorial slabs, it's hard to imagine that these represent just a few of the 3,300 people buried in the abbey and its cloisters.

When to Go The abbey is usually open to visitors daily except Sunday and on religious festivals, when it is for worship only, or special events. Opening hours vary; see the abbey website for details.

Planning Set aside at least two hours to do the abbey justice. Expect to wait in line. You will have to pay an admission fee. To make the most of your visit, pick up an audio guide or join a verger's tour, both at extra cost but worth it.

Websites www.westminster-abbey.org, www.visitlondon.com

HIGHLIGHTS

■ Every monarch since Edward II in 1308 has been crowned on the **coronation chair**, which sits on a plinth in the ambulatory near Henry V's tomb. Made in 1300, the chair has a shelf beneath the seat to enclose the Stone of Scone. Said to have been the biblical Jacob's pillow, the stone was moved in 1996 to Edinburgh Castle, where it now resides with other symbols of Scottish sovereignty.

■ Don't miss the exquisite early-16th-century **Lady Chapel** with its carved fan-vaulted ceiling, Tudor emblems, and nearly 100 statues.

■ **Poets' Corner** commemorates literary luminaries: Chaucer, Shakespeare, Tennyson, Dickens, Emily Brontë, and many others.

■ The **RAF Chapel** venerates Allied aviators who died during the Battle of Britain in World War II. Badges of 63 squadrons adorn the window.

■ Look out for the royal effigies and 13th-century painted oak altarpiece in the **Abbey Museum**.

EUROPE

FRANCE

Chartres Cathedral

This showpiece of Gothic architecture speaks of kings, artists, and figures of the Bible in a richly illustrated narrative of faith.

Rising above the level lands of the Beauce region, the spires of Chartres Cathedral (Cathédrale Notre-Dame de Chartres) have drawn travelers and pilgrims for more than seven centuries. Southwest of Paris on the River Eure, the Cathedral of Our Lady is a triumph of Gothic architecture. Earlier churches on this site were also devoted to the Virgin Mary. According to legend, in 876 Charlemagne brought to Chartres the *Sancta Camisa,* a part of the shawl Mary was said to have worn at Jesus' birth, as its holy relic. Created in just 30 years of intense activity, and consecrated in 1260, this is one of Europe's best preserved medieval cathedrals. It was a true collaboration of royalty and scores of artisans, although no names remain of the sculptors and artists who built it. Enter through the royal portal under the tympanum of Christ seated in glory. Step inside this stately Gothic sanctuary and be ready for glowing lessons—not only on the lives of Jesus and the saints, but also about the everyday activities of the various guilds that funded the cathedral. In fact, if you "read" the splendid windows as illuminated stories told across 28,000 square feet (2,600 square meters) of stained glass, these gemlike panels and rosettes of light will reward you with a plethora of inspiring tales, such as that on the Noah window, donated by coopers and carpenters.

When to Go Plan to arrive for the noon tour (fee charged). Take time to study the complex windows and sculpture, and return for a late afternoon tour of the crypt. Ideally, allow a couple of days, viewing one window and portal at a time. Visit on a cloudless winter day to see the colors at their most vibrant.

Planning Chartres is less than an hour's train journey from Paris's Montparnasse station—a pleasant trip through the Rambouillet woods onto the plains of the Beauce. Dress respectfully with arms and legs covered.

Website www.chartres-tourisme.com

EUROPE

HIGHLIGHTS

■ Of 186 original panes, 152 remain, forming the **world's most intact collection of medieval stained glass.** Each pane has a theme.

■ Look out for the world's largest and best-preserved **medieval labyrinth,** inlaid in the floor. Pilgrims would walk or crawl this "journey to Jerusalem" as a metaphor for life's passage to heaven.

■ Climb the elegant staircase to the 14th-century **St. Piat's Chapel,** built to enclose the Virgin Mary's relic.

■ The north porch, known as the **Door of the Initiates,** features a carved image of the Ark of the Covenant being transported in a cart. Some believe the Knights Templar carried the ark to Chartres and hid it under the crypt.

Chartres Cathedral is particularly beautiful and mysterious at night.

TEN STAINED-GLASS WINDOWS

With its vibrant, luminous colors, intricate patterns, and narrative threads, stained glass continues to uplift and inspire.

❶ Brown Memorial Church, Baltimore, MD

Defined by its royal-blue dome and shimmering stained glass, Brown Memorial Presbyterian Church is one of Baltimore's gems. Its 11 Louis Comfort Tiffany windows make it one of the finest Tiffany art collections still in its original setting. The designer's trademarks of vivid colors, intricate leading, and drapery techniques resonate with each piece.

Planning Zion Church at City Hall Plaza has a wealth of stained glass. www.browndowntown.org

❷ National Cathedral, Washington, D.C.

On sunny days the interior of the cathedral is transformed into a divine light show. The sun streams through the colored stained glass, bathing the gray stone inside in a kaleidoscopic display of scarlet, yellow, green, and purple.

Planning See the Seven Ages of Man at the Folger Shakespeare Library. By the same artist who did the National Cathedral's windows, it's open to the public on Shakespeare's birthday in April. www.nationalcathedral.org

❸ St. Mary's Cathedral, Sydney, Australia

Golden sandstone tracery bisects the impressive stained-glass windows shipped all the way from Hardman & Co. in England. The 15 "Mysteries of the Rosary" are depicted in the windows of the sanctuary and transept, while the nave contains scenes from the New Testament. The crowning touch is the great north window—a masterpiece of 19th-century design.

Planning The floor of the crypt tells the story of the Creation in mosaic terrazzo tiles. www.stmaryscathedral.org.au

❹ Abbell Synagogue, Jerusalem, Israel

When Marc Chagall dedicated his beautiful stained-glass windows to the synagogue in 1962, he said he was bringing his "modest gift to the Jewish people, who have always dreamt of biblical love, friendship, and of peace among all peoples." Jewish symbols and floating figures of animals, flowers, and fish dance across the 12 brightly colored windows.

Planning The synagogue is part of the Hadassah University Medical Center. www.hadassah.org.il

❺ St. Vitus's Cathedral, Prague, Czech Republic

Within the huge 110-acre (45 hectare) enclave of Prague Castle, St. Vitus's towers over the red-roofed city. On the north facade, Art Nouveau painter Alfons Mucha created stained glass to honor Saints Cyril and Methodius—look up to appreciate the rich reds, sapphire blues, and deep golds.

Planning Walk across the Charles Bridge and visit the Museum of Decorative Arts to learn about Bohemian glass. www.hrad.cz

❻ San Donato Cathedral, Arezzo, Italy

Begun in 1278, this noble cathedral rises above the serene Arno Valley in Tuscany, 50 miles (80 kilometers) southeast of Florence. The French artist Guillaume de Marcillat secured the commission to design the stained-glass windows, and it's one of the few surviving complete cycles of his work in Italy today. The series includes "The Baptism of Christ," "The Raising of Lazarus," and the "Pentecost" rose window.

Planning The cathedral is home to many works of art including the fresco "St. Mary Magdalene" by Piero della Francesca. www.toscanaviva.com

❼ Cuenca Cathedral, Cuenca, Spain

In the 1990s, a series of designs by four contemporary Spanish artists replaced the cathedral's delapidated medieval stained-glass windows. Bold, abstract blocks of color dapple the old stonework with bright reds, yellows, and blues, while other, more complex designs based on the local landscape create a haze of glowing colored light as sunlight streams in.

Planning The cathedral is in the medieval part of Cuenca, perched on a clifftop overlooking the Huécar Gorge. You can reach it from the newer section of the city at the bottom of the cliff by bus or on foot. There is no parking for nonresidents in the medieval city. www.euroresidentes.com

❽ Toledo Cathedral, Toledo, Spain

The 750 stained-glass windows, some dating from the 14th century, remain key to the light and shadows that characterize this cathedral. Gold, enhanced by accents of red and blue, stands out. Two softly colored rose windows surmount the north and south doors.

Planning Amble through the stone gate and thick fortifications of Toledo's city wall into the narrow streets of the old town, and enter a long-gone century. www.architoledo.org/cathedral

❾ Anglican Cathedral, Liverpool, England

The story of Christianity and the history of this vast cathedral, the U.K.'s largest, are played out in its stained-glass windows. At the entrance to the Lady Chapel, Liverpool's women are the theme. Local heroes are depicted alongside famous figures such as Elizabeth Barrett Browning and Grace Darling. The contemporary window on the west side has the magnificent Benedicite window at its crown.

Planning Visitors can see the great Benedicite window in close-up on the cathedral's Great Space tour. www.liverpoolcathedral.org.uk

❿ St. Martin's Church, Brampton, England

The luminous stained-glass windows, designed by the Pre-Raphaelite artist Sir Edward Burne-Jones and manufactured in the William Morris studio, portray the themes of worship, virtue, childhood, and paradise, as well as the Good Shepherd and heroes of the Bible in jewel-bright colors.

Planning This small market town is located 12 miles (19 km) from a part of Hadrian's Wall in Cumbria in northern England. www.stmartinsbrampton.org.uk

The Virgin Mary and a host of saints and holy men adorn this glorious light-filled stained-glass window from Spain's Toledo Cathedral.

The gargoyles of Notre-Dame double as drainpipes, gargling rainwater from gutters and disgorging it clear of the stonework below.

FRANCE

NOTRE-DAME DE PARIS

One of Europe's first great Gothic cathedrals
soars gracefully over the heart of Paris.

It's hard to decide which face of Notre-Dame, seat of the archbishop of Paris, best tells its story. Approach the massive west facade and it's a mighty fortress when seen from a distance, an intricate marvel of Gothic carving at closer range. From the Seine, a more elaborate Notre-Dame rises at the edge of the historic island, Île de la Cité, where Paris started life as a city. This is the perspective of intricate flying buttresses, the cathedral's nave and choir supported by arches of stone. Construction of Notre-Dame de Paris, dedicated to the Virgin Mary, began in 1163 on the site of a much earlier cathedral and lasted until about 1345. It's a towering example of French Gothic principles of verticality, in which walls became taller and taller to lead all eyes heavenward. Pillars grew slimmer, and arches took on points to better support the weight of ascending walls. And more light, filtered through greater swaths of stained glass, inspired the faithful. Today, entering Notre-Dame through its oldest door, the early-13th-century St. Anne portal on the west facade's south porch, one moves through every stage of the Gothic style.

When to Go Notre-Dame is open from 7:45 a.m. to 6:45 p.m. daily. Allow at least two hours for a visit and arrive early to beat the lines. Plan a visit to hear Gregorian chants, part of the 10 a.m. service on Sunday. The choir sings at the 10:30 a.m. and 6:30 p.m. services on Saturday. For a greater sense of the sanctuary as worshipers found it in years past, arrive on a Monday morning when staff remove chairs for cleaning.

Planning Notre-Dame is one of France's most visited sites. It is also a sanctuary that deserves respect from visitors. Women should keep their shoulders covered. Visits to the towers are popular but limited to 20 people at a time. The ascent to the top—a climb up 387 small steps—is inadvisable for people with heart conditions or breathing difficulties. Arrive early to avoid a long wait.

Websites www.cathedraldeparis.com, www.parisinfo.com

HIGHLIGHTS

■ Admire the **south rose window:** 43 ft (13 m) in diameter, it is one of Europe's largest stained-glass windows. Workmen removed the panes for safekeeping in 1939 and restored them after the war.

■ One of Notre-Dame's **two organs** is France's largest. During special services, the 13-ton **Emmanuel bell** rings in the south tower.

■ History buffs will love the **Archaeological Crypt of the Parvis of Notre-Dame**, a museum below the plaza opposite the cathedral, open Tuesday to Sunday, 10 a.m. to 6 p.m.

■ If you stand on the bronze star outside Notre-Dame, **point zéro**, marked in 1768 as Paris's Km 0, it is said that you will return to Paris.

EUROPE

FRANCE

SACRÉ-COEUR BASILICA

This glistening basilica stands on one
of France's most hallowed and oldest sites.

As if pasted against the northern edge of the Paris skyline, the rounded white domes of Sacré-Coeur Basilica mark the highest point of the City of Light. The butte of Montmartre, mount of the martyrs, has been sacred ground since ancient times. The Druid priests of the Gauls were followed by the Romans, who worshiped Mars and Mercury here. Later, Merovingian Christians built places of worship on the hallowed hill. During the Reign of Terror in the late 18th century, the revolutionaries drove out the Benedictines, destroyed their abbey, and guillotined the last abbess. The small Church of St. Peter, which vies with St.-Germain-des-Prés as the oldest church in Paris, is all that remains of the early structures on the butte. The basilica itself is a relatively recent arrival, built in a neo-Byzantine style and dedicated in 1919. Enter the dark narthex of Sacré-Coeur, and the first posted announcement reads: "This is a place of perpetual prayer." Through the day, people of all nations come here to worship. Domes lined with golden mosaics, side chapels lit by votive candles, a hint of incense in the air during services—all add a touch of mystery to this immense and remarkable church.

When to Go The basilica is open from 6 a.m. to 10:15 p.m., year-round. Allow at least an hour; try to time your visit for late afternoon to catch the sunset over Paris from the basilica's steps or terraces.

Planning No photos or videos are allowed inside the basilica. The crypt below the church—housing the treasury and tombs of bishops—is not open on a regular basis but is free of charge when it is accessible. Beware of persistent peddlers around the church. Ephrem, a nearby guesthouse, is a center for pilgrimage and retreat programs. It can house 100 people and has nine disabled-access rooms. Visitors to Ephrem may stay an hour, a day, or a week, meet with a priest or sister, and arrange individual or group retreats.

Websites www.sacre-coeur-montmartre.com, www.parisinfo.com

EUROPE

HIGHLIGHTS

■ Ride to the basilica on the **funicular railroad** from Place Suzanne Valadon. The *funiculaire* is a quick and scenic alternative to walking up Rue de la Vieuville and the steps of Rue Devret. However, the slower route does also open to a sweeping panorama from Place du Calvaire.

■ Step inside **St. Peter's**, an older parish church just to the left of the basilica, and note its Romanesque details as well as Roman columns.

■ Visits to the **dome**, best made in clear weather, are possible from 9 a.m. to 6 p.m. Climb 234 steps—some exterior—to enjoy one of Paris's headiest vistas.

One of the world's best-known buildings, Sacré-Coeur is constructed of travertine stone, which exudes calcite when wet and stays white as it ages.

The intricately carved Nativity Facade bears the most direct Gaudí influence.

SPAIN

Sagrada Família

Like a great medieval cathedral in scope and detail,
Gaudí's Expiatory Temple of the Holy Family will not be rushed.

With eight ornate towers tapering into Barcelona's skyline, the Sagrada Família is a totem of Catalonia's capital and Antoni Gaudí's most celebrated work. Begun in 1882, the church was his great passion: Gaudí worked on it tirelessly for more than 40 years until his death in 1926, but still could not finish it. Today, building continues following his (reconstructed) plans. Gaudí fans and Catholic pilgrims alike seek out the basilica to admire—or perhaps gasp at—the grandiose structure. Religious imagery permeates every nook and cranny. Inside and out, the building fuses intricate sculptures, vast stained-glass windows, and decorative details depicting geometric shapes and flora and fauna. Materials as varied as plaster, mosaic, iron, and stone merge in fantastical and technically complex designs. Two out of three facades are finished: the Nativity Facade on the east and the Passion Facade on the west. When complete, the Glory Facade will be the church's main front, looking south. Even with modern tools, progress is little faster than under Gaudí; the estimated completion date is 2026. But as Gaudí himself reportedly joked when asked when it would be ready, "My client is not in a hurry."

When to Go The basilica is open daily 9 a.m.-8 p.m., April-September and 9 a.m.-6 p.m., October-March.

Planning Allow two to three hours for a visit. A 45-minute group guided tour is available for an extra fee (hourly from 11 a.m. to 5 p.m. May to October; mornings only November to April). Dress respectfully.

Website www.sagradafamilia.org

HIGHLIGHTS

■ Gaudí completed the **Nativity Facade**, dedicated to the birth of Christ, before the Spanish Civil War interrupted work in 1935.

■ At the base of the facades are **turtle sculptures** symbolizing the stability of the cosmos. The one nearer the sea is a sea turtle; the one nearer the mountains a tortoise.

■ Ascend to the top of the towers and clamber around the walls to enjoy **jaw-dropping views** of the entire complex and the city.

■ The 12 **belfries**—four still unbuilt—will eventually represent the Twelve Apostles. At the pinnacle of each belfry, a double shield contains a golden cross inscribed with the initials of the apostle to whom the belfry is dedicated.

EUROPE

MEZQUITA

Córdoba's Great Mosque is a glory of the Islamic world and, without question, Europe's most magnificent Muslim monument.

From the eighth century to the 13th, the ancient southern Spanish city of Córdoba lay at the heart of the Islamic kingdom of Al-Andalus and witnessed a golden age of artistic creativity, intellectual sophistication, and an unusual degree of religious tolerance. To express their spiritual aspirations as well as their worldly ambitions, the city's emirs ordered the creation of the Mezquita—the Great Mosque. The austere outer walls of this huge complex on a plateau above the Guadalquivir River give little clue to the architectural wonders and spiritual inspiration within. Entering from a door in a sun-baked courtyard lined with orange trees, you first encounter only darkness. But as your eyes adapt to the change in light, a breathtaking vision unfolds. Hundreds of stone columns, set in sharply angled aisles and bearing double tiers of rounded, red-and-white striped arches made of alternating bands of brick and stone, vanish into the distance. At carefully calculated intervals, pools of light from rooftop domes illuminate this petrified forest. It is geometry elevated into poetry—or prayer. Venturing deeper into this strange, sacred landscape you will find further wonders: alcoves carved like marble seashells, Byzantine mosaics, Moorish tiles, and a 500-year-old Christian cathedral incongruously planted—as much because of Renaissance power politics as for worship—at the building's core. Even at the time many reportedly considered the cathedral an aberration.

When to Go The Mezquita is open daily all year; hours vary by season. Córdoba is pleasant nearly year-round, although it can be horribly hot in summer. In winter, opening hours extend into early evening.

Planning The Mezquita can be crowded for much of the day, especially on weekends and during vacation periods. If possible, plan for a return visit within the last hour before closing, when the bus tours have left and the atmosphere invites deeper contemplation. Allow two hours to cover everything.

Websites www.turiscordoba.es, www.cordoba24.info, www.guiasemanasanta.com

EUROPE

HIGHLIGHTS

■ At the heart of the mezquita is the exquisitely carved octagonal **mihrab** (prayer niche) with its glittering Byzantine mosaics and intricately arched dome.

■ In a side room near the mihrab, the **treasury** houses a number of Catholic masterworks. They include sculptures by Alonso Cano—the Spanish Michelangelo—and a 16th-century monstrance (Eucharist case).

■ Outside the Mezquita's walls, the **Barrio de la Judería** is a maze of ancient alleys once home to Córdoba's Jews. Calle de los Judíos has a **14th-century synagogue** converted after the Inquisition into a Catholic chapel.

■ Visit during **Semana Santa** (Easter week), when Catholic processions wind through the Mezquita's grounds.

Recycled from Visigothic and Roman ruins, many of the Mezquita's columns are far older than the mosque itself. According to legend, there were once 1,000 pillars in all.

TUNISIA

GREAT MOSQUE OF QAIROUAN

Qairouan's Great Mosque is North Africa's oldest Muslim place of worship and little younger than Islam itself.

On Tunisia's dry inland plain, the holy city of Qairouan greets you like a mirage. Even the Great Mosque is the color of the sand. It rises around the world's oldest surviving minaret, which has stood since about A.D. 730, soon after the Islamic conquest of the Maghreb. Started in 670 by Sidi Uqba, the Umayyad general who led the Arab conquest of the Maghreb, and rebuilt and enlarged the next century, the present structure dates largely from the ninth century, when for 100 golden years the Aghlabid dynasty ruled from Qairouan. With its buttressed walls and three-tiered minaret festooned with battlements and arrow slits, the mosque was both fortress and spiritual center. Imams preached, men studied, and in time of siege the populace took refuge here. The vast enclosure could shelter thousands; underground cisterns provided water. Step through the gate, lined with fine Koranic inscriptions, into the dazzling courtyard, all gleaming white marble and enclosed on three sides by cloisters and columns. Exquisite marquetry covers the doors leading to the prayer room. Beyond, look for the *minbar,* or imam's pulpit, sculpted in wood from Baghdad; the mihrab—a niche pointing in the direction of Mecca—covered in 162 mosaic tiles; and the massive chandeliers. Only Muslim men may enter the prayer hall, but everyone else can peep through the doors and see naves, bays, and another 414 columns. A popular saying is that if you cannot go to Mecca, seven pilgrimages to Qairouan might save your soul.

When to Go Spring or fall is best. The mosque is open from 8 a.m. to 2 p.m. daily except Friday (8 a.m. to noon). Non-Muslims enter through the main gate on Rue Okba ibn Nafaa.

Planning Allow 30-45 minutes for the mosque but a day to explore the city. Many Tunisians still speak French; polish your language skills and you'll get the best bargains. Without your own transportation, the best way to reach Qairouan is by shared taxi. Ask for the *louage* station, found in all main cities, and tell the attendant where you want to go. Within minutes, your car will be ready, along with traveling companions. Alternatively, there are bus services from coastal towns. Dress conservatively.

Websites www.tunisiaguide.com, www.tunisia.com

AFRICA

HIGHLIGHTS

■ In the courtyard look out for the **marble drain** with decorations that double as filters and a **sundial** that once indicated prayer time.

■ Enjoy the **bird's-eye view** from the terrace of the carpet shop opposite the Great Mosque. This is the best spot to appreciate the enormous size of the mosque and take photos. A small donation is welcome.

■ Visit the nearby **Aghlabid Pools** and, just outside the city walls, the **Cemetery of the Shurfa'** with its whitewashed tombs of holy men. *Shurfa'* (singular *sharif*) are descendents of the Prophet Muhammad's grandson Husayn.

■ The **Mawlid al-Nabi Festival** (also called Eid al-Mawlid) commemorating Muhammad's birthday occurs on a movable date determined by the lunar calendar. Although some conservative sects don't celebrate it, many Muslims mark the event by attending religious services and sharing a large feast with their families.

Opposite: Built around A.D. 730, the minaret is a very early example of Islamic architecture, far stockier than later versions. Above left: Many of the prayer hall's columns were recycled from Carthaginian buildings. Above right: Colonnades line three sides of the inner courtyard. Don't be tempted to count the pillars: according to lore, it could make you blind.

Great Mosque of Djénné

Like a giant, improbably audacious sandcastle, the word's largest, most striking mud-brick structure towers over an ancient Malian city.

AFRICA

Dusk falls over Djénné. As its streets darken and grow quiet, the prayer call echoes out from the Great Mosque's loudspeakers. Browsing the surrounding market square and alleys, you glimpse a muezzin's robed, turbaned figure moving shadow-like from corner to corner of the vast structure. Return next morning to take in the glories of the Great Mosque, which, although relatively young—the present structure dates from 1907—is a defining monument of the Sudanese-Sahelian style. A blend of African and Islamic traditions, its main construction materials are dried earth, rice husks, wood, and straw; maintained well, mud buildings last centuries. This is architecture that seems to grow out of the landscape. To stress its spiritual elevation over the temporal world, the mosque sits on a high plinth with six staircases rising from the market square. Along the mosque's four faces, series of vertical buttresses rise to pinnacles. Like any landscape feature, the mosque risks rain erosion and cracking in the heat, hence the bundles of palm wood bristling from its walls. Each year, before the monsoon, the outer plaster needs relaying to protect the structure from the coming rains. Women bring river water, and men swarm up the built-in palm-wood scaffolds to slap on new mud.

When to Go Winter (November–March) is best, with little rain and, often, a heat-tempering breeze. Avoid the sweltering rainy season—from May to September. Visit on a Monday to enjoy a colorful market.

Planning If using public transportation to reach Djénné, get off at the *carrefour de Djénné* (Djénné crossroads) and transfer to a waiting bush taxi to ride into town. A range of accommodations are available, from the height of luxury to simple comfort. While non-Muslims may not enter the Great Mosque, the exterior alone warrants the trip.

Websites www.officetourisme-mali.com, www.saudiaramcoworld.com/issue/199006

HIGHLIGHTS

■ Look out for the **ostrich eggs**, symbols of fertility and purity, capping all three of the mosque's 36-ft (11 m) tall towers.

■ The Great Mosque's annual **crépissage** (plastering) takes place in early April. The build-up begins days in advance as Djénné's inhabitants, in carnival mood, prepare the mud plaster in pits and young people party with music and dancing.

■ Hire a *pirogue*—a gondola-like riverboat—to travel to **Mopti**, the nearest large city, at the confluence of the Bani and Niger rivers. The trip takes three days and provides close-up and vivid encounters with wildlife as well as the people whose livelihood depends on the two rivers.

A mud-brick mosque has stood on this site since 1240, and the current building is one of Africa's most recognized landmarks.

President Felix Houphouët-Boigny spared no expense in building the $300-million basilica. The panes for its vast stained-glass windows were imported from France.

LANDSCAPES MEGALITHS & MYSTERIES CRADLES OF FAITH MAJESTIC RUINS SHRINES THE PILGRIM'S WAY CEREMONIES & FESTIVALS IN REMEMBRANCE RETREATS

DAILY DEVOTION

IVORY COAST

BASILICA OF OUR LADY OF PEACE

In this small West African state is a vast, modern Roman Catholic church that, in size, rivals St. Peter's in Vatican City.

Wide, empty boulevards run through Yamoussoukro, capital of the Ivory Coast, leading to the Basilica of Our Lady of Peace. The world's tallest and largest Roman Catholic church, it is a close replica of the Vatican's St. Peter's Basilica and was a project of former president, Felix Houphouët-Boigny. Pope John Paul II consecrated Our Lady of Peace in 1990 on the condition that it would be lower than St. Peter's and that a hospital for the poor be built. Though the Ivoirian basilica's dome is not quite as high as St. Peter's, the cross on top reaches a greater height—518 feet (158 meters)—and in 1990 the *Guinness Book of World Records* recognized it as the world's tallest Catholic church. The basilica's construction took only three years, but the hospital has yet to be built. Two embracing arms of high colonnaded walkways welcome worshipers arriving across a plaza of more than 7 acres (3 hectares) of Italian marble. Inside, morning sunlight throws a host of colors across the nave through 36 modernist windows made up of 79,700 square feet (7,400 square meters) of stained glass. The main aisle is flanked by circular, individually air-conditioned pews facing a central canopied altar, with seating for 7,000 people—and space for another 11,000 standing.

When to Go Visit in the cooler, dry season (November–February) but beware December's dust-laden winds.

Planning Set aside two hours to wander around the church—or a little longer if you plan on staying for a service. Check for a travel advisory before visiting as there has been periodic unrest in the Ivory Coast. Though not everyone speaks English, many understand it if you are talking about the people or country. The Ivory Coast is a malarial area: don't forget malaria pills and be sure to use insect repellent.

Websites www.africaguide.com, www.travel.state.gov, www.fco.gov.uk

HIGHLIGHTS

■ Look for the blue stained-glass window of **Jesus and his Apostles**. It includes Felix Houphouët-Boigny directly below Jesus—suggesting he is a 13th Apostle.

■ The **cornerstone** of the hospital laid by Pope John Paul II in 1990 remains abandoned in an adjacent field.

■ **Roadside stalls and cafés** provide excellent food and an opportunity to meet local people. Try *kedjenou* (chicken and vegetables in a mild sauce) with *attiéké* (fermented grated cassava). *Aloco* (fried plantain with onions and chilli) is also delicious.

■ **Senufo tribal masks** are a great buy but they come with a caution. Superstition surrounds their ownership and wearing, as they are believed to hold the souls of the dead.

AFRICA

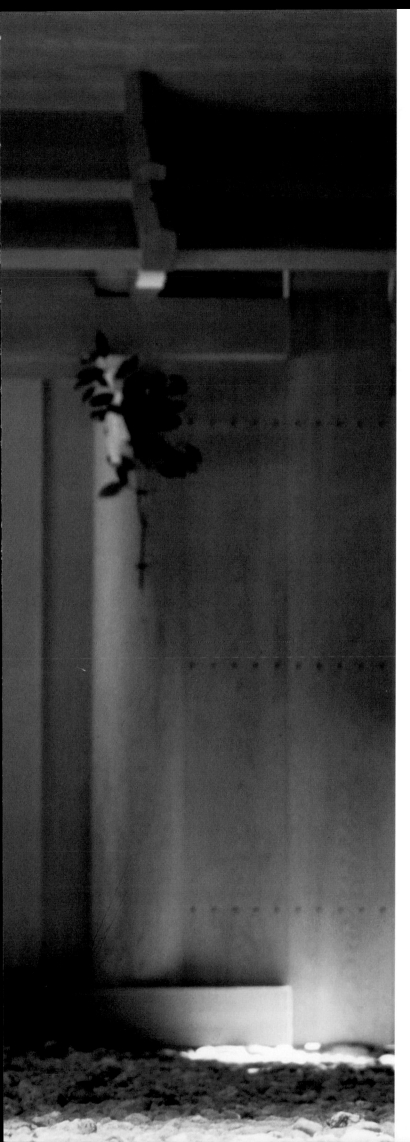

SHRINES 6

Some places are held sacred because of their connection with a particular religious event, a saint, a holy relic, or the presence of a god. These shrines take as many different forms as human spirituality itself, ranging from austere caves in lonely wilderness locations to magnificent temples in the hearts of teeming cities. Many are ancient landmarks with rich historical associations: these are the places where the founders and expounders of the world's great faiths have lived or died, the scenes of purported miracles and divine manifestations, the settings for holy events, the sites where relics are preserved and venerated. Others are more recent foundations, created by a faith community or individual donors to express a specific and powerful devotion. And some dramatically break down the barriers between separate belief systems, celebrating individuals revered equally by different traditions or fusing Christian symbolism with other traditions.

A Shinto priest, wearing traditional robes, *kanmuri* (ceremonial headdress), and *asagutsu* (wooden shoes), kneels in prayer at the Grand Shrine of Ise, the most sacred shrine in Japan.

Haida culture found expression through a rich oral history and the carving of totem poles from tall cedar trees.

CANADA

HAIDA GWAII

Carved and weathered totem poles silently face the sea
at an abandoned Haida village in a remote island wilderness.

On maps, this remote, wild archipelago off the coast of British Columbia, is called the Queen Charlotte Islands but to the indigenous Haida people it is known as Haida Gwaii, "Islands of the People." Native to the northwest coast, the Haida have lived here for centuries. At SGang Gwaay Llnagaay, misty silence, broken only by birdsong, surrounds the jumble of logs slowly being reclaimed by the rain forest. Once they were the longhouses of a Haida island village, now memorialized by the towering weathered totems carved with the faces of revered birds and mammals. Within Haida culture, totem poles denote lineage, illustrate family stories, welcome visitors, mark ownership of property, or designate a grave site. At K'uuna Llnagaay, the carved crests at the top of these tall cedar poles—frog, eagle, beaver, and killer whale—each signify a family that lived here in the mid-1800s. Now the poles are slowly weathering as they stand in tribute to the Haida who shaped them more than 150 years ago.

When to Go The Gwaii Haanas National Park Reserve is open all year. The climate is almost always cool and wet, however the driest and most pleasant time to visit is from mid-June through mid-August.

Planning Seven days allows sufficient time to visit the best island sites and also provides flexibility in case the weather is stormy. (Gwaii Haanas National Park Reserve can only be reached by kayak, boat, or seaplane, none of which operate in bad weather.) Flights to the Queen Charlotte Islands are available from Vancouver, while flights and ferries are available from Prince Rupert.

Websites www.pc.gc.ca/pn-np/bc/gwaiihaanas, www.haidaheritagecentre.com

HIGHLIGHTS

■ Walk through **the old growth forest of cedar trees** at Hlk'yah GaawGa. Look for the test holes in the trunks, made by Haida looking for the most suitable trees for carving a pole or forming a canoe.

■ Soak in the **healing thermal waters** at Gandll K'in Gwaayaay. The natural pools were held sacred by the Haida.

■ Delve into ancient and modern Haida culture at the **Haida Heritage Centre**. A modern totem pole, topped with three top-hatted watchmen, stands in front of the **Carving House**. It was made by a sculptor from the Skidegate community.

■ **Spend time alone** with the totem poles and the longhouses to sense the amazing power, deep peace, and spirit that lingers here.

WASHINGTON, D.C.

NATIONAL SHRINE OF THE IMMACULATE CONCEPTION

A place of pilgrimage and prayer, this is the main Marian Shrine in the United States and the largest Catholic church in the country.

NORTH AMERICA

Stone, brick, tile, and mortar are the only materials holding up the Basilica of the National Shrine of the Immaculate Conception in Washington, D.C. The imposing edifice, one of the ten largest churches in the world, was built entirely without structural steel beams, framework, or columns. Its Byzantine-inspired bright mosaic dome and 330-foot (100 meter) tall Knights' Tower distinguish it from both ground and air. Paying homage to the significance of the Blessed Virgin Mary to people from different countries around the world, the side chapels around the outside of the naves of the upper church and the crypt reproduce iconography and statues relating to famous Marian shrines, such as Our Lady of Czestochowa (Poland), Our Lady of Fátima (Portugal), Our Lady of Guadalupe (Mexico), and Our Lady of Lourdes (France), among many others. Some of the stonework, including the "Universal Call to Holiness" in the main church, was completed by Anthony Segreti, one of the master masons of the National Cathedral. More than 750,000 people make the pilgrimage to this site each year. Nevertheless, its immensity makes the basilica, with its Romanesque exterior and Byzantine interior, a place of great stillness and serenity.

When to Go The Basilica is open year-round; check the website for special services and events.

Planning Guided tours are always available, but if you are with a group of 15 or more people, a special visit can be arranged.

Website www.nationalshrine.com

HIGHLIGHTS

■ The seven main domes feature gilded **Byzantine-style mosaics.** The half dome in the North Apse shows Christ in Majesty come to judge the living and the dead. His right brow is raised to show that he judges justly; his left is relaxed to show his compassion.

■ The **Crypt Church** is decorated with beautiful mosaics depicting well-known female saints from throughout history, including St. Anne, St. Catherine of Alexandria, and St. Lucy.

■ The grounds include **Mary's Garden,** planted with white flowers to symbolize purity and leading to a fountain bordered with lines from the Magnificat, or Song of Mary.

The design and construction of the Basilica of the National Shrine of the Immaculate Conception took nearly a century to complete.

Worshipers climb up to stand at the feet of the 90-ft (27 m) alabaster statue of Padre Cícero.

BRAZIL

PADRE CÍCERO

This saint-like figure draws nearly two million pilgrims to the poor, unexceptional town of Juazeiro do Norte each year.

Pilgrims flock to the shrine of Padre Cícero, known locally as Padim Ciço. His devotees hope that he will one day be canonized by the Catholic Church and made a saint. Born in 1844, Padre Cícero Romão Batista was drawn to the priesthood from an early age. From the 1870s onward, as the local priest in Juazeiro do Norte, he became heavily involved in the community, paid personal visits to his parishioners, and spoke on issues that resonated with the lives of the people. In 1889, Maria de Araújo, a local woman, received communion from Padre Cícero. She claimed that the host turned to blood in her mouth, and this act of "heresy" left the young priest excommunicated by the Catholic Church. Nevertheless, his name spread among the poor rural Brazilians who came to hear him preach, and many people became convinced of his miraculous powers. These days, during Holy Week and on March 24 (Cícero's birthday), the town teems with the faithful, who travel from the rural interior to give thanks and ask favors of the revered figure. It is an intense display of prayer, belief, grief, and celebration, and a moving experience for both participants and spectators.

When to Go Pilgrims visit the sites throughout the year, but the most fervent celebrations take place during Holy Week, when thousands descend on the town.

Planning Juazeiro do Norte, in the dry semi-desert known as the sertão, is in the state of Ceará in northeastern Brazil. It can be reached by plane or bus from Fortaleza, the nearest city (the bus journey takes around eight hours). Please note that most of the region's income relies on religious tourism. You will encounter beggars and people singing or dancing for a few coins. The life of agricultural workers is tough, so don't begrudge them trying their luck with the wealthy travelers who visit.

Website www.braziltourism.org

HIGHLIGHTS

■ The **House of Miracles** displays a jumble of offerings—plastic and wooden arms and legs, letters of gratitude, photographs, and prayers for the priest. Such offerings reveal some of the problems that beset the people of this poor and deeply religious region.

■ Enjoy **the view from the Logradouro do Horto.** A giant statue of Padre Cícero carrying a hat and leaning on a stick stands on the summit.

■ Visit some of the **shrines erected in Padre Cícero's honor:** the church where he preached, the house where he lived and died, and the chapel where he is buried.

■ The **dramatic tableland of Chapada do Araripe** offers beautiful walks, with caves, natural springs, waterfalls, and misty cloud forest.

SOUTH AMERICA

GRAND SHRINE OF ISE

Japan's most sacred Shinto shrine attracts
more than six million pilgrims each year.

ASIA

Deep in a forest of giant sugi (Japanese cedar) trees stands the Grand Shrine of Ise, or Ise-jingu. The shrine is dedicated to the sun goddess, Amaterasu Omikami, and the goddess of agriculture and industry, Toyouke-no-Omikami. According to Shinto mythology, Amaterasu Omikami is the supreme deity and ancestor of the Imperial Family, including the current emperor. Centuries ago she gave the Japanese people their most important crop and source of survival—rice. Ise-jingu is comprised of two compounds, located almost 4 miles (6 kilometers) apart: the Naiku (inner shrine) and the Geku (outer shrine). The Naiku was established about 2,000 years ago to house a sacred mirror, which, according to legend, was given by Amaterasu Omikami to her grandson Ninigi-no-Mikoto when she sent him to rule Japan. The Geku was added in the fifth century A.D. in honor of Toyouke-no-Omikami, who is believed to have offered sacred food to Amateratsu. The wooden structures scattered across each compound are beautiful examples of simple Shinto-style architecture. Every 20 years, following a 1,300-year-old tradition, the Naiku and Geku are pulled down and rebuilt of cedar wood from the forest in exactly the same fashion—symbolic of the shrine being both ancient and perpetually new. The next, and 62nd, rebuilding ceremony will be in 2013.

When to Go The Shinto priests of Ise Jingu observe centuries-old rituals and ceremonies all year round, so check the website to see if you can time your visit to coincide with one.

Planning Trains run regularly from Nagayo, Kyoto, and Osaka to the two train stations in Ise; the trip takes 1.5-2 hours. The Geku is within walking distance of both stations, but you need to take a bus from the station to reach the Naiku. Ise does not have many places to stay, so make this a day-trip.

Website www.isejingu.or.jp

HIGHLIGHTS

■ The **Kan'name-sai Festival**, held in mid-October each year, is the shrine's most important festival. An imperial envoy offers the season's first harvest of rice crops, a five-colored silk cloth, and other sacred materials to the sun goddess.

■ A **font for ablution** is situated in front of the first *torii* (gate), marking the entrance to each shrine. Pilgrims must wash themselves before entering, a simple procedure that cleanses and purifies mind and body.

■ Near the Naiku, Oharai-machi is a **pedestrianized shopping street** that is an authentic replica of a Meiji-era (1868-1912) merchant's quarters. Try the *Akafuku mochi*—steamed rice cakes with azuki-bean paste.

Women in kimonos and rice straw hats dance in front of the shrine during the Kannamesai Festival.

The orange gateway is reflected in the still waters of the bay at high tide.

JAPAN

ITSUKUSHIMA

At high tide the giant vermilion gate of this Shinto shrine
appears to float on the waters of an island-studded bay.

Once considered a god, the entire island of Miyajima in Hiroshima Bay still
remains sacred. The Itsukushima shrine, set where the island's tides are at
their most extreme, was built on piers in the harbor to allow commoners to
come and worship without setting foot on the holy island itself. Forested Mount Misen
towers over the inlet, along the banks of which are several buildings, including Honden
(the main shrine), Haiden (the hall of worship), and a five-storied pagoda, all linked by
a roofed corridor. The high *torii* (gate) in the bay symbolizes the boundary between the
everyday and the infinite spiritual worlds. Founded in A.D. 592 during the Yamato period
(around A.D. 300–710), the shrine was completed in 1168 and has changed little since
then. It retains the delicate contours of the architectural style of the later Heian period
(794–1192). The brilliant orange, six-legged torii seems to stride out across the water at
high tide, but this great gate is equally striking at low tide, when it can be reached on foot
across damp sands where the Japanese photograph each other and dig for shellfish. The
current gate, dating from 1875, is the seventh and is a replica of its predecessors.

When to Go Year-round, but March, April, October, and November have the most comfortable weather.

Planning Allow two hours to see the shrine. Miyajima is reached by a ten-minute ferry ride from the
mainland port of Miyajima-guchi. Snacks on the island can be expensive so take a bento box or sand-
wiches with you, but keep them well wrapped and out of sight of the deer! The shrine is open from
6:30 a.m. to 6 p.m. and there is an admission charge, unlike other Shinto shrines.

Website www.jnto.go.jp

HIGHLIGHTS

■ Walk along the shrine's brilliantly
colored lantern-hung corridors to view
martial treasures, such as the swords
and armor of noted warriors, as well
as 1,000-year-old **paper and bamboo
fans**, more representative of the effete
Heian era.

■ Stay overnight on the island in order
to maximize your chances of seeing
a high tide and to view the lantern-lit
shrine and gate **illuminated at night**:
eerie but peaceful.

■ Enjoy the feeling of calm that
pervades the site, as **wild deer** graze
among stone statues by the shore.

ASIA

LABRANG MONASTERY

Join monks and pilgrims at a monastery in an intensely rural location,
where prayer flags flutter and the scent of yak-butter candles fills the air.

Set in a green valley on the edge of unspoiled grasslands in Xiahe County, the Labrang Monastery follows the Gelugpa (Yellow Hat) school of Tibetan Buddhism. The dazzling whitewashed buildings of the monastery are crowned with resplendent golden roofs, and within, Tibetan religious life flourishes: dark temples reverberate with the baritone voices of chanting monks, images of fierce-looking deities line the walls, and the flickering light of pungent yak-butter lamps illuminates the scene. The monks themselves are resplendent in their robes and distinctive yellow crescent-hats. Once 4,000 monks lived here; now there are several hundred, many of whom are students undergoing an intensive 15-year training before taking their final vows. A 2-mile (3 kilometer) long covered gallery extends around the perimeter of the complex: chanting pilgrims circumambulate the route clockwise, endlessly spinning the prayer wheels in the hope of gaining merit in the afterlife. The prayer wheels are richly decorated hollow drums containing printed prayers, or mantras. Each drum is mounted on a spindle, and each rotation is thought to be equivalent to reciting aloud all of the mantras within. Pilgrims also carry their own handheld prayer wheels, while row after row of larger wheels contain thousands more mantras. Follow the route, join in the chanting of "om mani padme hum," and listen to the hypnotic whirr and clack of the wheels.

When to Go Xiahe lies at an altitude of almost 2 miles (3 km), is extremely cold in winter, and pleasantly cool in summer. If you don't mind the cold, visit during the Tibetan New Year festival (Losar). Then stay another 3 days for the Great Prayer festival (Monlam Chenmo). Following the Tibetan Buddhist calendar, these fall in late February or early March. During periods of unrest, check the situation before traveling.

Planning Xiahe is a 6- to 7-hour bus trip from the large city of Lanzhou, which is linked by air and rail to major Chinese cities. Stay at a local hotel and allow at least 3 days to explore the monastery and its surroundings. If you are interested in Buddhism or learning Tibetan, this is a good place for a longer stay.

Website www.tibetinfor.com

ASIA

HIGHLIGHTS

■ View the six-story-high **Grand Sutra Hall**, one of 18 halls in the complex, which is big enough to hold 3,000 seated monks. The elaborate interior has portraits of the Buddha on the four walls, a dragon-embroidered silk canopy on the ceiling, and *nangka* paintings hanging from its 140 pillars.

■ Arrive early to stand with the monks as they gather on the steps of the main hall. Their **chanting** rings out in the still, clear air as they wait for the doors to open.

■ Visit the nearby **Sangke grasslands**, home to traditional Tibetan pastoralists caring for herds of yak. You can arrange to stay overnight with a local family. In summer, yellow Sangke flowers carpet the ground.

Opposite: Handheld prayer wheels and other devotional objects for sale in the local market. Above left: Pilgrims turn the prayer wheels while walking through the covered gallery that encircles the monastery. Above right: A dancer dressed as the god of the dead performs before a crowd during Losar, the Tibetan New Year festival.

Pilgrims, some barefoot and many wearing traditional red-pink scarves, trudge up the snowy hillside to the holy cave.

INDIA

Mata Vaishno Devi

Snow-capped peaks and dense forests provide the backdrop for an arduous pilgrimage to the mountaintop cave of a Hindu goddess.

Pilgrims come on foot or ponies, carried on litters, or even by helicopter, to show their devotion to the goddess Vaishno Devi. Loud, almost hypnotic, chants of "*Jai Mata Di*—Praise to the Mother" accompany them. Devotees claim that chanting these words gives them the strength to walk the steep 7.5-mile (12 km) trail. The shrine authority regulates every stage of the pilgrimage from the pathway to the summit to a complex ticketing system for entrance to the narrow cave. Inside the cave, natural rock formations, called the Holy Pindis, are said to be the incarnation of Mata Vaishno Devi in her three forms: Maha Kali, Maha Lakshmi, and Maha Saraswati. Other rock formations in the cave system are said to be some of the 330 million gods who have visited the cave to worship her. Visitors to the shrine believe that no one who visits the shrine and prays with a clean heart has ever returned empty-handed.

When to Go The temple is open throughout the year, but the peak season for visiting is either during the holy festival of Navratri (around April and October) or during the months of May, June, July, September, and October. In winter, heavy snowfalls can make the climb difficult.

Planning From Jammu (the nearest airport), take a bus or taxi 30 miles (48 km) to Katra, then hike the 7.5 miles (12 km) to the main cave. Allow one to two days for your visit to allow for waiting time to get into the cave—visit the website to see how many visitors are expected during your trip. Photography is not allowed inside the cave. This site is located in the state of Jammu and Kashmir, which has recently witnessed violent insurgent activity; check the political climate before you go.

Websites www.maavaishnodevi.org, www.mapsofindia.com

HIGHLIGHTS

■ Bathe in the **waterfall at Ban Ganga** near the start of the trek. Legend holds that it was created when Vaishno Devi shot an arrow into the ground to get water.

■ Stop to get Vaishno Devi's blessing at a small shrine said to house the **imprints of her feet**. The imprints are garlanded in bright yellow flowers.

■ Halfway up is Adhkuwari, with the **cave of the Eternal Virgin**. Only one person at a time can squeeze through its narrow entrance. It is believed that one visit here cleanses the soul of all sins.

■ Chant "Jai Mata Di" as you walk barefoot through the **icy stream** that flows through the cave: believers claim it makes the chill bearable.

■ Join the other pilgrims and sleep outside under the stars at the top near the cave's entrance. You'll wake in the clear dawn light to the sound of the **priests chanting their morning prayers** in the cave.

ASIA

INDIA

AMRITSAR

The most sacred shrine of the Sikh faith stands on a
stone island in the middle of a huge, square, man-made lake.

Lying at the heart of the ancient Punjab kingdom, the bustling city of Amritsar in northwest India is the spiritual and cultural hub of the Sikh religion. It is the lifelong ambition of every Sikh to travel to this holy metropolis and visit the Golden Temple (Harimandir Sahib) in the middle of the city. The temple precinct is surrounded by great halls of stone and marble that house and feed as many as 10,000 pilgrims every day. By day the pilgrims flock to the temple, reached via a long causeway across the lake from which Amritsar (Lake of the Nectar of Immortality) takes its name. Once inside the structure, devotees file past the Adi Granth, the holy book of the Sikhs, tossing rupee coins and flowers into the cordoned-off area where the tome resides. Some sit in meditation; others read aloud or chant. In the early evening, the sacred book is transferred to its nightly resting place in the Akal Takht Temple on the mainland, a procession that flows across the causeway and along the lakeshore to the beat of drums, the blare of trumpets, and the adulation of thousands of Sikhs who throw flowers and chant sacred hymns.

When to Go Set on the dusty plains of northwest India, Amritsar is sweltering hot in the summer and often surprisingly cold in winter as chilly winds blow down from the Himalaya. The best time to visit is probably the fall (October to November), when daytime temperatures fluctuate between 50 and 62ºF (10 to 17ºC).

Planning Be sure to stay in Amritsar at least one night so that you can see the vibrant procession that takes place in the temple precinct each evening. Since Sikhs believe that God rather than man is the provider of all things, visitors are invited to sleep and eat free of charge in the dormitories (*niwas*) around the Golden Temple. Amritsar has an international airport or can be reached by rail from Lahore (three hours) or Delhi (eight hours).

Websites www.darbarsaheb.com, www.sgpc.net

ASIA

HIGHLIGHTS

■ The holy book of the **Adi Granth** reveals the eclectic nature of the Sikh religion. Not only does it contain around 6,000 hymns composed by the first five Sikh Gurus between 1000 and 1606, but it also includes works by Hindu and Muslim holy men. The hymns are divided into 31 musical modes and are meant to be sung, except for the morning prayers, which are recited.

■ The **Central Sikh Museum** includes Sikh artwork, artifacts, and history dating back to the 16th century, when the temple was founded.

■ **Share a meal** at the Guru Ka Langar, the community kitchen which feeds all visitors to the shrine, regardless of creed or nationality, in the spirit of equality which is central to Sikhism.

An elderly Sikh man rests at the edge of a stone colonade beside the lake in front of the main building.

SHRINE OF A SUFI SAINT

One of the world's greatest parties, the anniversary of the death of Sufi saint Hazrat Lal Shahbaz Qalandar is a high-spirited celebration of peace between religions and people.

Built atop a conical hill beside the Indus, dusty Sehwan Sharif has been an important oasis town for at least 2,500 years. Today, it is best known as the site of a shrine sheltering the tomb of the Sufi mystic and poet Hazrat Lal Shahbaz Qalandar (1177-1274). Despite a privileged background, Lal Qalandar renounced materialism and traveled the world, promoting a message of dialogue between Muslims and Hindus before eventually settling in Sehwan Sharif. In the center of the old city, the shrine, first built in 1356, but rebuilt many times since, is a pilgrimage site for Muslims and Hindus, especially on his three-day *urs*, or death anniversary. His tomb rests beneath a silver canopy in a shrine covered in blue glazed tiles; mirrors reflect the glow from oil lamps. The days are quiet, but in the evening the mood becomes ecstatic, as devotees dance, pray, and sing to devotional music accompanied by the hypnotic beat of drums, cymbals, and horns. Qalandari Sufis, who especially revere Lal Qalandar, believe that altered states of consciousness bring them closer to God. Besides hypnotic dancing and singing, many take hashish as part of their transcendental journey, and the air at Sehwan Sharif is thick with it. Many conservative Muslims see them as dangerously liberal, but for many non-Muslims, they represent Islam at its most accessible.

When to Go The shrine is open daily from 4:30 a.m. to midnight. Go during the urs held from the 18th to the 21st day of the Islamic month of Shaban. Another major event takes place on the ninth and tenth days of the Islamic lunar month of Muharram, when Shiite Muslims form a self-whipping procession to mourn the anniversary of the death of Imam Husayn, grandson of the Prophet Muhammad. The weather is mildest from November to April. Summer, from May to August, is scorchingly hot.

Planning Sehwan Sharif is a four-hour drive from Karachi. Depending on the security situation, you can also reach it by train or bus. Check with your consular department before traveling overland in this often troubled part of Pakistan. If you are coming for the urs, book accommodations early, as hotels fill up months in advance.

Websites www.jhoolelal.com, www.tourism.gov.pk

ASIA

HIGHLIGHTS

■ In the morning, join devotees as they line up to pay their tributes to the saint, presenting garlands and green shrouds amid the smoke of **incense, burning joss sticks, and scented oil**, then circling the shrine in private contemplation.

■ See the ruins of **Kafir-Qila**, a huge fort said to have been built by Alexander the Great (356-323 B.C.) just outside Sehwan Sharif. Weary of Alexander's imperial expansion campaign, his army mutinied in what is now Amritsar and camped here on the homeward march to Macedonia.

■ Visit the boat villages of nearby **Manchhar Lake**, the largest freshwater lake in Asia and home to the Mohana fishermen. Although most anthropologists are dubious, the Mohana claim descent from Alexander the Great's troops.

■ Explore the remarkably well-preserved ancient city of **Mohenjo Daro**, a two-hour drive from Sehwan Sharif, which was the birthplace of the Indus Valley civilization some 5,000 years ago.

Opposite: Ecstatic pilgrims carrying banners make their way through the streets of Sehwan Sharif to the shrine where the Sufi saint Hazrat Lal Shahbaz Qalandar is buried. Above: A man bows his head in prayer at the grave of the saint as clouds of incense swirl up into the sky.

An altar stands in the crypt beneath the chapel.

SYRIA

Chapel of Ananias

The bare stone walls, simple altar, and light filtering in through high windows bring to life the simplicity of early Christian worship.

The streets narrow, and the noise of the city disappears, as you approach the arched metal gate near Bab Sharqi in the Christian quarter of Old Damascus. A small courtyard leads to the chapel dedicated to St. Ananias. Brilliant white statues depicting the baptism of St. Paul by Ananias stand in the shade, and steep steps lead down into the cool of the tiny underground chapel below. Wooden benches line the sides of the chapel, flanked by alcoves in the rough stone walls displaying paintings recounting the biblical story of Ananias, the man who restored St. Paul's sight after his conversion on the road to Damascus (Acts 9:11). Built on what is said to be the site of the House of Ananias, the chapel has been destroyed by non-Christian rulers (both Roman and Muslim) several times over the centuries. It was replaced with a pagan temple in the second or third century A.D. and later by more than one mosque before being bought in 1814 by the Franciscans and restored. Archaeologists have found remnants of an apse, columns, and other Christian religious artifacts dating to the fifth or sixth century.

When to Go Temperatures are moderate in Syria from April to June and September to November.

Planning The Chapel of Ananias is at 34 Sharia Hanania, 660 ft (200 m) from the junction of Bab Sharqi and Sharia Hanania near the Eastern Gate. You will need a visa to enter Syria (which will not be issued if your passport shows you have been to Israel). Hotel reservations need to be made in advance if you visit during Ramadan.

Websites www.ancientworldtours.com, www.blacktomato.co.uk, www.syriagate.com

HIGHLIGHTS

■ The chapel is at **Roman street level**, giving a sense of what the city was like in Biblical times.

■ Attend **Mass**; the Chapel of Ananias, run by the Franciscans, is one of the oldest Christian churches that continues to hold services.

■ Tour the other sacred sites along **"the Street called Straight"** (Via Recta) in Old Damascus, such as the Roman Temple of Jupiter, St. Paul's Chapel, and the Mosque of Hisham.

■ After your visit, try traditional **Middle Eastern food** such as falafel, baba ghanoush, tabbouleh, and hummus. For the best *shawarma* (kebab), try the first food stalls you come to in nearby Bab Touma.

ASIA

SYRIA

UMAYYAD MOSQUE

One of the largest and oldest mosques in existence,
Umayyad is also a masterpiece of Islamic architecture.

ASIA

Underneath lighting from elaborate chandeliers, worshipers facing Mecca kneel in prayer, while others sit absorbing the atmosphere within the ancient walls of the mosque. This mosque, built in Damascus in A.D. 705, stands on the site of a succession of places of worship dating back to the Aramaean Temple of Hadad (900 B.C.). Primarily a Sunni mosque, its innovative design is modeled on the house of the prophet Muhammad in Medina. Protected behind the deep green glass of an ornate domed shrine is the crypt, which is believed to contain the head of St. John the Baptist, known to Muslims as the prophet Yahya. This part of the mosque is sacred to both Christians and Muslims. Sunlight streams in through the high windows, casting a shower of primary colors onto the carpets covering the *haram* (prayer hall) below. The choral chant of the *adhaan* (call to prayer) is broadcast through the vast prayer hall and filters through the tall entrance doors into the great central courtyard beyond. White marble stretches across the open courtyard in contrast to the gilded mosaic panels inside and the mosaic-encrusted Beit al Mal (Dome of the Treasury) at the mosque's eastern end.

When to Go The mosque is very busy at Eid al Fitr (the end of Ramadan) and the feast of Eid al Adha (marking the hajj), but the atmosphere is vibrant and electrifying if you don't mind crowds.

Planning Women must be covered from head to foot when entering the mosque, and men should not wear shorts. You can rent a *galabiyya* (long gown) at the office next to the mosque. Respect the people attending worship, especially during prayer times, and always ask before taking photos. Please note that there are some areas of the mosque reserved only for women. Beware of pickpockets, particularly outside the mosque.

Websites www.syriatourism.org, www.silkroadandbeyond.co.uk

HIGHLIGHTS

■ Visit the **mausoleum of Saladin**, a prominent figure in Muslim history and great 12th-century leader.

■ Look for the shrine believed to contain the head of Husayn, the **Martyr of Karbala'**–it is marked by a heavily embossed silver plaque on the wall in the inner room.

■ Sit in the **courtyard**, and take some time to enjoy the tranquil atmosphere of the mosque.

■ Try to find the small room at the eastern end of the prayer room from which the **call to prayer** is broadcast.

The slender tower of the 13th-century Minaret of Jesus, the place where believers claim that Jesus will descend to earth on Judgment Day, is at the far right.

IRAN

HOLY SHRINE OF IMAM REZA

Built on the place where Imam Reza was martyred in A.D. 818, this shrine is the most sacred Shiite site in Iran.

In the Dar al Vilayah courtyard within the Imam Reza Shrine in Mashhad, the black flowing folds of chador-clad women brush past men kneeling in prayer. Children play on the patchwork of Persian prayer carpets next to their mothers, whose facial expressions reveal the intensity of their devotion. Every year more than 20 million Shiite Muslims visit the shrine of Ali ibn Musa al-Rida (Reza), the Eighth Imam of Shiite Islam; arrival at the shrine is the culmination of their pilgrimage. His mausoleum lies in the center of the shrine complex below a shimmering ceiling of colored and mirrored tiles under a great golden *muqarnas* (corbeled) dome. Twenty-one porches radiate from the mausoleum to the mosques, chambers, and courtyards of prayer, designated either for men, women, or families. Men scramble in their desire to touch or kiss the *zarih* (gilded latticework covering the shrine), and wailing and weeping emanates from the women's porches as they beat their chests. On the night before important festivals, to the sound of the Koran being recited, dignitaries sweep dust from the Imam's tomb with stately ceremony. The tomb is then washed with rosewater, and bags of the dust, which is believed to be sacred, are distributed to the faithful. The complex has been destroyed, rebuilt, and expanded over the centuries, each imam leaving his mark with additional chambers, mosques, courtyards, libraries, seminaries, and minarets.

When to Go April to June and September to November. Avoid Nowruz (Iranian New Year), which can be extremely busy; it falls on or around March 21 each year.

Planning Check your government's travel advisory service before traveling to Iran. Visas are not easy to obtain and may be easier to acquire if you book a tour. Credit cards and ATMs do not accept non-Iranian accounts; travelers checks are not accepted either. Take cash and change it at a bank, which has a better exchange rate than can be found on the street. Men and women must dress appropriately according to Islamic custom. Non-Muslims are only allowed to visit the shrine's main courtyards and the museum.

Websites www.magic-carpet-travel.com, www.iranparadise.com, www.imamreza.net, www.irpedia.com

ASIA

HIGHLIGHTS

■ Pilgrims in need of healing gather to pray through a silver window on the eastern side of the **Dar al Siyadah porch**, said to be the site of many miracles.

■ **Hear the Koran** read in daily ceremonies carried out each morning in the Dar al Huffaz hall.

■ **Saqqa Khaneh** (public water fountains) throughout the shrine complex commemorate the martyrdom of Imam Husayn and his 72 followers, who died of thirst near Karbala in the seventh century.

■ From the **drum tower**, trumpets and drums ring out to salute the rising and setting sun each day. The drums are also beaten when any person at the shrine is believed to have been miraculously healed.

Opposite: The Holy Shrine of Imam Reza is one of the largest ensembles of Islamic architecture in the world and is notable for the quality of its ceramics. Above: The sprawling shrine complex extends over seven courtyards, some still under construction. This one, built after 1979, is named for Imam Khomeini, founder of the Islamic Republic of Iran.

HILL OF CROSSES

The 50,000 crosses on this small hill mark a poignant pilgrimage site with both religious and political significance.

EUROPE

A small hill rises above the surrounding farmland, its slopes thickly forested with crosses and crucifixes. Made in all different sizes and styles, from crudely fashioned pieces of wood to elaborate and ornate carvings, the crosses are piled up or stuck one on top of another. Portraits of Lithuanian patriots rub shoulders with crude crosses made from license plates or Band-Aids; statues of Christ or the Virgin Mary are hung with rosaries; simple smaller crosses bear a huge range of intensely personal messages, memories, and wishes. The collection is constantly growing as each visitor leaves a cross or rosary. Although some claim that the tradition began during the Middle Ages, the first crosses on this site probably date from 1831 and commemorate those killed in a failed revolt against Russian rule. From then on the site was associated with Lithuanian defiance and independence. In the second half of the 20th century, the KGB used bulldozers to completely raze the site on three occasions, only to find further crosses, by now symbols not only of revolt against Soviet rule but against the communist repression of religion, erected in their place.

When to Go The site is open year-round. Easter sees the largest number of pious visitors.

Planning Allow an hour or so at the site. The Hill of Crosses, Kryziu Kalnas, is 7.5 miles (12 km) north of Siauliai. It can be reached by public buses en route to Riga in neighboring Latvia, or visited as a stop on a trip between Riga and Vilnius using the A12 highway. Taxi drivers will wait while you visit. There are plenty of places to stay in Siauliai itself, which also has several historic churches and museums (including ones dedicated to bicycles and photography).

Website www.lithuaniatourism.co.uk

HIGHLIGHTS

■ Pope John Paul II, who had Lithuanian ancestry, visited in 1993 and donated a cross himself. There is a **stone commemorating his visit** and thanking the Lithuanian people for their faith.

■ **Pagan symbols** lie among the Christian ones, characteristic of a region that was among the last in Europe to accept Christianity.

■ The **sound of the crosses and rosaries** swinging against each other in the wind is an evocative and moving one, not unlike wind chimes.

A pathway leads through the jumble of crosses and statues to the top of the mound; other smaller paths veer off at angles.

The dark stains on the faces and hands may be deliberate or a function of time and smoke from votive candles.

HIGHLIGHTS

■ The **Knight's Hall**, which once housed the Polish parliament, is lined with paintings including one recounting the arrival of the Black Madonna painting at Jasna Góra.

■ The monastery complex also includes a **library** containing more than 8,000 titles, a treasury, and a museum.

■ Drive the 100-mile (160 km) **Eagles' Nest Trail** between Częstochowa and Kraków to get a sense of a land under siege. The trail passes 15 medieval fortifications set atop limestone cliffs, proof that the Poles needed material as well as miraculous help as they were invaded time and again.

POLAND

THE BLACK MADONNA

The slashed and blackened face of the Madonna of Częstochowa has become a symbol of Poland and the spiritual center of the nation.

EUROPE

Around five million pilgrims a year flock to see the painting of the Black Madonna in the Jasna Góra Monastery. The image was supposedly painted by St. Luke himself on a cypress tabletop in the house of the Holy Family when Jesus was an infant. The tabletop was brought here in the 14th century, and the church and monastery were constructed to house it. The icon holds a special place in Polish hearts, purportedly having helped save the monastery from a 17th-century Swedish invasion. Since then it has become a focal point for national sentiment. It is hard to move within the crowded monastery corridors as you join the droves of the faithful visiting the icon, which is set in an altar of ebony and silver dating from 1650. The Virgin's expression is thoughtful, and the painting is often draped in pearls or a cloth of hammered gold. Offerings line the walls of the tiny chapel: crutches, jewelry, flowers, photos, and more, giving tangible evidence of the devotion of the Madonna's visitors.

When to Go In summer, Jasna Góra swarms with visitors, particularly during the annual pilgrimage in August on the Madonna's two feast days: August 15 and August 26. If you don't mind cold weather, go in winter, when there's snow on the hill; the monastery is strikingly lovely.

Planning Start from Kraków (60 miles/96 km away) and combine your visit with a drive along the Eagles' Nest Trail. Częstochowa is 140 miles (225 km) from Warsaw, a 2.5-hour drive along the main road towards Katowice, and can be visited in a day. Check the website for times of English tours.

Websites www.jasnagora.pl, www.czestochowa.pl

GERMANY

SHRINE OF THE THREE KINGS

A place of superlatives, Northern Europe's largest Gothic cathedral also contains the biggest and most famous reliquary in the Western world.

Soft beams of light filter in through the massive stained-glass windows of Cologne Cathedral, bathing the Shrine of the Three Kings (Dreikönigsschrein) in an ethereal glow. Believed to contain the remains of Melchior, Balthazar, and Caspar, the three Magi who traveled to Bethlehem for the birth of Jesus, this richly bejeweled, gilded sarcophagus is as magnificent as the Gothic cathedral built to house these holy relics. Modern-day pilgrims can view the reliquary, which also holds the bones of three martyred saints, in the 13th-century chancel behind the high altar at the cathedral's east end. Designed by Flemish goldsmith Nicholas of Verdun around 1190, this basilica-shaped masterpiece is 60 inches (152 centimeters) high, 43 inches (109 centimeters) wide, and 87 inches (221 centimeters) long, and took more than four decades to complete. Three large gems on the front of the shrine mark the location of the gold-crowned skulls of the Magi. On each of the four sides, embossed bas-relief figures portray scenes from the life of Christ, the Twelve Apostles, and Old Testament prophets. Medieval craftsmen also adorned the filigreed surfaces with more than 1,000 precious and semiprecious stones, along with colorful cloisonné and champlevé enamelwork and cameos, including one of Archbishop Rainald von Dassel, who brought the relics to Cologne in 1164.

When to Go The cathedral is open daily, although access is restricted during services. In addition, the chancel where the shrine is located is closed during confessions.

Planning One-hour English-language tours are offered. The nearest major airport is Frankfurt, and a high-speed rail line runs between the airport and Cologne; the trip takes about an hour.

Websites www.koelner-dom.de, www.koeln.de

HIGHLIGHTS

■ Examine the reliquary's meticulous craftsmanship, noting its **exquisite lapidary and metalwork.**

■ The **original wooden Shrine of the Magi** can be viewed in the cathedral's treasury, along with liturgical vestments, chalices, crosses, and other religious artifacts.

■ View **"The Adoration of the Magi" altarpiece** by Stefan Lochner, a 15th-century German artist.

■ Tour the twin-spired **cathedral,** completed in 1880, 632 years after construction began. Marvel at its colossal size and architectural detail, as well as its other treasures including the Gero Cross and the Madonna of Milan.

■ Attend Mass or just sit quietly in the nave to fully appreciate the grandeur of the cathedral and all the stunning **stained-glass windows.**

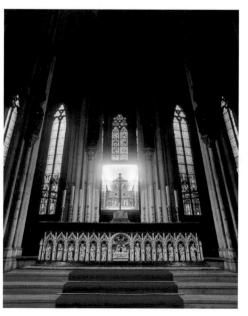

Opposite: The front of the reliquary shows the baptism of Christ, which is celebrated on January 6, the feast day of the Magi. Above left: This stained-glass window, showing the conversion of St. Paul on the road to Damascus, was destroyed in World War II and then reconstructed in 1992-94. Above right: The reliquary in its place behind the main altar.

Ten Reliquaries

From entire buildings constructed to hold sacred objects to small but elaborately decorated jeweled boxes, reliquaries hold the holy of holies.

❶ Gothic Reliquary, New York, NY

This sumptuous reliquary once housed in the convent of the Poor Clares of the Order of St. Francis of Buda (today part of Budapest) now graces The Cloisters, New York's home for all things medieval. In the shape of an elaborate Gothic interior with pointed arches and gilded silver, the doors open to reveal a charming Madonna and Child with angels.

Planning The Cloisters is in Fort Tryon Park. Take the A train to 190th Street, then walk north for ten minutes along Margaret Corbin Drive; or take the M4 bus from Madison and 83rd, and get off at the last stop. www.metmuseum.org

❷ Kyaikhtiyo Pagoda, Mon State, Myanmar

Legend holds that a single strand of Buddha's hair has kept the gilded Golden Rock from falling from its precarious perch for thousands of years. It is claimed that the huge boulder, just barely resting on a cliff over a gorge, was placed there by two mischievous Nats (Burmese spirits). A stream of pilgrims brings squares of gold leaf to rub onto its surface.

Planning Reaching the pagoda is physically arduous. A bus takes visitors to base camp; from there it's a steep truck ride to the foot of the ridge, followed by a 1.5-mile (2.5 km) hike to the top. Only men are allowed to touch the Golden Rock. www.goldenlandpages.com/hotspots/kyaik.htm

❸ Dubrovnik Cathedral, Dubrovnik, Croatia

It is said that Blaise, a third-century Armenian bishop, became Dubrovnik's patron saint after he saved the city from Venetian attack by appearing to a priest in a dream. Since then, the cathedral's magnificent treasury has claimed to be home to the saint's skull, arm, and leg. Encased in a 12th-century crown of silver and gold filigree, the skull is the star attraction on February 3, the saint's feast day, when his relics are paraded around the city's streets before excited crowds.

Planning An impressive statue of St. Blaise stands over Pile Gate, the entrance to the old town. From there, you can walk along Dubrovnik's ancient city walls overlooking the Adriatic. www.dubrovnik-online.com

❹ Topkapi Palace, Istanbul, Turkey

Istanbul's Topkapi Palace is home to an important collection of the Prophet Muhammad's relics. Housed in a suite of richly tiled, domed rooms, the relics are preserved in ornate caskets and are said to include the Prophet's Holy Mantle, hairs from his beard, soil from his grave, his sword, bamboo bow, and his footprint in stone. The Koran has been recited continuously next to the relics since their installation.

Planning Topkapi Palace Museum is open 9 a.m.-7 p.m. every day except Tuesday. www.topkapisarayi.gov.tr

❺ Santa Croce in Gerusalemme, Rome, Italy

In A.D. 320, St. Helena, the mother of Rome's first Christian emperor Constantine, founded the Basilica of Santa Croce to house relics she brought back from the Holy Land. She went to find the cross on which Jesus was crucified and brought back three fragments and a nail, which she believed to be part of the True Cross, as well as thorns said to be from Jesus' crown.

Planning Don't miss the beautiful vegetable garden in the adjoining monastery. www.basilicasantacroce.com

❻ Cappella della Sindone, Turin Cathedral, Italy

The Turin shroud, which bears the faint outline of a man's face, is believed by some to be the burial cloth of Jesus Christ. A replica is in the church; the shroud itself is now preserved in a climate-controlled case built by an aerospace company. The church's museum holds earlier reliquaries, such as a 15th-century velvet-lined box adorned with silver nails.

Planning The shroud itself will not be exhibited again until 2025. www.sindone.org

❼ The Iron Crown of Lombardy, Monza, Italy

Both the 8th-century Emperor Charlemagne and Napoleon were crowned with a slender band of plain iron set within a jeweled crown. Beaten from a nail alleged to come from the True Cross, the band is only 0.4 inch (1 cm) thick—enough for two emperors to establish their connection to Christ.

Planning The cathedral where the crown is housed is in Monza—just north of Milan. www.hellomilano.it/Index/Monza/HistSites.htm

❽ Shrine of St. Ursula, Bruges, Belgium

St. Ursula was a devout Christian princess who avoided marriage by embarking on a cruise to Cologne accompanied by 11,000 virgins. They were all slaughtered on the way home by Huns. Her unlikely tale is remembered by Hans Memling in six delicately painted scenes on her wooden reliquary.

Planning St. Ursula's reliquary is in The Memling Museum, part of the St. John's Hospital complex. www.trabel.com/brugge-m-memling.htm

❾ Abbey of St. Foy, Conques, France

Once in the rival Agen monastery, the relics of St. Foy were spirited to Conques in A.D. 866 by a jealous monk. The monks built a golden reliquary in the shape of a 3-ft (90 cm) high, heavily jeweled, seated figure to house the stolen goods.

Planning The church and Treasury Museum are open daily. www.conques.com

❿ San Lorenzo de El Escorial, Madrid, Spain

King Philip II was an obsessive relic collector, amassing more than 7,500 in his lifetime, including ten entire bodies; he even instructed that his favorites surround his deathbed. Today, his collection can be seen throughout the Escorial complex.

Planning Escorial is easily reached by bus or train from Madrid. www.patrimonionacional.es

Precariously balanced on the cliff edge, this huge gilded rock can be wobbled from side to side allowing a thread to slide beneath it. Kyaikhtiyo Pagoda, placed on top of the rock, was built in 574 B.C.

Above the whitewashed entrance of the shrine enclosing the Cave of the Apocalypse, a mosaic shows St. John dictating his revelation to his disciple.

GREECE

THE CAVE OF THE APOCALYPSE

St. John allegedly wrote the Book of Revelation, the final chapter of the New Testament, in a cave on a hilltop in the Dodecanese Islands.

Brooding over the white houses, barren hillsides, and deep blue bays of the tiny Aegean island of Pátmos, the 1,000-year-old fortress monastery of St. John the Divine (Agios Ioannis Theologos) is one of the great holy places of the Eastern Orthodox world. Yet below the monastery's massive, black stone walls is a smaller and even more sacred site—the Cave of the Apocalypse. It is believed that St. John made his home here after being exiled to the island by the Emperor Domitian in A.D. 95. A colorful mosaic of St. John dictating his visions received from Christ to his disciple, Prochoros, surmounts the entrance. Within the cave are glorious frescoes and icons, some dating from as early as the 13th century. The walls and ceilings are darkened by the soot of votive tapers and hung with dozens of the small silver votive plaques that devout Greek villagers use to beseech the saint's intercession. Guides point out the rock that Prochoros may have used as a writing desk, the worn stone that St. John is said to have used as his pillow, and the fissure in the rock from which the saint heard the voice of God. The cave is often crowded with pilgrims and tourists, but it is also still a regular place of prayer for the villagers of Chora, as it has been for so many centuries.

When to Go Easter through October. Pátmos becomes crowded with pilgrims during Greek Easter (which usually falls in April) and the mid-August religious festival of the Dormition, or Assumption, of the Virgin.

Planning Most accommodations on Pátmos are in and around the harbor village, Skala, or nearby Grikos. The cave is about halfway between Skala and Chora, the mountaintop village that is home to the monastery. Allow two hours to walk each way. Of if you prefer, take a taxi or shuttle bus from Skala. Pátmos has no airport but there are frequent ferries and hydrofoils from nearby islands, including Léros, Sámos, or Kos.

Websites www.gnto.gr, www.dolphins.gr

HIGHLIGHTS

■ Chora, the hilltop village that surrounds the ancient walls of the Monastery of St. John, is one of the loveliest of traditional Greek island settlements. More than 40 tiny **churches and chapels** are hidden among a labyrinth of stone-cobbled lanes and dazzling white houses.

■ The Monastery of St. John houses a fine collection of sacred **reliquaries and icons**.

■ From Chora, enjoy the **panoramic views** of the tiny, nearby islands of the Ikarían Sea, the mountains of Ikaría and Sámos to the north, and—on a clear day—the Turkish mainland to the east.

■ Visit the village of **Grikos**, with its clear blue water, long sweep of sand and pebbly beach, and cluster of tavernas serving just-caught fish.

EUROPE

Basilica of St. Francis

Masterpieces of Italian art and an elaborate church mark the last resting place of a saint who rejected riches and embraced poverty.

The interior of the Lower Basilica of St. Francis in Assisi is suffused with the yellow hues of candlelight and dimly lit by floor lamps. In the gloom, you can make out semicircular Romanesque arches. The whispered prayers of brown-cassocked friars echo through the ancient side chapels, where frescoes created by the giants of 13th-century Italian art, most notably Cimabue and Giotto, blanket the walls. The frescoes were created following the completion of the Lower Basilica in 1230. The low ceiling of midnight blue in the central nave is scattered with bright stars bridging the scenes on opposite walls painted by the unknown artist Maestro di San Francesco. The scenes depict similarities between the life of Jesus and the life of St. Francis. On the transept wall, Cimabue painted what many claim is the closest likeness to the saint in his "Our Lady enthroned with St. Francis" (1280). From the nave, a stone stairway leads down into the crypt beneath, where the remains of St. Francis lay hidden until 1818. After the dimness of the crypt and the Lower Basilica, the Upper Basilica, completed in 1253 in the Gothic style, is bright and full of light, decorated with more frescoes attributed to Giotto and Cimabue and their schools of artists. Giotto's 28 frescoes of the life of St. Francis in the Upper Basilica draw many visitors here.

When to Go All year round. In spring and fall the weather is more moderate, although the site can get busy; summer is quieter but can be very hot; winter, although cold and wet, is the quietest time.

Planning Closed on Sunday mornings. There is a strict dress code—wear long trousers or skirts and long-sleeved shirts. Photography is not allowed. Buses run from the train station to the basilica. Assisi is very busy during the Calendimaggio springtime festival (first Thursday in May after May 1) and on August 2, when Catholics go to the Basilica of Santa Maria degli Angeli to receive the Pardon of Assisi.

Websites www.italyheaven.co.uk, www.bellaumbria.net

EUROPE

HIGHLIGHTS

■ Visit the **Hermitage of the Carceri** outside of town to see the caves where St. Francis and his companions lived.

■ Look for the **frescoes** of Obedience, Chastity, and Poverty: the vows by which St. Francis lived his life.

■ Notice the **patches on the ceiling** in the Upper Basilica above the altar and front entrance. In 1997, an earthquake damaged the building and killed four people; repairs took two years. Frescoes attributed to Cimabue and Giotto were badly damaged.

■ As a young man, Francis was praying before a crucifix and seemed to hear Christ speak to him from the cross, saying: "Francis, repair my falling house." He gave money to repair the church and was disowned by his father. This **crucifix** is now in the Church of Santa Chiara in Assisi.

St. Francis, the mark of the stigmata visible on his hand, and St. John the Evangelist look on at the Madonna and Child in this 14th-century fresco by Pietro Lorenzetti.

SHRINE OF PADRE PIO

Throngs of the devout and the curious flock to a small town in the spur of Italy to visit the shrine of a much-revered 20th-century saint.

In 1916, Padre Pio was sent to the quiet mountain town of San Giovanni Rotondo in the Gargano to recover from tuberculosis. Instead, the Capuchin friar became famous for the stigmata he reportedly received while praying inside the church on September 20, 1918. He bore the stigmata—open wounds that mirror those on the crucified Jesus—for the next 50 years. In his cell, an austere white room, visitors can see his fingerless gloves, bandages, and a scab from the wound. For many years, church authorities were reluctant to believe that his wounds were miraculous, but in 2002, 34 years after his death, he was made a saint. The little town now bustles with 7 million pilgrims and is home to a vast ultramodern church designed by architect Renzo Piano, who also designed the Pompidou Center in Paris. The interior of the radical semicircular structure, with its soaring green copper roof, spirals in ever-decreasing circles like a snail shell. It is filled with crisscrossed rows of giant riblike stone arches and can house up to 6,500 seated worshipers inside and another 30,000 outside.

When to Go April through October offers the best weather conditions and an opportunity to mingle with Padre Pio's thousands of devotees. From November to March, it is colder, there are fewer visitors, and the site is less crowded.

Planning The shrine at San Giovanni Rotondo, near Foggia, Is 180 miles (290 km) southeast of Rome. It takes at least five hours to get there via bus or train. You can also drive, or combine your visit with a trip to Naples or Bari. Stay at least one night. The visitor information office at the Lady of Grace Church provides guidebooks, tours, and assistance. All visits are free. Avoid Sundays if you want to stay clear of the many locals who are on pilgrimage.

Websites www.conventopadrepio.com, www.italytraveller.com

EUROPE

HIGHLIGHTS

■ Walk the **Via Crucis** as it winds up the slopes of Monte Castellano through pine woods. The faithful pray before sculptures of the stations of the cross and statues of the Virgin, Padre Pio, and Christ resurrected.

■ Visit the nearby **Foresta Umbra**, which has been a protected woodland for more than a century. Beeches, limes, oaks, and chestnuts shelter many species of birds and animals.

■ Drive up a winding road to **Monte Sant'Angelo**, or St. Michael's Mount, an ancient place of pilgrimage.

One wall of the ultramodern shrine is a vast stained-glass window that lets light flood into the building.

A nun from the Monastic Communities of Jerusalem order prostrates herself in prayer before the altar in the crypt.

FRANCE

SHRINE TO MARY MAGDALENE

Long popular with pilgrims from all corners of Europe, this church is said to hold relics of Mary Magdalene.

The gently rolling hills of Burgundy's Morvan region provide a picturesque backdrop for the Basilica of Vézelay, set above neat woodlands and Vézelay's cobbled village streets. In 878, Pope John VIII founded an abbey church on this hill, and in 1146, Bernard of Clairvaux stood at the pulpit, inspiring the faithful to go on the Second Crusade. Vézelay was one of four major starting points for pilgrimages to Santiago de Compostela in Spain, and modern pilgrims still begin the long trek to Spain from this church. The building of this Romanesque church was completed in 1215. Light pours into the church from the windows set high up above the pale stone arches. Stone stairs, worn to a gloss by centuries of footsteps, descend to the Carolingian crypt, where a golden reliquary is said to contain a single finger of Mary Magdalene. This is the heart of the shrine, where more than 800,000 visitors come each year. Other alleged relics of the saint held in this church were burned during the Wars of Religion in the 16th century. During most of the year, services led by the Monastic Communities of Jerusalem are held in the abbey chapel.

When to Go Easter and August are very crowded, while a visit in April, October, or over Christmas is pleasantly peaceful. The festival of St. Mary Magdalene is observed annually on July 22.

Planning Contact the Vézelay Tourism Office for help finding suitable accommodations in or around Vézelay. There is no train station in the town; take a taxi from the nearest station, Semicelles. There is a music festival in August and organ recitals Sundays at 4 p.m. from mid-June to mid-September.

Websites www.vezelaytourisme.com, www.burgundytoday.com

HIGHLIGHTS

■ Stop in the dim light of the narthex to study the carved **tympanum** above the central door, with its depiction of "The Mission of the Apostles," before moving into the luminous nave.

■ **Sculpted capitals** on the columns in the nave are a kind of Bible in stone. They tell stories from the Bible and the lives of the saints alongside profane allegories, from violent to amusing.

■ Stroll behind the church, past ruins of the old abbey and the well-tended terraced gardens. A sweeping **panorama of the Morvan hills** lies beyond.

■ Other notable **cathedrals** in the area are at Sens, Auxerre, and Autun. The Cistercian abbey at Fontenay is also worth a visit.

EUROPE

Ten Marian Shrines

The Virgin Mary is venerated by pilgrims around the world, who flock to the many shrines, artworks, and churches created in her honor.

❶ Our Lady of Aparecida, Aparecida, Brazil

The small dark figure of Our Lady of Aparecida, just 16 inches (40 cm) tall, was found in the Paraíba River in 1717 by three local fishermen. Topped with an oversize golden crown and swathed in a robe adorned with the Brazilian flag, the statue is housed in the magnificent Basílica de Nossa Senhora Aparecida—the largest Marian shrine in the world.

Planning The feast day of Our Lady of Aparecida is held every year on October 12. www.aboutsaopaulo.com/city/aparecida/our-lady.html

❷ Weeping Madonna of Rockingham, Australia

An unassuming statue in a private Australian residence has been a site of international pilgrimage since 2002. Rockingham's effigy of the Madonna is said to weep tears and the scent of roses to fill the air; a number of people have experienced "miraculous events" after visiting the shrine. The statue has been subject to scientific testing, but the source of the liquid and the lingering sweet smell remains a mystery.

Planning The statue can be viewed by appointment only. Rockingham is less than an hour's drive south of Perth. www.weepingmadonna.org

❸ Our Lady of Vladimir, Moscow, Russia

Russia's national icon, Our Lady of Vladimir, dates from the 12th century and is a model of Byzantine art. The exquisite colors of the egg tempera have dulled over time, but the baby Jesus still presses his cheek devotedly to his mother's face while the Virgin Mary continues to hold our gaze.

Planning The icon is on display at the Church Museum of St. Nicholas in Tolmachy, part of the State Tretyakov Gallery. www.tretyakov.ru

❹ House of the Virgin Mary, Ephesus, Turkey

Surrounded by green forest, this simple stone chapel on Mount Koressos is considered to be the last home of the Madonna. According to the Bible, she traveled to the spot with the Apostle John in the years after the Crucifixion, remaining there until her death. The site is sacred to both Muslim and Christian faiths.

Planning The House of the Virgin Mary is near Ephesus, one of the best preserved of Turkey's ancient cities. www.tourismturkey.org

❺ Santa Casa di Loreto, Loreto, Italy

A humble stone house, purported to be the birthplace of the Virgin Mary and witness to the Annunciation, has beckoned pilgrims for centuries. According to legend, it was carried by angels all the way from Nazareth, arriving in the small Italian hill town in 1295. The shrine attracts thousands each year.

Planning The house is inside the Basilica of Loreto; don't miss the beautiful frescoes that decorate the dome ceiling. www.santuarioloreto.it

❻ Shrines of the Madonna, Malta

The figure of the Madonna is very popular in Malta, attested to by the many churches and icons dedicated to her. Gozo's church, Ta'Pinu, was the scene of an alleged apparition in 1883, when a local woman purported to have heard the voice of the Virgin. Outside, spare and beautiful statues wind their way up the hill marking out the 14 stations of the cross.

Planning The best time to visit Malta is on Good Friday, when colorful processions throng the streets. www.visitmalta.com, www.tapinu.org

❼ Notre-Dame de La Salette, Grenoble, France

High up in the French Alps in 1846, two frightened children claimed to have seen a vision of the weeping Virgin in a mountain pasture. Since then the site has become popular with pilgrims and many claim to have been healed by Our Lady of Salette. Starting at the imposing mountainside basilica, visitors can follow the walking trail through breathtaking Alpine scenery up to the "Valley of the Apparition."

Planning The village of La Salette is 50 miles (80 km) south of Grenoble, and the shrine of La Salette can easily be reached by car, bus, or taxi. www.lasalette.cef.fr, www.grenoble-isere-tourisme.com

❽ Black Virgin, Rocamadour, France

This delicate walnut statue of the Virgin Mary holding the infant Jesus on her knee helped turn the town of Rocamadour into a major site of Christian pilgrimage during the Middle Ages. The town, with its seven chapels, clings to a limestone cliff, seemingly defying gravity. Pilgrims and tourists alike converge on the town to climb the 200 weathered steps of the Grand Escalier—the devout on their knees—up to the Chapelle Notre-Dame, where the statue is housed.

Planning The town is a two-hour drive from Toulouse. www.villes-sanctuaires.com, www.rocamadour.com

❾ Italian Chapel, Orkney Islands, Scotland

During World War II, a group of Italian prisoners of war were held on the windswept island of Lamb Holm. Led by Domenico Chiocchetti, the prisoners transformed two Nissen huts into a chapel dedicated to the Madonna, Queen of Peace, with only the raw materials to hand. Chiocchetti was so devoted to the chapel that when the Italians were freed in 1945, he stayed behind to finish the font. Today, the unique building attracts more than 100,000 visitors a year.

Planning There are regular flights to Kirkwall airport from the mainland. The Orkney Islands can also be reached by ferry from John o' Groats and Aberdeen. www.undiscoveredscotland.co.uk/eastmainland/italianchapel

❿ Our Lady of Fátima, Portugal

In 1917, three shepherd children claimed to witness a number of manifestations of the Virgin Mary. The town of Fátima and its shrines have since become one of the most famous modern-day sites of Marian apparition.

Planning An estimated four million people visit the town each year; the busiest times are May and October. www.santuario-fatima.pt

On the 84th anniversary of the children's vision at Fátima, the holy image of the Virgin Mary stands in front of thousands of pilgrims whose candles make pinpoints of light in the darkness.

Touching the globe that La Moreneta holds in her right hand is thought to bring believers the Virgin's blessing.

LA MORENETA

The statue of a dark-faced Madonna
and child is venerated in Catalonia.

Nestled high in the rugged hills northwest of Barcelona lies the small town of Montserrat. According to legend, an image of the Virgin Mary was found in a cave here in the year 880 after shepherds had seen bright lights and heard voices in the area. The place rapidly became a Christian pilgrimage site, with churches, chapels, a Benedictine monastery, and a basilica all constructed for the visiting faithful. Most of the complex was destroyed by the French in 1811; the present church was built in the 1850s. La Moreneta is now behind glass, only the golden orb exposed for the faithful to touch. Newlyweds come to ask Mary's blessing, then join other worshipers in prayer and reflection in the adjacent chapel. Flickering votive candles on the way out illuminate a host of personal possessions left by people seeking cures for various ills.

When to Go April 27 is particularly busy, as this is La Moreneta's feast day. The shrine is open year round, but is quieter in winter.

Planning Montserrat is 35 miles (56 km) northwest of Barcelona. It's possible to visit on a day-trip from Barcelona, but stay overnight if you want to explore the site and its natural surroundings thoroughly. Trains to Montserrat leave hourly from Barcelona-Plaça Espanya Station. On arrival at the base of the mountain, you can make the 1,969-ft (600 m) ascent to the monastery on foot, by rack rail, or by cable car. The town lies at just over 4,000 ft (1,220 m), so it is wise to take warm clothing at all times of the year.

Websites www.montserratvisita.com, www.barcelona-tourist-guide.com, www.abadiamontserrat.net

HIGHLIGHTS

■ The Santa Cova, the **sacred cave** where the original image of the virgin was found, is a 40-minute walk from the monastery, along a mountain path lined with religious statues. A chapel now stands on the site.

■ **Mountain trails** surround the monastery, allowing visitors to go exploring on hikes that range from 15 minutes to more than 3 hours. Bring binoculars to admire the views and to spot wildcats, sparrow hawks, peregrine falcons, and other mountain wildlife.

■ The Sant Joan funicular rises farther up the mountain from the monastery to the **Sant Joan chapel**, which has commanding views of the surrounding landscape. The walk back is a 45-minute downhill stroll.

■ The choir school here is the oldest in Europe, and the 50-voice **Escalonia boys choir** sings every day, except Saturday, in the basilica.

EUROPE

SPAIN

CONVENT OF ST. TERESA

The patron saint of Spain, known for her reforming zeal
and miraculous visions, is venerated in the city of her birth.

A ring of 82 semicircular towers and nine gates encircle the old city of Ávila; these walls appear today very much as they did when constructed in the 11th century. A walk along the top of the walls lets you appreciate Ávila as a fortress-city, built to withstand attack by the Moors. Among its "newer" buildings is the Convent of St. Teresa, which was built in 1636 at the birthplace of Teresa de Cepeda y Ahumada, known as St. Teresa of Ávila, or in Ávila simply as "La Santa." The daughter of a wealthy family, Teresa led a pious life, experienced religious ecstasies, wrote several influential books, and played a major role in reforming the Carmelite order of nuns. The naves of the church are adorned with statues of St. Teresa and her friend St. John of the Cross; a chapel within the Baroque church at the convent marks the site where St. Teresa was born. A Sala de Reliquias—relic room—displays St. Teresa's ring finger; after her death, many of her followers believed that her severed hand had the ability to perform miracles. Each year, Ávila hosts a week of religious, civic, and cultural activities to celebrate St. Teresa's feast day, October 15. On that day, a mass is held at the convent and a proclamation is read from the City Hall balcony.

When to Go Anytime except winter, when it is bitterly cold. October 15 is St. Teresa's feast day, when religious festivities combine with concerts, bullfights, and Flamenco Week. Religious festivities also occur during Easter Week (Semana Santa) and on May 2 in honor of San Segundo, the town's patron saint.

Planning Located 70 miles (113 km) northwest of Madrid, Ávila can be easily toured on a day-trip from the capital city. Trains leave from Madrid's Chamartín station, buses from the Estación Sur de Autobuses.

Websites www.spain.info, www.avilaturismo.com

HIGHLIGHTS

■ In the **Monasterio de la Encarnación**, where St. Teresa lived for 27 years, you can visit her cell and a small museum dedicated to her life and writings.

■ Stop to see the 12th-century **Ávila Cathedral**–built soon after the Reconquista in a mixture of Romanesque and Gothic styles.

■ Visit the burial place of **Tomás de Torquemada**, the Grand Inquisitor of the Spanish Inquisition.

■ St. Teresa's tomb is in the nearby town of Alba de Tormes in the **Convento de Carmelitas**. Her heart, which believers claim has not decayed, is also there.

A stained-glass window of St. Teresa at prayer in the Convent of St. Teresa.

THE PILGRIM'S WAY

7

Every visit to a sacred place is a kind of pilgrimage, but in many spiritual traditions the journey itself becomes an act of faith. In Islam, one particular pilgrimage is a religious obligation. Every pious Muslim able to travel aspires, at least once in a lifetime, to join with millions of co-religionists from all over the world on the annual hajj—a demanding but inspiring journey to the holy sites of the Saudi Arabian city of Mecca. Christians make pilgrimages in search of spiritual renewal, physical healing, or as an act of repentance. Penitents climb the rocky mountain of Croagh Patrick in Ireland, often barefoot or on their knees. Others visit the French shrine of St. Bernadette at Lourdes in hopes of miraculous cures. Jews from all over the world come to pray at Jerusalem's Western Wall—the last remnant of King Solomon's Temple, while on the Indonesian island of Java, the eighth-century temple of Borobudur receives a host of pilgrims for the annual celebration of the Buddha's birthday.

Thousands of Muslim pilgrims from all over the world gather for evening prayers at the Grand Mosque in Mecca during the annual hajj, squeezing into every nook and cranny to be close to the Kaaba–Islam's holiest place.

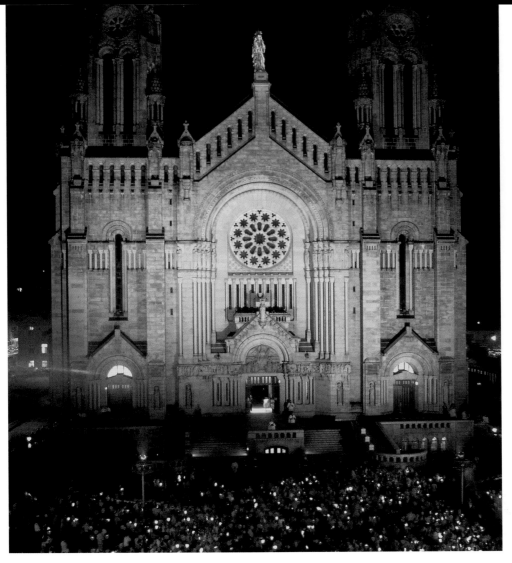

Pilgrims gather in front of the basilica, which houses one of Canada's most visited Christian shrines.

CANADA

STE.-ANNE-DE-BEAUPRÉ

This beautiful basilica built in honor of St. Anne
is one of the oldest pilgrimage sites in North America.

In 1658, during a storm on Canadian waters, French sailors cried out for protection to their patron St. Anne. Because they were spared from shipwreck, they built a chapel in honor of their beloved saint on the bank of the St. Lawrence River to the east of Quebec City, close to the spot where they had landed. Today, the towering Basilica of Ste.-Anne-de-Beaupré, completed in 1926, represents the fifth house of worship on this site dedicated to the woman who, according to Catholic tradition, was the Virgin Mary's mother. More than 1.5 million visitors and worshipers, mainly from North America, go to great lengths to get a glimpse of the 12-foot (3.7 meter) high gilded oak sculpture, atop the facade, of St. Anne embracing her daughter. Some pilgrims offer prayers; others, seeking a miracle, leave flowers, medals, and petitions. As Quebec's patron saint, she is revered by Catholics as a healer, and devotees tell anecdotes of people who were once crippled, paralyzed, or blind leaving the sanctuary cured. Inside the basilica lie piles of canes and crutches, abandoned by those whose bodies she allegedly restored.

When to Go The shrine is open throughout the year and holds daily Mass in several languages. The pilgrimage season runs from June to early September, with the largest annual event held on July 26, the Feast of St. Anne. The museum is open from June to October from 9 a.m. to 5 p.m.

Planning Allow a whole day to see the basilica, museum, and other displays.

Website www.ssadb.qc.ca

HIGHLIGHTS

■ The basilica crowns a complex of several fine attractions, including a **memorial chapel** commemorating an earlier church, which welcomed pilgrims from 1676 to 1876.

■ Summer visitors can pray at the **stations of the cross**—a pathway with fine religious sculpture winding up the hill next to the basilica. Close by is a replica of Rome's **Scala Santa**—the staircase that Jesus Christ is said to have climbed in Pilate's palace and St. Helena later supposedly took from Jerusalem to Rome.

■ The **St. Anne Museum** contains many beautiful works of religious art dedicated to the saint, including the altar of the third church.

■ The basilica's lower floor holds the **Immaculate Conception Chapel**, which has a statue of the Virgin Mary standing under a starry dome and a replica of Michelangelo's "Pietà" in St. Peter's in the Vatican City.

NORTH AMERICA

MEXICO

CABALGATA DE CRISTO REY

A modern horseback pilgrimage in central Mexico
draws cowboys from across the continent.

Every January, thousands of hooves pound the ocher turf of the Mexican central sierra as a procession of cowboys makes its way on horseback to the statue of Cristo Rey del Cubilete on top of Cubilete Mountain, 10.5 miles (17 kilometers) from the city of Guanajuato. The riders wear bright shirts and wide-brimmed hats pulled low over their faces, their spurs glinting and alligator-skin boots glistening in the winter sun. The object of their devotion is the 196-foot (60 meter) high statue of Christ that sits with arms outstretched on top of the mountain. Anticlerical government forces destroyed the original statue in the 20th century, but the figure was rebuilt with donations from Guanajuato's devoted rural population. Beneath the statue is a small chapel where Mass is held daily. In this deeply religious country, a procession that began in 1952 with just 25 riders has grown each year, and numbers are now in the thousands. They come in community and family groups, riding for three or four days through adobe villages and across wide agave-dotted plains in a spiritual reenactment of the journey of the three wise men to welcome the Christ Child. Most travel up the mountain paths on horseback, but some pilgrims complete the climb on their knees.

When to Go The pilgrimage takes place in early January, culminating on Epiphany (January 6).

Planning Respect the harsh climate here. The sun is extremely powerful, but temperatures drop dramatically at night. Afternoons often bring strong winds; so take adequate layers and sunscreen. Guanajuato is 230 miles (370 km) northwest of Mexico City. There are frequent buses from the capital and the journey takes around five hours. It is roughly the same distance from Guadalajara.

Websites www.aboutguanajuato.com, www.whatguanajuato.com, www.guanajuatocapital.com

HIGHLIGHTS

■ On the **eve of Epiphany**, the worshipers bed down beneath the desert sky, light fires, grill meat for their supper, and share tequila. The atmosphere is celebratory, convivial, and emotional.

■ Marking the geographical center of Mexico, the statue is renowned for its **expressive hands**, symbolically stretching out over the whole country.

■ Guanajuato has fantastic examples of **Spanish colonial architecture**. The winding streets, elaborate mansions, and baroque churches are evidence of a city made rich by the silver the conquistadores mined from the neighboring Sierra Madre Mountains from the mid-16th century onward.

A long, colorful cavalcade of pilgrim riders makes the journey to a mountaintop statue of Jesus to celebrate the Feast of Epiphany.

BOM JESUS DA LAPA

This subterranean sanctuary in the Brazilian state of Bahia provides a focus of impassioned devotion for local people.

SOUTH AMERICA

The hot, damp air, profound silence, and raw organic architecture of this natural cathedral create an atmosphere unlike that found in most man-made structures. The interior of the limestone cave features strange rock formations and ancient, oozing stalactites and stalagmites supporting hundreds of religious statues and images. This unusual site of Catholic devotion lies at the foot of a dramatic 300-foot (90 meter) cliff in the small town of Bom (Good) Jesus da Lapa in eastern Brazil. According to legend, a young Portuguese philanderer, Francisco de Mendonça Mar, left Salvador on foot and wandered for many months before finding the cave—and his faith—in the Bahian interior. Here he set out to pray, repent, and live the life of a hermit. Word of his piety spread, and soon rural Brazilians and the incoming silver miners who were flocking to the region came to regard him as a miracle worker. It was not until after Francisco's death in 1722, however, that the cave became a focus of intense devotion. More than 800,000 pilgrims visit each year, arriving on foot and by truck from rural communities throughout the state to ask for intervention, to pray, and to give thanks.

When to Go Pilgrims arrive steadily from May to October, but the most fascinating festivities take place from August 1 to 8, when celebrations include a novena (a devotion that involves praying for nine consecutive days asking for special favors) and a procession. August 5 is Pilgrims' Day, when a huge Mass is held in the cave.

Planning Hotel prices triple during the first week in August—check rates before traveling. It's advisable to book accommodations well in advance to be sure of securing the place of your choice. Buses run the 500 miles (800 km) from Salvador and take around nine hours; there is also a small airport just outside town. You will need to spend a couple of days here to get the flavor of the town and observe the many religious ceremonies and acts of worship. You can combine your stay with a trip covering the interior of Bahia, which has dramatic landscapes, some beautiful villages, and lovely walks.

Website www.braziltour.com

HIGHLIGHTS

■ Explore the mazelike caverns that make up the limestone cathedral. The two main caves of devotion are **Nossa Senhora da Soledade** and the smaller **Senhor Bom Jesus.** A winding tunnel connects the two.

■ Mounting the walls of the Sala dos Milagres, or Cave of the Miracles, are hundreds of **body parts** made from wood or wax. People offer them in supplication for particular cures or miracles and in gratitude for prayers answered. You can buy the little models to hang in the cave for around $4 outside the shrine.

■ The surrounding area is extremely beautiful; you can **hike** into the hills beyond the cave and take **boat trips** along the São Francisco River.

Offerings from pilgrims festoon the Sala dos Milagres (Room of the Miracles).

Some pilgrims find demanding ways to approach the sanctuary. The one on the right is balancing a model of the building on his chest.

CHILE

VIRGEN DE LO VÁSQUEZ

This annual spectacle draws thousands of Christian pilgrims, who find ever more extraordinary ways to show their devotion.

Chile's Feast of the Immaculate Conception is an annual event that one could describe as "extreme pilgrimage." Each December, hundreds of thousands of the faithful arrive in Valparaiso, a port city 58 miles (93 kilometers) northwest of Santiago. From Valparaiso, they make their way 20 miles (32 kilometers) southwest along Route 68 to the sanctuary of the Virgen de Lo Vásquez, which displays a statue of the Virgin Mary dressed in white with a blue cape. The journey itself is not particularly arduous—the labor lies in the devotees' manner of travel. Some walk the last few miles barefoot; some crawl, carrying bunched candles that burn down to stubs; some bear crosses; and some travel the final stages inching along on their backs, huge replica churches strapped to their chests. Tourists join the festivities, lining the streets to marvel at the pilgrims' suffering. After performing their prayers, bruised and bloodied participants can find relief and refreshment at the bazaar. A huge temporary market sprawling along the road past the sanctuary, it sells food, drink, and all kinds of religious offerings. The single-towered shrine, reconstructed in 1913 after an earthquake, is the third to stand on the site. It is elegant, but small, and not designed to accommodate many visitors; so pilgrims must take turns with their prayers.

When to Go The Feast of the Immaculate Conception takes place on December 8.

Planning The feast is a public holiday in Chile, and so almost all normal commercial facilities—excluding the market—shut for the day, and Route 68, which connects Valparaiso and Santiago, is closed to vehicular traffic. Book accommodations well in advance and be prepared for holiday crowds.

Websites www.enjoy-chile.org, www.chile.travel

HIGHLIGHTS

■ The streets and architecture of **Valparaiso** are an attraction in themselves. The city rises up from the harbor at such a sharp incline that pedestrians often use outdoor elevators to transit up and down the steep hills.

■ Give yourself enough time to explore **La Sebastiana**, home of Chile's Nobel Prize-winning poet, Pablo Neruda, and to visit Chile's **Congress** building, which has a visitors' gallery.

■ For a change of pace, visit Valparaiso's twin city, **Viña del Mar**. Just a 20-minute bus ride away, it offers upscale shopping and beaches as a counterpoint to bohemian "Valpo."

SOUTH AMERICA

PERU

PILGRIMAGE FOR THE SNOW STAR

Peru's pre-Columbian culture merges with Catholicism in a spectacular and noisy pilgrimage high in the snowbound Andes.

Every year after the harvest, thousands of pilgrims representing farming communities all over the Andean highlands converge on the Sinakara Valley, perched at an altitude of 15,420 feet (4,700 meters) on the slopes of Mount Ausangate near Cusco, the ancient home of the Quechua, Aymara, and Inca peoples. They come for a three-day festival celebrating the Lord of Qoyllur Rit'i (Snow Star), an ancient mountain god associated with the fertility of the land, at a place where, in 1783, a miraculous vision of Jesus is said to have appeared to a local boy. A Catholic chapel, the Capilla del Señor, marks the spot. Escorted by dancers and musicians, pilgrims trek to the glacier-fringed valley dressed in colors unique to their villages, pitch camp, and settle in for the celebrations. The main ceremony, which honors Jesus in the chapel, incorporates processions of dancers in local costume accompanied by loud music played on Andean flutes. While some people wait to visit the chapel, others venture onto the glaciers to plant crosses and perform age-old Andean rituals. On the second night, a select group of pilgrims known as *ukukus,* or bear men, ascend to the summit of the mountain, where they pay homage to the mountain gods and cut blocks of ice from the glacier, which feeds the headwaters of the Amazon and other rivers that rise in the Andes. After Mass at the chapel everyone sets off for home, carrying the glacial ice to provide holy water to sprinkle on their lands before planting new crops.

When to Go The date of the festival varies from year to year but takes place in late May or early June.

Planning The starting point for the pilgrimage is the village of Mahuayani, about four hours' drive from Cusco. Allow a full day for the journey from Cusco and the trek to the festival site. Organized treks—with a guide, cook, pack animals, supplies, and equipment provided—are available starting from Cusco. The temperature is just above freezing during the day but can drop to 23°F (- 5°C) at night—take plenty of warm clothing.

Websites www.cuscoperu.com, www.thinairoutfitters.com

SOUTH AMERICA

HIGHLIGHTS

■ As well as the ukukus, representing bears, **dancers** in costumes called *pabluchas*, representing alpacas, and other guardians of the mountain spirits, sway in long processions around the Catholic shrine.

■ On the final morning, greet the **colorful procession** returning from the mountain carrying blocks of ice.

■ While in Cusco, visit the **Monasterio y Museo de Arte de Santa Catalina** to find out about how the local art represents a mix of indigenous and Spanish cultures.

Opposite: A select band of pilgrims, their identities concealed beneath costumes and masks, makes a midnight ascent of Mount Ausangate to collect ice from a dangerous glacier. Above left: A pilgrim returns carrying blocks of ice to provide holy water. Above right: Costumed dancers representing mythological characters perform throughout the festival.

A stone stairway leads past statues of the Niou—the guardians of the shrine, literally "two kings"—on the way to Futago-ji Temple.

JAPAN

KUNISAKI PENINSULA PILGRIMAGE

Trek through a precipitous volcanic landscape following a prayer route taken by generations of Japanese monks.

The Japanese call Kunisaki Peninsula the "remote island." This spiny projection, extending into the Seto Inland Sea on the eastern island of Kyushu, came to be as a result of an ancient eruption of the volcanic Mount Futago. So rugged and isolated is the peninsula that it had only limited road access until the second half of the 20th century. In the eighth to 14th centuries this inaccessibility made it of interest to ascetic Buddhists, who built dozens of temples and established a pilgrimage route between them that simply ignored the land's contours, swooping up to every high point, then dropping down to the next place of worship as it circled the 2,360-foot (720 meter) remains of Mount Futago. The original trail has almost vanished, and what remains is a series of penitential—yet rewarding—climbs and descents. Slender ridgetop paths mix thrilling drops with panoramic views across tangled green valleys to the Inland Sea. In places the route follows an ancient highway made of centuries-old paving stones tilted this way and that by tree roots. But more often the way is apparent only to the guide, who leads you up slopes ankle-deep in wildflowers and bracken, or hacks a path through typhoon-felled bamboo.

When to Go March, April, October, and November have the best weather for trekking.

Planning Mount Futago is in Oita Province. Allow three to four days for the circuit. The path is sometimes invisible and the trek largely impossible without local guides. Tour companies send on your luggage by taxi while you take the high road and arrange access to traditional inns—some of which are unaccustomed to foreigner visitors. Trekkers should have a head for heights.

Websites www.walkjapan.com, www.jnto.go.jp, web-japan.org/nipponia

HIGHLIGHTS

■ Pray for a safe journey at **Futago-ji Temple** before the image of the fearsome Fudomyoo, a locally popular deity whose statue appears at several temples en route.

■ Don't miss **Mumyo-bashi**, a slender stone arch across a deep chasm; the fainthearted crawl across on hands and knees.

■ Spend a night with monks at **Monjusen-ji**, a temple perched on a cliff face.

■ Visit **Kumano Magaibutsu**, the oldest and largest Buddhist relief carvings in Japan.

ASIA

INDONESIA

BOROBUDUR

The eighth-century temple of Borobudur is an annual destination for pilgrims celebrating the Buddha's birthday.

Indonesia may be the largest Muslim nation, but it also has one of the world's most important Buddhist shrines—the temple of Borobudur. Just outside the old royal city of Yogyakarta on the island of Java, the stone monument squats amid bright green rice fields with smoldering live volcanoes as a backdrop. Dating from around A.D. 800, the temple has several claims to fame, including being the world's largest Buddhist stupa and the largest stone monument in the southern hemisphere. Built like a step pyramid, with six square and three circular platforms, it represents a mandala—a symbolic representation of the cosmos. Pilgrims follow a winding, 2-mile (3.6 kilometer) route from the base of the temple along corridors and up stairways to the top, on a journey that takes them through the three levels of Buddhist cosmology from Earth to nirvana—Buddhist heaven. Each year, thousands of Buddhists gather at the temple for the culmination of the Vesak pilgrimage celebrating the birth of the Lord Buddha. Setting off in the early evening from Mendut Temple, 5 miles (8 kilometers) away, saffron-robed monks carrying flower offerings walk to Borobudur. As dusk falls, they light candles and begin praying and chanting along the route.

When to Go The temple is open all year. Check the date of the Vesak Festival; it generally falls in May but some years in June.

Planning You can explore the temple in half a day, but will need a week to see all the sights in the area, including Yogyakarta and Prambanan. You can reach Yogyakarta from Bali and Jakarta by air, from Bali by road, or from Jakarta by rail. Borobudur is an hour by car from Yogyakarta. Amanjiwo Resort, a 35-suite luxury hotel with remarkable stone architecture inspired by the ancient temple, is a short drive from the ancient ruins.

Websites www.borobudurpark.com, www.amanjiwo.com

ASIA

HIGHLIGHTS

■ Lining the route up the terraces are 1,460 carved **reliefs** illustrating scenes from the life of the Buddha and of human desires that good Buddhists strive to overcome. They serve as a spiritual guide for pilgrims to study as they ascend the temple.

■ Eleven miles (18 km) east of Yogyakarta, **Prambanan**'s ninth-century Hindu complex, part of the Borobudur archaeological park, has three towering *candi* (temples) covered in intricate stone sculpture.

■ Nightly from May to October, 250 actors and a full gamelan orchestra perform a **stupendous open-air production** of the Hindu epic the *Ramayana* on a stage beside the Prambanan ruins.

Seventy-two stupas, each containing a statue of the Buddha, occupy Borobudur's top platform.

Pilgrims come from all over Tibet to circumambulate Mount Kawakarpo.

CHINA/TIBET

MOUNT KAWAKARPO

A sacred destination for Tibetan Buddhists, Mount Kawakarpo, or Snow White Mountain, is also a spectacularly rewarding trek.

Deqin is the last stop in China's Yunnan Province before the Tibet Autonomous Region, and it has the feeling of a border town. Hairy-faced yaks amble down a street packed with Tibetan farmers who have come to complete the *kora*—or circuit—around Yunnan's highest peak, the 22,112-foot (6,740 meter) Mount Kawakarpo. Buddhists worldwide revere the mountain as the physical embodiment of the Buddha's mind, and there are two pilgrimage routes from which to choose. The inner route you can complete in a day or so with transportation to take you to and from the trailhead. This route passes the Xidang Hot Springs, the Sacred Waterfalls, and the impressive Mingyong Glacier. The 186-mile (300 kilometer) outer route takes the pilgrim on a hard but rewarding journey through alpine meadows and forest groves, and up steep, scree-covered tracks to 13,000-foot (4,000 meter) passes. The wondrous desolation of these passes is relieved by the hundreds of prayer flags draped around the shrines. The mountain is a virgin peak, which no one has ever scaled successfully, but the Tibetan pilgrims have no interest in climbing. They believe the circumambulation can earn them a better life in their next incarnation.

When to Go Visit from May to June or September to October. Fall has the clearest, driest hiking weather.

Planning The inner route takes anywhere from one to five days, depending on how you approach the trek. Allow 12 days or more for the outer route. Trekking companies offer packages leaving from Kunming that include stops in Lijiang, to explore its old town, and Gyalthang on the way to the trek starting point.

Websites www.khampacaravan.com, www.snowlion.com

HIGHLIGHTS

■ Look out for the old **caravan paths** as you drive toward the trailhead on the inner route. On these dusty roads, the muleteers of old used to carry tea and textiles to trade between Lhasa, Kunming, and Darjeeling.

■ Spend time at the **historic caravan stopping point** of Gyalthang, located at over 10,000 feet (3,300 meters). This ethnically diverse town, set in an area of great natural beauty, has customs and dialects found nowhere else. While acclimatizing to the altitude, you can visit the 17th-century Sumtsenling Monastery and the nearby Gyalwa Ringa Temple.

■ Try some local **yak butter tea**—it slips down better if you think of it as a thin cheese soup.

ASIA

INDIA

SABARIMALA

Every year millions of pilgrims trek through the jungle of Kerala to the remote hilltop shrine of Lord Ayyappa.

On a remote, forested hilltop at Sabarimala in the Western Ghats of Kerala is a temple dedicated to Lord Ayyappa. Born from the union of Lord Siva and Mohini, Lord Vishnu's female incarnation, Ayyappa is to Hindus a symbol of religious unity. Each January, millions of pilgrims—mostly men and a few older women—climb the hill barefoot. As they near the Patinettampadi—18 holy steps up to the temple—they chant Ayyappa's name in ever rising tones, and the whole mountain reverberates with the sound of their fervor. Hindus consider each pilgrim to be a representation of the Lord himself, having achieved this status through observance of rules of cleanliness and self-denial for 41 days preceding the journey. On reaching the temple, the pilgrims wait—sometimes days—to glimpse Lord Ayyappa's statue in the inner sanctuary. Sabarimala's foremost event is Makara Jyothi (usually on January 14), when a scion of the Raja of Pandalam in a palanquin brings the sacred jewels of Lord Ayyappa to the temple and hands them to the priest, who places them on the divine image and performs a sacred ritual to complete the ceremony. Devotees believe that, at the same moment, the gods perform the same rite to worship Ayyappa in the hills northeast of the temple, where a brilliant burst of light—the Jyothi—will appear. Viewing it is said to be a gateway to bliss.

When to Go The temple is open mid-November to mid-January, and for a few days a month during the rest of the year.

Planning The temple is open to people of all faiths, except women between the ages of ten and 50. Pamba—where the 2.5-mile (4 km) climb to the temple begins—is 8 miles (13 km) from the city of Chalakkayam but is the closest that cars and buses can get to Sabarimala. Some pilgrims reach Pampa by hiking along mountain trails from Erumeli (a distance of about 31 miles/50 km).

Websites www.sabarimala.org, www.ayyappa.com

HIGHLIGHTS

■ Pilgrims perform **Neyyabhishekam**, a ritual pouring of sacred ghee on the idol of Lord Ayyappa, to symbolize the merging of Jeevatma (the soul) with Paramatma (the infinite).

■ Each evening the temple's annually selected chief priest, the *mel santhi*, sings the *Harivarasanam*, a **lullaby composed for Lord Ayyappa**, before closing the temple doors.

■ Visit the shrine of **Vavurswami**, a Muslim warrior whom Ayyappa defeated and subdued, although they later became close associates.

■ At the shrines of the serpent god and goddess, musicians and dancers satisfy the deities with a **snake dance**, so as to protect devotees from harmful bites.

Devotees of Lord Ayyappa perform a ritual dance on the journey to Sabarimala.

NEPAL

SWAYAMBHUNATH STUPA

Kathmandu's Swayambhunath attracts a mix of Buddhists, Hindus, and tourists to its golden shrine.

Perched on a solitary hill on the western edge of Kathmandu is the golden shrine of Swayambhunath. It has been a place of pilgrimage and prayer for at least 2,000 years and is now a totemic symbol of Nepal. To reach the shrine, many devotees and secular visitors clamber up the 365 steps of the eastern stairway through a grove of trees inhabited by quiescent monks, souvenir sellers, and assorted simians who give the place its colloquial name—the Monkey Temple. Affording what many believe is the best view of the Kathmandu Valley, the present shrine is one of Nepal's oldest Buddhist temples. King Vrsadeva erected it in the fifth century A.D., around the time that the Roman Empire was coming to an end. It is probable that an earlier temple existed on the site, which was then an island in a lake that filled most of the valley. According to legend, a single lotus grew out of this lake, and when the lake drained away the plant magically morphed into a hill and the flower into the famous stupa. The name Swayambhu (Self-Created) derives from this ancient myth. Nowadays, the crowded temple precinct throbs with activity as peasants from the nearby rice fields, pilgrims who have ventured from far afield, yellow-robed monks spinning copper prayer wheels, and camera-clad tourists snapping photos explore the many buildings and statues around the stupa. Swayambhunath is sacred to Hindus as well as Buddhists, and several whitewashed Hindu shrines lie scattered among the Buddhist ones.

When to Go The weather is best suited to sightseeing in spring and fall. It's best to visit Swayambhunath in the early morning, when the temple precinct hosts more religious devotees than tourists.

Planning To reach the temple either drive or take a taxi to the western entrance at the top of the hill or walk up the stairway on the eastern side. An hour is enough time to see the temple grounds, but you will need at least half a day to get a full sense of Swayambhunath's place in Nepalese religion and culture.

Websites www.welcomenepal.com, www.nepal.com, www.hotelvajra.com

HIGHLIGHTS

■ The gold-plated **central stupa** is rich in symbolism: the whitewashed dome at the base represents the world; the eyes signify the wisdom of looking within oneself; the "question mark" nose is the Nepali symbol for the number one, representing the unity of the cosmos; and the 13 gold tiers symbolize the path to enlightenment.

■ The **Harati Devi Temple** is dedicated to the Hindu goddess of smallpox and other epidemics. This pagoda-style shrine reflects the way in which the Nepalis have blended aspects of Buddhism and Hinduism to produce a unique view of the cosmos.

■ Climb to the roof of the *gompa* (monastery prayer room) for a **bird's-eye view** of the temple grounds. Farther afield, the **rooftop Pagoda Bar** at the nearby Hotel Vajra is an excellent perch from which to contemplate the temple mount over afternoon tea or sunset drinks.

■ About a ten-minute walk from Swayambhunath, the **National Museum of Nepal** contains many of the nation's religious and artistic treasures, including exquisite wooden sculptures, paintings, and metalwork.

Opposite: A pair of stone footprints near the bottom of the eastern stairs are said to be those of either the Buddha or the Bodhisattva Manjusri, who made the site a place of pilgrimage. Above left: Statues and shrines line the stairs up the wooded hillside. Above right: The central stupa has a commanding view of Kathmandu and the surrounding mountains.

A royal male elephant carrying a casket symbolizing the Tooth Relic leads the Kandy Perahera Festival procession.

SRI LANKA

TEMPLE OF THE SACRED TOOTH

This lakeside temple is a major pilgrimage destination and the focus of an annual festival famed for its colorful exuberance.

In A.D. 313, a princess called Hemamala is said to have smuggled the Sacred Tooth—the Buddha's upper left canine, retrieved by devotees from his funeral pyre in India—into Sri Lanka, where Buddhists treated it as a precious relic. According to lore, whoever holds the tooth holds the country. After becoming king in 1592, Wimaladharmasuriya I moved the relic to his new capital, Kandy. Its initial home was a wooden temple, which later gave way to the current one. Over the years, the tooth took on additional significance as a symbol of Sri Lankan independence. The Temple of the Sacred Tooth inside the old royal compound is now the focus of daily worship. Continuously open, it is chockablock with devotees day and night stoking joss sticks and oil lamps, donating food and other offerings to the shrine and the monks, or staring in wonder at the golden casket housing the world's most famous tooth. Each year, the Perahera Festival takes over the town. This ten-day Relic of the Tooth celebration includes a parade with dancers, drummers, and around a hundred silk-clad elephants strung with electric lights. It's a jolly spectacle but one undertaken with deep religious devotion.

When to Go At around 1,600 ft (500 m) above sea level, Kandy has a cool, highland climate offering year-round relief from the steamy Sri Lankan coast. The Perahera Festival is in July or August; the exact date varies according to the phases of the moon.

Planning Allow two to three days to cover all the temples, palaces, and museums in Kandy and its environs. If you want to scale Adam's Peak nearby, several adventure tourism agencies offer guided treks.

Websites www.daladamaligawa.org, www.srilankaecotourism.com

HIGHLIGHTS

■ The **Relic of the Sacred Tooth** lies in a jeweled casket on a throne within the shrine, which has two huge elephant tusks guarding it.

■ The former dwelling places of the Sinhalese monarchs now serve other purposes. The King's Palace is now the **Archaeological Museum**, while the superb **Kandy National Museum** was once the Queen's Palace.

■ Next to the temple, the Alut Maligawa Pavilion of the Sri Dalada Museum showcases **historical documents, artifacts, and gifts** from prominent people offered to the Relic of the Tooth over the years. Among the museum's other treasures are royal garments, ancient murals, silver caskets, and Buddha statues.

ASIA

IRAQ

Shrine of Imam Husayn

The magnificent mausoleum of this holy martyr
is a focus of religious passion for Shiite pilgrims.

Every day, thousands of pilgrims make their way through the narrow streets of Karbala' in central Iraq, across a broad, palm-shaded plaza, and through vast arched gateways into the Shrine of Imam Husayn. This is one of Shiite Islam's holiest sites. The shrine's golden dome and twin minarets hover above the grave of Husayn ibn 'Ali—the revered second grandson of the Prophet Muhammad and the third Shiite imam—slain by Arab rivals during the Battle of Karbala' in A.D. 680. Visits to the grave began immediately after his death, and a mosque soon went up over it. In later years, the shrine was destroyed several times by fire, pillage, and religious upheaval. Construction of the present building began in the 11th century, and it has been much enriched ever since. Because Imam Husayn is an enduring symbol of liberation and redemption through suffering, his tomb has become a focus of overt grieving, self-flagellation, and even bloody reenactments of the massacre in which he fell. Processions to the shrine can be noisy, with black-clad devotees clapping, shouting, ululating, and beating their chests at what Shiites believe to be one of the Gates of Heavenly Paradise.

When to Go Certain times are especially crowded: more than a million devotees can fill the shrine precinct and surrounding streets during annual religious festivals, such as Ashura and Arba'in. On 10 Muharram in the Islamic lunar calendar, the day of Ashura commemorates the martyrdom of Husayn ibn 'Ali and his 72 companions. Arba'in is 40 days later. Saddam Hussein banned observance of both holy days; public celebration only restarted in 2003 after his regime fell.

Planning Karbala' and the Shrine of Imam Husayn are an easy day-trip from Baghdad, which frequently takes in the very important Shrine of Imam 'Ali in Najaf. Security concerns in Iraq are ongoing. Visitors wanting to travel to Karbala' should check on the situation with the U.S. State Department or their Foreign Ministry. Make the trip only with an experienced local guide.

Websites www.al-islam.org, www.atlastours.net

HIGHLIGHTS

■ Beneath the golden dome, the **tomb of Imam Husayn** is a study in early Islamic architecture. The opulent gold-and-silver structure has metal walls etched with ornate geometric patterns.

■ At the opposite end of central Karbala's huge plaza, the **Shrine of 'Abbas** holds the grave of Imam Husayn's half-brother, who also died at the Battle of Karbala'.

■ To Shiites, **Najaf**, 30 miles (48 km) south of Karbala', is the world's holiest site after Mecca and Medina. Covered in gold bricks and rebuilt in the 16th century, the **Shrine of Imam 'Ali** covers the tomb of Muhammad's cousin and son-in-law. To Shiites he was the first legitimate imam or caliph; a violent dispute over succession after his death led to the Sunni-Shiite split.

A group of Shiite women visit the shrine of Imam Husayn.

ISRAEL

WESTERN WALL

One of Judaism's most sacred sites, for centuries the Western
(or Wailing) Wall has drawn Jews to pray alongside its massive stones.

The Western Wall was once part of the Second Temple, built in 515 B.C. on the site of the ancient First Temple that Solomon intended to be the final resting place of the Ark of the Covenant. Jews still lament the loss of their Second Temple, and this gave rise to the name Wailing Wall. Chiseled rocks seem to vibrate beneath any hand that presses against the wall. Perhaps it is from centuries of oral prayers or the colorfully written pleas stuffed between the wall's cracks. Littering the ground are random scraps of paper from the stone's crevices, now tightly sealed with newer messages. The exposed wall is only about 187 feet (57 meters) long and sits at the end of a large square platform. A remarkable engineering feat, the wall—around 62 feet (19 meters) high—is made of limestone boulders, some weighing 100 tons, joined without mortar. Around 19 B.C., King Herod enlarged the Second Temple, but the Western Wall is the only part to survive Roman destruction in A.D. 20. Today, the area is almost always full of devotees. Men pray on one side, women on the other, each trying to touch the giant pitted stones. The wall is a coveted spot for Jews and Muslims and has been the object of many bitter disputes—hence the armed guards who patrol the area. Some visitors pray here for hours, some for just a few minutes. A few depart smiling; others leave crying. But all seem to leave grateful to have finally stood there.

When to Go The wall is always open but it's best to go during the day. Armed Israeli guards are on patrol and search visitors. Electronic items are banned on Saturdays. The weather is usually pleasant all year.

Planning Your mood will decide how long you stay. You may wish to bring pieces of paper and a pen to leave words of thanks or a prayer. Sometimes there are tiny spaces left by former messages that have decayed and disintegrated. It's easier for tall people to find spaces since colorful messages fill the middle and bottom. Be respectful of those who are praying. People usually move aside or try to make room, but some won't budge. Pushing is unacceptable. Expect thousands on Jewish holidays. Men must wear a yarmulke (skullcap) or hat, and women a long skirt. The custom is to walk away from the wall backward.

Websites www.thekotel.org, www.goisrael.com

ASIA

HIGHLIGHTS

■ On **Tisha B'Av** (in July or August), tens of thousands of Jews throng the Western Wall to mourn the sacking of the First and Second Temples.

■ Explore the **Western Wall tunnel**. Excavated between 1967 and 1988, it reveals parts of the Western Wall that are currently underground, as well as a complex of Roman and medieval vaults. Book guided tours in advance.

■ Visit the nearby **Jewish Quarter**, which brings to life the rich historical period of the Second Temple, more than 2,000 years ago. Here you will find Herodian mansions and four Sephardic synagogues, all restored. In the most magnificent of the synagogues the Sephardic chief rabbi used to be appointed.

Opposite: Crevices in the Western Wall overflow with messages delivered in person—or even sent by fax or email. Above: Tens of thousands of Orthodox Jews gather at the wall for the Blessing of the Priests during the festival of Sukkot. This commemorates the wandering of the Israelites in the desert after their exodus from Egypt.

HOLY SEPULCHRE CHURCH

In Jerusalem's Old City, the world's holiest Christian site has survived destruction three times—and centuries of rivalry between sects.

ust inside the entrance, devoted Christians touch and kiss the worn, rose-hued slab called the Stone of Unction. Along with some historians, they believe this is where Jesus' body was prepared for burial after he died. In the church's center, priests—Catholic, Orthodox, and Armenian Apostolic—hold services at different times. Crowds of tourists wander under the rotunda and through the vast multilevel church, with its tombs, Byzantine wall etchings, and other artifacts. Most visitors come to climb the steps leading to the Rock of Golgotha (also called Calvary), now in the Greek Orthodox section, where Jesus died on the cross, according to the New Testament. It was to enshrine Golgotha that Constantine the Great, Rome's first Christian emperor, commissioned the basilica in A.D. 326. It withstood fires in 614 and 1808, and destruction by the caliph in 1009. Rebuilding work by the Crusaders onward enabled the church to survive and expand, and today it dates mainly from about 1810. Every day, Christians kneel under an opening at Golgotha's altar, which is smothered almost garishly in icons. There they pray and approach the spot where Jesus uttered his last words. A few steps away the Chapel of Adam enshrines the side of the same rock, that some say split as Jesus died. What appear to be bloodstains speck the tall stone. The Gospels leave no doubt about the crucifixion site, but no one can be sure if the cave nearby was Jesus' tomb—though it is likely because of its proximity to Calvary.

When to Go The church is open 5 a.m.-9 p.m, April-September, and 4 a.m.-7 p.m., October-March.

Planning Allot plenty of time to visit. Even an entire day may not be enough. The church is always busy. Easter Mass is a high point of the year and includes a procession of clergy through Jerusalem.

Websites www.goisrael.com, www.bibleplaces.com

HIGHLIGHTS

■ Attend a **service.** The church is seat of the Greek Orthodox patriarchate of Jerusalem, although various Christian sects are responsible for different parts of the church. The Greek Orthodox church has the most rights and services, followed by the Armenian Apostolic and Roman Catholic churches, while the Coptic, Ethiopian, and Syriac Orthodox churches have the least.

■ Five of the 14 **stations of the cross** along the Via Dolorosa (the Way of Suffering) are inside the church. Pick up an information pack here about the other nine. While most are within Jerusalem's old city walls, the actual crucifixion was outside the city.

■ Look out for the **rotting ladder** below a window in the upper part of the entrance. A testament to interchurch rivalry, it has been there since at least the 19th century as the sects cannot agree what to do with it.

For many centuries Orthodox Christians have gathered in the Church of the Holy Sepulchre to celebrate the Orthodox Easter ceremony of the Miracle of the Holy Fire.

Hajj pilgrims walk around the Kaaba seven times and try to kiss it, but not everyone can do so because of the huge crowds. Pointing at it is an acceptable second best.

SAUDI ARABIA

THE HAJJ

A great social leveler, the hajj unites Muslims of all colors, nationalities, and classes in the oneness of God and of mankind.

Mecca abounds in historical and religious significance. Muslims the world over turn in its direction five times a day when praying, and millions visit to perform the annual pilgrimage, the hajj, but it was sacred even before Muhammad's birth around A.D. 570. Adam and Abraham, potent figures from the Abrahamic traditions, have strong links to the city. Abraham's life was a series of trials of his faith in God and these inspire some of the ceremonies that Muslims perform during the hajj, such as sacrificing a sheep. Muslims with the means and ability are expected to visit once in a lifetime for the hajj, known as the fifth pillar of Islam. Although now empty, an ancient granite cube, the Kaaba, has housed a series of religious artifacts over the centuries and incorporates a stone—a meteorite, according to Islamic tradition—in its walls. Within the Holy Mosque, or Masjid al Haram, and covered by a black cloth embroidered in gold, it is the centerpiece of the hajj. Pilgrims begin and end their hajj by walking around it seven times. Alongside religion, commerce has always been a core part of Mecca's activities, and trade was crucial to its development. The city, which had a natural well, was a stop on the caravan route from the Nile Valley to the Mediterranean Sea. In 2007, around four million people descended on Mecca, which has modernized rapidly to meet the demand for better amenities.

When to Go Although the hajj is the obligatory pilgrimage, Muslims can visit Mecca at any time of the year for *umrah* (the "lesser" pilgrimage) or just to visit friends or family. Mecca is closed to non-Muslims.

Planning The minimum stay to complete the religious ritual cycle for either the hajj or umrah is three days. The longest visit allowed is one month. Visitors must arrange trips through a travel agency approved by the Saudi government; independent travel is not possible. To make the most of the hajj, allow for several months' spiritual preparation. Women under 45 need a male escort.

Websites www.saudiembassy.net, www.hajinformation.com, www.hajjguide.org

HIGHLIGHTS

■ Holy water from the **Zamzam Well** slakes thirst as well, it is said, as sating hunger and curing illness. The well was supposedly revealed to Abraham's slave and concubine, Hagar, by their baby son, Ismail. At the end of the hajj, millions of pilgrims carry the water home in 2.5-gallon (10 liter) jerry cans.

■ **Jabal al Nur**, to the northeast, is the site of the cave where Muslims believe Muhammad received the first verse of the Koran from the archangel Gabriel.

■ Mecca glories in its ancient merchant traditions and is famed for its **shopping malls and bazaars**; the alleys leading off the main courtyard heave with stalls. Gold jewelry is a good buy.

ASIA

Ten Historic Pilgrimages

Follow in the footsteps of pilgrims past, journeying through remote, isolated landscapes or historic cities in search of peace.

❶ March for Jobs & Freedom, Washington, D.C.

Photos of the 1963 March on Washington for Jobs and Freedom show a sea of people flooding the National Mall and enjoying the festive mood. More than 250,000 joined the rally between the Washington Monument and the Lincoln Memorial, some having traveled up from the Deep South. Their reward—Rev. Dr. Martin Luther King, Jr.'s "I Have A Dream" speech—is surely one of the most stirring orations ever delivered.

Planning The National Mall and Memorial Park is open 24 hours a day. A ranger is on hand from 9:30 a.m. to 11:30 p.m. to answer questions. www.crmvet.org, www.africanamericans.com

❷ Mormon Pioneer Trail, United States

In 1846, more than 70,000 Mormons, driven by a wish to find somewhere they could follow their creed in peace, traveled west from Nauvoo, Illinois, to Salt Lake City, Utah. Using wagons and handcarts, they crossed 1,300 miles (2,092 km) of rough terrain. The lucky ones reached Utah in 1847.

Planning The trail passes through Iowa, Illinois, Nebraska, Utah, and Wyoming; Wyoming has some original trail segments that are still unspoiled. www.nps.gov/mopi

❸ Bodh Gaya, Gaya District, Bihar, India

India's spiritual center of Buddhism is Bodh Gaya, whose *bodhi* (fig) tree, it is said, sheltered the meditating Buddha Gautama for seven weeks in his quest for enlightenment. Today the tree (a descendant of the original) and the nearby pyramid-shaped Mahabodhi Temple are among Buddhism's holiest sites.

Planning Visit in October to April. Nearby Patna is also associated with Buddha, and its museum houses his ashes. www.buddhanet.net

❹ Salt Satyagraha, India

In 1930, Mahatma Gandhi set out with 78 followers from Sabarmati Ashram to walk to the sea at Dandi, Gujarat, in nonviolent protest against the British salt tax. The 248-mile (400 km) Salt Satyagraha march lasted from March 12 to April 5 and instigated widespread resistance to British rule of India.

Planning The Sabarmati Ashram houses a museum of Gandhi's life. Both are open daily 8:30 a.m.-6 p.m. www.saltmarch.org.in

❺ St. Paul Trail, Turkey

This rugged 310-mile (500 km) trail partly follows St. Paul's footsteps as he set out to preach Christianity. Leading from Perge or Aspendos, both near Antalya, to Antioch in Pisidia, near Yalvaç, the route forges through dramatic landscapes—from fragrant forests of pine to crystal clear lakes.

Planning Red and white blazes mark the paths. www.stpaultrail.com

❻ Route of Saints, Kraków, Poland

Nowhere else in Europe mingles religion and royalty more richly than Wawel Hill. The dreamy 14th-century cathedral has 18 chapels and an alluring cluster of tombs—one of Poland's patron, St. Stanislaus. The cathedral museum has a 500-year-old robe, Kmita's chasuble, embroidered with intricate scenes from his life. Away from the hill, follow Kraków's Route of Saints, linking its 16 beautiful churches.

Planning Climb the cathedral's Sigismund Tower to see its famed bell, tolled only on special occasions and audible 50 miles (80 km) away. www.wawel.krakow.pl, www.cracow.org

❼ Canterbury Cathedral, Kent, England

A pilgrimage to Canterbury pays homage to a beloved saint, a glorious cathedral, a giant work of literature, and simple human history. Archbishop Thomas Becket's murder on the altar by four knights of Henry II in 1170 almost immediately secured his fame as a miracle worker. His shrine drew pilgrims seeking cures—or simply a roistering good time—as immortalized in Chaucer's *Canterbury Tales*.

Planning Take any route you like. Although Chaucer's pilgrims set out from the erstwhile Tabard Inn in London's Southwark, he did not disclose their route. The cathedral has tour guides. www.canterbury-cathedral.org

❽ Eleanor Crosses, England

Devoted to Eleanor of Castile, his queen and the mother of his 17 children, Edward I was distraught when she died of a sudden fever in 1290. He had her body carried from Lincoln to London, 108 miles (174 km) south, for the funeral. He ordered a memorial cross to be built wherever the cortege rested. One even gave its name to London's official center, Charing Cross.

Planning Of the 12 original crosses, just three remain—at Geddington, Hardingstone (Northamptonshire), and Waltham Cross (Hertfordshire). www.historic-uk.com/DestinationsUK/EleanorCrosses.htm

❾ St. Patrick's Footsteps, Ireland

Retracing St. Patrick's steps in Ireland is serious spiritual—and physical—exercise. You can undertake an austere retreat on the island of Lough Derg, or you can climb—barefoot is the painful custom—Croagh Patrick. But other sites associated with him require less effort to visit, such as the Northern Irish town of Downpatrick, with his grave, near the ancient Down Cathedral, and a museum with an exhibition dedicated to the saint.

Planning Start at Campbell's Pub in Murrisk, County Mayo. www.loughderg.org, www.saintpatrickscountry.com

❿ Moffat Mission, Northern Cape, South Africa

In 1838, missionary Rev. Robert Moffat set up his thatched-roof "Cathedral of the Kalahari," aiming to convert the locals to Christianity. He arduously translated the Bible into Setswana, printing it on a press still in use at the mission.

Planning The mission is open to the public daily. To trace Moffat's steps, read his *Missionary Labours and Scenes in Southern Africa* or *Rivers of Water in a Dry Place*. www.places.co.za

Founded by St. Augustine in A.D. 597, Canterbury Cathedral continues to welcome all worshipers, many of whom come to pay homage at the site of St. Thomas Becket's martyrdom.

Masjid al Nabawi

The Saudi city of Medina is a popular if not
mandatory stop on the way to or from the hajj.

ASIA

A s the burial place of Muhammad and the city where the Prophet and his followers fled after attacks against them in Mecca, Medina is the second holiest site in Islam to Sunnis and Shiites alike. Like Mecca, it allows only Muslims to enter, and millions visit each year to pray at the Masjid al Nabawi (Prophet's Mosque). This act is said to be worth more than a thousand prayers at any other mosque, even though it is not part of the hajj nor a duty for Muslims. The image of the mosque, with its distinctive green dome, adorns prayer mats in Muslim homes, making it instantly recognizable to believers. A lack of compulsion—together with a freedom from ritual—makes the mood here less chaotic. It is also easier to appreciate Islam's diversity because, unlike at Mecca, pilgrims wear their normal clothes. Most of the current mosque dates from the 19th and 20th centuries. Muhammad, who built the original, lies buried under the green central dome, beside the first two caliphs, Abu Bakr and Umar. Prayer and reflection at the mosque start before sunrise, lasting throughout the day, giving way to socializing, eating, and shopping after dark. Increased visitor numbers have led to an ambitious expansion of the mosque, which is far bigger than it was during the era of Muhammad, who died in A.D. 632. It can now hold more than half a million worshipers, and it uses technology—such as Teflon umbrellas—to counter the blasting heat of summer.

When to Go Muslims can visit Medina any time of the year, although the days before and after the hajj are the most crowded. Ramadan, the month of fasting, is also a busy period.

Planning Two or three days are long enough to see the major sites. Avoid the hottest months, June through September. Medina is less than an hour by air from Jeddah, or about four hours by car.

Websites www.al-islam.org, www.saudiembassy.net

HIGHLIGHTS

■ Opposite the Masjid al Nabawi, the stark **Jannat al Baqi Cemetery** shelters the remains of several early Muslim leaders.

■ The **Masjid al Qiblatain** (Mosque of the Two Qiblahs), 2 miles (3.2 km) northwest of the Masjid al Nabawi, is unique in the Muslim world. Marking the shift in prayer direction, or *qiblah*, from Jerusalem to Mecca in Islam's earliest days—ordered to Muhammad in a vision—it has two mihrabs (prayer niches), one pointing to Jerusalem, the other to Mecca.

■ The **Tomb of Hamza bin 'Abdul Muttalib**, 3 miles (5 km) north of Medina, honors Muhammad's uncle and close adviser, who died at the Battle of Uhud in 625, one of the first battles in the history of Islam.

The Masjid al Nabawi has ten minarets, more than any other mosque in the world. It initially had none but various rulers added them in expansion projects over the years.

According to legend, St. George personally asked King Lalibela to build a church dedicated to him.

ETHIOPIA

LALIBELA ROCK CHURCHES

Ethiopia has been a Christian land since the fourth century—these rock-hewn churches rank among its greatest architectural treasures.

Hewn from red volcanic rock high in the mountains of Ethiopia, the stately churches of Lalibela stand beside a traditional village crowded with beehive huts. The location is remote and isolated, but these rocky slopes gazing out over huge horizons of green and brown foothills brim with people. Generations of priests, resplendent in their robes and with ornamental crosses in hand, tend the churches, while crowds of pilgrims come to worship. Follow in their footsteps and you'll pass along deep corridors, carved downward into the cliffs, leading to these medieval monuments. Legend has it that their builder 800 years ago was a pious king, Lalibela, seeking to create a new Jerusalem, a place of pilgrimage, here in the highlands. Recent research suggests their history is much older, stretching back to the seventh century. The most imposing of the 11 main churches has the shape of a giant monolithic cross, rising from a pit 36 feet (11 meters) deep, with its roof at ground level. Walk into the candlelit interior, and you'll find columns and grottoes richly decorated with Christian images alongside the church's—and Ethiopia's—patron, St. George, slaying a dragon.

When to Go Just after the rains in October is an especially good time to visit, when Ethiopia is vividly verdant and carpeted with wildflowers. Try to visit during a key festival, such as T'imk'et, in mid-January, but beware that you'll need to book early to secure accommodations and flights.

Planning Allow two to three days to see the main highlights, or longer if you wish to explore further and properly soak up the atmosphere. Most of the churches are unlit—remember to take a flashlight with batteries. Visiting all the churches entails much walking, often up steep hills. If you are going for a festival, note that Ethiopia has its own calendar. All dates given here are in the Western calendar.

Websites www.perillos.com, www.tourismethiopia.org

HIGHLIGHTS

■ Attend a **festival**. Ethiopian Christmas (January 7 in the Western calendar), Easter (April or May), and above all, T'imk'et (Epiphany, January 19), are incredibly colorful and exuberant times to visit. Crowds of the faithful, in bright white or multicolored gowns, arrive at Lalibela from all points on the horizon to chant and sway in time to traditional music.

■ Go for a trek. Put on your walking boots or hire a mule and head off into the surrounding mountains. See some local villages, discover remote historical wonders like the **Church of Ashetun Mariam**, and sate yourself with vast panoramas.

■ Attend a **church service** and marvel at the architecture while priests chant from ancient tomes and censers sweep frankincense into the air.

■ The holiest church, the **Selassie Crypt**, said to have once held the Ark of the Covenant, is so sacred that few but senior priests have ever entered it.

AMBOHIMANGA

This hilltop destination has been a sacred center
for the Malagasy for more than 500 years.

AFRICA

A site of spiritual and nationalistic pilgrimage, the Royal Hill of Ambohimanga lies on the peak of one of the 12 sacred hills surrounding Madagascar's capital, Antananarivo. Also known as the Blue Hill, it was the ancient seat of the Merina Kingdom. Here King Andrianampoinimerina (a somewhat abbreviated version of his official name, meaning "the beloved prince of Imerina who surpasses the reigning prince")—or Nampoina for short—ruled from 1787 to 1810, uniting factions from neighboring regions and enforcing the abolition of slavery. His success paved the way for his son Radama I to unify the island country and become Madagascar's first recognized king. The relics of this ancient, verdant city include the *rova* (royal enclosure), burial sites, a natural spring, pools, a forest, and the *fidasiana* (gathering place). King Nampoina's tall and narrow wooden house stands majestically near his queen's summer residence and the sacred lake of Amparihy, reserved for the *fandroana* (royal bathing) rituals. In Malagasy tradition, ancestors have power over the living. You can often see pilgrims approaching the sacred enclosure barefoot—so as not to soil the sacred earth—and taking symbolic cleansing showers before ritual ceremonies.

When to Go April-May and September-November are the best times to visit. Avoid the January-March cyclone season.

Planning Ambohimanga is 12 miles (19 km) north of Antananarivo (locally known as Tana). You'll need a day at Ambohimanga Hill to explore the rova and surrounding area. Take a bus from the northern bus station for the 45-minute ride. You can hire guides from near the royal enclosure's main entrance—set a price before you start your tour. No alcohol is allowed into the royal enclosure. The private lemur park at the moated village of Soavinandrimanitra is a 30-minute walk from Ambohimanga.

Website www.air-mad.com

HIGHLIGHTS

■ Marvel at the **massive stone disk** at the enclosure's entrance—it took 40 men to maneuver the rock into the doorway to seal the entrance.

■ Look out for animist **sacrificial altars** throughout the enclosure—evidence of a society with deep-rooted beliefs in *fady* (taboo), *tody* (karma), and *tsiny* (negative forces).

■ In Malagasy tradition, ancestors watch over the living. You can pray to the **spirit of Nampoina** in the sacred northeast corner of his house. You must enter it with your right foot first and leave with your left one first.

■ Walk round to **Ambatomiantendro Rock** to see the grid of *fanorona*—the traditional Malagasy board game—etched in the stone.

Until the French occupation of 1895, foreigners were forbidden from passing through this or any other of the seven gates leading to the Royal Hill of Ambohimanga.

Centuries of pilgrims have climbed this beech-lined hill to the site where St. Francis supposedly received his stigmata.

ITALY

Chapel of the Stigmata

Built on a rocky mountain outcrop in Tuscany, this magnificently situated chapel complex is dedicated to St. Francis of Assisi.

In 1224, during a 40-day fast combined with intense prayer and a hunger to identify with Christ, St. Francis of Assisi is said to have achieved his wish. Followers believe he acquired the stigmata: the supernatural appearance of wounds on his hands, feet, and side. As written accounts relate, he saw a brilliant six-winged seraphim and a crucified Christ. The vision was said to be so magnificent that Assisi's body suddenly— and permanently—bore marks known as the Five Holy Wounds. The trek to Mount La Verna, site of the event, is a personal quest for many Catholics. Its Chapel of the Stigmata is one of eight chapels at the Franciscan Sanctuary, a quadrangle of holy buildings around a stone piazza. The chapel itself is a small room with a 13th-century marble relief over the door showing the seraphim with wings wrapped around Christ; St. Francis kneels with hands outstretched. A red marble frame and wooden cross mark the spot where devotees believe Francis received the stigmata. While simple in design, the chapel has an intricate glazed terra-cotta of the Crucifixion by Andrea della Robbia (1435–1525). On the Feast of the Stigmata (September 17), some 3,000 pilgrims ascend the steep slope to pray and honor St. Francis, following in the steps of generations.

When to Go You can visit at any time of year, but the best weather is from April through October.

Planning Linger a day or two—the mountain has more than 20 ancient buildings. If you ask, the Franciscan friars and sisters will gladly give you a tour. You can stay overnight at La Verna guesthouse, a spiritual retreat in the sanctuary complex. Guests should maintain an atmosphere of solemnity. It's worth reading St. Bonaventure's *Life of St. Francis* to appreciate the site, the chapel's traditions, and its artifacts.

Website www.santuariodellaverna.com

HIGHLIGHTS

■ While the climb to the sanctuary is not easy, it is rewarding. Along the way, you pass a number of historic relics, including a **statue of St. Francis** asking a boy to release turtle doves intended for sale at the market.

■ Be sure to stop at the **basilica**, the compound's largest church, with its **campanile**. Its most revered relic is a stained cloth said to have covered the bloody wound on St. Francis's side. As well as the **chapel**, the sanctuary features a guesthouse, a **16th-century well**, and a **massive cross** made of two logs that permanently marks the sky.

■ Watch the **friars** of Mount La Verna as, each afternoon, they proceed to the chapel during their liturgical exercises.

■ **Mass** is conducted throughout the year, three times a day on weekdays, six on Sundays.

■ Take a hike through the adjacent **forest** that is part of a national park. Dense beech, fir, maple, and ash trees drape the lush valley.

EUROPE

While fervent pilgrims climb to the peak on their knees, others satisfy themselves with the easy walk to the granite statue of St. Patrick outside Murrisk.

IRELAND

CROAGH PATRICK

This rocky outcrop strongly associated with St. Patrick inspires some Irish Catholics to perform extreme acts of penance.

The bare rocky pathway ascending 2,100 feet (640 meters) to the summit of the holy mountain of Croagh Patrick on Ireland's west coast has drawn pilgrims since the Stone Age. Pre-Christian Celts who worshiped the deity Crom Dubh believed the crag to be his home, which they named Cruachan Aigle. Later, it is said, St. Patrick—who introduced Christianity to Ireland and became its patron saint—spent 40 days and nights fasting and praying at the peak for Lent in A.D. 441. While there, according to a popular legend, he banished all snakes and demons from Ireland. Ever since, this has been Ireland's foremost Catholic pilgrimage site. On Reek Sunday, the last Sunday in July, pious Catholics fast before making a predawn ascent—some barefoot, others on their knees—along the trail from the village of Murrisk. Pausing at three pilgrimage stations to pray and do penance, they reach the peak for sunrise. Their reward is not only spiritual but also visual: the mound of Leaba Phádraig (Patrick's Bed) at the crest overlooks the town of Westport, 365 islands in Clew Bay, and the Atlantic beyond.

When to Go For the most pleasant weather, go from April to September.

Planning Allow two to three hours to reach the summit and 90 minutes to descend. Festival days get very busy; 30,000 pilgrims climb the mountain each Reek Sunday. Services at the peak take place on Reek Sunday, Garland Friday (the last Friday in July), and the Feast of the Assumption (August 14). Croagh Patrick's visitor center, Teach na Miasa, has bathrooms, a restaurant, and a gift shop, and can arrange guided tours with advance notice. It also has lockers and showers. Avoid reaching the peak (where the path narrows) around noon, as it gets crowded and the pace slows. Take a rain jacket, hiking shoes—if you're not attempting the climb barefoot—sunblock in summer, and plenty of water. Check weather conditions before the outset and let someone know your estimated return time. A walking stick is useful: you can rent or buy one in Murrisk or at the visitor center. You can drive only as far as the visitor center.

Websites www.croagh-patrick.com, www.fantasy-ireland.com

HIGHLIGHTS

■ The **first pilgrimage station**, Leacht Benáin—named after St. Patrick's disciple St. Benignus—is a small circular cairn at the base of the mountain; the **second station** is at the peak and comprises the summit church and Leaba Phádraig; the **third station** is on the western descent at the three cairns of Roilig Mhuire (Mary's Grave).

■ On the summit, look for the **stone oratory** dating from A.D. 430 to 890. It is one of Ireland's oldest stone churches. Archaeologists discovered it in 1994.

■ Visit the **Celtic hill fort** that the archaeologists also uncovered in the excavations around the summit.

■ Along the path near the summit, look out for the **Neolithic rock art** on Leaba Phádraig.

EUROPE

FRANCE

TRO BREIZ

This medieval pilgrimage in honor of the seven founding saints of Brittany has artfully reinvented itself for modern times.

EUROPE

In medieval lore, a pilgrimage to the seven churches of Brittany's founding saints assured passage to paradise. Those who did not complete this seven-step journey were doomed to hike a longer trail every year after death. The 373-mile (600 kilometer) route remains the same, but the Pilgrimage of the Seven Saints of Brittany has adapted to the times, taking on a new Breton title—*Tro Breiz, Tour of Brittany*—in 1994, and allowing pilgrims to take one of the seven steps each year. The steps vary in length. St. Malo, for example, is a starting point for the trek to Dol-de-Bretagne, a relatively short tour of 18.5 miles (30 kilometers) stretched out over five days. The next year, a more challenging seven-day pilgrimage of 115.5 miles (186 kilometers) leads from the vast cathedral of St. Samson in Dol-de-Bretagne on the north coast to Vannes in southwestern Brittany. Tro Breiz (also spelled *Breizh*) takes in more than a thousand walkers of all ages and categories, but united in spiritual intent. Each day starts with Mass and breakfast before pilgrims set off, singing prayers and hymns along the way. An open-air picnic lunch revives hikers, as do chapel stops en route. Evening music sessions, in the lively Breton Fest Noz (Festival of the Night) tradition, are common before the lights go out at ten, as fiddlers' refrains give way to the songs of frogs and crickets.

When to Go Tro Breiz runs annually in late July, though shorter retreat hikes in other seasons are on parish programs across Brittany.

Planning The organized pilgrimage takes up to seven days, depending on the route. Reserve a place by June at the latest and meals by early July. To lighten each person's load, the organizers transport sleeping bags and personal gear during the day to the next stop. Rain gear is indispensable. For information about annual processions ask in local Catholic churches or tourist offices.

Website www.brittanytourism.com

HIGHLIGHTS

■ From rugged seacoast through wooded lanes, Brittany's **natural beauty** is a high point of the spiritual adventure for many.

■ Look for the **Tro Breiz stained-glass windows** in churches such as St. Vincent's Cathedral in St. Malo.

■ The churches of Brittany's founding bishops—most no longer cathedrals—all merit a visit: **St. Malo** at St. Malo, **St. Samson** at Dol-de-Bretagne, **St. Brieuc** at St.-Brieuc, **St. Tugdual** at Tréguier, **St. Pol-Aurélian** at St.-Pol-de-Léon, **St. Patern** at Vannes, and **St. Corentin** at Quimper.

■ Annual parades or **pardons** bring out Bretons on saints' days. Participants often don richly embroidered traditional suits and lacy Breton caps, especially for *grands pardons*—though these parades don't occur every year.

Revived in 1994, the Tro Breiz originally took more than a month to complete—but pilgrims can now cover a less arduous stage each year.

FRANCE

Mont-St.-Michel

For nearly a millennium this magnificent island abbey has drawn pilgrims across its wild, tidal bay.

The Abbey of Mont-St.-Michel—a marvel of medieval Gothic architecture—rises from the peak of a natural granite island off the shore of France's Normandy coast. Since the tenth century, pilgrims—known as *miquelots*—have braved the island's tidal mudflats to draw strength from the archangel Michael for their spiritual struggles. Catholics know him as St. Michael the Archangel, the arbiter of good and evil—the weigher of souls—and often portray him in art with scales in his hand. Medieval kings walked from Chartres Cathedral to seek his counsel, in the company of other miquelots whose pilgrimage was a penance. The first abbey on the mount dates from 1023 to 1028. A later addition, a three-tiered complex known as *La Merveille* (The Marvel) went up in the early 13th century after a fire destroyed parts of the abbey. It later fell into a long period of decline and even served as a prison after the French Revolution, but by the late 19th century, pilgrims were again at the gate. Below the abbey, a village curls steeply around the mount, providing shelter, sustenance, and souvenirs for pilgrims and visitors—as well as its 41 residents. The mount was once accessible only by a natural land bridge, covered at high tide, but today a causeway links it to the mainland. Nevertheless, each year on the archangel's feast day, Michaelmas (September 29), thousands of pilgrims (accompanied by local guides) take the hard way, wading the almost 2 miles (3 kilometers) across the bay to and from the mainland.

When to Go The abbey is open year-round; winter visits offer a chance to take in the ageless tranquillity of the mountain. In early spring and late fall it's a good spot to see migrations of shorebirds. It's possible to see the highlights in an afternoon, but a longer visit—with overnight stays—is worthwhile for pilgrims.

Planning Pack a pocket flashlight, as passageways inside the abbey are not well lit. It will also come in handy after dark in the village's narrow streets. It's useful to check a table of the tides before arrival and to park in the causeway parking lot when low tide is certain. The abbey offers simple rooms to those seeking a retreat.

Websites www.ot-montsaintmichel.com, www.baie-mont-saint-michel.fr

EUROPE

HIGHLIGHTS

■ Spend a night in one of the many small hotels and inns below the castle walls. Then rise early for a truly spectacular **morning view** from the ramparts across the bay. Look upward as the first light of day shines on the winged figure of the archangel Michael atop the abbey church spire.

■ Attend a **church service** on the mount. The Monastic Communities of Jerusalem, an international order of Roman Catholic monks and sisters, reside in the abbey and lead services daily except Monday.

■ Visit the town of **Avranches**, south of the bay. Its municipal library holds more than **200 illuminated manuscripts** from Mont-St.-Michel's medieval scriptorium.

■ If you visit in spring, arrive two hours before high water to watch the highest—and fastest—**tides** in Europe.

Opposite: Mont-St.-Michel can be dangerous to approach as the difference between low and high tide often reaches 49 ft (15 m). Above left: This stone carving depicts St. Michael burning St. Aubert's head with his finger to persuade him to build Mont-St.-Michel. Above right: The tiny Chapel of St. Aubert lies outside Mont-St.-Michel's fortifications.

Lourdes' Basilica of the Rosary commemorates St. Bernadette's vision of the Virgin Mary carrying a prayer bead.

FRANCE

LOURDES

A religious site with reputed curative powers, this
Pyrenean town is a year-round pilgrimage destination.

A mere wisp of a poor peasant girl, Bernadette Soubirous bore no saintly marks. Yet,
the unsuspecting, uneducated 14-year-old's visions of the Virgin Mary charted
Lourdes' course as a spiritual center. After 150 years, throngs still crowd the site
of Mary's 18 reported apparitions. Here, a statue of the Holy Mother peers out from a
slice of rock high above the winding River Gave. True to Bernadette's account, a blue sash
encircles the white folds of the Virgin's gown. A delicate, yellow rose rests on each bare
foot. Bernadette attested that Mary showed her a hidden spring inside the grotto. Now
piped into marble bathing pools, the chilly water is said to heal the sick, and devotees
tell stories of extraordinary cures. Mary is said also to have directed Bernadette to tell
the town's priest to build a chapel—and one begot others. Rising above the grotto, the
Domain of Our Lady complex now includes three distinct overhanging churches, linked
by two curving ramps. Ironically, Bernadette suffered asthma and other ailments and
died at 35 in a convent in Nevers. In 1933, Pope Pius XI canonized her.

When to Go The pilgrimage season runs from April 1 to the end of October. In July, August, and
September, there's a daily pilgrimage service. Gather by the Crowned Statue at 8:30 a.m., follow your
guide to Mass, and walk in Bernadette's footsteps. Stop at the kiosk near St. Joseph's Gate and rent an
MP3 player, earphones, and a map for a nominal charge.

Planning To make the most of your visit, spend at least two days in Lourdes—longer if you want to
explore the surrounding attractions. Direct trains run from Paris, Bordeaux, Toulouse, Marseille, and Lyon.

Websites www.lourdes-france.com, www.lourdes-infotourisme.com

HIGHLIGHTS

■ Legend has it that Charlemagne
overtook the **fortified castle** of
Lourdes in 778. Learn about the
castle's history and archaeology as
you wander around.

■ The **Pic du Jer**, the beginning of
the Pyrenees, overlooks Lourdes.
Take the 100-year-old funicular
railway 3,280 ft (1,000 m) through
the pine trees. At the top, you can
rent mountain bikes or hike.

■ Explore the **Bétharram caves**,
about 9 miles (15 km) from Lourdes.
Here, you'll see five floors from
five different time periods. Take
the family-friendly tour (partially
by boat) and see huge limestone
deposits and gushing waterfalls.

■ Visit the **National Museum of the
Château de Pau**, birthplace of Henry
IV of France, nearly 20 miles (32 km)
from Lourdes. Guided tours in English
showcase historical and decorative
art collections.

EUROPE

SPAIN

WAY OF ST. JAMES

One of Europe's great journeys, this Pyrenean pilgrimage offers an abundance of spiritual, cultural, and natural wonders.

EUROPE

The pilgrim's way to Santiago de Compostela Cathedral, sheltering St. James's relics, has drawn devotees for almost 1,200 years. In fact there are several routes, converging from north, east, and west. In medieval times many north European pilgrims came by sea, walking only the final leg and wearing—as a badge—scallop shells symbolizing the apostle. As pilgrims descend from the Pyrenean passes, the first town they reach is Pamplona, with a fine Gothic cathedral of mellow, ocher-colored stone. A little way west, the French and Aragonese routes to Santiago meet at Puente La Reina, crossing a graceful 11th-century bridge. Medieval pilgrims paused at Santo Domingo de la Calzada's hospice, now a hotel. Burgos, dominated by a splendid 13th-century Gothic cathedral, is the next major town. Farther west, León Cathedral has a light, airy interior illuminated by superb stained-glass windows. Relics exist, too, of stormier aspects of the region's past, such as Ponferrada's massive Templar castle. At the trail's climax, Santiago de Compostela, the Baroque cathedral's towering spires dominate Praza do Obradoiro, a wide square amid a treasury of medieval architecture.

When to Go It is best to undertake the pilgrimage in spring or early summer (April-June) or fall (September-October). Winter can be cold and wet; high summer can be too hot for pleasant walking.

Planning Allow at least two weeks to cover the 484 miles (780 km) from Roncesvalles to Santiago de Compostela. Bring waterproof clothes as it can rain heavily in northern Spain at any time of year. There are many places to eat along the way. Some pilgrims' hostels are free if you register in advance, but they don't take reservations and can fill up early. All urban centers en route have good public transportation.

Websites www.caminosantiago.com, www.santiagoturismo.com

HIGHLIGHTS

■ On a clear day, the steep, forested **descent into Spain** from the watershed of the Pyrenees at Roncesvalles offers heady views of snowcapped mountains.

■ After a long day's walk, enjoy well-deserved wine and tapas at one of the many **open-air cafés**.

■ Since the Middle Ages pilgrims have felt elation at the first glimpse of Santiago Cathedral's **majestic Baroque spires** at the end of the journey.

■ Spain's least spoiled **coastline** is between Vigo and La Coruña.

■ **Pamplona** is famed for its annual running of the bulls, held daily during the festival of San Fermín (July 7-14).

Santiago de Compostela Cathedral is said to be the burial place of St. James, who brought Christianity to the Celts of Iberia.

8
CEREMONIES & FESTIVALS

All the world's great religions honor their gods with sacred celebrations. For Buddhists, Christians, Hindus, Jews, Muslims, Sikhs, and devotees of other faiths, these events shape communal calendars and private lives. Many of the festivals on the following pages are exuberant explosions of color and pageantry. Others are somber—even shocking—in their intensity. Some festivals draw believers on pilgrimages to sacred locations, such as India's Kumbha Mela, when Hindus take part in the largest religious gathering on Earth. Others mark defining moments in the history of a faith, such as the birthday celebrations for the Buddha in Seoul, South Korea. And still others break down boundaries between worlds, as in Japan's Obon Festival, when lanterns are lit to guide loved ones visiting from the realm of the dead. Each ceremony opens a window into the hearts and souls of peoples and places in ways that no traveler will ever forget.

In the Himalayan kingdom of Bhutan, monks take part in the brilliant annual *tsechu*, or mask-dance festival, that lasts for several days and celebrates the life of Guru Rinpoche, who brought Buddhism to their country.

The mission church was completed in 1640 by Franciscans during the Spanish colonial period.

NEW MEXICO

FEAST OF ST. STEPHEN

This annual festival in an ancient pueblo set in a stunning landscape offers visitors a glimpse into the mystique of ancient traditions.

The people of Acoma, so it is said, were led by their ancestors to "Sky City" atop a 370-foot (113 meter) sandstone mesa. They called their city Haak'u, which means "a place prepared." They traveled through the lands of what is now New Mexico, periodically calling out the name of the city, and when they heard it echoed back, they settled in the place of their destiny. Although they endured the oppression of Spanish colonial rule, the Acoma people kept faith with the spiritual world of their ancestors. Yet they also made certain Catholic traditions their own. Every year on September 2, the bells of the San Esteban del Rey (St. Stephen) Mission Church ring in the feast day of their patron saint. After Mass, the saint's icon is paraded to the public square. Then music and dancing take over, representing different aspects of the landscape, wildlife, and environment. For visitors the festival reveals a rare blend of ancient beliefs with Catholic celebration. Don't ask for explanations, just enjoy immersion in the Acoma way of life.

When to Go September 2; the timing is set by religious leadership. Call the Haak'u Museum in advance for an idea of when to arrive. Add on two extra days for a full experience of Acoma.

Planning Acoma is 45 minutes west of Albuquerque. Take Exit 102 off I-40 and follow the signs for the Haak'u Museum and Sky City Cultural Center in the valley. The center runs tours of the pueblo. Photo permits are required. Video cameras and tripods are prohibited. You will not be allowed to photograph inside the mission or cemetery area.

Website www.acomaskycity.org

HIGHLIGHTS

■ The massive **stone and adobe edifice** of the mission church encloses a sublime space decorated with parrots to denote beauty, corn as the staple food, and pink for the color of the earth.

■ Take a **walking tour of the pueblo** with an Acoma guide from the Sky City Cultural Center. This is a chance to learn about Acoma history and culture. Their society is matriarchal, with decision-making falling to the youngest daughter in the family.

■ Acoma's location on top of the mesa brings stunning **360° views**. Afterward descend via the original **hand-carved stone stairway,** for centuries a primary way of reaching the village before the road was built.

■ The Haak'u Museum in the valley below has permanent and temporary exhibits on Acoma history and art. Here you will find examples of **very fine pottery**, decorated in geometric patterns.

NORTH AMERICA

CANADA

KAMLOOPA POWWOW

A weekend of the most spectacular dancing in Kamloops, British Columbia, celebrates the culture of many North American tribes.

A respectful silence falls over the audience as members of the lead drumming circle, or host drum, start pounding and chanting in unison, signaling the start of the Grand Entry at the Kamloopa Powwow. Spectators rise to their feet as the 6-foot (1.8 m) long eagle staff of the Secwepemc (Shuswap) nation, host of the event, is carried into the arbor (dance arena). This is followed by the Canadian and American flags and the staffs of the participating First Nations (Native American tribes). Now the dancers, lined up according to dance style and gender, enter in single file, the men leading the procession. Dressed in colorful regalia, they move in a clockwise direction to mirror the sun's path, their cadenced steps and motions in harmony with the rhythmic drum beat. Once the gathering has been blessed with songs and an invocation, intense competition for prize money begins. The arena becomes a swirling sea of color as the men mimic the hunt or acts of bravery with graceful athleticism. The women's fancy shawl dancers twirl their fringed shawls as they execute rapid steps, while the jingle dancers, their dresses covered with tin cones, move in time to the drums. The outfits and headdresses are as beautiful as the dancers' fluid movements, each one unique, the colors, patterns, and beadwork reflecting family traditions or personal stories.

When to Go The powwow, held in late July or early August at the Special Events Facility in Kamloops, runs Friday night through Sunday. The Grand Entry, which precedes each powwow session, is at 7 p.m. Friday and Saturday, and noon Saturday and Sunday.

Planning Weekend and single-day admission tickets may be purchased at the gate. If you wish to stay in the area, book your hotel early as more than 15,000 visitors attend the powwow each year. Kamloops lies in a beautiful region of lakes and rivers and is a good base for exploring nearby wilderness areas.

Websites www.kib.ca/powwow.htm, www.secwepemc.org, www.bcadventure.com

HIGHLIGHTS

■ Feast your eyes on the gorgeous **competitive dances**, which include traditional, jingle dress, grass dress, chicken, fancy feather, and fancy shawl dances. Non-native spectators are invited to join in the intertribal dances.

■ Nearly 1,300 members of **more than 30 tribes** from British Columbia, Saskatchewan, Alberta, and the northern United States participate in the powwow, which is hosted by the Kamloops Indian Band, a community of Shuswap people. Explore their history and culture at the nearby **Secwepemc Museum and Heritage Park**.

■ The festival also features a **Powwow Princess pageant**, with a Sunday coronation, and vendors selling food, jewelry, and native crafts.

Intensive drumming contests, accompanied by chanting, are a major feature of the Kamloopa Powwow.

DIWALI

The national Hindu street festival of this island nation
is a feast of light, sound, color, and taste.

Hush settles over normally raucous streets, as hundreds of tiny flames flicker like dancing fireflies. The flames emanate from oil-filled clay pots that line the streets of Aranguez, just outside the capital city of Port-of-Spain, fill the driveways and windowsills of Chaguanas, in central Trinidad, and perch on doorsteps and throughout the yards of San Fernando, in the island's south. It's Diwali (Festival of Light) time, and these little oil lamps, known as *deyas*, celebrate Lakshmi, goddess of light, wealth, and prosperity, and commemorate the return of Lord Rama after 14 years of banishment. Inside their houses, Hindus—more than 40 percent of Trindad and Tobago's population is Indian—gather at an altar to perform Lakshmi Puja, a worship ceremony. Friends assemble over feasts of Indian food—all vegetarian, in keeping with the solemnity of the holiday. In tiny villages like Felicity and Patna, the anticipatory quiet breaks as crowds throng the streets to watch night performances of Indian music and dance, and to feast on traditional foods. In an atmosphere that's somehow both festive and solemn—and strictly alcohol-free—musicians bang drums and steel pans to a hypnotic beat and fireworks pierce the sky with light and sound. As the spectacle ends, the deyas are the only lights left burning in the darkened night.

When to Go Diwali is in October or November.

Planning Plan to spend at least four days on Trinidad to participate in Diwali Nagar, and the newer festival of Diwali Sammelan in San Fernando, and to visit such Hindu landmarks as Chaguanas's Temple in the Sea. Book accommodations in advance, as hotels fill up. You'll need a car to visit such areas as Chaguanas, San Fernando, and smaller villages—and steel nerves to face the traffic jams heading to Diwali Nagar. Trinidad and Tobago bans gay visitors.

Websites www.diwalifestival.org, www.gotrinidadandtobago.com

HIGHLIGHTS

■ Celebrations begin with **Diwali Nagar**, a huge nine-day fair near Chaguanas. Watch performances by Trinidad's leading Indian artists, from Shiv Shakti's glittery fusion of traditional and contemporary dance to the stirring music of Karma.

■ Sample Indian and Trinidadian **delicacies** from *roti* (flat bread often filled with curry) to *gulab jaman* (a scented doughnut).

■ In Waterloo, visit the world's only **Indian Caribbean Museum**.

■ Browse local neighborhoods and survey the amazing array of **deyas**, often fashioned into phantasmagoric designs on elaborate bamboo frameworks in friendly competitions among neighbors.

Women set out deyas at Diwali. In the week preceding the holiday, they can be bought from street vendors across San Juan, Chaguanas, and San Fernando.

Nyabinghi drummers wear the Rastafarian colors—red, green, and gold—as they celebrate Bob Marley's birthday.

JAMAICA

RASTAFARIAN NYABINGHI

Born of poverty and oppression, Rastafari finds many reasons to celebrate—not least the life of its great apostle, Bob Marley.

Drums beat out a mesmeric rhythm. The chanting begins, a simple refrain repeated again and again. Often, this is apocalyptic-sounding: "Burn down Babylon," "Babylon, your throne gone down." Or it can be exhortative: "Awake, Zion, awake," or just, "Read your Bible." Bodies sway to the beat. The men shake their manes of dreadlocks. Somebody calls out, "Fire!" And the pipe with the "sacred herb" ("ganja," cannabis) is solemnly lit and passed from person to person, each in turn disappearing into a cloud of smoke. This is a *nyabinghi* (or *binghi*), a Rastafarian spiritual celebration in which the drumming, chanting, and "herb" are intended to lead to heightened awareness. Even for an outsider, it is almost impossible not to be stirred. As faiths go, Rastafari is modern—it emerged in the 1930s from one of the worst slums in Jamaica's capital city, Kingston—but aspects of its teachings can touch everyone's experience. You may not believe that the late Ethiopian Emperor Haile Selassie was (or is) a manifestation of God, but most people have probably known some kind of "downpression" (oppression) in their lives. As the drumming and chanting continue, the call to freedom of spirit, freedom from exploitation and a corrupt order (Babylon), and for the return of an exiled people to their own land (Zion), is bound to resonate.

When to Go February is officially "Reggae Month." Rastas mark Bob Marley's birthday (February 6) with a festival. Other festival dates are: April 21, "Grounation Day," the anniversary of Haile Selassie's visit to Jamaica in 1966; July 23, Haile Selassie's birthday; August 17, birthday of the Jamaican-born black rights' leader, Marcus Garvey; and November 2, anniversary of Haile Selassie's coronation.

Planning The most authentic nyabinghis take place in Jamaica's rugged interior and you have to be invited. But during the important festivals, public events are often held on beaches and in towns. Although considered sacramental by Rastas, cannabis use is, strictly speaking, illegal in Jamaica.

Websites www.nyahbinghi.com, www.bobmarley.com

HIGHLIGHTS

■ The village of **Nine Mile**, in the green hills of St Ann's Parish on Jamaica's North Coast, is where Bob Marley was born and now lies buried in a mausoleum. It has become something of a **shrine to the Rastafarian superstar**. It is also an excuse for a trip through small towns and villages and attractive inland scenery, little visited otherwise by tourists.

■ In Kingston, you can visit the **Bob Marley Museum** in his former home, a fine old town house on the capital's Hope Road. **Memorabilia** on display include his favorite Gibson guitar. You can also see bullet holes in a back wall left by a failed assassination attempt.

■ Try the **Queen of Sheba Restaurant** on the grounds of the museum, which serves vegetarian food, including some of **Marley's favorite dishes**.

NORTH AMERICA

MEXICO

Day of the Dead

This three-day festival explodes with all the vitality of a cabaret driven by music, dance, and food, and for a brief, brilliant moment takes the sting out of death.

The scene could not be more enchanting: thousands of people polishing tombstones and arranging golden and scarlet floral displays in a cemetery in Oaxaca. As the sun sinks over southern Mexico, the graveyard takes on a carnival air, with families picnicking, hawkers selling wax skulls and other ghoulish artifacts, and children tossing firecrackers. All around there's music—teenagers with stereos, troubadours with guitars, and elderly women chanting religious tunes as everyone settles in for the night around the open fires. Mexico's Day of the Dead, or *Día de los Muertos*, is not exclusive to Oaxaca, but this is certainly one of its more important manifestations. Although largely based on Catholic tradition, the ritual also draws inspiration from an Aztec festival in which human sacrifices ensured the rebirth of deceased kinfolk. Throw in a touch of Halloween—Mexican kids dressed like witches, vampires, and goblins—and you have the makings of a truly macabre fiesta. The reality, though, is far from gruesome. Brass bands parade around the square, trailed by troupes of dancers in outrageous costumes; women compete to make the best cactus moonshine; and people break into witty *calavera* (death's head) songs and poems. Indeed, it's the spirit of life that infuses Oaxaca during the Day of the Dead.

When to Go Day of the Dead celebrations take place over October 31 (All Souls' Day), November 1 (All Saints' Day), and November 2. Arrive in Oaxaca a few days early to get the lay of the land and visit the pre-Columbian ruins on the outskirts of the city.

Planning Oaxaca is alive with special events in the last week of October, so set aside at least four days for a complete experience. Flights to Oaxaca and many of the city's better hotels can fill up well in advance of the holiday, so make your reservations early. The elevation here is fairly high and nights can be surprisingly cool, so pack accordingly. Pre-arrange a local taxi or hotel car to take you to the cemeteries and other after-dark attractions, and then back to your hotel before dawn. Some local travel agencies also offer guided tours, but these are often restricted to three hours rather than the whole night.

Website www.go-oaxaca.com

NORTH AMERICA

HIGHLIGHTS

■ The huge **Panteón General Cemetery** near the city center is decorated with thousands of candles, floral tributes, and elaborate calavera displays.

■ The municipal cemetery in Xoxocotlán village on the southern outskirts of Oaxaca is probably the best place for visitors to partake in the **traditional all-night vigil.**

■ Many of the holiday essentials, like food, flowers, firecrackers, and wax skulls, are sold at more than 700 stalls in the sprawling **Benito Juárez Market** near the main square (*zócalo*). Part of the market is reserved for local handicrafts, including the rich wood carvings and textiles for which Oaxaca is well known.

■ Masses take place in the **Spanish Baroque cathedral** (Catedral Metropolitana de Oaxaca) on All Saints' Day (November 1), a Roman Catholic holy day of obligation. The courtyard outside is a venue for local artists to create sumptuous *tapetes de arena*—sidewalk "carpets" made from sawdust, chalk, glitter, and colored sand.

Opposite: Celebrations allow for some contemplative moments, as seen in the attitudes of Mexicans in prayer at the candlelit tomb of a loved one in Xoxocotlán Cemetery, outside Oaxaca. Above: Grinning skeleton "characters," dressed up and adorned with ribbons, exemplify the many imaginative ways that Mexicans laugh at death.

VENEZUELA

DRUMMING FEAST OF ST. JOHN

Throughout June, the small towns around Caracas and along the nearby Caribbean coast come alive to honor St. John the Baptist.

I t is a hot, humid night and sweat drips down the young woman's neck as she gyrates to the sound of pounding percussion in a heady display of sensuality and power. From the clapping crowd encircling the girl, a suitor approaches to seduce her but she turns away, nose in the air, dancing for the onlookers, and before long a rival replaces him. The festivities in the area, especially in Barlovento, once the site of a concentration of slave plantations, are Catholic in origin but owe much to traditional African rituals. The drums, too, are of African derivation. Notable is the large wooden *mina*, astride which the player sits, beating the skin at one end while others beat the sides with sticks. St. John the Baptist is patron saint to many on the Caribbean coast, and his statue is kept all year round in a special niche—garlanded with flowers and colored paper—in the house of one of the villagers. The usually sleepy towns begin to gear up for his festival in early June, and pulsating rhythms can be heard on every street corner throughout the month. Different towns distinguish themselves with their own beats; the drummers are famous for complex harmonies, often accompanied by group chanting. Drumming opens the festival, and on the following day, after Mass, it drives the all-night celebrations with intense, hypnotic beats that often cause revelers to fall into trancelike states.

When to Go The festival of St. John the Baptist runs continuously from the night of June 23 to June 25.

Planning Various towns celebrate the festival; all are close to Caracas and accessible by bus. The main events take place in Guarenas, Guatire, Santa Lucía, Ocumare del Tuy, Barlovento, and Curiepe. All are participatory affairs and tourists are encouraged to join in the dance. Local celebrants are friendly and encouraging, but they don't understand outsiders' reticence. You don't need to be able to move, but you have to be willing to try!

Website www.rbv.info

HIGHLIGHTS

■ On June 24, a Mass is held for the saint, after which there is a **street parade** of his statue, which onlookers sprinkle with rum along the way. He is known locally as San Juan Borrachero (St. John the Drunkard).

■ Pay a visit to one of the **local drum makers**. These craftsmen, who can demonstrate how the avocado wood drums are made, often have much to say about the history of drumming in the village.

■ The small town of **Curiepe** is renowned for its exuberant festival. More than 20,000 people flood in and make up a tumultuous procession. The spirituality of the occasion, and possibly the rum, give them the energy to dance in the streets for days on end.

At the three-day festival in Curiepe, the celebrations explode onto the streets with nonstop drumming and dancing.

Women in bowler hats and traditional skirts, or *polleras*, whirl in unison in Copacabana's main square as festivities commence.

BOLIVIA

VIRGIN OF THE CANDLES

The most venerated image of the Virgin Mary in Bolivia is at the heart of riotous celebrations that last for three days.

Gleaming white Moorish arches loom over the modest main square and the streets are strewn with flower petals. Drunken revelers in traditional costume spin to the sound of flutes, pipes, and rhythmic drumming of traditional Aymara music while Lake Titicaca shimmers just beyond. Sitting on the end of a peninsula projecting into the southwestern waters of the lake, the small town of Copacabana is home to the Basílica de la Virgen de Candelaria (Basilica of the Virgin of the Candles). Legend has it that in 1576 the Virgin Mary saved local fisherwomen from a terrible storm. An Inca craftsman, Tito Yupanqui, sculpted her image from the dark wood of the maguey cactus and placed her in the chapel, where she gained a reputation throughout Peru and Bolivia for working miracles. She came to be known also as the Dark Virgin of the Lake. Her chapel was enlarged by the Spanish and the present basilica completed in 1805. The Fiesta de la Virgen (Festival of the Virgin) is celebrated over three days in February, when pilgrims come from all over the country to give thanks to her. In a frenzy of color and noise, a replica of the Virgin is paraded around the town in a glass coffin and taken by boat onto the lake to bless the waters.

When to Go The festival is held during the first few days of February, but blessings and Mass are held daily at the basilica.

Planning Copacabana is a small town and can be visited in just a few days. It is worth taking more time to explore Lake Titicaca and also La Paz, Bolivia's vibrant first city. The altitude here—12,648 ft (3,855 m)—means that temperatures drop suddenly when the sun goes down, so make sure you pack enough warm clothes. There are a number of hotels in and around Copacabana. Hostal La Cupula and Rosario del Lago are both on the lakeshore and have lovely views.

Website www.itisnet.com/english/e-america/e-bolivia/e-copaca/e-copacabana.htm

HIGHLIGHTS

■ The statue stands in an illuminated niche set into the **ornate Baroque altarpiece**. It is an impressive sight, especially at night, when the candles of the faithful light up the darkness.

■ On the third day of celebrations, **bulls are rounded into a corral** outside town, and the crowd cheers as the brave and the inebriated jump in and try to escape without being gouged.

■ Daily throughout the year, buses, cars, and trucks, decked in flowers and ribbons, park in front of the basilica to receive a **ritual blessing** in the Benedición de Movildades. Offerings of alcohol are poured over the vehicles to protect them.

LORD OF THE MIRACLES

A huge annual gathering honors Lima's patron saint, a local representation of Jesus believed to possess miraculous powers.

Octber in Lima is known as the purple month. Many of the faithful dress in this color, which for Catholics symbolizes penitence. The focus of veneration is a painting of Jesus, known locally as "Cristo de Pachamamilla" (a Quechua word referring both to an earthy color and godliness). It originally occupied a chapel wall in a poor area of Lima that survived the powerful earthquake of 1746, as if by a miracle. The Church of Las Nazarenas was built around this wall, and the painting is kept here. Today, belief in its miraculous powers extends right across South America, and the annual parade of the image draws hundreds of thousands of the faithful to honor the Señor de los Milagros (Lord of the Miracles). The night before, people sleep in churches until dawn, when Mass is celebrated. Then the procession sets off through downtown Lima toward the Church of La Merced. A select, purple-robed brotherhood carries the litter with the massive painting showing Jesus crucified, the Virgin Mary at his feet, and God and the Holy Spirit watching from heaven. Amid clouds of incense and the sound of prayers and chanting, the procession—which includes hymn singers, musicians, penitents, and peddlers—weaves through the streets before the eyes of myriad devotees.

When to Go The celebration begins on October 18, with the procession itself taking place on the following day. Allow as much extra time as you can to make the most of seeing this historic capital.

Planning Lima's airport, Jorge Chávez, has flights from North and South America and Europe. Most people get around the country by bus; avoid night buses, and take a taxi rather than drive. The cheaper hotels are in the less salubrious city center; more desirable are the neighborhoods of Miraflores and Barranco. Lima is renowned for its delicious food, including seafood.

Website www.peru.info/perueng.asp

HIGHLIGHTS

■ Try the delicious **Turrón de Doña Pepa**, a traditional candy associated with the procession, that is eaten all through October.

■ Join the locals at the **music and dance performances** at La Candelaria, a club in the bohemian neighborhood of Barranco, to see some of Peru's traditional costumes and customs.

■ Visit the Museo Arqueológico Rafael Larco Herrera, for more glimpses into **Peru's indigenous past**. The collection includes ancient textiles, archaeological artifacts, and ceramic and gold objects used in religious ceremonies and everyday life.

The streets of Lima are transformed into a sea of purple, as worshipers throng around the silver-mounted painting of Jesus, revered for its healing powers.

At the end of Obon, lanterns are floated away on water to light spirits back to the other world.

JAPAN

OBON

Dancing and floating lanterns feature in a series of Buddhist rituals to welcome the spirits of the dead into the home.

At the time of Obon, or the Festival of Lanterns, Japanese Buddhists return to their hometowns and villages to honor their ancestors with religious rites, especially if a family member has died recently. According to Buddhist belief, this is when the spirits of the dead return to the living world and briefly reunite with their families. People therefore visit family graves to "call back" the spirits to their ancestral homes. They guide the spirits by lighting fires at their gates and placing paper lanterns at the *butsudan* (ancestral shrine)—having, of course, cleaned their homes and made offerings of rice, fruit, vegetables, flowers, and incense in front of the butsudan. Obon is based on the legend of Buddha's disciple Maha Mogallana, who rescued his mother from the hell of hungry ghosts by meditating, practicing compassion, and giving offerings to the monks. When his mother was released, Mogallana danced for joy, which is thought to be the origin of *bon odori*, or folk dancing, that is a frequent sight during Obon.

When to Go Obon may occur in either July or August, depending on which calendar is followed—the Gregorian (western) calendar or the solar (seasonal) calendar. Timing may vary according to the region, but it is most commonly celebrated now from August 13 to 16.

Planning Most businesses are closed during Obon. Aim to arrive before the start of the festival since all long-distance trains, domestic airlines, and most accommodations are booked solid at this time. This is Japan's main summer holiday, and the weekends before and after the festival are also likely to be crowded. Major cities like Tokyo or Osaka will be more empty than usual, however, as most Japanese head to home towns and the countryside.

Website www.jnto.go.jp

HIGHLIGHTS

■ Participants clad in light cotton kimonos flock to temple grounds or town squares for **bon odori**. This dance varies from region to region, but dancers usually move in a circle to the beat of taiko drums. Anyone can participate—just join in the circle and follow what others are doing.

■ In many areas, Obon ends with *Toro Nagashi*, the **lantern floating ceremony**, to guide the ancestors' spirits back to the other world. A flotilla of paper lanterns inscribed with calligraphy and illuminated with candles is launched on rivers and lakes leading to the ocean. This ceremony is usually followed by a fireworks display.

■ Towns often hold **huge carnivals** featuring rides, games, and food.

■ At the end of the festival on the hillsides around Kyoto, people light fires in the shape of **five giant characters** from Japanese script, or *kanji*. This spectacular sight can be seen from various viewing points.

ASIA

TEN NOCTURNAL FESTIVALS

All around the world, festivals take place in the dead of night. While some of us are sleeping, others are celebrating with music and dancing.

❶ Noche de la Primavera, Mexico City, Mexico

Mexico City welcomes the arrival of spring in style. All through the night, the streets and plazas pulse with music and dancing. Mexican folk rhythms mingle with Latino pop, while acrobats, theater troupes, and animators entertain the revelers until dawn.

Planning Festivities begin at 5 p.m. on the eve of the spring equinox, so about March 20. www.visitmexico.com

❷ Noche de Brujas, Veracruz, Mexico

Catemaco's annual celebration, the Night of the Witches, is a spectacle of all things magical. Witches, wizards, fortune-tellers, and healers gather together, stalls are set up, and the streets bustle with activity. For the right money, you can cast a spell, bestow a curse, or cure your ills with herbs.

Planning The witches' congress takes place annually on the first Friday of March. The nighttime celebrations begin on the preceding Thursday evening. catemaco.info/activities/brujos/index.html

❸ New Year's Eve, Rio de Janeiro, Brazil

On the last night of the year, more than two million revelers flock to Copacabana Beach to watch the fireworks and dance the samba. Just before midnight the locals, dressed mostly in white, cast out offerings to Iemanjá, the Goddess of the Sea. Perfume, flowers, and rice are set adrift in paper boats while thousands of floating candles light up the night sky.

Planning The beach is close to the center of Rio de Janeiro and easily accessible by train or bus. www.ipanema.com

❹ Chichibu Yomatsuri, Chichibu City, Japan

Six ornate floats, each representing one of the city's protective gods and decorated with lanterns, tapestries, and carvings, are hauled on ropes by hundreds of chanting devotees toward the city hall. Stalls selling snacks and rice wine line the crowded streets, and fireworks blast colors through the black skies.

Planning The festival takes place every year on December 2 and 3. Chichibu is a 90-minute train ride from central Tokyo. www.jnto.go.jp

❺ Lantern Festival, China

On the 15th night of the first month of the new Chinese year, towns and villages across China are bathed in the glow of lanterns. Traditional red-paper globes take their place among illuminated butterflies, dragons, and birds, each posted with a riddle—those who solve the puzzles win a prize.

Planning The Lantern Festival takes place across China in February. www.chinavoc.com

❻ Tet, Vietnam

New Year's Eve in Vietnam, where families await midnight with expectation, is a time of renewal. Houses are swept clean and festooned with colorful decorations. Those who stay at home whisper prayers for their ancestors, while in the parks, there are celebratory firework displays. Throughout the country the troubles of the past year are forgotten.

Planning Tet observes the lunar cycle and falls on a different date each year, usually in late January or early February. The official celebrations last three days, though they can last longer. www.thingsasian.com/stories-photos/1253

❼ Laylatul-Bara'ah, Pakistan

The Night of Salvation falls in Sha'aban, the eighth month of the Islamic calendar. It is a time for the faithful to repent to Allah and seek pardons for their sins. Some spend the night at the mosque, others visit the cemetery to pray for the departed. It is also a time for fasting.

Planning Laylatul-Bara'ah is observed throughout the Muslim world. members.tripod.com/worldupdates/newupdates10/id69.htm

❽ Jani, Latvia

The residents of the Latvian town of Kuldiga mark the start of midsummer, or *Jani*, by running naked through the streets. Elsewhere, they don crowns of flowers or oak leaves and celebrate with medicinal Jani-herbs and bonfires. These are lit before sunset and stoked until dawn. Specially prepared straw torches are used to drive away evil spirits.

Planning The bonfires are lit on Midsummer's Eve, and the festivities last for two days. www.inspirationriga.com/main.php?gid=4&sid=15&cid=163

❾ San Juan, Spain

During the Festival of San Juan, Spain is ablaze with fire and music fills the streets. People spend the afternoon building bonfires that burn throughout the night to welcome in the summer. According to tradition, jumping over a bonfire three times on San Juan night will burn all your troubles away.

Planning The San Juan festivals in Spain differ in date from region to region, but they all run for several days around June 23. www.donquijote.org/culture/spain/fiestas/sanjuan.asp

❿ Summer Solstice, Glastonbury, England

Glastonbury Tor (or hill) has been sacred for millennia, its legend dating back to Arthurian times. Now this mystical hill, rising strangely above its flat surroundings, is a focal point for the Druid community and the setting for their solstice ceremony. On Midsummer's Eve, hundreds of people gather on the Tor in a circle—children throw petals, holy water is sprinkled, and the service is blessed with fire.

Planning Glastonbury Tor is managed by the National Trust. It's open countryside with no admission charge or opening hours. www.nationaltrust.org.uk, www.glastonburytor.org.uk

As night falls on Rio's Copacabana Beach, people carry floral offerings into the sea and set them afloat for the goddess Iemanjá in the hope of securing good luck for the following year.

NEBUTA MATSURI

One of Japan's biggest and rowdiest festivals has evolved from purification rituals into an elaborate preparation for the harvest.

ASIA

Every August, Aomori, the northernmost city on Japan's Honshu Island, attracts some three million people who marvel at giant illuminated lanterns in the shape of samurai, demons, and spirits parading down the streets. Nebuta, which means drowsiness, is a high point of the national calendar and may have started as a way of preparing or "waking up" people for the fall harvest season. The festival also celebrates the end of the short summer in northern Japan. Every evening, around 20 floats, their lanterns lit within by hundreds of lightbulbs, are pulled along a 1.5-mile (2.4 kilometer) course. The spectacular character shapes—some 26 feet (8 meters) high, 50 feet (15 meters) wide, and weighing in at 4 tons (4 tonnes)—are constructed from wood and wire, meticulously covered in paper on which the designs are traced, and then painted in brilliant colors. Dwarfed by the warriors and spirits leaping, crouching, snarling, and grimacing overhead, more than 200,000 *haneto* (dancers) clad in vivid costumes weave in and out of the floats and gyrate to the sound of drums, flutes, and cheering crowds chanting, "*Rasse-rah, rasse-rah!*—Hooray!"

When to Go August 1 is the eve of the festival, which runs until August 7. The first two days are dedicated to children, and August 4 and 5 see the highest concentration of parade floats.

Planning Sitting at the base of Mutsu Bay, Aomori is accessible by plane, boat, bus, and train. Japan Airlines flies from Tokyo's Haneda Airport to Aomori. The city center has many business hotels but is short on budget hotels. Consider staying in nearby Hirosaki instead. Booking accommodations in advance is essential during the Nebuta Festival. Join in the fun as a haneto by renting a costume from a local shop and be ready with the other dancers 30 minutes before the parade starts.

Website www.nebuta.or.jp/english

HIGHLIGHTS

■ The **lantern shapes** are inspired by famous generals and other historical figures, as well as by characters from kabuki plays, but the designs are original. They are so elaborate that work begins on the next year's themes immediately after the current year's festival has ended.

■ On the final day the procession starts in the afternoon, and later that evening the top three lanterns are mounted on ships for a **cruise around Aomori Bay** to a spectacular backdrop of fireworks. This is a reminder of the earliest times, when candles were floated out to sea to carry away illness, bad luck, or any other impediment to a good harvest.

Gigantic illuminated samurai dominate and delight the crowds on the darkened streets of Aomori.

Ornate, bedecked shrines are carried to Senso-ji Temple for the Saturday purification rite.

JAPAN

SANJA MATSURI

Three wild days honor deities enshrined in Senso-ji, one of Tokyo's historic temples, and bring good luck to the old quarter of Asakusa.

Some 13 centuries ago, it is said, three fishermen netted a statue of the goddess Kannon. Senso-ji Temple in Tokyo was built to display the statue. The three men acquired holy status and are remembered in a festival attracting 1.5 million Japanese and tourists. They pour into Asakusa, the traditional haunt of geisha and *yakuza* (gangsters), to follow gilded and lacquered shrines, in which the gods are believed to ride. It is an honor to be chosen to carry the *mikoshi* (shrines). On the first day, Friday, groups of bearers wearing matching, tunic-style jackets parade the mikoshi around three main districts of Asakusa, amid chanting, clapping, whistling, and drumming. Alcohol, festive music, and crowd participation fuel the revelry. Floats carry musicians, beautiful geisha walk alongside yakuza, and traditional dances are performed. On the second day, the mikoshi are carried to the temple precinct for a purification rite. On the third day, the three great temple shrines representing the three fishermen are taken around the streets to bless the community. Emotions run high as people fight to grab the poles bearing the shrines, which pitch and toss about. Yet, the more tipsy the ride, it is believed, the more luck will be scattered around.

When to Go The festival is held on the third Friday, Saturday, and Sunday in May. Each day brings a new range of events. If you can stand the crowds, stay for all three days.

Planning Driving in this area is chaotic—take the train and arrive early to get a decent viewing position. Asakusa station is on the Ginza and Toei Asakusa lines and in the festival neighborhood. You can buy full festival gear at local shops, such as Nakaya, and attend a geisha performance on Saturday or Sunday.

Website www.jnto.go.jp

HIGHLIGHTS

■ Feel the power of **taiko drumming** by watching the parade on Friday, or catch the performance at the temple on Saturday. The show starts after the last mikoshi leaves the temple.

■ Watch **tiny children**, also clad in matching festival jackets, pulling the strings of miniature shrines in the Saturday parade.

■ See the yakuza bare their **elaborate body tattoos** (they strip down to loincloths to parade), balance precariously on top of the larger shrines, and dance to throbbing drums and piercing flutes. You can even buy sweatshirts that mimic the all-over tattooed effect.

■ Feast on **festival fare**: freshly toasted rice crackers cooked in front of you, doughy octopus balls, and Japanese-style pancakes (*okonomiyaki*) can be picked up from street vendors near the shrine.

ASIA

Buddhist women in traditional costume hurry through the streets of Seoul to join the lantern parade.

SOUTH KOREA

Lotus Lantern Festival

Every year South Korea's capital hosts a very special birthday party for Siddhartha Gautama, a Nepalese prince better known as Buddha.

To date, the founder of Buddhism has been honored with more than 2,500 birthday parties in east Asia. The biggest and brightest is the Lotus Lantern Festival in Seoul, where people light traditional paper lanterns to carry their prayers. This joyous festival, known locally as the "day when Buddha arrived," attracts Korean and foreign Buddhists and visitors, and includes celebrations, parades, and exhibits. You can take impromptu lessons in Zen meditation, lantern-making, and printing classic Korean patterns. In the afternoon children in costume act, sing, and play music, and around Jogyesa Temple monks perform dance and instrumental works that are particular to Korean Buddhism. At the festival's climax, the streets fill with light and color as more than 100,000 lanterns are carried through the city at dusk. All kinds of people join the parade. Monks and nuns dressed in traditional *hanbok* clothing walk alongside lay worshipers and tourists. They carry 70 different types of lantern—each one designed to make a certain wish come true—varying in size from delicate handheld lotus flowers and butterflies to gorgeous dragons carried by several people and huge lantern floats bearing elaborate elephants and Buddhas. The procession begins at the city's Dongdaemun Gate and takes 90 minutes to snake through the streets to the giant Jogyesa Temple. On arrival, the crowd unites by singing and dancing in the *Dongdae*, or Being Together.

When to Go Buddha's birthday is the eighth day of the fourth month of the Chinese lunar calendar. Most years this falls in May.

Planning The festival runs for three days and culminates in the lantern parade and Being Together celebration. Book hotel accommodations well in advance as hundreds of thousands of people arrive in Seoul for the festival. During the celebrations, the city's Buddhist temples provide simple meals for free.

Website www.llf.or.kr

HIGHLIGHTS

■ A daytime **street festival** takes place in the run-up to the lantern parade. Visitors can try their hand at *hanji*, the Korean art of folding paper, and make their own lantern.

■ In the week before the festival begins, Bongeunsa Temple displays an **exhibition of lantern art**. The exhibition is opened with the lighting of a giant lotus lantern nearby at the Seoul City Hall Plaza.

■ On the eve of the festival, a **carnival atmosphere** comes to Jogyesa Temple as supersize lanterns are put on show.

■ Held to open the main lantern parade, a **religious ceremony** draws representatives from temples across South Korea.

ASIA

PHILIPPINES

WAY OF THE CROSS

San Fernando, northwest of Manila, is the annual host of a
Passion play in which penitents submit to living crucifixions.

s early as 6 a.m. on Good Friday, flagellants fill the streets in the barrio of San
Pedro Cutud, just outside San Fernando, whipping their backs with *burilyos*—
bamboo sticks tied to braided ropes. Boys as young as ten take part in this all-
male ritual; like their elders, they believe in the power of penance to absolve sins or gain
divine favors. Before noon, residents begin a street performance of *Via Crucis* (Way of the
Cross)—the only Passion play in the world where participants are actually nailed to a
cross. It has been enacted in San Fernando annually since the 1950s, but its present form
took shape in 1962, when local artist Artemio Añoza volunteered to be nailed on a cross
to gain divine approval. After depicting his arrest, trial, scourging, and condemnation,
the volunteers portraying Jesus and the other participants, followed by flagellants,
crossbearers, and penitents on their knees, traverse the 2-mile (3.2 kilometer) route in
the scorching heat of noon toward the crucifixion site. Three penitents at a time are
nailed to a cross and stay suspended anywhere from several seconds to ten minutes.
Stretchers are ready to receive them when they descend. Each crucifixion represents an
act of faith whereby the penitent hopes that their prayers will be answered.

When to Go Easter falls at different times each year, but is usually in March or April. Allow a few days on
either side of the festival to explore the region.

Planning Travel before Good Friday as bus terminals are closed then. Victory Liner buses leave every
hour from Cubao, Quezon City. Get off at the tourist office at Pakuhan, and hire a jeepney to take you to
San Fernando, five minutes away. San Fernando itself does not have the best range of accommodations.
Most travelers opt to stay in nearby Clark, 15 to 20 minutes away, where there's a much wider choice of
rooms. Be prepared for spending long hours in temperatures up to 100ºF (38ºC). Bring lots of water,
a hat, and sunscreen.

Website www.cityofsanfernando.gov.ph

HIGHLIGHTS

■ **Well-preserved Fernandian rituals**
take place throughout Holy Week:
the melodious chanting of *Pasyon Ni
Kristo*—Christ's Passion, Death, and
Resurrection—sung a cappella; the
solemn meditation on the stations of
the cross; processions; and many
faith-healing rituals.

■ In the **Good Friday evening
procession**, elaborate floats festooned
with flowers and lamps carry statues
of saints, wearing black vestments as a
sign of mourning, through the streets.

■ On Easter Sunday, the Resurrection
is celebrated with an elaborate
dramatization of **Jesus' reunion with
his mother**, followed by Mass at the
Metropolitan Cathedral.

Hooded penitents seek to gain absolution for their sins by following in the steps of Jesus to an improvised Calvary.

CHINA/TAIWAN

MATSU FESTIVAL

Songs, gongs, and firecrackers are just a fraction of the birthday celebrations that take place across southern China and Taiwan in honor of the Taoist Goddess of the Sea.

Fishermen and sailors revere Matsu as their protectress. This goddess derives from a legendary figure named Lin Moniang. According to the story, while a typhoon raged Lin Moniang fell into a trance or a profound dream and saved her brothers from drowning at sea by reaching out to them in the dream. As the account spread, fishermen made Matsu the object of their prayers, and they now devoutly mark the occasion of her birthday by decorating their boats with colorful flags and ribbons and taking part in or watching ceremonies at the local temple dedicated to her. The largest Matsu festival takes place on Meizhou Island in Fujian, China, the goddess's mortal home. The celebration attracts more than 100,000 pilgrims annually and centers on her original temple, which marks the spot where Lin Moniang is believed to have been taken up into the clouds. The temple is situated on the slopes of Mount Maifeng, where a 50-foot (15 meter) statue of the goddess gazes down from the summit. Almost all Matsu festivals feature displays of local arts and crafts, as well as dance performances with folk songs. The local Matsu temple is, naturally, the focal point, but there is a great deal of activity in the surrounding streets, too, with the emphasis on volume: loud fireworks displays, dragon dances accompanied by Chinese drummers with cymbals and gongs, alongside kite-flying and calligraphy, crafts, and local cuisine.

When to Go The birthday festival takes place on or around the 23rd day of the 3rd lunar month (any time between mid-April and mid-May). In 2009, this equates to April 18, in 2010 to May 6. Lower-key ceremonies marking her death take place on the 9th day of the 9th lunar month (August or early September).

Planning Most of the festivities last just a day, but the Meizhou Festival, and some of those in Taiwan, can continue for a week or longer. Meizhou Island lies just off the central part of the Fujian coast, between Quanzhou and Putian. There are regular ferries from both cities.

Website www.chinahighlights.com/travelguide/festivals/mazu-festival.htm

ASIA

HIGHLIGHTS

■ The centerpiece of the festival is the **parade** of a statue of Matsu to the temple, where she is welcomed by the deafening racket of thousands of firecrackers.

■ A huge variety of **folk arts and crafts, performances, and parades** make this a wonderful opportunity to discover the many facets of southern Chinese maritime culture.

■ In **Taiwan**, where Matsu is the most worshiped of all the Chinese deities (there are around 1,000 temples dedicated to her across the island), the largest celebration takes place at **Chaotien Temple in Peikang**. Another notable temple is at Tachia, in Taichung County, the focus of an animated festival.

■ In **Hong Kong**, the liveliest celebration is at Joss House Bay in Sai Kung, New Territories, and involves **fantastically decorated boats**, dragon dances, drums, and lots of noise. The temple of Tin Hau (the Cantonese name for Matsu) overlooks the seashore, and the most delightful way to arrive and get an overall view of the scene is by boat from Hong Kong harbor.

Opposite: In Tachia, Taiwan, the statue of Matsu is removed from her temple by worshipers who include politicians and officials. It is paraded in a gilded sedan chair for eight days along the island's west coast. Above left: A young celebrant is decked out as a warrior. Above right: Fishermen's boats, decorated with flags, gather for the festival in Hong Kong.

A Hindu ascetic, festooned with limes hung from hooks, is set to pay homage to Lord Murugan at the Batu Caves near Kuala Lumpur.

MALAYSIA

THAIPUSAM

At an extraordinary Hindu celebration, pilgrims engage
in elaborate body piercing to mark the birthday of Lord Murugan.

Thaipusam is not a festival for the faint of heart. Celebrated by the Tamil community in several Malaysian states, it commemorates the birthday of the Hindu deity Lord Murugan (also called Subramaniam) as well as the victory of good over evil. It was on this day that the goddess Pavarti gave her son an invincible lance with which he destroyed evil demons. From the end of January (the date coincides with the full moon in the tenth month of the Tamil Hindu calendar), more than one million people gather at Kuala Lumpur alone, including pilgrims who give thanks for prayers answered and atone for their sins. Women and children carry offerings of milk, coconuts, flowers, and peacock feathers; men attach rows of fruit to their bodies with hooks, or hoist *kavadis* (mobile altars) on both shoulders. The most striking kavadis are large, ornate steel frames attached to the body with metal skewers and hooks that pierce the skin, cheeks, and tongue. Once pierced, devotees feel imbued with spiritual strength and are often able to accomplish incredible feats. They carry their tinsel- or flower-covered kavadis in a deep trance, some dancing and chanting, from the Sri Mahamariamman Temple in the heart of the city to the Batu Caves, a distance of 8 miles (13 kilometers), over eight hours. The journey culminates in a flight of 272 steps to the temple at the top of the caves, where the pilgrims fulfill their vows or seek favors.

When to Go Around the end of January or the beginning of February.

Planning Thaipusam also takes place in Pinang, where some half a million pilgrims and tourists trek from temples in George Town to the hilltop temple in Waterfall. From Kuala Lumpur, you can take an internal flight or a half-day bus ride to George Town. Both cities offer plentiful accommodations from budget to luxury, but for Thaipusam you must book months in advance. To be at the heart of things, stay in Kuala Lumpur's Golden Triangle, the commercial hub, or in the historic commercial center in George Town.

Websites www.tourism.gov.my, www.tourismpenang.gov.my, www.kualalumpur.gov.my

HIGHLIGHTS

■ On **the eve of Thaipusam**, the ceremonial "bath" of Lord Murugan takes place at the Sri Mahamariamman Temple in Kuala Lumpur. His statue is dressed with elaborate offerings and colorful flowers before being placed on a silver chariot drawn by two oxen to lead the procession to the Sri Subramaniam Temple at Batu Caves.

■ In Pinang, on the evening after Thaipusam Day, the image of Lord Murugan on his silver chariot travels from Waterfall back to George Town on an overnight journey. This **chariot procession** has concluded Thaipusam celebrations since 1857. Devotees flock around the chariot, carrying offerings amid undulating music, while children are lifted up to be blessed and coconuts are smashed before the statue of the deity.

ASIA

INDONESIA

TEMPLE ANNIVERSARY FESTIVAL

With festivals throughout the year, the Balinese temple complex
of Pura Besakih is a fine place to party Hindu-style.

ASIA

With dozens each day, Bali could easily be called the island of festivals. The most common are the *odalan* marking the anniversary of a temple. Celebrated every 210 days—equivalent to six months in Bali's Hindu *wuku* calendar—the odalan are a time of solemn sacrifice and prayer, colorful religious processions, and joyous feasting, music, and dance often lasting well past midnight. Odalan can last from a single day at secluded rice-country villages to several days at major shrines like Pura Besakih, Bali's "mother temple," perched at 3,215 feet (980 meters) in the central highlands. The temple is at the base of Mount Agung, mythical abode of the main Balinese gods, on a spot where prehistoric animist rites took place before Hinduism came to Bali. Comprising 22 major temples and shrines, some as old as the 14th century, Besakih is the wellspring of nearly everything the Balinese hold sacred. Each shrine holds its own festival; Besakih thus hosts an odalan nearly weekly. Processions vary but usually include hundreds of people clad in sarongs and other traditional garb. Joining them are gamelan orchestras and dancers, who will later appear at the open-air performances that punctuate every odalan.

When to Go Bali's climate is tropical, with hot temperatures, high humidity, and frequent afternoon showers, although Besakih is fairly cool. Blue skies are most likely in the dry season (June-September).

Planning A day will do to cover the temples and attend an odalan, but allow a week to explore the highlands thoroughly. If you miss a Besakih odalan, try another major shrine, such as the clifftop Pura Uluwatu, the island temple of Pura Tanah Lot, or Pura Ulun Danu Batur, high up a volcano above the crater lake. Odalan guests should follow dress rules—sarongs, not shorts—and not obstruct any ceremony.

Website www.bali.com

HIGHLIGHTS

■ Besakih's ritual heart, **Pura Penataran Agung**, is dedicated to the Hindu god Siva. This large temple complex spans six earthen terraces linked by stone stairways. The lowest level contains pavilions for music and dance at festivals, while the second is the heart of daily worship, including a place where priests prepare holy water and a shrine housing the legendary Padmatiga (Triple Lotus Throne).

■ Dedicated to Vishnu, the **Pura Batu Madeg** (Temple of the Standing Stone) sits over and around a large sacred rock and is the oldest extant Besakih shrine. Like the other main temples, it also represents a cardinal direction (north) and a sacred color (black).

Brilliantly dressed women bearing food and flower offerings attend an odalan at Besakih.

A *tsechu* dance performance dramatizes the life of the Second Buddha and his triumph over evil.

BHUTAN

TSECHU

This sacred dance festival centers on Guru Rinpoche, known in Bhutan as the Second Buddha, and awards merits to the faithful.

Masked dancers bouncing on the cobbles; gowns of brocade and silk; garlands of skulls; peacock feathers and incense—the annual *tsechu* (tenth day) pours life into the *dzong* (temple-fortress) of Paro and other monasteries dotting this tiny Himalayan kingdom. Villagers come from afar, some walking for days, all wearing their finest clothes and shoes—otherwise the policeman at the gate might sting their legs with nettles. The courtyard is packed with extended families squatting around picnic baskets, boy monks giggling, dignitaries smiling, jesters dangling rope phalluses in front of pretty girls. There are serious episodes, when you line up for a blessing or a drop of holy water; hilarious times, when you watch the antics of irreverent clowns; nail-biting moments, when demons and death masks stare you in the face; and myriad prayers and religious tales to wipe away your sins. And all around drums, cymbals, conch shells, and horns made of human thighbones accompany the cavernous chanting of monks.

When to Go Spring or fall are the best times to visit. Tsechus are held across the country at different times of year, so check dates to plan your itinerary.

Planning Tsechus can last up to five days. Attend at least one full day, plus the last morning if a thongdroel is unfurled. You can only visit Bhutan by booking through a registered tour operator. The daily tourist charge set by the government includes full board, services of a qualified guide, internal transportation—whatever your itinerary—and all entrance fees. Longer stays and groups attract discounts.

Websites www.tourism.gov.bt, www.bluepoppybhutan.com

HIGHLIGHTS

■ The heart of the festival is the **Dance of the Eight Manifestations of Guru Rinpoche**. Unchanged for more than 1,000 years, it is performed by monks and lay dancers in gorgeous costumes.

■ At dawn on the last morning you will see, in some major dzongs such as Paro or Trongsa, the **unfurling of a giant appliqué image of the Guru**, called the *thongdroel*, worshiped with prostrations, offerings, and prayers. They say that setting eyes on the thongdroel purifies your soul.

■ Make the most of **people-watching**: mothers feeding babies, monks blowing bubblegum, old men chewing betel nut, crowds rolling with laughter as jesters remind everyone of the importance of safe sex. It's education, fun, and religion all in one.

■ The **women's and men's gowns** (*kiras* and *ghos*), often homespun and woven in bright intricate patterns, reflect the skills of the Bhutanese, who consider work an act of worship.

ASIA

INDIA

HOLI

Spring fever takes a boisterous and semi-erotic turn in Brindavan and other places in Uttar Pradesh, where Krishna spent his childhood.

ASIA

Here the young divine, Krishna, jealous that he was dark and his beloved Radha fair, is said to have smeared her face with red powder to match up their skin color. During Holi every male seems to imbibe his spirit, and every woman is his Radha. They fling brilliant *gulal* powders and colored sprays at each other to the accompaniment of music, punctuated by the beating of the *dholak* (hand drum) and cries of "*Holi hai!*"—"It's Holi!", while folk dancing depicts the love of the divine couple. Men wear white to reveal the colors thrown at them; women dress brightly to signify spring and youthful beauty. Visitors could well be caught in the crossfire and receive a rainbow soaking. Families prepare for the festival by arranging colors on silver plates and making candy and snacks. The night before, the triumph of good over evil is celebrated with the symbolic burning of the demoness Holika. Spring banishes the winter cold as dry twigs crackle in the blaze, and the season of plenty replaces the season of want. The actual festivities begin with a ritual smearing of red gulal powder on the faces of the idols of Radha and Krishna. There is no other worship, but Krishna is present in every mind, urging revelers to let down their guard and be at one with all.

When to Go Holi falls in the month of March, and it is necessary to know the date of the full moon to make exact travel plans. In Hindu terms, the festival begins on the 12th day of the waxing moon of the month of Phalgun. Arrive a week before the festival to take in the entire mood and travel through the small villages that made up the area that was Krishna's realm in his playful youth.

Planning Take the train from Delhi to Mathura and from there a taxi to Brindavan. Hundreds of visitors crowd into Brindavan during Holi, so you should book a place through a travel agent. There are decent lodges all over the town, but the ones near the Radha Raman Temple in old Brindavan are recommended.

Website www.holifestival.org

HIGHLIGHTS

■ Symbolic of Krishna visiting Radha, men come from the village of Nandgaon to play Holi with the women of **Radha's village, Barsana**, 25 miles (40 kilometers) from Mathura. Any man who gets trapped by the women, as he tries to hoist his village flag in Barsana, has to wear women's clothes and dance and sing to his female "captors."

■ The night before Holi, a **huge bonfire** is lit in the village of Phalen to commemorate the victory of good over evil. You will witness how the local priests walk through the lighted fire and come out unscathed!

■ Visit the **500-year-old Radha Raman Temple** in Brindavan: of the many dedicated to Krishna, it is the one with the strongest sense of history.

Colors flung back and forward by the crowds turn the very air into a haze of shimmering hues during Holi in Uttar Pradesh.

KUMBHA MELA

Known as the largest human gathering on the planet, the Kumbha Mela (Pitcher Festival) occurs every three years in one of four different cities in India.

Named after a pitcher containing the elixir of immortality, this Hindu festival rotates among four locations: Allahabad, Haridwar, Ujjain, and Nasik. Legend has it that when the gods tried to save the pitcher from demons, drops of the elixir fell in these places. Tens of millions from around the globe attend the festival, including *sadhus* (holy men), preachers, sages, devotees, media, and politicians. People arrive from all over India, too, some carrying their meager belongings on their heads. Others are entrepreneurs who come to make money—astrologers, palm readers, snake charmers, barbers (it is considered especially sacred to shave your head before entering the water), and food vendors. Evenings are smoke-filled as cooking fires are lit, and the noise of the throng is deafening at most times. The zealous *naga sadhus*, a Hindu sect who wear dreadlocks and smear ash over their naked bodies, are a major attraction; people follow them into the waters of Hinduism's holy rivers and listen to their discourse. The festival at Ujjain always coincides with a planetary conjunction believed to charge the Shipra River with supreme healing forces. There are five days designated by astrologers as especially auspicious for the baths, the last at the time of a full moon. Devotees must take a dip on these days to wash away their sins and take one step nearer salvation.

When to Go The next Kumbha Melas are in Haridwar in the foothills of the Himalaya in March–April 2010 and in Allahabad in January–February 2013. The festival lasts for around 41 days.

Planning Weather will vary from city to city and according to the time of year of the Kumbha Mela. When the festival is held in early January the weather can be treacherously cold in the evenings. While there are toilet facilities for the pilgrims, they are really inadequate, so be prepared. Also, the festival entails a lot of walking and there are no seating arrangements. If you need to rest, you may just have to sit on the ground. Don't be surprised to see many sadhus and ascetics smoking chillums (special smoking equipment) filled with marijuana. With tens of millions of people, it is easy to get lost, so if you are going with others, prepare a plan and stick to it. Cell phones make it a little easier, but the crowds can be overwhelming.

Websites www.kumbhamela.net, www.spirit-of-india.com

HIGHLIGHTS

■ While people engage in discussions and prayers in groups, it is a common sight to see **men praying on their own** and performing religious devotions for hours and even days on end.

■ The festival witnesses **extraordinary manifestations of devotion**—people have written about sadhus they have seen or met who have been holding up a hand for 27 years, or taken a vow of silence, or who sleep buried in the sand, and even one who has been standing on one foot for several years.

■ Indian drama and theatrical groups in elaborate garb perform **religious dances and classical plays** on temporary stages.

■ After bathing, **women lay their saris out to dry**, an exceptionally beautiful and colorful sight.

Opposite: Two holy men shade themselves from the sun during celebrations by the Ganges River. Above left: Veiled devotees pray while sitting within circles of burning cow dung. Above right: The Shipra River at Ujjain hosts initiation ceremonies for new disciples of the *juna akhara* sect, who must symbolically die and be reborn in its waters.

Chariot Festival

Under a blazing Indian sun, Lord Jagannath—the Hindu Lord of the Universe—is wheeled on a towering chariot to his summer retreat.

ASIA

Temple bells sound, the air is heavy with the scent of incense and flowers, and voices are raised in prayer and praise of Lord Jagannath (an emanation of Lord Krishna), his sister Subhadra, and brother Balabhadra. This is Puri, on the Bay of Bengal, and the temple of Jagannath is the starting point of the 2-mile (3.2 kilometer) route to the Gundicha garden temple, where the three gods will briefly reside. The crowds cheer and surge forward as priests bring out the garlanded statues and load them onto three gigantic chariots to the sound of gongs crashing. Hundreds of hands grasp the ropes on Balabhadra's chariot, and it lurches into motion. The chariot begins its slow journey flanked by holy men, families, parties of peasants, boys spraying water to assuage the heat, peddlers, and lepers begging for alms. Next comes Subhadra's chariot, and finally Jagannath's, each one brilliantly colorful but distinct. To those who take part in the ritual, the road represents an entire lifetime. Devotees believe death at this juncture leads to salvation, and in the past some threw themselves under the chariot wheels. This gave rise to the term "juggernaut," or destructive force, coined by British rulers around the early 19th century. It does not happen today—believers content themselves with observing Lord Jagannath on his chariot, itself an assurance of eternal beatitude.

When to Go The festival falls on the day of the full moon in the Hindu month of Ashadha (June–July).

Planning Fly or take the train or bus to Bhubaneswar, the state capital of Orissa. Puri is 40 miles (64 km) by road from Bhubaneswar and can be reached by bus or taxi. Accommodations include luxury and budget hotels, lodges, *dharma shala* (inns for the pious, usually free of cost), and youth hostels, most of them along the beach. Book well in advance as the crowds are unimaginable. You can buy tickets for seats at the festival or a pass for the cordoned space along the route.

Websites www.orissatourism.org, ws.ori.nic.in/jagannath

HIGHLIGHTS

■ Admire the **temple of Jagannath**, which soars to 213 ft (65 m) and is rich in sculptures of graceful men, women, and animals. The temple is typical of the Orissan style of architecture and is mirrored in the classical, very lyrical Odissi dance of the same region.

■ Take up a position on the roof of a nearby building for **stunning views** not just of the chariots as they roll slowly along, but also of the sea of humanity below.

■ Buy **exquisite local crafts** for which the region is renowned: miniature wall hangings on religious themes, such as the life of Lord Jagannath—called *patta chitra*—stone carvings, silver filigree, and metalwork.

Thousands from all over India and the rest of the world seethe around the three great chariots of Balabhadra, Subhadra, and finally, Lord Jagannath (right to left).

Pilgrims of all castes and ages travel on foot across the state of Maharashtra to Pandharpur, singing hymns and playing instruments along the way.

INDIA

PANDHARPUR TEMPLE FESTIVAL

A sleepy village comes alive as pilgrims gather to pay homage
to a cherished image of Lord Vithoba, an incarnation of Krishna.

Thunder, lightning, and sudden showers alternate with the pure sultriness of the monsoon season, but groups of pilgrims, many of them humble farmers, come singing, dancing, and chanting hymns, walking over rough terrain for three weeks. They carry flags and palanquins of saints, and play cymbals and drums in time to the singing. Women carry water, food, or the sacred *tulsi* plant on their heads. The fervor is infectious and sustains people during the long walk, itself part of the centuries-old ritual. Along the way the pilgrims are even welcomed by people of other religions. The pilgrims' goal is the festival of the god Vithoba, which takes place at his picturesque temple on the crescent-shaped Bhima River. In the inner sanctum, the deity stands on a brick, arms akimbo, his consort, Rukhmini, alongside him. It is believed that 250,000 pilgrims, called *warkaris*, arrive on foot and the sacred occasion itself could witness a crowd of 700,000 worshipers, all of whom take their turn to bow at the god's feet and receive a blessing. The idol, about 5,000 years old and standing 3.3 feet (1 meter) tall, is made of black stone and said to be self created. Certain daily rituals are held at the temple, including early morning prayers, offerings of food, dressing the deity in robes, and waving lights in front of him. All of them are symbolic of the love felt for Vithoba.

When to Go The festival takes place in June or July, so check for exact timing. Two days is long enough to feel the devotional atmosphere and explore the village.

Planning The closest international airport is Mumbai, 250 miles (400 km) away, and the closest domestic airport is Pune, 125 miles (200 km) away. Pandharpur is easily reached from Mumbai by direct train or bus, which depart daily. Arrange to stay in low-cost Birla cottages (free to pilgrims) or free hostels called *dharma shala*. Travel light, be careful with your valuables, money, and camera, and be prepared for a rustic lifestyle—Pandharpur is an old village that has changed little since the 15th century.

Website www.maharashtratourism.net

HIGHLIGHTS

■ Six main gates lead into the temple, each dedicated to a saint or god. There are **quaint and beautiful stories** about the gates, each one exemplifying simplicity and faith. Make a point of wandering through these gates to get a feel of the place.

■ Inside the temple complex, visit the "hall with four pillars" and the **"hall with 16 pillars"** (or Solkhambi Mandapa). The pillars are carved with figures of kings, snake gods, lotuses, and elephants, but the most exquisite is the inner pillar, which is clad in silver. There is also an assembly hall, where singers sometimes assemble for devotional songs.

■ There are 24 temples, 18 hermitages, eight bathing ghats, and five mansions in the village. They each have their own **atmosphere** that is different from anything else the country has to offer.

ASIA

Purim Parade

Purim is Judaism's most joyous festival, nowhere more so than in Israel, where it resembles a cross between Halloween and Mardi Gras.

To the beat of pounding drums and blaring music, tens of thousands of revelers line the streets of Holon, a town just south of Tel Aviv, to cheer a crazy, ever-changing kaleidoscope of giant floats, twirling dancers, strutting acrobats, marching bands, and thousands of other merrymakers bedecked in feathers, spangles, balloons, and other flashy finery. They are celebrating Judaism's most joyful holiday, Purim, which marks the salvation of the Jewish people from annihilation nearly 2,500 years ago in ancient Persia. On this day, Jews eat special treats and recount the story of the holiday—but tradition also requires them to party like mad, stage comic skits, masquerade in bizarre costumes, and even get drunk. Men, women and, above all, children of all ages don fancy dress and whoop it up at street fairs, carnivals, and colorful parades. The name for these festivities is *Adloyada*, from the Hebrew expression meaning "Until we can't tell." The term is a reference to the copious alcohol intake: you're supposed to drink until you can't tell the difference between good and evil, hero and villain. The biggest Adloyada takes place in Holon.

When to Go Purim falls on the 14th day of the Jewish month of Adar and is usually in March. Adloyada parades and other festivities often take place in the days before and after the actual holiday.

Planning The Holon Adloyada parade kicks off around noon, preceded by various other open-air events. Festivities last through the afternoon and into the evening. You can get to Holon easily from Tel Aviv. Given the crowds, it's a good idea to get there by 10 or 11 a.m. to enjoy pre-parade events and secure a spot with a good view along the parade route, which currently wends down Sokolov and Weizman Streets to City Hall, but can change from year to year.

Websites www.wordtravels.com/Travelguide/Countries/Israel, inisrael.com

HIGHLIGHTS

■ Each year the Holon Adloyada has a different **specific theme**, ranging from children's stories and cartoon characters to ethnic costumes and international peace.

■ Go to temple and **hear the Megillah**, or biblical Book of Esther, read out loud in Hebrew. Kept as a long scroll, the Megillah recounts how Queen Esther and her uncle Mordecai sabotaged Haman's plot to annihilate the Jews. Each time the celebrant mentions Haman's name, congregants drown it out with **shouts and noisemakers** called *graggers*.

■ Eat **Purim treats** called *hamantashen* (Haman's pockets) or *oznei Haman* (Haman's ears). These are triangles of pastry stuffed with sweet fillings.

Girls parade in costume, making a sea of shining yellow.

Each movement of the dervishes' whirling symbolizes a stage on the spiritual journey toward selfless love.

TURKEY

WHIRLING CEREMONY

In a ritual that goes back 800 years, members of the Whirling Brotherhood spin ecstatically to achieve mystical union with God.

Konya in central Turkey is the scene of the famed ceremony that takes place during the festival to commemorate the death of Mevlana Rumi. This 13th-century Islamic mystic founded the Mevlani Sufi order in the city. Rumi's son founded the Whirling Brotherhood, whose characteristic movement came from Rumi's habit of occasionally spinning for joy in the streets. At the start of the *sema*, or whirling ceremony, the dervishes enter dressed in long white robes (symbolizing the shroud of the ego), black cloaks, and conical hats (symbols of worldly tombs and tombstones). The master chants a prayer for Mevlana and a verse from the Koran, a kettledrum strikes up, and a reed flute begins its mournful wail. The dervishes walk around the hall three times, drop their black cloaks—signifying the relinquishing of earthly attachments—and, one by one, begin to whirl across the floor, arms folded across their breasts and heads on one side. As they revolve faster and faster, they hold out their arms, right palm up to receive blessing from heaven, left palm down to transfer the blessing to earth. They repeat the dance four times, and the ceremony ends with readings from the Koran.

When to Go The festival is held over a week in mid-December each year, culminating on December 17.

Planning Konya is about 150 miles (240 km) south of Ankara. Flights to Konya and hotel rooms are in high demand during the festival, so book at least a year in advance. Some companies run small group tours centered on the ceremonies, which take place in the Mevlana Cultural Center in Konya. Whirling can also be seen at other locations at this time. Photography is not allowed during the ceremonies.

Websites www.argeus.com.tr, www.helloturkey.net/konya.html

HIGHLIGHTS

■ The **haunting, mournful music** that accompanies the sema is highly evocative even to those who don't understand the chants.

■ The **smooth, graceful movement** of the dervishes as they travel like a slow-moving constellation of spinning stars mesmerizes the audience.

■ The Mevlana Müzesi, located in the monastery where the Mevlevi order lived, houses a **museum and shrine** containing the tombs of Rumi, his father, son, and other leaders of the Mevlevi Dervish order.

■ The oldest known Neolithic settlement in the world, **Çatalhöyük**—which lies 30 miles (48 km) southeast of Konya—dates from 7500 B.C.

ASIA

GERMANY

PASSION PLAY

The idyllic Alpine town of Oberammergau has become synonymous with a reenactment of the life of Jesus that takes place every decade.

The quiet streets of Oberammergau are lined with painted houses that look like they're straight from a fairy tale. They are decorated with frescoes known as *Lüftmalerei* (which literally means "air paintings"), many on religious themes. That's natural in a village dedicated to a world-famous religious performance. The Passion play has its roots in the year 1633, when almost every family in Oberammergau was devastated by the plague. Survivors then made a vow to God that if they were spared in future they would regularly perform a "Play of the Suffering, Death, and Resurrection of Our Lord Jesus Christ." From 1634, they kept this promise, acting the play in the cemetery where the plague victims had been buried. In modern times the Passion play has been held in the last year of the decade and continues to involve actors, musicians, designers, and technicians from the town. Only the direction is done by professionals. In the year 2000, almost half the village, or more than 2,000 townspeople, took part. For this production the text was thoroughly revised, new music composed, and new sets and costumes created. The theater had been completely renovated and rededicated in 1999 with a renewal of the plague oath. Perhaps most critically, the timing was moved so that the Crucifixion would take place at night, allowing for more dramatic lighting. The play, which includes several elaborate *tableaux vivants* of Old Testament scenes, is performed daily for five months, and each time a sell-out audience is caught up anew in the unique story on which rests the foundation of Christianity.

When to Go The next Passion play is in 2010. Performances run daily from May to October.

Planning Bookings are taken two years ahead of time. Whenever you choose to go, allow days around the play to make the most of the Alpine region. You can rent hiking and climbing gear from nearby Garmisch-Partenkirchen.

Website www.oberammergau.de

HIGHLIGHTS

■ Watching the impossibly large yet **surprisingly intimate spectacle** can make you lose touch with the material world. The actors never leave character, even when the unexpected occurs. In 2000, the donkey who carried Jesus into Jerusalem was pregnant. When she gave birth, the foal became part of the cast.

■ The new text includes more of **Jesus' teaching**, including the Beatitudes, bringing to life both the New Testament and the figure of Jesus.

■ Oberammergau is renowned for its **wood carving**. Carvers' shops dot the town: be sure to ask to see the more detailed hand-carved figures.

■ Visit nearby **Linderhof Castle**, particularly for its room of mirrors. This tiny, elaborate palace, completed in 1878, was the favorite residence of the unstable King Ludwig II.

Opposite: The play is performed outdoors against the backdrop of sky and mountains, most impressive for the trial and death of Jesus. Above left: The painted houses underscore the village's religious associations. Above right: Recent productions are often ground-breaking and imaginative.

ORTHODOX EASTER

Just after midnight on Easter Saturday, a serpent of light curves down the hill of Lykavittos, Athens—the light of a myriad candles.

EUROPE

They are carried by thousands of people who have ascended to the tiny chapel of Agios Giorgios to hear the holy words "*Christos anesti*—Christ is risen" to which the response is "*Anesti enei*—Truly He is risen." Each flickering taper, lit from the chapel's holy flame, is brought home. The next morning the lintel of every house, as elsewhere in Greece, will bear a cross of soot from that candle flame, which will also be used to light votive tapers before the household's icons. Easter in Greece is the great Orthodox festival—a time of solemn church services, rites, and processions that have remained unchanged since the Byzantine Empire. It begins (after up to a week of fasting) on Good Friday, when Greeks visit their local church to see the icon of Christ lifted down from the Cross, wrapped in linen, and placed in a flower-covered bier that is then paraded through the streets. Easter Saturday is a day of devotion that ends on the stroke of midnight with the lighting of the candles and an eruption of fireworks. After this a quiet meal at home symbolizes the end of the Lenten fast. On Easter Sunday, families gather for a day of feasting, starting with red-dyed, hard-boiled eggs (a pre-Christian tradition) and a glass from the first cask of the previous year's vintage retsina, before a slow dinner of whole roast lamb or kid—a fortifying prelude to music and dancing.

When to Go The timing of Greek Easter varies, but it usually falls in April or early May.

Planning Allow at least five days. Book transportation and accommodations well ahead. Transportation to and within Greece is at a premium over Easter, when many expatriate Greeks return to their homeland and city-dwellers return to their ancestral islands or mainland villages. Athens, like all Greek cities, has plenty of hotels and guesthouses, ranging from simple pensions to luxury hotels. Days are normally warm 64-77°F (18-25°C), evenings cool to chilly. It can rain heavily, so take light rain gear and an umbrella.

Website www.gnto.gr

HIGHLIGHTS

■ Lykavittos, 910 ft (277 m) above sea level, is the highest point in Athens. From the top, there are **superb views of the ancient Acropolis,** rising above a sea of modern buildings. The mount's name means "path of light," suggesting that the Easter procession of lights descends from a much older, pre-Christian religion.

■ Easter is celebrated similarly, though on a smaller scale, in every city and village in Greece. Particular to Corfu is the **parade of the mummified body** of the island's patron saint, Spyridon, believed to perform lifesaving miracles.

■ In Crete, many villagers burn an effigy of Judas over a public bonfire. The island's **fireworks** eclipse those anywhere else in Greece.

As the period of Jesus' entombment draws to a close on Easter Saturday, the faithful light tapers in Agios Giorgios, Athens.

The charming underwater Madonna of the Sea at Zoagli is the focus of a beautiful nighttime ceremony.

ITALY

MADONNA OF THE SEA

The veneration of the Virgin Mary as protectress of seafarers takes place in tiny fishing villages and coves along the Ligurian coast.

Communities east of Genoa worship the Virgin Mary in quite different ways. In August, at steep little Zoagli tucked into its neat bay, a torchlit procession after a solemn Mass makes its way to the sea. Divers descend 30 feet (9 meters) to a bronze underwater statue of the Madonna del Mare (Madonna of the Sea) and small lamps are set afloat on the water. Farther along, in the isthmus village of Sestri Levante—the legendary home of mermaids—the feast of the Madonna del Carmine (Madonna of Mount Carmel) is celebrated with High Mass. Afterward, the church's golden Madonna, resplendent with jewels and decorated with grapes, is paraded around the streets by men in simple brown tunics. She is venerated for prayers answered and thanked with jewelry, wedding rings, and personal tokens. At the end of the day, the sea reflects a dazzling explosion of fireworks, shot into the darkening sky overhead.

When to Go Taking place in July and August, these religious festivals are often not listed with tourist activities, their focus being primarily with the parish. The festival of the Madonna of the Sea at Zoagli takes place on the evening of August 6, Christ of the Abyss on the last Saturday in July, and the Madonna of Mount Carmel on July 16.

Planning Aim to spend the day. For lunch, reserve a table in a local trattoria—families arrive in large groups for festive meals together. Many Ligurian towns are set into steep hillsides, so parking is best closest to the main road; then walk down to the towns by the sea where festivities take place. Trains on the Pisa-La Spezia-Genoa line serve most of these towns and offer a practical alternative to tight streets with little or no parking available.

Websites www.promoliguria.it, www.tangoitalia.com/turismo/liguria/sestrilevante.html

HIGHLIGHTS

■ Similar ceremonies ripple along the coast all summer, most in honor of the Virgin Mary, but some dedicated to Jesus. At Camogli in a nighttime festival, a wreath is placed over the underwater sculpture of "Cristo degli Abissi" (Christ of the Abyss), patron saint of scuba divers. This is preceded by a **procession of torchlit boats**.

■ Zoagli's marine Madonna, in her rock and seaweed home, is a favorite subject for divers to photograph. Take the plunge and enroll in one of the **underwater photography courses** for which the town is known.

■ Towns such as Rapallo have **fireworks display contests** with traditional firecrackers called *mortaretti*, which are very noisy and smoky.

TEN HARVEST FESTIVALS

Some festivals are extravagant, riotous affairs, others more somber—all are rooted in gratitude for a successful harvest.

❶ Thanksgiving, Plimoth Plantation, MA

Thanksgiving, a U.S. holiday on the fourth Thursday of November, originated in the fall of 1621, when Pilgrims celebrated their successful wheat crop and overflowing store cupboards with a three-day feast. The hosts shared their meal of partridge, wild turkey, and fish with the Massasoit and Wampanoag Native American tribes. Abraham Lincoln declared Thanksgiving a national holiday in 1863.

Planning Plimoth Plantation, a historic recreation of the 17th-century English settlements, serves Thanksgiving dinner with typical foods, such as Indian pudding and roast wild turkey. www.plimoth.org

❷ Vendimia, Mendoza, Argentina

On the final Sunday of February, the Archbishop of Mendoza sprinkles the season's first grapes with holy water and offers the new vintage to God, setting off a month of celebrations in Argentina's Mendoza region. Crowds line the streets to watch a parade of competing beauty queens atop their regional floats, and the festival culminates with a spectacular show at the amphitheater—musicians, entertainers, and dancers take to the stage before a Harvest Queen is chosen amid a backdrop of spectacular fireworks.

Planning Mendoza is hot during summer (winter months in the northern hemisphere), but cools off at night, so bring an evening cover-up. www.greatwinecapitals.com/mendoza/index.html

❸ Rice Harvest, Bali, Indonesia

Dewi Sri, the rice goddess, is venerated as a matter of course in Bali, where rice is the staple crop. During the harvest, villages are festooned with flags, and simple bamboo temples dedicated to the goddess are erected in the upstream, most sacred corners of the rice fields. Small dolls of rice stalks representing Dewi Sri are placed in granaries as offerings.

Planning Due to Bali's favorable climate, rice is planted and harvested several times a year. April and fall are likely times to observe a Bali rice harvest. bali.sawadee.com

❹ Chanthaburi Fruit Fair, Chanthaburi, Thailand

Chanthaburi is known for gemstones—and for its profusion of beautiful native fruits, as colorful as jewels. During the summer harvest, the annual Fruit Fair exhibits exotic durians, rambutans, longans, and mangosteens in vibrant arrangements as elaborate as Buddhist mandalas. There are produce competitions and art displays, and the opening-day parade features floats made from thousands of tropical fruits and vegetables.

Planning The month of the Fruit Fair varies according to the peak ripeness of fruit; check with the Thailand tourist ministry. www.thailandgrandfestival.com

❺ Sukkot, Jerusalem, Israel

Sukkot celebrates Israel's bountiful harvests and recalls the time when the Israelites wandered the desert living in temporary shelters. Families build makeshift huts, or *sukkah*, with roofs open to the sky. Here they eat, and sometimes sleep, for the next seven days. Wands of willow, myrtle, and palm, together with a citron (a kind of lemon), are shaken every day in all directions to honor the gifts from the land.

Planning The festival starts after Yom Kippur, in September or October. Join the pilgrims who visit Jerusalem every year during Sukkot. Look up to see sukkah big and small on the town's balconies and rooftops. www.virtualjerusalem.com/jewish_holidays/sukkot/index.htm

❻ Blessing of the Sea, Greece

At Epiphany, which recalls the visit of the three Wise Men to the infant Jesus, processions set off from local churches to the ocean, where a priest blesses a gold cross before hurling it into the waves. Men leap in to be first to retrieve it; the victor achieves grace, and banishes old spirits from the new year.

Planning Epiphany ceremonies occur all over Greece on January 6. Piraeus (near Athens) is known for its festivities. www.greeka.com

❼ Olivagando, Magione, Italy

Magione's two-day festival in November celebrates both the feast day of St. Clement and the local olive harvest, bringing together everyone involved in the production of olive oil. A priest blesses the new oil at a special Mass, and the town hosts a lavish medieval dinner at its 12th-century castle.

Planning Book early for the medieval dinner at the Castle of the Knights of Malta. www.inumbria.it/articoloeng-37471.html

❽ Lammas Festival, U.K.

Lammas marks the beginning of the harvest season, when food is abundant and the light begins to wane. Early Britons baked bread from the new crop to leave on church altars, and corn dolls decorated bounteous feast tables.

Planning Today, Lammas is a widely celebrated Celtic holiday—Eastbourne's festival is held yearly on the seafront. www.lammasfest.org

❾ Madeira Flower Festival, Madeira, Portugal

Funchal's April flower festival fills the air with fragrance and marks the arrival of spring. Each of the island's children brings a bloom to create the colorful Muro da Esperança (Wall of Hope), and intricate flower carpets line the streets.

Planning Bring a bathing suit as the water temperature in Madeira is comfortable year-round. www.madeiratourism.org

❿ Incwala, Swaziland

In late December, men journey to the sea to gather water so Incwala can begin. Branches from the sacred *lusekwane* tree are woven into a bower for the king, and only when he eats the first fruit can his people partake of the harvest.

Planning Visitors are allowed at the ceremony, though photography requires a permit. www.gov.sz

In a Jerusalem market, orthodox Jews select prime specimens of *etrog* (citron) for Sukkot. The fruit—along with myrtle, palm, and willow—accompanies the daily blessing, prayers, and processions.

CHRISTMAS MIDNIGHT MASS

St. Mark's Basilica, a Byzantine treasure in Venice, makes a gorgeous setting for Roman Catholic High Mass in celebration of the Nativity.

EUROPE

The basilica's sonorous bells ring out over the city to announce the service on this momentous night. The congregation has been gathering for over an hour, and now people are thronging the aisles on the geometric marble floor—visitors and locals, children running about, babies asleep in their parents' arms. The golden walls and domes swathed in breathtaking mosaics—an endowment of Venice's ties with the Orthodox Church—lend an Eastern aura to the pageantry. Dominant is the central Ascension Dome, a mosaic of Christ Pantocrator (Ruler of the Universe), while below 1,000 candles create their own flickering patterns of light. Presided over by the patriarch, the celebration begins half an hour before midnight with psalms and readings followed by the chant of the ancient Kalenda, a résumé of biblical and historic dates before the birth of Jesus. The archdeacon brings an image of the child Jesus before the patriarch, who sings the Gloria as a herald to the service. The interior is illuminated to symbolize the divine light of God, and a sermon explains the importance of the Nativity. Only Catholics partake of the sacrament, but the atmosphere is one of communal celebration.

When to Go Make the most of pre-Christmas Venice by arriving a couple of days in advance—and stay as long as you like!

Planning No tickets are required for Midnight Mass, but it is highly recommended that you arrive no later than 10:30 p.m. Entrance is through the north facade. The Latin responses are rehearsed beforehand and everyone can join in the singing. The service is printed in Italian, with English, French, and German translations for visitors. Wear appropriate and warm clothing, and do not tote any luggage. No photos or videos are allowed. Over this period many churches host glorious concerts, and you'll see postings about these throughout Venice. Restaurants often close for Christmas, so check which ones will be open and reserve for Christmas dinner.

Websites www.basilicasanmarco.it, www.italiantourism.com

HIGHLIGHTS

■ This is a wonderful chance to see the golden mosaics of the **basilica's interior** in all their illuminated glory and to reach corners that are normally inaccessible to the public.

■ Savor the deep sense of **ecclesiastical history** of this unique service. The patriarch wears vestments embroidered in silver and gold, a gift of Pope Alexander VIII to the basilica in around 1690.

■ Getting lost is part of Venice's allure. Explore the narrow, winding alleyways, and discover the "real" Venice with half the tourists and trinket sellers of high season. Don't miss the **Christmas fairs and markets**, such as the one on elegant Campo Santo Stefano.

The magnificent, domed interior of St. Mark's Basilica glows with mosaics of Old and New Testament themes dating from the 11th to the 16th century.

From the loggia of St. Peter's Basilica, Pope Benedict XVI delivers his Easter message to the faithful in 2007.

VATICAN CITY

EASTER MASS

Romans, pilgrims, and tourists gather to celebrate the most joyous day in the Roman Catholic calendar, the climax of Easter's holy days.

From early in the morning, as the pearlized sky turns blue, the great curving expanse of St. Peter's Square welcomes some 100,000 people, most but not all Catholic, a rainbow mixture of ages and nationalities. A sense of anticipation underlies the chatter. At 10:30 a.m., to a peal of bells and melodious strains from the choir, the pope makes his entrance and greets the gathering from the steps of St. Peter's Basilica. Here an altar has been set up, surrounded with red, orange, and yellow flowers, which are almost rivaled in brightness by the orange and blue uniforms of the Papal Swiss Guard. The pope honors an icon of Christ, an ancient custom revived by John Paul II, and opens this celebration of the Resurrection and the newness of life. Pilgrims, tourists, and choir make the liturgical responses together, and some of the faithful read out prayers. At noon, the pontiff appears on the basilica's central balcony to deliver the traditional *Urbi et Orbi* message, Latin for "to the city [of Rome] and to the world," and which he takes as an occasion to speak of world issues. Finally, with outstretched arms, the pope offers greetings in dozens of languages, to the delight of the crowd, and gives his blessing. The conclusion of the benediction is announced by the pealing bells of St. Peter's, answered by the cannons at the Castle of St. Angelo.

When to Go Arrive several days before Easter weekend and enjoy this beautiful and historic city in spring. Catholic Easter always falls between early March and late April.

Planning Flights are more expensive at this time, and the city is packed with visitors, so book travel and accommodations well in advance. To obtain free tickets for seats at Easter Mass in St. Peter's Square, contact the chancery office of your local Catholic diocese, or the American seminary in Rome. You do not need a ticket if you arrive very early and claim a spot to stand. Places need to be reserved for other rites and services led by the pope. To avoid standing in line, join a tour to visit the Vatican museums.

Websites www.vatican.va, www.romaturismo.it

HIGHLIGHTS

■ The Sunday Mass is the culmination of the Holy Triduum—the three days from the evening of Holy Thursday to Easter Sunday. If you plan in advance, you can be present at the evening **Mass of the Lord's Supper** on Holy Thursday in the Basilica of St. John Lateran, at which the pope washes the feet of 12 priests in memory of Jesus' act of humility at the Last Supper.

■ On Good Friday the pope leads afternoon services that include the veneration of the cross and, in the evening, the **stations of the cross** in the Colosseum. On Holy Saturday evening, the **Easter Vigil** includes a Midnight Mass in St. Peter's celebrated by the pope and senior cardinals.

■ Take the opportunity on other days to visit the **Vatican museums**, which are open over this period (except for Easter Sunday and Monday).

EUROPE

Ten Pre-Lenten Celebrations

Pre-Lenten festivals have evolved from solemn religious rites into flamboyant last-gasp indulgences before the abstinence of Lent.

❶ Mardi Gras, New Orleans

Napoleon may have sold Louisiana to the Americans, but French traditions endured, most notably Mardi Gras (Fat, or Shrove, Tuesday), the raucous carnival that really defines New Orleans. Beginning with a masked ball on the Feast of the Epiphany (January 6), festivities pick up steam all the way to the start of Lent, culminating in five days of parties.

Planning Visitors can ride on Mardi Gras floats organized by private clubs, or "krewes." The Corps de Napoleon offers membership to out-of-towners. www.mardigras.com, www.napoleonparade.com

❷ Carnival, Trinidad and Tobago

Trinidad and Tobago celebrates carnival the way it was meant to be: not a big slick commercial stadium show, but a party of the people—a spontaneous outpouring that plays out in flashy costumes, parades, dance shows, food festivals, and battle-of-the-steel-band competitions. The French launched carnival in the late 1700s as a masquerade ball for the island elite, but the event soon grew into an egalitarian street spectacle. Over the years, immigrants of all faiths have added to the hoopla, and today carnival is a multicultural extravaganza.

Planning Carnival week includes the finals of two island-wide musical competitions-*Panorama* for steel bands and *Dimanche Gras* for calypso-Trinidadian versions of "American Idol" that have been around for more than 40 years. www.gotrinidadandtobago.com

❸ Carnival, Martinique

It's the devils who come marching in when Martinique revs into carnival mode, a pre-Lenten celebration dedicated to all things mischievous. Five days of parties and processions ensue, and dressing in drag for mock weddings is the norm. Shrove Tuesday is Red Devils Day, when red-and-black costumes are donned for a fiendish parade through the streets of Fort-de-France. Carnival culminates with Ash Wednesday's symbolic mourning of King Carnival, or *Vaval*, whose effigy arrives at a funeral pyre via a parade of floats and dancing she-devils. His death marks the end of the year's merriment.

Planning The lead-up to Carnival begins in early January with weekend parties; there is even a mini-carnival in mid-Lent. www.martinique.org

❹ Fiesta de las Flores y las Frutas, Ecuador

Set against a backdrop of snowcapped Andes, Ambato's Festival of Flowers and Fruits pays homage to the agricultural bounty of the region with flamboyant costumes, elaborate floats, fireworks, and lots of peach-flavored wine. On the Saturday before Lent, Mass is held outside Ambato's whitewashed cathedral.

Planning Ambato is located about two hours south of Quito. www.ecuador.com

❺ Carnival, Rio de Janeiro, Brazil

The world's most famous carnival is an extravagant four-day celebration finishing on Shrove Tuesday. One of the highlights is the lively Rio Samba Parade, taking place at the impressive 70,000-seat Sambódromo stadium.

Planning Tickets to the Sambódromo parade should be purchased well in advance because they *will* sell out. www.rio-carnival.net

❻ Patras Carnival, Greece

A meeting of myth and reality, Patras Carnival draws its inspiration from ancient Greece—in particular, Dionysus, the god of wine. St Anthony's Day (January 17) is the official start of a carnival season that stretches into early March, finishing with a lavish parade and a kite-flying competition.

Planning Patras makes a great base for exploring the ancient sites of Olympia and Delphi. www.iexplore.com/dmap/Greece/Event/9044

❼ Carnevale, Venice, Italy

An event that inspired many others around the world, the flamboyant Venetian Carnevale originated in the 13th century and reached a decadent peak during the Renaissance. Although rooted in Catholicism, the carnival has always been a secular extravaganza, an excuse for Venetians to act out their fantasies behind the anonymity of disguise.

Planning Carnival week is cold and sometimes even snowy; pack appropriate clothing with your mask. www.carnivalofvenice.com

❽ Fasching, Germany

The six-day Fasching Festival takes place all over southern Germany and is a joyous affair. Each village or district has its own unique costume and the variety is astounding—spiders and witches, animals and jesters. The high point comes on the Monday before Ash Wednesday, when a rowdy pageant of fools is followed by an all-night carnival ball.

Planning Base yourself in the lakeside town of Friedrichshafen and rent a car to tour carnival parades. www.friedrichshafen.ws

❾ Karneval, Cologne, Germany

The carnival season begins on November 11 and flows all the way through winter to the eve of Lent. In Cologne alone there are more than 500 carnival events including parades, balls, concerts, and traditional variety shows.

Planning Rose Monday, just before Lent, sees a grand parade. The city's carnival museum gives an excellent history. www.koelnerkarneval.de

❿ Carnaval, Sitges, Spain

For one week each year, sun-splashed Sitges transforms from a sleepy beach town into a carnival heaven. Festivities kick off on Fat Thursday with a waterfront ceremony to raise King Carnestoltes from the dead, and ends with a procession of thousands marching through the medieval quarter.

Planning The Sunday and Tuesday night parades are high points. Look out for folk dances and traditional carnival fare. www.sitgestour.com

Members of a Brazilian samba school perch on an elaborate float during Mardi Gras celebrations in Rio de Janeiro. Groups vie to be named the most imaginative.

Marchers carry one of the floats displaying the life of Christ into Trapani's church at the end of the Mysteries Procession on Easter Saturday.

ITALY

GOOD FRIDAY IN TRAPANI

On the most solemn day in the Christian calendar, a town in Sicily remembers the Passion in a day-long ritual.

At 2 p.m. on Good Friday, the doors of the Church of Purgatory in the town center open and bearers called *massari*, carrying large wooden statue groups that represent the stations of the cross, lurch forward to the tune of a funeral march. It is the start of Trapani's Processione dei Misteri (Mysteries Procession), and for the next 24 hours, the massari will transport these tableaux on their shoulders around the streets of Trapani. Each of the 20 tableaux is carried by ten or twelve men, members of one of the town's guilds, and they march to the instructions of their leader who flourishes a handheld wooden *ciaccula*—similar to castanets. Before them, a phalanx of hooded men walks slowly, in mourning, while a marching band follows behind playing a funeral dirge. This same procession has taken place for more than 400 years, although today's statues were made in the 18th and 19th centuries. The heads, with their expressive, often tormented, faces, and the hands and feet are carved from wood. The statue groups, which are borne on wooden platforms, are decorated with silver jewelry and flowers. The streets of Trapani fill with crowds to see the procession, while from balconies along the route people throw down flower petals. The next day the statues are returned to the church, and the joyous part of the Easter celebration begins.

When to Go Easter weekend. Springtime is perhaps the best time to visit Sicily. The temperature is mild and the wildflowers and almond trees are in bloom.

Planning Fly to Palermo and rent a car at the airport or take the shuttle bus into the city. Trains and buses run from Palermo to Trapani; buses are frequent and probably the more efficient option. In Trapani, the railroad and bus stations are on the edge of the city center, which is small enough to walk around. It also has a small airport for domestic flights, and you can take a ferry to the nearby islands from the port. Easter is a very popular time to visit Sicily, so arrange transportation and accommodations well in advance.

Websites www.processionedeimisteri.it, www.sicilynet.it

HIGHLIGHTS

■ Experience **the ultimate in fast food** when one of the guilds arrives to eat as you enjoy dinner in a little backstreet restaurant. The moment the men sit down, dishes laden with pasta are brought to the table; 15 minutes later the men take up their burden and resume their weary march through the streets.

■ The **nocturnal section of the procession** is particularly eerie, and afterwards the haunting sound of the funereal music will invade your dreams.

■ From the **medieval mountaintop village of Erice**, on a clear day, you can see as far as Tunisia, 50 miles (80 km) away, and Mount Etna. A cable car runs from Trapani to Erice, a maze of cobbled streets surrounded by ancient walls.

EUROPE

FRANCE

Gypsy Pilgrimage

The coastal town of Saintes-Maries-de-la-Mer on the sea-swept Camargue is an annual destination for thousands of Roma (Gypsies).

Coming from all over Europe and beyond, they gather to honor the saints Mary Jacobe, the Virgin Mary's half-sister and Jesus' aunt, and Mary Salome, the mother of the disciples James and John the Evangelist. In these ceremonies the Roma also venerate their patron saint, Sara. Egyptian, or perhaps Gypsy, she is believed to have disembarked here with the two Marys, as well as Mary Magdalene and three others, all fleeing persecution for following Christ. Legend says that their simple boat had neither sail nor rudder, but Providence guided it to a safe shore. The first two Marys and Sara stayed on the coast while Mary Magdalene traveled inland to a cave to pray. The town's Romanesque church, Notre-Dame-de-la-Mer, holds relics of St. Sara in its crypt, which has become a place of pilgrimage as well as a popular baptism and wedding venue during the festival. Celebrants carry the statue of St. Sara and a small brown boat holding the figures of Mary Jacobe and Mary Salome from the church to the sea, symbolizing their miraculous arrival. Banner-bearing Camargue horsemen on white steeds and women in Provençal dress follow, and as music and church bells fill the air, the crowd cheers: "Vive Sara! Vivent les Saintes Maries!"

When to Go The festival proper lasts from May 24 to 26, although many people stay longer. A second, very colorful, and more local, festival takes place in mid-October. Church services, processions to the sea, and traditional costumes are important features of this *Fête de Marie Salomé*. Allow time to relax on the 19 miles (30 km) of sandy beach.

Planning To reach Saintes-Maries-de-la-Mer, drive or take a train from Avignon to Arles and then a 45-minute bus ride. On the way, admire the rice fields and reed-thatched rural homes. Check timetables at the Arles visitor center. There are only three buses a day.

Website www.saintesmaries.com

EUROPE

HIGHLIGHTS

■ Late in May for about ten days, both **motorized and horse-drawn caravans** of Roma surround the town in their annual pilgrimage.

■ During the festival, Roma commemorate local poet and bull-breeder, Folco, Marquis de Baroncelli-Javon (1869–1943), who campaigned for official recognition of the festival and of Roma rights in general. They pay their respects at the marquis' tomb, then honor him with folk dancing and **bull runs in the streets**.

■ Look out for the **ranches**, where *gardians*, similar to cowboys, raise black bulls and white Camargue horses. Some of these buildings are still in the traditional whitewashed and reed-thatched roof tradition.

Camargue horsemen form part of the Roma procession that carries the statue of their black saint, Sara, into the sea and back to the local church.

Young women in traditional costume carry a decorative tribute to the Virgin during the October fiesta.

SPAIN

FIESTAS DEL PILAR

This festival in honor of Zaragoza's patron saint combines perfectly with the Spanish love of partying for days (and nights) on end.

In A.D. 40, the faithful say, St. James the Apostle was praying by the banks of the Ebro River in Aragón when the Virgin Mary appeared to him. She gave him a statue of herself, and a pillar (*pilar*, in Spanish) hewn from jasper, and told him to build a church around it. Over the centuries, her followers have created, on the Plaza del Pilar, a basilica of extraordinary beauty to which modern-day devotees throng to kiss the column—now encased in marble—after which every woman called Pilar is named. Celebrations come to a head each October with the Fiestas del Pilar, which celebrate Zaragoza's patron saint. Participants offer huge quantities of flowers and fruit to the Virgin, and a procession of giant papier-mâché figures, the Giants and the Bigheads, parades through the town each day. But this is a Spanish fiesta, so music and dancing fill the streets. There's bullfighting and theater. And, in the evenings, revelers make their way to El Tubo, the city's bar district, and continue the celebrations through the night.

When to Go The festival runs for nine days, beginning on the Saturday preceding October 12 in the Plaza del Pilar amid music, theater, circus, and revelry.

Planning Arrive at Zaragoza by air, road, or rail. Several bus lines operate within the city and locally, but it may be helpful to rent a car. The heart of the old city lies south of the Ebro River, where you will find the Plaza del Pilar with its basilica and most of the city's churches, monuments, hotels, and restaurants. Thousands of visitors visit Zaragoza for the festival, so be sure to reserve accommodations early.

Website www.fiestasdelpilar.com

HIGHLIGHTS

■ Music forms an important part of the festival, with a **large number of groups** playing everything from folk and pop to reggae, tango, and jazz at venues across the city.

■ If you can't master the tango, try the traditional Aragonese dance, the *jota*. **Folkloric music and dancing** take place daily at the Fuente de Goya in the Plaza del Pilar.

■ There are **fireworks displays** each evening. The one on the final evening of the festival, which takes place at the Parque de Macanaz on the banks of the river, is particularly striking.

■ **Sound, light, and water** shows transform the Parque Primo de Rivera each evening.

■ For the thirsty, the Parque de Atracciones hosts a **beer festival** throughout the days and nights of the fiesta.

EUROPE

SPAIN

HOLY WEEK IN SEVILLE

Catholics throughout Spain celebrate Holy Week with parades, but nowhere with more spectacle than in the southern city of Seville.

For eight days each spring, the ancient city streets pulsate with religious pageantry. From Palm Sunday to Easter Sunday, around 50,000 members of the city's religious brotherhoods form 59 processions to make the journey from their parishes to the city's cathedral. Most brotherhoods carry two richly decorated floats. One represents the Passion and Resurrection of Jesus, the other carries the Virgin Mary. The statues wear gold crowns and ornate velvet and brocade robes, and the floats' frames include intricate silverwork. They can weigh more than 2 tons (2 tonnes)—and the processions last up to eight hours. Stand close enough and you can hear the tired grunts of the carriers hidden behind floor-length curtains. Following behind is a trail of penitents in white tunics with long pointed hoods and covered faces (only God knows their identity), carrying full-size crosses, banners, and candles. From the balconies, singers intone emotional flamenco laments. The spectacle reaches its peak in the early hours of Good Friday, when the most important and most lavishly adorned of the floats make their way through the narrow, cobbled streets. Two days later, Seville marks the Resurrection of Jesus and brims over with joy once more.

When to Go If you can't stay for the whole week leading up to Easter, try to be there for the ceremony in the early hours of Good Friday. The exact timing varies every year, but is always March or April.

Planning Accommodations get booked up well in advance, as the Holy Week processions attract around a million spectators. If you want to be sure of a comfortable night, make your reservation early. The local newspapers give details of which brotherhood will process on each day, and the time it will leave its home church. As many as ten brotherhoods can process at one time, so arm yourself with a map of the city and a good pair of walking shoes. The trick is to navigate the winding streets to see as much as possible—but without running into a procession that blocks your way.

Websites www.guiasemanasanta.com, www.sevillaonline.es

EUROPE

HIGHLIGHTS

■ If you're in town a few days early, visit the **churches** to see the brotherhoods making their preparations.

■ On one level the Holy Week processions are solemn religious events. But the *sevillanos* like to party, and the **bars** lining the brotherhoods' routes do brisk business. Make sure you allow some time for refreshment to soak up this alternative atmosphere.

■ Try *torrijas*, the local **Easter delicacy**. It's a kind of French toast soaked in eggs, wine, and honey.

Penitents of the Resurrected Brotherhood prepare for the Easter Sunday procession at Seville's church of Santa María la Blanca.

IN REMEMBRANCE

9

To understand a people's beliefs and values, examine how they honor their dead. All societies create sacred spaces to revere the departed. Some are somber and reflective, others vibrant, even joyful—but all tell stories. In Egypt's Valley of the Kings, see how archaeologists have recreated the lives of pharaohs who died 3,000 years ago. In China, visit silent mounds guarding rulers who built one of the world's most enduring civilizations. Discover tales of passion, as told by the tombs of star-crossed lovers Heloïse and Abelard in Père Lachaise Cemetery, Paris. Hear tales of war, in military cemeteries such as Arlington, where the United States honors its fallen. Closer to our own times, reflect on the lives swept away by tyranny and terror, in the Peace Park on the site of the A-bomb attack in Hiroshima, or Jerusalem's Holocaust memorial, Yad Vashem. But also savor locations celebrating life, like Romania's Merry Cemetery, with its exuberantly painted gravestones.

Founded during the Civil War, Arlington National Cemetery is one of two U.S. national military cemeteries under army administration. It is a place of mourning with nearly 100 graveside services held each week.

L'ANSE AMOUR MOUND

The remote and tiny settlement of L'Anse Amour attracts visitors in search of solitude, nature, and a mysterious ancient burial site.

NORTH AMERICA

No one knows the name or the sex, but what we do know about the youth is this: roughly 7,500 years ago, an adolescent from northeast Canada died and was carefully laid facedown in a deep pit, his body enshrouded in bark. The head was aimed westward, and elders had sprinkled red ocher on the back and laid stone implements and weapons in the grave. They then lit fires around the body, finally filling the pit with rocks. Such an elaborate ritual required perhaps a week of preparation and suggests that this young person was an important member of the community. Today, the hallowed rock-covered circle, 26 feet (8 meters) in diameter, is North America's oldest known burial mound. This youth lived in the Maritime Archaic era among a community of sea-mammal hunters known as the Red Paint People who occupied the subarctic Atlantic coast. Near the tiny fishing hamlet of L'Anse Amour, on Labrador's southern tip, the mound was excavated in 1974 and later restored to its original shape. L'Anse Amour—Cove of Love in French—has a mere eight inhabitants. Yet every summer, some 10,000 visitors come to satify their curiosity about this remote location.

When to Go The weather is best in the summer, from June to September, when you can bike, hike, and visit the lighthouse. A scenic coastal drive on Highway 510 is highly recommended.

Planning Allow a day to see the mound, museum, and lighthouse—or two if you also plan to visit the Red Bay National Historic Site, a 16th-century Basque whaling station. To reach L'Anse Amour, fly to Lourdes-de-Blanc-Sablon airport in Quebec. Rent a car, drive eastward, and you'll be there within 30 minutes. A lucky few can spend the night at the three-bedroom Lighthouse Cove Bed & Breakfast, a 20-minute walk from the burial site. Unsurprisingly, it's L'Anse Amour's only lodging; reservations are advisable.

Websites www.destinationlabrador.com, www.pointamourlighthouse.ca, www.labradorstraitsmuseum.ca

HIGHLIGHTS

■ From mid-June through mid-October, visit the 109-ft (33 m) tall **Point Amour Lighthouse**, built in 1857. It's Canada's second largest lighthouse and the tallest along its Atlantic seaboard.

■ Bring binoculars to spy **humpback whales and year-round icebergs.** For hikers, L'Anse Amour's Spooner Cove, Battery, and Overfall Brook trails range from easy to medium difficulty.

■ Visit the **Labrador Straits Museum** to understand early domestic life and see how women have contributed to Labrador's progress over the past 150 years. It also has replicas of items found during excavations and exhibits on the Maritime Archaic era.

Still very much in use, Point Amour Lighthouse has an automated beacon and now doubles as a maritime museum. Climb its 128 steps to enjoy fine marine views.

An eternal flame burns at the tomb of President John F. Kennedy.

VIRGINIA

ARLINGTON NATIONAL CEMETERY

Symbols of national identity abound at this resting place of some 300,000 servicemen and women and their family members.

Flanked by granite pillars at each end, the entrance's semicircular retaining wall bears the Great Seal of the United States. Vehicles pass through ornate wrought-iron gates marked with six gold stars and military seals. A sea of simple white crosses envelops you in a somber, respectful quietude. With a tree-lined expanse before it, the white marble sarcophagus of the Tomb of the Unknowns stands as a tribute to those unidentified U.S. soldiers who served in all wars. Around the clock an official Army Honor Guard keeps watch. On a slope just below Arlington House, the grave of President John F. Kennedy forever flickers with the eternal flame. A walk among the headstones chronicles American history, from the World War II Iwo Jima Memorial to 367 Medal of Honor recipients and astronauts lost in space. The cemetery is full of those who gave their lives but about whom most of us know nothing.

When to Go The cemetery opens at 8 a.m., 365 days a year. It closes at 7 p.m. from April to September, and at 5 p.m. the rest of the year.

Planning Allow two to four hours to walk around the cemetery, which covers 624 acres (253 ha). There is a visitors' center by the entrance with a bookstore. The site doesn't provide wheelchairs or strollers and cars are not normally allowed inside. Ample parking is accessible from Memorial Drive. You can reach Arlington by the year-round narrated Tourmobile bus from Washington landmarks, such as the White House, or the Metro's blue line. Be respectful of burials taking place.

Websites www.arlingtoncemetery.org, www.nps.gov/arho, www.washington.org

HIGHLIGHTS

■ Featuring a curved gateway with a roof of glass tablets in front of a reflecting pool, the **Women in Military Service for America Memorial** honors nearly two million women who have served in defense of the U.S., including nurses. It's the only such memorial.

■ Two simple **memorial markers** a few feet (meters) apart commemorate the **14 astronauts**–13 American and one Israeli–who died when the U.S. space shuttles *Challenger* and *Columbia* broke apart in 1986 and 2003, respectively.

■ There are major **memorial services**, all open to the public, at 11 a.m. on Memorial Day (the last Monday of May) and Veterans Day (November 11), and at sunrise on Easter Sunday.

■ The 19th-century **Arlington House** was originally intended as a living memorial to George Washington and once housed Robert E. Lee. While the adjoining tract became a national cemetery in 1864, Congress bought the home from Lee's son in 1883.

NEW YORK

GROUND ZERO

After several years of debate, a memorial
museum now rises on the ruins of the World Trade Center.

Though today it resembles an ordinary construction site, there is no more hallowed place in New York City than Ground Zero, the former site of the World Trade Center. For many, the world changed forever when 2,980 people perished here on September 11, 2001, in the first foreign attack on the continental United States. In a suicide mission planned by the terrorist group al Qaeda, two hijacked American passenger airplanes crashed into the city's two tallest towers, causing fires so severe that metal supports melted and the buildings crumbled to the ground. Taking shape on the former site of the Twin Towers are a new Freedom Tower—to be the city's tallest at 1,776 feet (541 meters)—three other office towers, and the National September 11 Memorial & Museum at the World Trade Center. This will include the museum building, two reflecting pools with cascading waterfalls, and a contemplative area of more than 300 oak trees, a forest oasis in the city. By 2008, all 50 U.S. states, 30 foreign countries, and scores of individuals and organizations had raised a total of more than $325 million toward the $350 million needed for the memorial complex. While the buildings go up, the Tribute WTC Visitor Center, across from the Twin Towers site, offers tours, exhibits, and programs, linking visitors who want to understand better the events of the day, universally known as 9/11, with the people who experienced them. It is a project of the September 11th Families' Association formed by relatives of victims.

When to Go The site and Tribute WTC Visitor Center at 120 Liberty Street are open daily all year. The visitor center hours are Monday and Wednesday-Saturday, 10 a.m.-6 p.m.; Tuesday, noon-6 p.m.; Sunday, noon-5 p.m. Allow at least two hours for the visitor center and a walk around the area.

Planning The visitor center offers walking tours Sunday through Friday at 11 a.m., 1 p.m., and 3 p.m., and on Saturday at 11 a.m., noon, 1, 2, and 3 p.m.

Website www.tributewtc.org

NORTH
AMERICA

HIGHLIGHTS

■ **Walking tours** led by survivors of 9/11 are moving recreations of the events of that day and its aftermath.

■ A **walkway** around the building site provides an overview of the vast area.

■ Five galleries at the **Tribute WTC Visitor Center** trace the history of the World Trade Center with photos, film, artifacts, and recordings before, during, and after 9/11.

■ The mangled remains of Fritz Koenig's **"Sphere,"** which once stood between the Twin Towers as a symbol of global peace, is evidence of the devastation of the terrorist attack and a memorial to its victims. The bronze sculpture, 15 feet (4.6 m) in diameter and weighing 4,500 pounds (2,041 kg), was damaged by falling debris. It was moved to Battery Park, a few blocks south of Ground Zero and an eternal flame lit on the first anniversary of the attacks.

Opposite: Badly damaged on 9/11, Fritz Koenig's "Sphere" now rests in Battersea Park. Above left: Construction of the Memorial & Museum at the World Trade Center started in 2006. Above right: Two days after 9/11, workers found this steel cross beam in the debris of the World Trade Center. They later erected it on a pedestal as a shrine.

SERPENT MOUND

Surrounded by mystery and magic, the Great Serpent slithers across a ridgetop high above the rolling farmlands of rural Ohio.

NORTH AMERICA

The great writhing serpent undulates for a quarter-mile along a prominent ridge, through verdant green woodlands high above the lush pastoral farmlands of Ohio. The largest effigy mound ever discovered is now encircled by a meandering walkway through grassy fields dotted with trees. The path begins at the tightly coiled tail and follows the sinuous curves of the massive body for around 1,370 feet (418 meters) to the mighty oval-shaped mound just beyond the head of the serpent. The mound's very existence raises the question of what ancient culture built it and why. The Serpent Mound's head aligns with the summer solstice sunset, while the coils of the body mark aspects of the lunar and solar solstices and equinoxes, indicating that skilled astronomers directed the placement and construction. Most likely, this great serpent dates from A.D. 1000 or earlier. The astrological alignments, coupled with ancient serpent mythologies, seem to link it to the once important task of maintaining the fragile balance between the forces of day and night, summer and winter, and the magical powers of the upperworld against the demonic forces of the underworld.

When to Go The weather is most pleasant in late spring and early fall, when the museum is open only on weekends. Summer days can be hot and humid, so visit in the morning when it is cooler. You can explore the museum and mound in a day trip from Cincinnati or Columbus, Ohio.

Planning The Serpent Mound is in Adams County about 80 miles (129 km) east of Cincinnati and 100 miles (161 km) south of Columbus. The memorial park is on State Route 73 about 20 miles (32 km) south of Bainbridge. The mound is open all year, Wednesday through Sunday. The museum's opening hours vary, and it is closed from November to March.

Websites www.ohiohistory.org, www.adamscountytravel.org

HIGHLIGHTS

■ The **museum** has exhibits on the unique geology of the area, the astronomical alignments of the mound, and the ancient people who created it.

■ The alignment of the center of the coiled tail to the base of the serpent's head is **true north**.

■ Climb the observation tower for a **panoramic view** of the entire serpent mound, and marvel at the creativity of the ancient peoples who lived here centuries ago.

The origins of Serpent Mound remain wrapped in mystery.

Imported from India, the black granite for the Vietnam Veterans Memorial was deliberately chosen for its reflective properties.

WASHINGTON, D.C.

VIETNAM VETERANS MEMORIAL

Although at first a controversial reminder of a controversial war, over time this memorial has firmly gained in Americans' affection.

Y ou start by walking past a tiny sliver of black granite etched with a handful of names; as you move forward, the buzz of nearby Constitution Avenue slips away and an awed hush falls over visitors. As the tapered wall grows taller, you gaze up at a sheer face of names carved in stone, and this tribute to those who fell or went missing during the Vietnam War becomes a mesmerizing record of history. The two intersecting triangles, both 247 feet (75 meters) long and set into the earth, make no political statement about this very political war—the wall simply honors those who served and died. Here simplicity rules: the wall lists 58,256 names chronologically by the day of casualty or disappearance, but that's the only distinction; all are the same size, without rank or decoration. Some visitors make pencil rubbings of names, some leave flowers, mementos, or letters, some merely stop and stare at the reflective granite: to view the names means to see your own image among them. At its apex, where the chronological sequence from 1959 to 1975 begins and ends, the wall climbs to more than 10 feet (3 meters). As you walk on, its height starts to shrink and you begin your ascent back to the world of the living. From its inception, the wall was a political and emotional battleground. Its designer, Yale University student Maya Lin, and her design sparked much controversy, yet a panel of judges chose her vision from among more than 1,400 entries. The wall now draws millions every year.

When to Go The memorial is open 24 hours a day, every day. Fall is beautiful here, though spring is the best time to visit, when the surrounding area is abloom with colorful cherry blossoms. Allow 30 to 45 minutes to spend time gazing at the names and exploring the accompanying sculptures.

Planning The memorial is at the intersection of Henry Bacon Drive and Constitution Avenue. The closest Metro stop is Foggy Bottom. Rangers are on duty from 9:30 a.m. to 11:30 p.m. daily to answer questions.

Websites www.nps.gov/vive, www.viewthewall.com, www.thewall-usa.com

HIGHLIGHTS

■ The wall was completed in 1982, but the site has several later additions: a statue of **"The Three Servicemen,"** the **Vietnam Women's Memorial**, and the **In Memory Plaque**, recognizing everyone who served.

■ Although the wall records names chronologically by date, then by alphabetical order, the sheer number makes it almost impossible to locate an individual name. There is a **directory** of names at the end of the wall. Plus marks on the wall indicate those Missing in Action.

■ A remembrance ceremony, with wreath laying, music, and speeches, takes place here every **Veterans Day**, which always falls on November 11.

NORTH AMERICA

Ten War Memorials

Those who have sacrificed their lives fighting for their country hold a special place in a nation's heart.

① National War Memorial, Canada

In the center of Ottawa's Confederation Square, 22 bronze figures from all branches of the military advance through a tall granite arch under the gaze of Canada's parliament buildings. Unveiled in 1939, the memorial, crowned with bronze statues of Peace and Freedom, represents the "Great Response" of the thousands of Canadians who served and fell in World War I. The site now commemorates all those who have given their lives for the country.

Planning Confederation Square is in the heart of downtown Ottawa, Ontario. Canada's national mourning ceremony takes place here each year on Remembrance Day (November 11). www.vac-acc.gc.ca

② Korean War Veterans Memorial, Washington, D.C.

Nineteen figures, some emerging from trees, patrol Washington's National Mall through juniper bushes and over granite obstacles. The statues, made of reflective stainless steel, come to life in sunlight and turn ghostly after dark. The memorial honors the Americans who served and gave their lives in the Korean War from 1950 to 1953.

Planning The memorial is on French Drive, near the Foggy Bottom Metro station. www.nps.gov/kwvm

③ Liberty Memorial, Kansas City, Kansas

Four stone statues—symbolizing Courage, Honor, Patriotism, and Sacrifice—ring the top of the Memorial Tower, while the "Great Frieze" charts the progress from war to peace. The Liberty Memorial was built following World War I and restored and reopened in 2002. The National World War I Museum opened at the same site in 2006.

Planning Located on Kessler Road in Penn Valley Park, the site is open Tuesday through Sunday, from 10 a.m. to 5 p.m. www.libertymemorialmuseum.org

④ Little Bighorn Battlefield National Monument, Crow Agency, Montana

In June 1876, Sitting Bull's Sun Dance alliance of Lakota, Cheyenne, and Arapaho warriors defeated Lt. Col. George A. Custer and the Seventh Cavalry Regiment. The U.S. Secretary of War designated the land a national cemetery in 1879, but it wasn't until 1991 that Congress commissioned a memorial. Now the site bears witness both to the dead and to the final efforts of the Native Americans to preserve their heritage.

Planning The monument is open daily except for New Year's Day, Thanksgiving, and Christmas Day. The visitor center holds talks on the battle throughout summer. www.nps.gov/libi

⑤ U.S.S. Arizona Memorial, Honolulu, Hawaii

Japan's sinking of the U.S.S. *Arizona* at Pearl Harbor on December 7, 1941 prompted the United States' belated entry into World War II. The sunken ship is the final resting place of 1,177 servicemen; their bones still lie entombed in the hull.

Planning No tickets are sold in advance; they are allocated on a first-come, first-served basis. Waiting times can be long—take the chance to visit the Pearl Harbor Memorial Museum. www.pearlharbormemorial.com

⑥ Anzac Commemorative Site, Turkey

In 1915, during World War I, Allied troops fought the Ottoman Empire for control of the Gallipoli Peninsula. Their campaign failed, with terrible losses on both sides, including 8,709 Australians and 2,721 New Zealanders. The site features informative panels, walking routes, and battlefield tours. Memorial services take place annually on April 25.

Planning Most visitors base themselves at Çanakkale, a 30-minute ferry ride from the peninsula. www.anzacsite.gov.au, www.anzac.govt.nz

⑦ Warsaw Uprising Memorial, Warsaw, Poland

The Warsaw Uprising of 1944 against Nazi rule saw thousands of Poles killed and much of the old town razed. This memorial honors the heroes. One group shows battling insurgents; the other, "Exodus," depicts broken soldiers fleeing into sewers.

Planning The monument is in Warsaw's Krasiński Square. www.1944.pl

⑧ Normandy American Cemetery and Memorial, France

Overlooking France's Omaha Beach lie the graves of thousands of Americans killed in World War II, most on D-Day (June 6, 1944); the Walls of the Missing bear a further 1,557 carved names. A poignant bronze statue entitled "Spirit of American Youth" stands at the center of the memorial.

Planning The site is in Colleville-sur-Mer, near Bayeux. www.abmc.gov

⑨ Thiepval Memorial, France

The Thiepval Memorial honors British and South African servicemen who lost their lives on the Somme battlefields during World War I. The world's largest British war memorial, it lists the names of 72,085 missing soldiers.

Planning Located near Amiens, the Thiepval visitor center is open daily except from Christmas to New Year's Day. www.thiepval.org.uk

⑩ Cenotaph, London, England

Designed by Sir Edwin Lutyens, the Cenotaph (literally "empty tomb") in Whitehall, central London, was erected in 1919 to honor the fallen of World War I. Every year on Remembrance Sunday, the monarch and public figures lay poppy wreaths, and veterans and the armed forces parade to salute all British and Commonwealth soldiers killed in battle since 1914.

Planning The nearest tube stations are Charing Cross and Westminster. The ceremony takes place at 11 a.m. on the second Sunday in November, the nearest to Armistice Day. www.roll-of-honour.com

The U.S.S. *Arizona* Memorial straddles the battleship that sank on December 7, 1941, when the Japanese bombed Pearl Harbor.

DEC. 29, 1890
CANKPE OPI EL TONA
WICAKTE PI GUN HE CAJEPI KIN
23 SPOTTED THUNDER
24 SHOOTS THE BEAR
25 PICKED HORSES
26 BEAR CUTS BODY
27 CHASE IN WINTER
28 TOOTH ITS HOLE
29 RED HORN
30 HE EAGLE
31 NO EARS
32 WOLF SKIN NECKLACE
33 LODGE SKIN KNOPKIN
34 CHARGE AT THEM
35 WEASEL BEAR
36 BIRD SHAKES
37 BIG SKIRT
38 BROWN TURTLE

In 1903, surviving relatives and other Sioux erected this memorial in English and Lakota to victims of the 1890 massacre.

SOUTH DAKOTA

WOUNDED KNEE

The prairie winds and the grassy plains hold memories of the Lakota people and the tragedy that befell them one cold winter morning.

Chief Big Foot, High Hawk, Shading Bear, and Long Bull lead the long list of names carved onto all four sides of a simple stone monument atop a lonely little hill. Known as Wounded Knee, this was the site of the massacre of a band of Lakota on December 29, 1890. Pursued by the Seventh Calvary, the tribe of 300 had fled from their home in the Badlands across the cold wild plains. Here on the Pine Ridge Reservation they hoped to find a place to practice their ancestral ways in peace. Instead the army encircled them, forcing them to disarm. The search for weapons was prolonged as the Lakota resisted giving theirs up, and finally a gun went off, inadvertently provoking carnage. Today a small cemetery marks the site where most of the tribe perished in what is often called the last of the Indian Wars. The site's power lies in its vastness. Here grasses rippling in the wind fade into the distant horizon under a cornflower blue sky so deep and timeless that it seems to hold the echoes, chants, and prayers of those slain here.

When to Go The Wounded Knee Museum opens daily from late May to early October.

Planning Summers are very hot, with temperatures often exceeding 100°F (38°C), and usually dry. However, the weather can change rapidly and temperatures may plummet or a violent thunderstorm strike. Dress in layers, wear sturdy walking shoes and sunscreen, and carry water when traveling to the Pine Ridge Reservation. In the town of Wall, 55 miles (89 km) east of Rapid City, the Wounded Knee Museum provides directions to the massacre site and a self-guided tour map. With an early morning start, a day is enough to explore the museum leisurely, eat lunch in Wall, and then visit the Wounded Knee site.

Website www.woundedkneemuseum.org

HIGHLIGHTS

■ At the Wounded Knee Museum, see **original photographs** taken that grisly day and a **model of the massacre site**, and then read eye-witness accounts and contemporary newspaper clippings. Listen to the **recorded voice** of massacre survivor Dewey Beard, a Lakota warrior.

■ Note the four large **Hotchkiss guns** still standing on the hill. The soldiers used these to shoot indiscriminately into the Lakota encampment.

■ Since 1936, **Wall Drug Store** has been attracting ever greater hordes of visitors with its garish billboards and offer of free ice water. The enjoyably kitsch shopping mall now employs around a third of Wall's population of 800 and attracts two million visitors a year.

NORTH AMERICA

LOUISIANA

New Orleans Cemeteries

New Orleans' unusual topography has given rise
to inventive methods of disposing of its dead.

New Orleanians call them the "Cities of the Dead." Lined with tall tombs and elaborate crypts, the narrow avenues of New Orleans' many cemeteries conjure eerie visions of the thousands of dead residing here. Some of the family tombs resemble small houses, complete with iron fences. Elaborate ironwork, crosses, and statues adorn many tombs. On holidays, votive candles line the graves as tributes from the living to their dead forebears. In other places, graves are usually located underground, with memorials marking the spot. In New Orleans, however, the low water table means that coffins are unsafe below ground. Aboveground burials became the norm in 1789, beginning with the St. Louis Cemetery No. 1, where bodies were laid to rest inside the tombs. In family tombs many relatives may share the space. They can do so because the city's subtropical climate causes the tombs to become virtual ovens, with cremation-like heat that causes bodies to decompose rapidly. Within about a year, only bones remain. Cemetery workers sweep these into an opening in the floor of the tomb, which is then ready for its next occupant. The name and date of each person then go onto a plaque or headstone.

When to Go New Orleans is at its best from October through mid-April; heat and humidity can make the city uncomfortable the rest of the year. Tours of individual cemeteries usually last an hour.

Planning For a full appreciation of the cemeteries' history and legends, a guided tour is best. Safety is another reason to join a group: narrow lanes and tall tombs make good hiding places for thieves. Tours given by Save Our Cemeteries, a nonprofit group dedicated to preserving and restoring the burial grounds, are highly recommended.

Website www.saveourcemeteries.org

HIGHLIGHTS

■ Marie Laveau, the notorious **Voodoo Queen** of New Orleans, is believed to be buried in St. Louis Cemetery No. 1. Admirers leave gifts and mark her likely tomb with Xs. Some say devotees still perform secret rites there.

■ **Lafayette Cemetery No. 1** is the most visited graveyard and the one most often seen in films such as *Double Jeopardy* and *Interview with the Vampire*. It's also the graveyard featured in *The Vampire Chronicles* by local novelist Anne Rice.

■ **St. Roch Cemetery** is the city's oldest. Full of mementos of his supposed cures, its chapel honors St. Roch for purportedly saving lives in an 18th-century yellow fever epidemic.

Before the practice of aboveground burial became the norm in New Orleans, coffins would rise up out of the ground after a storm because of the high water table.

TOMBS OF ROYAL SIPÁN

This South American village is the New World
equivalent of Egypt's Valley of the Kings.

SOUTH
AMERICA

Outside archaeological circles, the name Sipán doesn't normally send the pulse
racing. But this dusty village in the northern desert of Peru is an extraordinary
place of sumptuous treasures and ancient religious rites that scholars have yet to
decipher fully. Sipán flourished from A.D. 200 to 600 as a cultural and spiritual hub of the
Moche civilization. Many of the city's leaders, secular and sacred, were buried in mounds
beside large mud-brick pyramids. Unlike many pre-Columbian sites in the Americas,
the Moche tombs—and their priceless gold and silver contents—were essentially lost
and forgotten for more than 1,400 years. Not until 1987 was the first tomb discovered,
that of a high-ranking noble. He was quickly dubbed the Lord of Sipán. In later years
archaeologists found ten more, including tombs of a high priest, the Old Lord of Sipán,
a shaman's assistant, and a high-ranking warrior. Of the graves open to visitors, the Lord
of Sipán's is the most intriguing, filled with replicas of original gold accoutrements, as
well as clay funeral pots, which once contained food for the dead to eat in the afterlife,
and adobe bricks with distinctive brands. Scholars think these may have been memorial
tablets donated by Sipán's powerful families or clans.

When to Go Temperatures in the northern desert often hit 90°F (32°C) in summer (December–February).
The other three seasons offer much milder climes, with mostly clear skies and little rain.

Planning The city of Chiclayo is the best base for visits to Sipán, 22 miles (35 km) to the southeast, and
the region's other archaeological sites, such as the vast mud-brick metropolis of Túcume, where 26
pyramids loom above a cactus-studded landscape. Although you can easily see the royal tombs at Sipán
in a couple of hours, you need several days to visit all the major archaeological sites of north coastal Peru.

Websites www.peru.info, www.go2peru.com

HIGHLIGHTS

■ Two large **mud-brick pyramids**
(*huacas*) dominate the Sipán
archeological zone. Visitors can scale
the larger of the two for a view of the
ruins. Scholars believe the smaller
pyramid was probably a royal palace,
the larger one a religious building.

■ In Chiclayo's northern outskirts,
the excellent **Royal Tombs of Sipán
Museum** has many original artifacts.
The collection is especially rich in
Moche ceramics, many decorated
with scenes from everyday life.

■ In a corner of the Mercado Modelo
in downtown Chiclayo, the **Shaman's
Market** is an emporium stocking
everything a shaman might need,
such as snake skins, toucan beaks,
voodoo dolls, crucifixes, aphrodisiacs,
and hallucinogenic plants.

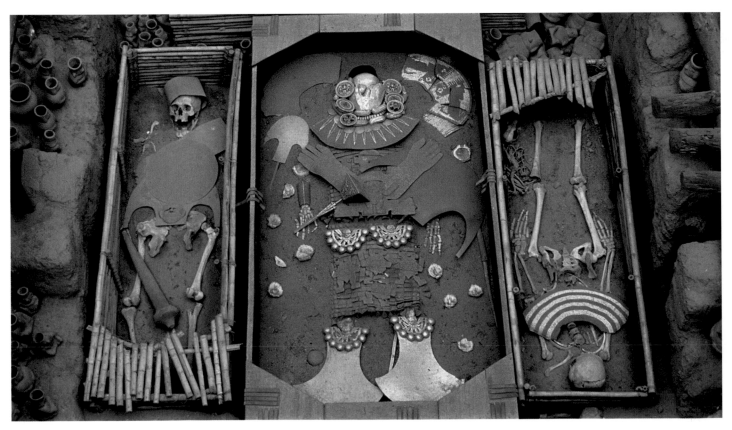

The Lord of Sipán was buried with gold artifacts and attendants for the afterlife on either side.

The Children's Peace Monument celebrates the hopes of a girl who died of leukemia after the A-bomb explosion.

JAPAN

PEACE MEMORIAL PARK

A glimpse into the apocalyptic past of Hiroshima—declared
a Peace Memorial City in 1946—gives hope for the future.

HIGHLIGHTS

■ Pray for world peace with the locals at the **Memorial Cenotaph**, and feel touched when you see young children and their families kneel down in unison.

■ Visit the **Peace Memorial Museum**. It depicts history through reconstructions, photographs, and charred remains from the blast.

■ Capture the memory on film by taking a **photo through the cenotaph**, lining up the peace flame and the A-Bomb dome.

■ Ring the **Peace Bell**, while paying attention to the map on its surface. Designed to symbolize one world, the map has no national boundaries.

■ Bring origami paper to fold your own cranes for the **Children's Peace Monument**. Sadako Sasaki only managed to fold 644 cranes before she died, but her schoolmates—and then peacelovers worldwide—carried on the tradition.

ASIA

O n August 6, 1945, the world's first atom bombing left Hiroshima in ashes. Amid annihilation one prominent structure remained—the Industrial Promotion Hall, renamed the A-Bomb Dome. A crumbling ruin of its former glory, the shell illuminates Hiroshima's bleak past and rosier present aspirations. It rests on one bank of the Motoyasugawa River, facing the memorial park. A wide pillar-lined bridge links the two, leading to the Children's Peace Monument. Here there is a statue of a young girl lifting a crane skyward, while a bronze boy and girl hang precariously on opposite sides of the towering pedestal. Below, an inscribed stone reads: "This is our cry; this is our prayer—for building peace in this world." Origami cranes in clear cages ring the monument. Each attests the hope of Sadako Sasaki, a young local leukemia patient who attempted to fold a thousand cranes believing that doing so would make her wish to recover come true. Well-trimmed hedges and wide stone paths guide visitors, engaged in muffled conversation, through the park. The flame at the concrete Memorial Cenotaph will burn till the destruction of the world's last nuclear weapon. People bow down to an epitaph reading: "Let all souls here rest in peace; for we shall not repeat the evil." From rubble to beauty, the park both mourns the dead and inspires the living.

When to Go The weather is most pleasant in spring (early April) or fall (around October). A poignant date to visit is Memorial Day on August 6, though you can expect massive crowds at this time.

Planning Allow one to two full days. The park's tourist information booth provides maps and brochures.

Websites www.pcf.city.hiroshima.jp, www.city.hiroshima.jp

TEN SACRED GARDENS

These quiet places of contemplation offer a welcome reprieve from the distractions and stress of modern life.

❶ Mt. St. Sepulchre Monastery, Washington, D.C.

When the political world becomes too profane, find an antidote in this peaceful monastic garden set in the midst of urban Washington, D.C. Wander around the beautiful Rosary Portico with its 15 chapels dedicated to the lives of Jesus and Mary, or take the rising path through trees and flowers, and seek out the full-scale replica of the grotto at Lourdes.

Planning The grounds are open daily, from 10 a.m. to 5 p.m. Don't miss the eerie catacombs in the monastery crypt. www.myfranciscan.org

❷ Japanese Tea Garden, San Francisco, CA

The beloved project of Makoto Hagiwara, who lived at and landscaped it from 1895 to 1925, this verdant garden in Golden Gate Park has a history progressing through war, prejudice, and exile, to peace. After Hagiwara's death his family carried on as the garden's guardians, though it fell into neglect in World War II, when the U.S. interned them as Japanese Americans.

Planning Enjoy a meditative brew at the beautiful teahouse, open daily. www.jgarden.org

❸ Sacred Temple Gardens, Kauai, HI

Tread the Straight Path to God to a Hindu temple enshrining a 200-year-old, 6-ft (1.8 m) bronze of the god Siva, set amidst 458 cultivated acres (185 ha) near the foot of an extinct volcano. Monks tend the ashram garden's ayurvedic plants, exotic blooms, and a *rudraksha* (tears of God in Sanskrit) forest; the name refers to the trees' seeds, used to make prayer beads.

Planning The monks provide free tours, starting at 9 and 11 every morning, but donations are welcome. Visitors should dress modestly—no T-shirts, shorts, short dresses, or tank tops. www.himalayanacademy.com

❹ Jardín Etnobotanico, Oaxaca, Mexico

Set on the grounds of the Santo Domingo Cultural Center, and hidden behind imposing walls, Oaxaca's ethnobotanical garden contains more than 1,300 native plant varieties, including a large collection of cacti and agaves. Knowledgeable guides are on hand to reveal the plants' many medicinal uses.

Planning Tours in English are on Tuesday, Thursday, and Saturday. Get there early to sign up. www.oaxacainfo.com/oaxaca/story-plants.htm

❺ Ryoan-ji Rock Garden, Kyoto, Japan

This late-15th-century dry rock garden teases the mind with its opacity. Fifteen rocks in an abstract arrangement are set in neatly raked lines of gravel, yet from whatever direction you view them, you can see only 14. Legend says that when you attain enlightenment, the hidden rock will reveal itself.

Planning Ryoanji is in northwest Kyoto. www.ryoanji.jp

❻ Daisenin Teien, Kyoto, Japan

A fine example of the *karesansui*—or "withered landscape"—style of dry garden, Daisenin Teien's narrow gardens envelop its Zen temple, Daitokuji. The northeast corner features a miniature tree-and-rock landscape with a stone bridge and a gravel waterfall that "flows" around a corner to an austere raked "ocean," from which two ambiguous gravel cones rise.

Planning Visit early so that crowds don't disturb your contemplation at this popular site. It is open from 9 a.m. to 5 p.m., March-November, and 9 a.m. to 4:30 p.m., December–February. www.jgarden.org

❼ Palace Garden, Pasargadae, Iran

Only the ghostly outline of a garden remains at Pasargadae, the sixth-century B.C. heart of the Achaemenid Empire. Built by Cyrus the Great, it was to be the prototype for the classical Persian garden. You can still discern the stone irrigation channels of a four-quadrant layout. Use your mind's eye to see it as it once was, thick with pomegranates and roses.

Planning The Pasargadae archaeological site is northeast of Persepolis, near Shiraz. Check with your government's travel advisories before traveling to Iran. www.gardenvisit.com/garden/pasargadae

❽ Jahan Nama Garden, Shiraz, Iran

The 13th-century Jahan Nama Garden, recently restored, is a typical example of a walled Persian garden—four wide pathways radiate outward from a stone pavilion and fountain at the center. The garden is a popular spot to linger at dusk thanks to its many benches and the sweet scent of the orange trees, roses, and cypresses bordering the paths.

Planning Open most days, the garden is a two-minute walk from the Tomb of Hafez, close to the town center of Shiraz. www.gardenvisit.com/garden/jahan_nama_garden, www.shirazcity.org

❾ Garden of Gethsemane, Jerusalem, Israel

The massive, gnarled, and twisted trunks of this garden's eight ancient olive trees seem to express the pain that Christ suffered in their midst—Gethsemane, from the Hebrew *gat shemanim*, or oil press, is the site of Jesus' night-long agony, betrayal by Judas, and arrest. Experts agree that the trees here are between one and two thousand years old.

Planning Open-air services take place at the altar in the garden on Maundy Thursday, the night of Jesus' betrayal. www.christusrex.org

❿ Generalife, Granada, Spain

This imaginative sequence of courtyards, paths, and fountains was at first a pleasure garden for Islamic Nazarite sultans, the early rulers of Granada. Originally from arid lands, they treasured water, and it is everywhere here—from the crisscross fountains of the Patio de la Acequia (Courtyard of the Conduit) to the magical Escalera del Agua, a staircase with rivulets of cascading water in place of handrails.

Planning Combine a trip to Generalife with a visit to the wondrous Alhambra adjoining it. Both open daily except December 25 and January 1. www.alhambra.org

Originally laid out during the reign of Sultan Muhammad III of Granada (1302-09), Generalife is one of the world's oldest extant Moorish gardens and a sublime triumph of Islamic landscaping.

Despite its modern urban backdrop, Daisen Kofun retains an unruffled air of ancient mystery and majesty. It probably dates from the fifth century A.D.

JAPAN

DAISEN KOFUN

Little known outside Japan, Daisen Kofun is one of the world's largest tombs of any kind and remains too sacred to excavate.

An expansive mound of earth, covered in greenery and carefully crafted into the shape of a keyhole, rests in the middle of a wide, still moat. The urban sprawl that expands around this trench belies the sacred grounds at its center. Yet it is hard to miss this tumulus, known as Daisen Kofun. Spanning 1,594 feet (486 meters) in length and 115 feet (35 meters) in height, the tomb measures more than double the length of the base of the Great Pyramid of Giza. But despite its grand presence, the probable site of Emperor Nintoku's burial grounds is no tourist playground. Daisen Kofun is one of more than 10,000 mound tombs scattered across Japan, some as old as the third century A.D. Their shapes vary throughout the land and include the keyhole, a square front and round back, and a square front and back, as well as the rare eight-sided tomb. They were resting places for the country's elite, and archaeologists believe that the keyhole shape designated an imperial grave, where the ancient Japanese entombed their emperors in heavy stone chambers. Lining the mounds, and protecting their entrances, are *haniwa*—clay figures depicting animals, humans, weapons, and other objects. No one knows their exact purpose. One discredited theory is that they replaced human attendants who would once have been buried alive with their masters to serve them in the afterlife.

When to Go Visit in spring (March-May) or fall (September-November).

Planning Base yourself in Osaka or Nara and spend a couple of days exploring the kofun of Nara and surrounding Osaka, areas rich in tombs. Research which have museums nearby—or on the grounds—as these typically house the burial artifacts and give more detailed explanations. Not all kofun are open to the public and you may need special permission to visit. Some are still covered, while others have been excavated. Ask at any Japanese tourist office for more information. Daisen Kofun is a 20-minute train ride from central Osaka, on the JR Hanwa Line to Mozu, followed by a five-minute walk.

Websites www.t-net.ne.jp/~keally/kofun.html, www.jnto.go.jp

HIGHLIGHTS

■ Take a 30-minute stroll around Daisen Kofun's circumference to appreciate its **sheer size**. Three moats surround it. By order of the imperial household, archaeologists have never excavated the mound, and visitors may not walk on it.

■ For an impressive collection of haniwa, visit the **Shibayama Kofun Museum** near the airport at Narita. Take a shuttle bus from terminal 2.

■ Rent a bicycle at Kintetsu Asuka railroad station and take in the temples, tombs, and museums inside **Asuka Historical National Government Park**.

■ Visit Saito, in Miyazaki prefecture, for the **Kofun Matsuri** (Burial Mounds Festival) in fall. The area comes to life with a fire festival and torch parade around the kofun.

ASIA

INDONESIA

CLIFF TOMBS OF TANA TORAJA

The Torajans honor their dead with giant celebrations
and not one funeral but two.

D ank mausolea, decomposing coffins, and animal sacrifice may not appeal to everyone's sense of propriety, but the morbid sights of Tana Toraja do have a surreal draw. A tapestry of hills and valleys marks this sacred region in central Sulawesi, where water buffalo roam among verdant paddy fields and visitors come to see fascinating cliff tombs. Torajans believe that these final resting places are homes for the afterlife, where their deceased family members live on. Over the years dozens of coffins have entered the vaults, which the Torajans treat as family mausolea. The most famous sites lie off the 11-mile (18 kilometer) road between the main towns of Rantepao and Makale. At Lemo, royal tombs with long balconies are carved into soaring cliffs 98 feet (30 meters) high. Coffins on platforms are suspended from overhanging rock faces near Kete Kesu. The entrances to two caves at Londa are piled high with coffins and bones, and strewn with tobacco and liquor offerings. At many tomb sites, you'll see *tau tau*—wooden effigies of the dead—positioned nearby. Also look out throughout Tana Toraja for extraordinary *tongkonan,* traditional houses, and *alang,* rice barns.

When to Go Visit during the funeral festival season—roughly from July to September—when Torajans traditionally hold a second, larger funeral, doubling as a giant party.

Planning A bus is the only way to get to Tana Toraja, with Makale and Rantepao connected to all points around Sulawesi. From Makassar, buses (some quite luxurious and air-conditioned) leave day and night from the Daya bus terminal. Flights into the airport near Rantepao may resume in the near future. Rantepao is the best place to look for reasonably priced lodgings. Outsiders should have an invitation to participate in a festival or a funeral, and a local guide can introduce you. If you don't have one, just turn up at the event and hang around until someone offers to be your host. And always bring an offering such as coffee, cigarettes, or palm wine, as gift-giving is an essential part of Torajan ceremonies.

Website www.my-indonesia.info

HIGHLIGHTS

■ Visit Lemo between 8 and 9 a.m. to view its **tau taus** in the best light.

■ Witness a **traditional ceremony or funeral** during the festival season. Funerals last several days, with the parading of the coffin, buffalo fights, and major animal sacrifice–sometimes up to 24 buffalo–followed by the laying of the coffin to rest on the last day.

■ On the doors of some tombs, there hang **hats or purses**, or other personal relics. The Torajans believe the dead use these items in the afterlife.

■ Kambira, 13 miles (21 km) from Rantepao, is the site of numerous **baby graves**. When an infant dies before starting to teethe, the family buries him or her inside a niche carved out of a tree. Eventually, the tree patches itself and grows around the baby.

Lemo is famed for the sheer number of tau taus lining its tomb balconies. Clad similarly to the dead people they depict, the statues are almost life-size.

EASTERN QING IMPERIAL TOMBS

South-facing towers line the feet of green mountains, guarding the elaborate tomb complexes of some of China's greatest emperors.

When the Manchus took control of Beijing in 1644, they buried the last Ming emperor at the Ming tomb complex to the north before establishing their own Qing-dynasty mausoleum 77 miles (125 kilometers) east of the capital. Although some later emperors lie buried in a second complex to the southwest, the Eastern Imperial Qing Tombs remain the most extensive and intact in China. Altogether, five emperors, 15 empresses, 136 concubines, three princes, and two princesses rest here. Agriculture has now invaded the vast walled enclosure, and seas of maize or apple blossom separate the "soul towers" that dominate the fortified tomb mounds. You approach each of these towers through a multi-courtyard complex of ornate halls used for the preparation of sacrifices and performance of respectful ritual. The most elaborate resemble the Forbidden City in miniature and are reached over marble bridges that cross streams now diverted for irrigation. Local farmers make a secondary income from ferrying visitors around in converted tractors, but it is possible to visit many tombs on foot. Take a long walk up the site's main "spirit way," lined with seated and standing human and animal figures, the first resting between watches, the second on guard against the approach of intruders.

When to Go Visit in late spring or early fall to avoid the worst of the humid summer and the chilly, desiccating winter. The first weeks of May and October, both seven-day national holidays, are very busy.

Planning You can reach the site on a one-day trip from Beijing, although farmers offer very modest lodging on site. Cold drinks and ice cream are widely available from vendors, but the restaurants are basic and poor value. Bring a picnic. From April 7 to October 15 there are government-run bus tours at low prices with a discount entry ticket included. These leave from just northwest of Xuanwu Men subway station in Beijing, between 6:30 and 8:30 a.m., on Saturdays, Sundays, and public holidays, take three hours each way, and allow three hours at the site before returning.

Website www.travelchinaguide.com

HIGHLIGHTS

■ Explore the **burial chamber of the fourth Qing emperor** to rule China. It is reached through multiple pairs of carved marble doors and arched halls engraved with more than 30,000 words of Buddhist sutras in Tibetan and Sanskrit.

■ Less gaudy than the others, the main hall of the **Dowager Empress Cixi's tomb** features top-quality dark woods that have been carved with innumerable gilded characters.

■ Look out for the slightly overgrown and forlorn **tumuli of the Qianlong emperor's 55 concubines**, together in one courtyard.

■ Enjoy the **views** across the vast site from the top of one of the soul towers.

■ Walk out to remoter **tombs of lesser royalty**, where you may find yourself alone with only birdsong and the distant sound of a tractor.

Opposite: This stone statue of a military mandarin overlooks the "spirit way" of the imperial tomb complex. Above left: A large white marble archway marks the main entrance to the tombs. Above right: Incorporating gold dragons, this imperial crown is one of several on display in the site's exhibition room.

TAJ MAHAL

No one can fail to feel awe at the sheer beauty
of this shimmering testament to love.

ASIA

In Agra, on the banks of the Yamuna River in northern India, the Taj Mahal stands tall in all its symmetrical grandeur as a monument to the undying love of Mogul emperor Shah Jahan for his favorite wife, Mumtaz Mahal, who died while giving birth. Built by 20,000 workers who labored for more than 20 years, the Muslim mausoleum was completed around 1654. Walk through the magnificent dark red sandstone gatehouse and its curved archway until you suddenly catch a glimpse of the Taj Mahal, and its otherworldly beauty, glistening in the distance. Stroll down an avenue of deep-green, spired cypress trees lining a limpid blue pool that reflects the awe-inspiring building in its waters. As you approach the monumental Taj, you gaze at intricate latticework, the gleaming white marble facade, and masterful calligraphy created from shining, inlaid precious jewels decorating the walls with selections from the Koran. The gardens, symbols of paradise to Muslims, have four main sections, each subdivided again into four parts, because that number is sacred in Islam. Inside, sacred geometric patterns line the floor, ornate decorations fill the walls and ceilings, and interior rooms cast soft light on more adornments.

When to Go To avoid the drenching monsoons as well as the hottest times of the year, it's best to visit India between October and March. The Taj is closed to non-Muslims on Fridays.

Planning The *Taj Express*, a special air-conditioned luxury train, runs daily between Delhi and Agra, leaving Delhi in the morning and returning at night. There are also buses to Agra from Delhi and many other Indian cities. Agra has an airport, with flights from Delhi, Jaipur, and Jodhpur.

Websites www.asi.nic.in, www.incredibleindia.org

HIGHLIGHTS

■ During a **full moon**, stay until closing time, when the Taj Mahal's marble shimmers and seems to float in the soft moonlight.

■ The Taj Mahal is the backdrop for the annual ten-day **Taj Mahotsav** festival, usually in February. Watch bejeweled elephants and camels parade; let classical and folk dancers entertain you. Don't forget to sample some of the local crafts and foods.

■ Don't miss the **tombs of Mumtaz Mahal and Shah Jahan** in the crypt, below the Taj Mahal's main entrance.

■ Ornate red sandstone **mosques**, with their own reflecting pools, stand on either side of the Taj Mahal.

A boy rides a camel across the shallow Yamuna River by the Taj Mahal.

One of the most visited tombs in Tikhvin Cemetery is that of novelist Fyodor Dostoyevsky, who died in 1881.

RUSSIA

ALEXANDER NEVSKY MONASTERY

Some of the greatest luminaries in Russian history lie in the sedate grounds of this monastery.

Teeming with boisterous activity, Nevsky Prospekt runs through the heart of St. Petersburg. At one end of this wide, main boulevard, you enter the sedate world of the Alexander Nevsky Monastery. The 13th-century saint and Russian prince lends his name to this complex of five churches founded by Peter the Great in 1710. Step through the cream-colored arched gateway, and pay homage to the Russian greats who rest in the two tree-lined cemeteries. On the right, the Tikhvin Cemetery contains some of the most famous and ornate graves—many are works of art. Walk to the far right-hand corner and reflect at Tchaikovsky's resting place. Adorned with two winged angels, the bronze tombstone bears a bust of the composer. Follow the brick pathways under a canopy of trees toward the back wall. Here you'll view Dostoyevsky's grave surrounded by a diminutive wrought-iron fence. Topped with a cross, the soaring monument holds a bust of the bearded novelist. Besides artists, musicians, scientists, and conductors, you'll come across Russian royalty, such as Natalya Alexeevna, a daughter of Tsar Alexis I and sister of Peter the Great.

When to Go The monastery is open daily from 11 a.m. to 7 p.m., except Tuesday and Saturday. It gets crowded in summer. The famed White Nights, when twilight lasts all night, peak from mid-June to July 1.

Planning Centrally located, the monastery is easy to find. The nearest subway station is Ploshchad Alexandra Nevskovo. Enter from Alexander Nevsky Square, and buy tickets just outside the main gate. Also request a map of the cemeteries.

Websites www.saint-petersburg.com, www.russia-travel.com

HIGHLIGHTS

■ As you traverse St. Petersburg's main street, **Nevsky Prospekt**, you'll find restaurants, shops, kiosks, museums, and the baroque grandeur of the Winter Palace and the Hermitage. Along the way, there are so many denominations of churches that French author Alexandre Dumas dubbed it the "street of religious tolerance."

■ Several of the city's celebrated architects rest in peace in **Lazarus Cemetery**, across the way from the monastery. An unadorned, gray granite stone marks the grave of Carlo Rossi, who designed the Senate and Alexandrovsky Theater. A simple stone likewise seems oddly modest for fellow Italian Giacomo Quarenghi, who created three lavish royal palaces.

■ With some thousand rooms, the **Hermitage**, at the other end of Nevsky Prospekt, remains one of the world's top art museums. Built in 1764, it encompasses several buildings and more than three million works of art.

■ Stroll through **Alexander Garden**, just opposite the Hermitage and right behind the Admiralty. Note the illuminated musical fountain. St. Petersburg has more than 200 **parks and gardens** and 700 **verdant squares**.

EUROPE

"Fight to the Death" captures the determination of the Soviet forces. "Mother Motherland" is on the hilltop beyond.

RUSSIA

Mamayev Hill Memorial

A complex of exhibition halls and monumental statues in socialist realist style honors the Soviet heroes of the Battle of Stalingrad.

During the failed German assault on Stalingrad in 1942–43, Mamayev Hill was the scene of some of the fiercest fighting, and in 1967 a large complex of memorials and monumental statues opened here in honor of the victory. Square of the Heroes has a reflecting pool flanked by six 20-foot (6 meter) high sculptures of pairs of figures representing military values such as comradeship and patriotism. The reliefs on the symbolic ruined walls illustrate scenes from the battle. In the Hall of Valor, 43 red basalt panels record the names of 7,200 soldiers, representing all those who died defending Stalingrad. From the Hall of Valor the path leads through the Square of Sorrow, its main monument a mourning mother cradling her dead soldier son, and on to the hill on which Volgograd's totemic landmark stands. Two hundred granite steps, one for each day of the battle, lead to the summit, where a towering, 269-foot (82 meter) high statue of Mother Motherland (the Soviet term for Mother Russia) raises her massive sword in victory as she watches over the graves of 34,505 war dead in the cemetery at her feet.

When to Go The memorial complex is always open. Large crowds gather on days when special ceremonies or events take place, such as Victory Day (May 9), or the anniversary of the end of the Battle of Stalingrad (February 2).

Planning Volgograd is 560 miles (900 km) southeast of Moscow. Allow two to three hours to explore the whole site. Stroll through the complex at night to enjoy the statues illuminated by colored lights.

Websites www.mamayevhill.volgadmin.ru, volgograd.russiantravelguides.com

HIGHLIGHTS

■ Observe the hourly **changing of the guard** at the Hall of Valor. In the center of the hall a large hand cast in concrete holds an **eternal flame**, while Robert Schumann's "Reverie" plays in the background.

■ The statues in **Heroes' Square** represent the true heroes of the battle—soldiers and medics. A soldier supports another who is wounded. A nurse helps an injured soldier off the battlefield. Two soldiers, one young and one old, toss symbols of fascism into the Volga River.

■ The Volgograd **State Panoramic Museum** on the Volga River houses "The Defeat of the Fascist Armies at Stalingrad," Russia's largest narrative painting, and a large collection of artifacts from World War II.

EUROPE

TURKEY

NEMRUT DAĞI

On a remote mountaintop in eastern Turkey, a collection of giant stone heads guards the burial site of an ancient king.

A bitter wind whips round the 7,000-foot (2,150 meter) summit of Nemrut Dağı (Mount Nemrut) in the eastern Taurus Mountains, as people huddle under blankets waiting for the dawn. At last a pink glow appears and spreads along the eastern horizon. The landscape lightens, revealing barren hills that stretch away as far as the eye can see. As the brilliant orange-red sun rises in the sky to cheers from the waiting crowd, warm-colored light catches a row of giant stone heads, each the height of a person, arranged along the base of a 164-foot (50 meter) high, man-made tumulus. This is the burial site of Antiochus I, ruler of the small territory of Commagene in the 1st century B.C. Five of the heads come from a nearby row of huge seated stone figures identified from inscriptions as the ancient Greek gods Apollo, Tyche, Zeus, and Heracles, as well as Antiochus himself. A ceremonial way leads along the north side of the tumulus to the western terrace, which is still in shadow and cold in the early morning. The same sequence of statues originally stood here, but the heads are all that remain, gazing toward the west. Antiochus created this sanctuary of the gods as a place "where my divinely loved soul will sleep for eternity." Archaeologists think the rock beneath the tumulus conceals his burial chamber, but have yet to find it.

When to Go Visit from May to early October. In winter, snow can block the roads to the summit.

Planning Nemrut Dağı is 53 miles (85 km) east of Adıyaman and 31 miles (50 km) from the village of Kahta, where there is a campsite. You can book tours to the summit in Adıyaman, Şanlıurfa, or Malatya. From the summit parking lot, there's a 30-minute walk to the top. Allow a minimum of three hours. Some organized tours take in other remains of the Commagene civilization as well.

Websites www.adiyamanli.org, www.nemruttours.com, www.turkeytravelplanner.com

ASIA

HIGHLIGHTS

■ Row upon row of hills crisscrossed by ancient tracks stretch away to the horizon on all sides. The **views**, and the site, are particularly spectacular at sunrise and sunset.

■ The **stone heads** are around 6 ft (1.8 m) high and wear Persian headdresses. **Zeus** sports a beard and a coronet decorated with stars. **Antiochus** had himself represented as a young man.

■ A stela bearing a carved relief of a lion decorated with stars and beams of light is thought to be the **world's oldest horoscope**. It describes the position of the planets Jupiter, Mercury, and Mars on July 7, 62 B.C., representing the day on which Antiochus died, expecting to take his place among the gods.

The heads of Apollo, Antiochus, and Zeus catch the late afternoon sun on the western terrace.

ISRAEL

YAD VASHEM

This national memorial documents the history of the Holocaust through the names and stories of individual victims.

Yad Vashem, meaning "a memorial and a name," is an apt name for the cluster of museums, monuments, and archives that make up the Holocaust Martyrs' and Heroes' Remembrance Authority complex on Jerusalem's Mount of Remembrance (Har Hazikaron). The place is a lushly landscaped area with trees planted over the years since the establishment of the site in 1953 to honor the Righteous Among the Nations, non-Jews who had risked their lives to help Jews during the Holocaust. Ashes of the dead, collected by survivors from killing sites and camps, have a final resting place in the Hall of Remembrance. The stark, modern Holocaust History Museum tells the story of the Holocaust from a Jewish and personal perspective. Screens here play testimonies recorded by survivors describing horrific crimes against dead family members and the Jewish community in general. The stories and names of people and their hometowns echo through the cavernous building. When it all becomes too much to bear, and the heart has been assailed from all directions, the tour ends on a balcony overlooking Jerusalem's peaceful, sun-drenched hills. Here anguish-filled visitors find hope that if we remember and recognize the past, such horrors truly might never happen again. This is Yad Vashem's message and Israel's gift to the world.

When to Go Yad Vashem is open every day except Saturdays and Jewish holidays. On Sundays to Thursdays, the whole complex is open from 9 a.m. to 5 p.m. On Thursdays, the Holocaust History Museum stays open until 8 p.m. On Fridays and the eve of holidays, the site is open from 9 a.m. to 2 p.m.

Planning The entrance is near Mount Herzl. Buses run from central Jerusalem and several other places to the Mount Herzl bus stop. From there a free shuttle service runs to Yad Vashem during opening hours. Car parking is available. Entry is free and advance reservation is not necessary except for groups, who can book online. The visitors' center at the entrance offers information, maps, and audio guides, and free guided tours in English leave daily at 11 a.m. For private guided tours, fill in the online reservation form.

Website www.yadvashem.org

HIGHLIGHTS

■ The **Hall of Names** in the Holocaust History Museum displays 600 photographs and a sample of the more than two million "Pages of Testimony" preserved in the Hall of Names. Eventually, the hope is to honor the names and stories of all the six million Jewish Holocaust victims.

■ Hollowed out from an underground cavern, the **Children's Memorial** pays tribute to the roughly 1.5 million Jewish children who died during the Holocaust. Mirrors reflect memorial candles infinitely in a dark and somber space, giving the impression of millions of stars shining in the sky. In the background one hears the names of murdered children, their ages, and countries of origin.

■ The **Memorial to the Deportees** features an original cattle car, perched on rusted railroad tracks jutting out from the hill. It is one of many the Nazis used to transport Jews to the death camps.

■ At the **"Valley of the Communities"** monument, the names of more than 5,000 Jewish communities destroyed or damaged during the Holocaust are engraved on 107 stone walls.

Opposite: "Korczak and the Ghetto's Children" honors Polish-Jewish orphanage director Janusz Korczak, who voluntarily accompanied his charges to Treblinka in 1942. Above: The "Memorial to the Victims of the Concentration and Extermination Camps" is by Nandor Glid.

ROYAL MOUNDS

This burial site of ancient pagan kings is also
one of Sweden's oldest national symbols.

EUROPE

On the outskirts of Uppsala, to the north of Stockholm, in the village of Gamla Uppsala ("Old Uppsala"), three stately mounds of earth rise from a broad plain where two to three thousand burial mounds once stood. In pre-Viking times, Gamla Uppsala was the residence of Swedish kings, a center of worship of the Norse gods, and the site of the *Thing*, or general assembly, of the Swedish people. Excavations of the mounds, which date from about 1,500 years ago, have revealed the remains of burnt bones, ornate weapons and clothing, and sacrificial offerings. These are evidence of the pagan Norse belief that cremation brought the deceased soul to Valhalla, the hall of the Norse god Odin. From the contents of the graves, archaeologists believe the mounds are the resting places of ancient kings. As you stroll along the narrow paths that wind around the three tumuli—known as the Eastern, Middle, and Western Mounds—imagine the Gamla Uppsala of old with its glittering golden temple to the Norse gods Odin, Thor, and Frey and its sacred grove where human and animal sacrifices took place. The nearby Assembly Mound is a geological formation resembling the burial sites but without the remains of either gods or kings.

When to Go Visit during spring, summer, or early fall to avoid Sweden's chilling winters.

Planning Uppsala is about 30 miles (48 km) from Stockholm. Trains run regularly between the two cities; the trip takes about 45 minutes. The Royal Mounds are 2.5 miles (4 km) from the center of Uppsala. You can reach the site by bus or, on warm days, on foot or by bicycle. Entrance to the site and the church is free, but there is a small admission charge for the museum. Check opening hours before visiting; they vary throughout the year.

Websites www.uppland.nu, www.uppsala.world-guides.com

HIGHLIGHTS

■ The nearby **Gamla Uppsala Museum** houses items uncovered in the mounds. The exhibits include models of the area's landscape through the centuries.

■ Visit **Gamla Uppsala Church**, parts of which date back to the 12th century. Legend holds that the church occupies the site of an ancient pagan temple. During his Nordic tour of 1989, Pope John Paul II celebrated Mass in this church.

■ The 13th-century **Uppsala Cathedral** is Scandinavia's largest church.

Ancient Swedes built the Royal Mounds along a ridge with a commanding view of the area.

Harald Bluetooth's stone, on the left, bears a mixture of runes and Christian symbols and is sometimes known as Denmark's birth certificate.

DENMARK

JELLING

Two large inscribed stones record the transition from pagan to Christian belief.

In the quiet countryside of central Jutland, two burial mounds, a collection of mystical runic inscriptions, and a small church tell the story of the first king of one of Europe's longest continuing monarchies. For it was here in Jelling (pronounced YELL-ing)—a capital city and power center in pre-Christian Denmark—that belief in the old Viking gods yielded to Christianity. As you approach the village two imposing, grass-covered burial mounds come into view. They belong to Gorm the Old, a very early Danish king—and possibly the first—who lived from the late ninth century to 958, and his wife Thyra. Between the mounds stands a modest Romanesque church. It occupies the site of an older, wooden church built by Gorm's son, Harald Bluetooth, following his conversion to Christianity, and in which Harald had his father reburied. Directly in front of the church are two tall, inscribed stones. The smaller one bears words recorded by Gorm the Old. Mystic runes—ancient hieroglyphs used for communication and magic—memorialized Thyra upon her death. The larger, three-sided stone was erected by Harald, who succeeded his father as king. One side proclaims Harald as king of Denmark and Norway, while another side brims with florid depictions of a lion and a serpent. The third side shows a melding of old Viking decorations with the first Danish representation of Christ and runes bearing witness to Harald Bluetooth's conversion of his subjects to Christianity.

When to Go Jelling's winters can be cold and dreary. Plan to visit between May and October.

Planning Jelling is in east Jutland, west of Copenhagen. Trains from the capital take three hours. If you want to spend the night, the village has a small inn.

Website www.visitdenmark.com

HIGHLIGHTS

■ The nearby museum, **Kongernes Jelling** (Royal Jelling), chronicles the history of the area. Exhibits include a full-sized cast of Harald Bluetooth's rune stone painted in the bright colors that may have originally adorned the monolith.

■ Visit the travertine-walled **church**, where Gorm the Old lies buried. The frescoes, which were restored in the 19th century, were originally created in the 12th century.

■ Each summer, you can view the **Jelling Orm**, a full-sized replica of a Viking ship, anchored in Fårup Lake just south of Jelling.

EUROPE

BEŁŻEC MEMORIAL

The site of one of the Nazis' notorious death
camps lay hidden in a forest for 60 years.

EUROPE

arth do not cover my blood; let there be no resting place for my outcry! So reads a quotation from the Book of Job on a memorial wall at the entrance to the onetime Bełżec death camp. Rusty iron letters form the words; red stains drip from them like bloody tears. Here, between February and December 1942, the Nazis murdered half a million people, most of them Jews from territory currently straddling southeast Poland and western Ukraine. They buried the bodies in mass graves and later tried to destroy all evidence of the horror. For decades, the remote site lay abandoned and all but unmarked, but in 2004 the American Jewish Committee and the Polish government jointly inaugurated a vast and haunting memorial here. Industrial slag covers the entire area of the camp, creating a bleak wasteland over the mass graves. Cutting through it, a corridor edged by jagged, rusty iron sinks deeper and deeper into the ground, like a path of no return. It ends at a memorial wall engraved with hundreds of names. Above, a walkway skirts the perimeter of the desolate field. Along it, iron letters spell out all the towns and villages whose Jewish residents died here. These letters, too, have rusted; they, too, now seem to drip tears of blood.

When to Go The Bełżec Memorial is open during daylight hours year-round; admission is free. As it is an open-air site, winter visits can prove tough. Ask at the on-site museum about guided tours of the complex.

Planning Since Bełżec is in a rather remote location in southeast Poland near the Ukrainian border, it can be difficult to visit as a day trip from Warsaw or Kraków. But the beautiful Renaissance city of Zamość, about 30 miles (50 km) away, has good hotels and makes a comfortable base. In Zamość you can see the former fortress synagogue, a few steps from the graceful, arcaded market square.

Websites www.deathcamps.org, www.visit.pl

HIGHLIGHTS

■ The **town and village names** along the perimeter walkway are in both Polish and Yiddish, the language once spoken by most Jews in the region.

■ The **museum** provides a vivid account of the camp's history and role in the Holocaust. Scholars believe at least 434,500 Jews and unknown numbers of non-Jewish Poles and Roma (Gypsies) died here.

■ Rail cars shipped victims into the camp and took bodies from the gas chambers to mass graves. When the Nazis destroyed the camp in 1943, they exhumed bodies and burned them on pyres made of railroad track. Near the memorial entrance, a **monument made of railroad track** recalls both the trains and the pyres.

Bleak and lonely, Bełżec Memorial reflects the camp's murderous history.

The bone sculptures in the ossuary include this coat of arms of the Schwarzenberg family.

HIGHLIGHTS

■ Examine the ingenious artistry of the ossuary's many bone sculptures. The large **chandelier** is said to contain at least one of every type of bone in the human body.

■ Visit the **cemetery** and the **upper chapel** of the Church of All Saints, also known as the Church of Bones.

■ Kutná Hora has a **Museum of Silver and Medieval Mining**, which offers guided mine tours, and beautiful medieval architecture, including the five-naved **Church of St. Barbara.**

CZECH REPUBLIC

SEDLEC OSSUARY

A local woodcarver applied his skills to creating extraordinary decorations out of human bones.

EUROPE

A well-worn stairway descends past a pair of giant chalices made from human bones into the bowels of the Church of All Saints in Sedlec, where a macabre sight awaits the visitor—a room filled with decorations and sculptures made from human bones. The 40,000-odd skeletons used for this ghoulish art came from the adjacent cemetery, which was a popular burial place in the Middle Ages after a Cistercian abbot scattered soil there from Golgotha, site of Jesus' crucifixion. In the 1500s, with thousands of people succumbing daily to the Black Death, the older graves were dug up to make room for new burials, and the church's lower chamber stored the recovered skeletons. The church later came into the ownership of the Schwarzenberg family, who in the 19th century hired a woodcarver, František Rint, to create order out of the thousands of bones heaped in the ossuary. Rint strung garlands of bleached-white skulls and crossbones across the ceiling, fixed more to walls and pillars, and created a huge, bell-shaped mound of bones in each corner. Not wanting his work to go unacknowledged, Rint left his signature in finger bones on a wall near the entrance.

When to Go The ossuary is open daily, except December 24 and 25. Hours vary throughout the year. Plan on 30 minutes to an hour to see it, longer if you want to tour the entire church.

Planning Sedlec is on the outskirts of Kutná Hora. You can get there by train from Prague, 44 miles (71 km) to the west. The ossuary is a ten-minute walk from Kutná Hora-Sedlec station.

Websites www.kostnice.cz, www.prague.cz

Siret's wonderfully carved Jewish tombstones are some of the prettiest in eastern Europe.

ROMANIA

SIRET'S JEWISH CEMETERIES

This remote, quiet corner of northeastern Romania
has a rich collection of old carved Jewish tombstones.

Rearing lions, mythical griffins, doves, grapevines, hands placing money into charity boxes, flowers—these are just some of the rich sculptural motifs on the Jewish tombstones in this quiet little town on Romania's border with Ukraine. No Jews live here anymore. But Jews often refer to their cemeteries as "houses of the living," and Siret's three Jewish cemeteries—one founded in the late 18th century or earlier, one from the 19th century, and one from the 20th—form haunting congregations of stone. The hundreds of gravestones bear some of the finest and most varied examples of Jewish symbolic art to be found in eastern Europe. The ornate symbols refer to the name, family lineage, or inherent personal traits of the deceased, and frame elegantly carved Hebrew epitaphs. You can see diverse styles of carving here, from the austere to the rococo, and here and there you can recognize the work of individual artists.

When to Go Siret is fairly cool by Romanian standards. The best weather is from April to September. Grass and weeds sometimes overgrow the cemeteries in late spring and summer.

Planning A car is the best way to explore this far northeastern corner of Romania. Half an hour's drive from Siret, Rădăuți has several small hotels, as well as a beautiful Jewish cemetery. The Old Cemetery in Siret is behind a high wall near the center of town; to find the newer two, cross the road and turn down the lane. Contact the Jewish community in Rădăuți (tel. +40 (0)230 561333) to visit Siret's synagogue. Men should cover their heads in the cemeteries (and synagogue).

Websites www.radautz-jewishheritage.org, www.romanianmonasteries.org/bucovina

HIGHLIGHTS

■ Commonly found symbols include **two hands raised in blessing**, denoting a *cohen*, or descendant of Aaron, the first Jewish high priest, and a **pitcher**, denoting a descendant of the Levite tribe. **Lions** may denote names such as Lev or Leib, or may represent the Lion of Judah.

■ Note the sometimes extremely elaborate **braided candlesticks** on some gravestones. They mark the graves of women, as they traditionally light and bless the Sabbath candles.

■ The **synagogue in Siret**, now disused, has brilliant interior decoration, including a large representation of the zodiac and paintings of animals. These represent the Talmudic exhortation to be "as strong as a leopard, as light as an eagle, as fleet as a stag, and as brave as a lion to perform the will of thy father who is in heaven."

EUROPE

ROMANIA

THE MERRY CEMETERY

This unusual cemetery in the bucolic region of Maramureş celebrates the lives of dead villagers with humor and joy.

Deep in the countryside of northern Romania, in the village of Săpânţa, is a most unusual graveyard, its cheerily painted wooden crosses exuding a decidedly sunnier outlook than the normal somber ranks of mossy tombs and solemn epitaphs. The carved images, of which there are more than 800, have been colorfully painted with disarmingly simple portraits and scenes from the lives of the deceased. And as this is one of the least developed areas in Europe, they typically commemorate local people engaged in time-honored livelihoods: shepherds with their sheep, farmers tending the soil, bakers, blacksmiths, and weavers, always with the emphasis on the celebration of a life. A few scenes are less joyful: the alcoholic drinks from a bottle, and an image of a road accident marks the grave of the young girl who died in it. The majority of crosses also feature a pair of white doves and include an epitaph, often in the form of a limerick—most, but not all, lighthearted. Almost all are written in the first person, as if in the words of the deceased. The majority of crosses were the work of a local wood-carver, Stan Ioan Pătraş, who died in 1977; his grave is in front of the church entrance. Pătraş's apprentice still creates around ten new headstone images a year.

When to Go Visit from April to October; although July and August can be hot, the heat is rarely as intense as it is in southern Romania. Orthodox Easter, generally celebrated later than Easter in western Europe, is a good time to visit. There are many local festivals in summer.

Planning Săpânţa is 9 miles (15 km) northwest of Sighetu Marmaţiei, from where there are several buses each day. Villagers rent out rooms—arrange them either directly with the occupants or through Antrec, a Romanian agritourism agency. To explore the Maramureş region fully, allow at least five days.

Websites www.romaniatourism.com, www.antrec.ro

EUROPE

HIGHLIGHTS

■ Look out for the paintings of the **shepherd** with his dog and flock in a flower-filled orchard, the **contented farmer** and his horse, and the **barber**.

■ **Stan Ioan Pătraş** made his own cross before his death. He inscribed it with the words *Creatorul Cimitirului Vesel* (the Creator of the Merry Cemetery). Some outsiders ask to be buried here, but the cemetery is for villagers only.

■ Pătraş's apprentice works at his former cottage behind the cemetery. The building doubles as a **museum** of Pătraş's folk art.

■ The churches at **Bârsana**, to the east of Săpânţa, and at **Ieud**, merit a visit.

Colorful painted wooden crosses made of oak, and decorated with images and traditional folk-art patterns, fill the cemetery at Săpânţa.

A mural of a procession of horses decorates the tomb of a Thracian princess at Kazanlak.

BULGARIA

THRACIAN TOMBS

A large collection of richly decorated tombs lies concealed beneath the Bulgarian countryside.

Beneath Bulgaria's pastoral landscape, Thracian rulers and nobles rest in eternal sleep, their *mogili* (burial tombs) filled with an incalculable cache of treasures reflecting the colossal wealth of an ancient civilization. Archaeologists have excavated more than 50 tombs, revealing elaborate friezes and vibrant frescoes, as well as burial masks, jewelry, drinking vessels, and other ceremonial offerings, many crafted from gold, silver, and other precious metals. Several of the tombs open for public viewing are located in the Valley of the Thracian Kings in central Bulgaria. The tomb at Kazanlak—a third-century B.C. beehive tomb—is significant for its unsurpassed pictorial decoration, the country's best-preserved example of Hellenistic art. Northwest of Kazanlak, the Ostrusha tomb, part of an extensive necropolis along the Shipka Pass road, has an unusual granite sepulchral chamber resembling a Greek temple. The tomb at Sveshtari is one of the most impressive tombs with its unique architectural design and decorative carvings, including the ten caryatids, or sculpted female figures, on the walls of the main chamber. Archaeologists unearthed a magnificent golden funeral wreath and armaments of battle, including bronze shields and swords, in the double chambers of the tomb-temple at Starosel near Plovdiv, exemplifying the rich funerary culture of the ancient Thracians.

When to Go April through September is the best time to visit, although July and August will be hotter, drier, and more crowded.

Planning Without a rental vehicle, the only way to reach some of the sites is on a guided tour. Check with local tour operators and area museums, including Iskra Historical Museum in Kazanlak. To protect the artwork in the Kazanlak tomb, a replica was set up next to the original for visitors. With advance notice, it is possible to arrange a private guided tour of the original tomb through the Iskra Historical Museum along with visits with an archaeologist to the tombs near Shipka.

Websites www.bulgariatravel.org, www.kazanlaktour.com

HIGHLIGHTS

■ The **exceptional murals** at the Kazanlak tomb portray the life and death of a powerful Thracian ruler.

■ Examine the fine **architectural detail** used in the various tomb designs, including the square versus round burial vaults.

■ Local **museums**, as well as the National Archaeological Museum and National Museum of History in Sofia, house treasures from several tombs in the area, some of which are not open to the public.

EUROPE

GERMANY

Berlin Holocaust Memorial

A field of 2,711 simple gray plinths commemorates
six million murdered European Jews.

There's no entrance, no exit, and it's never closed. You can walk into the memorial from any of the four sides, and suddenly a field of concrete cubes surrounds you. Their heights shift as you cut your own path through the unsettling, undulating terrain. Sleek and gray, the slabs—or stelae—all have a slight tilt and sit on uneven, sloping ground. They are all unique in size and shape, some being only 0.75 inches (2 centimeters) high, others more than 15 feet (4.8 meters) tall. Although they follow a grid pattern, they cover a 205,000-square-foot (19,000 square meter) area, and can make visitors wandering through them feel overwhelmed and lost. Built between the East and West Berlin of the Cold War, the memorial—also known as the Memorial to the Murdered Jews of Europe—was dedicated in May 2005, 60 years after the end of World War II. The result is a stark reminder of the horrific events of the Holocaust. The stones are featureless, and the entire field bears no names and no plaques (though an underground information center holds the names of all known Jewish Holocaust victims). Its creator, American architect Peter Eisenman, envisioned the memorial not as a holy shrine, but as an everyday place. Still, while some children play among the stones, other people walk slowly, in silent remembrance.

When to Go Berlin is most beautiful in the spring and fall. Plan to spend an hour wandering among the stelae and another in the information center.

Planning The memorial is in Cora-Berliner-Strasse, near the Brandenberg Gate. The Field of Stelae is open 24/7; the information center is open daily except Monday, between April and September, from 10 a.m. to 8 p.m., and between October and March, from 10 a.m. to 7 p.m. Take subway line U2 to Potsdamer Platz or Mohrenstrasse.

Website www.holocaust-mahnmal.de

EUROPE

HIGHLIGHTS

■ One room in the permanent underground exhibition focuses on **individual life histories** of hundreds (and eventually thousands) of Holocaust victims from all over Europe. Their biographies are recited over loudspeakers as their names and personal information are projected on each wall.

■ The quotation in the information center's lobby, from Auschwitz survivor **Primo Levi**, has the following translation: "It happened, therefore it can happen again: this is the core of what we have to say."

■ The **New Synogogue** in Berlin's Jewish district now functions as a museum of Jewish history. Services are also held here.

The slabs tip this way and that, creating a disorientating effect for visitors walking among them.

HAL SAFLIENI

An underground burial chamber, for thousands of years a well-kept secret, also functioned uniquely as a Neolithic temple.

EUROPE

Unusual spiral designs in blood-red ocher grace the limestone surfaces of the oracle room of this hypogeum, or underground burial chamber, in Paola. The mystical artwork adorns several other rooms in the subterranean honeycomb of interconnected chambers, including the "holy of holies" chamber, believed to be an inner sanctum. First discovered in 1844, the necropolis was quickly sealed and soon forgotten, until 1902, when workers laying the foundation for a house broke through the surface and nearly tumbled into what they thought was a natural cave. Excavation revealed a vast complex of rock-cut rooms, crypts, stairways, and corridors extending 33 feet (10 meters) below ground on three levels, each from a different period between 3600 and 2500 B.C. Archaeologists unearthed the remains of about 7,000 people, many in burial chambers on the upper level (3600 to 3300 B.C.), along with amulets, pottery, and other personal possessions. Similarities to the interiors of Maltese megalithic temples, including such features as massive trilithons, linteled doorways, and corbeled ceilings, support the belief that the hypogeum also served as a temple, probably for fertility rites.

When to Go Tours take place daily, except on major holidays, every hour starting at 9 a.m., with the last one at 4 p.m. They last about an hour and include an exhibit of artifacts and an introductory audiovisual presentation in addition to the 45-minute guided tour.

Planning Advance reservations are necessary. If available, you can buy tickets in person at the hypogeum or the National Museum of Archaeology. However, pre-booking online is highly advisable as tours, each limited to ten people, often sell out weeks in advance. Last-minute tickets are available on a first-come basis at the hypogeum for that day's noon tour only. Expect to pay double what you would for prepaid tickets.

Websites www.heritagemalta.org, www.heritagemaltashop.com

HIGHLIGHTS

■ Examine the **remarkable workmanship** of the world's only known prehistoric underground temple. Craftsmen carved the chambers out of the living rock using tools of flint and animal horn.

■ Visit the **National Museum of Archaeology** in Valletta to view the "Sleeping Lady," a 5-inch (12 cm) rotund clay figure excavated from one of the hypogeum's innermost chambers. Other figurines, necklaces, and pottery also are on display.

■ Note the similar architectural aspects of the nearby **Tarxien Neolithic Temples** built between 3800 and 2500 B.C., roughly the same time as the hypogeum.

Hewn from soft limestone, the interior of the main chamber of the hypogeum resembles a honeycomb on a giant scale.

The Renaissance Church of San Michele, the masterpiece of Mauro Codussi, is one of the jewels in the lagoon.

ITALY

SAN MICHELE

This island cemetery under the blue Venetian sky is the fascinating burial place of famous visitors and anonymous local residents.

The vaporetto glides to its stop at the stillness of San Michele Island, just minutes north of the center of enchanting Venice. Behind the ecru brick walls lies a tightly packed cemetery dotted with slender cypress trees and a series of understated gardens. Beyond the water-taxi landing, the Church of San Michele stands as one of Venice's first Renaissance structures, resplendent with a facade of white Istrian marble. Built in 1469, the church features turquoise and royal blue mosaics inside. Its cloister leads into the cemetery proper. Walls separate Protestant, Catholic, Orthodox, and Jewish sections. Left of the central path in the Protestant area, American poet Ezra Pound rests in a rectangular grave that resembles a flower bed. Family members chose a plain white Orthodox gravestone for the composer Igor Stravinsky and his wife; while ballet slippers decorate the impresario Sergei Diaghilev's two-tiered, white-columned site. Aptly, Italian sculptor Antonio dal Zotto's final resting place is a work of art—a crypt surrounded by a semicircle of a dozen narrow pillars. Joseph Brodsky, Nobel Prize winner and former U.S. poet laureate, who died in 1996, has a simple white stone festooned with flowers. As you meander the peaceful walkways of the cemetery, you'll happen upon a touching children's section, an area of humble memorials to nuns, and a partition devoted to gondoliers.

When to Go Visit all year, but in high summer Venice is at its hottest and most crowded.

Planning Rather than the expensive water taxi, take the reasonably priced water bus (vaporetto), either the 41 or 42 from Fondamente Nuove toward Murano, and stop at Cimitero—only a few minutes' ride. The cemetery is open Tuesday-Sunday, from 9 a.m. to 1 p.m. and 3:30 to 7:30 p.m; Monday, 3:30 to 7:30 p.m.

Websites www.veneto.to, www.italiantourism.com

HIGHLIGHTS

■ Although very crowded, the cemetery is still in use. Most who are buried here now have their remains transferred to a common grave or comingled with the remains of other family members after 12 years. Look out for the **funeral gondolas** draped in black and bedecked with flowers.

■ Above the portal of the Church of San Michele, look out for the **statue of St. Michael**, protector of the island, holding a set of scales in one hand and slaying a dragon with the other.

■ After visiting San Michele, hop back on the water taxi toward **Murano**. Since 1291, the island has been the center of Italian glassmaking. Tour the glass museum (Museo Vetrario), and visit one of the remaining glass factories.

EUROPE

ROMAN CATACOMBS

Originally created as collective Christian burial grounds, the catacombs are a fascinating record of early religious life and art.

EUROPE

Narrow stairs lead deep into the cool, dank underbelly of Rome to an endless network of passageways, each lined with row upon row of rectangular recessed niches hollowed out of the porous tufa rock. The multilevel underground city of the dead covers more than 600 acres (243 hectares) and extends 65 feet (19.8 meters) below ground. Tens of thousands of Christians were buried here from around A.D. 150 to 450, their sepulchral chambers adorned with beautiful mosaics and frescoes, many depicting baptism or the Eucharist. The sealed slabs of the tombs bear epigraphs, showing the name, age, and often profession of the deceased. Of the 60-odd known catacombs, five are open to the public, including three on Via Appia Antica, Rome's first *via consularis*, or royal highway, built in 312 B.C. Most people visit the catacombs of St. Callistus, the official cemetery of the early Church of Rome, which contains the remains of third-century pontiffs, many buried in the Crypt of the Popes. Visible in the catacombs of St. Sebastian, invocations scrawled by early pilgrims to the martyred saints Peter and Paul are not unlike graffiti.

When to Go The site is open year-round except Easter, Christmas Day, and New Year's Day. Hours vary, but all the catacombs are closed one day a week and for at least two hours at midday, as well as one month in winter for restoration. Tours run from 40 minutes to an hour, depending on the site and guide.

Planning A separate admission fee applies for each of the catacombs, with tickets available at the entrance. Visitors may not enter without a guide, and the wait for the next English-language tour may be long, especially in summer. The catacombs on Via Appia Antica are the most popular and can be very crowded. Instead explore the less visited catacomb of Priscilla, which date to the second century and are among the oldest and largest of Rome's catacombs.

Website www.catacombe.roma.it

HIGHLIGHTS

■ Admire the **early Christian art**, including the well-preserved third-century religious frescoes in the Cubicula of the Sacraments in the catacombs of St. Callistus.

■ Tour **St. Domitilla Church**, a fourth-century sunken basilica built over the catacombs. The only place where visitors can see bones, the catacombs of Domitilla feature an exquisite second-century **"Last Supper"** fresco.

■ View **sculptured sarcophagi**, including the impressive *sarcofago del bambino* (sarcophagus of the child) in the Trichorae, a triple-apsed, aboveground mausoleum near the entrance to the catacombs of St. Callistus.

The catacombs of St. Sebastian are believed to have temporarily housed the remains of Sts. Peter and Paul.

The memorial, whose designer was British architect Sir Reginald Blomfield, stands 80 ft (24.4 m) high.

BELGIUM

MENIN GATE MEMORIAL

Every evening, under a memorial arch, buglers pay a moving tribute to the soldiers who died in the Ypres Salient during World War I.

T he crowd grows silent as the first plaintive strains of the "Last Post" bugle call echo around the Menin Gate Memorial to the Missing in Ypres (Ieper), Belgium. This tribute, performed by Ypres fire brigade's band, honors British and Commonwealth soldiers who died in the three battles of Ypres between 1914 and 1917. The limestone-and-brick memorial straddles the Menin Road, the route that hundreds of thousands of soldiers took to the front line. Above its east entrance, a recumbent stone lion holds silent vigil over bygone battlefields. At the opposite end, a flag-draped sarcophagus and wreath face the town. The monument includes the Hall of Memory, its inner walls, stairways, and upper loggias inscribed with 54,896 names, listed by regiment, of soldiers from Britain and Commonwealth countries (except New Zealand) who have no known grave. Another monument, the Tyne Cot Memorial, at the nearby village of Passchendaele, site of the Third Battle of Ypres (or Battle of Passchendaele), lists the names of 34,984 missing British and New Zealand soldiers.

When to Go You can visit the memorial anytime. The "Last Post" ceremony is at 8 p.m. every night and may last minutes or more than an hour depending on the number of groups laying wreaths and other special tributes. On Armistice Day (November 11) extended ceremonies take place at 11 a.m. and 8 p.m.

Planning Allow several hours to visit the memorial, nearby battlefields, and World War I museums. Arrive by 7:30 p.m. to secure a good viewing spot for the "Last Post" ceremony. It is considered disrespectful to applaud after the ceremony.

Websites www.lastpost.be, www.visitbelgium.com

HIGHLIGHTS

■ Visit the **In Flanders Fields Museum** in Cloth Hall (Lakenhalle) on the Market Square (Grote Markt), and the museum and preserved trenches at Sanctuary Wood (Hill 62), to learn about World War I and the three battles of Ypres.

■ Wreaths of poppies left by visitors to memorial ceremonies flank the staircase entrances to the **Hall of Memory.** In the war years, red poppies grew profusely from the churned soil of the battlefields, especially of Ypres, and so became an emblem of the fallen soldiers. You can search the on-site Memorial Register for relatives' names to locate them in the Hall of Memory.

EUROPE

PÈRE LACHAISE CEMETERY

A city cemetery set into a hill on the eastern edge of Paris, this is the final resting place of some of the world's most celebrated figures.

Named for Louis XIV's confessor, Père François de la Chaise, the cemetery received its official designation from Napoleon in 1804. The largest of three cemeteries in Paris, it contains around 300,000 graves as well as a columbarium, or urn depository, for those cremated. Musicians, painters, and writers, men and women of science, military strategists, heroes and heroines, and people of political and industrial fame rest here. A columned roof shelters the tombs of the medieval lovers, Heloïse and Abelard, whose remains were brought here in the early 19th century. Another romantic pair, the actors Yves Montand and Simone Signoret, share a simple headstone. Chopin's tomb, like that of many musicians, continually bears garlands. Fresh flowers decorate the black marble slab of a much-loved French writer; the inscription reads simply: Colette. Elaborate carved sepulchres, like those of the influential Haussmann and Pleyel dynasties, lie alongside modest stones with names the elements have long since worn away. Walking through Père Lachaise on a windy fall afternoon, you trace two centuries of European history and meet with both the eminent and the unknown. Fallen leaves scuttle along the walkways, their nostalgic, brittle whispering broken by the sharp sound of shovels driven into hard ground: the grave diggers are at work.

When to Go The largest park in Paris, Père Lachaise is open daily but the hours vary slightly. Allow a couple of hours to visit the cemetery's 118 acres (48 ha).

Planning The Porte des Amandiers (Almond Tree Gate) leads directly from the Père Lachaise metro stop inside the gates, where an orientation map is posted. Line 2 metro Philippe Auguste and line 3 Gambetta stops are also convenient. A visitor center provides an informative map, numbered to indicate the tombs of the cemetery's most famous occupants.

Websites www.pere-lachaise.com, www.paris-tourisme.com

HIGHLIGHTS

■ Take a moment to study the old as well as modern **carved tombstones** of such figures as Miguel Ángel Asturias, a Guatemalan author and Nobel Literature Prize laureate.

■ One of the most renowned—and graffiti-covered—graves is that of the hugely influential singer-songwriter **Jim Morrison**. Security guards are often on duty here, as occasional visitors attempt to deface the stone or take parts as memorabilia.

■ Explore the long **avenue of Jewish graves** close to the shrine of Heloïse and Abelard.

■ Enjoy the cemetery's sheer **diversity** of cultures, languages, and religions. It represents people from all disciplines and all walks of life, from all corners of the world.

Opposite: Although the cemetery was named for Louis XIV's confessor, it's a nondenominational burial ground, with graves of Jews, Muslims, and Buddhists as well as Christians. Above left: Romantic painter Théodore Géricault's bust holds a palette and brush. Above right: Geranium pots and wreaths adorn singer Edith Piaf's plain marble tomb.

The 12th-century Church of St. Honorat was once an important shrine because of its many relics of early martyrs.

■ The **Museum of Ancient Arles** has a collection of sarcophagi that is second only to Rome's, illustrating the transition of imagery and style from pagan to Christian times.

■ At the end of the walk through the Alyscamps, the ruined Romanesque **Church of St. Honorat** stands on the site of several successive churches, including the sixth-century Monastery of St. Césaire.

■ From the gates of the Alyscamps, walk toward the old **city walls** to appreciate the expanse of land once covered with tombs.

FRANCE

ALYSCAMPS

Roman and early Christian tombs line the route through this ancient necropolis.

EUROPE

In Roman times, the sarcophagus sculptors of Arles in southern France were in great demand. Thousands of tombs had to be carved for burials in the western world's foremost cemetery, which was located outside the city walls. It was popular because St. Genesius of Arles, a highly revered third-century Christian martyr, was buried here. Blocks of marble were transported here from Greece and from Italy's Carrara cliffs along the Via Aurelia. Regulations of the day restricted graves to land outside the city walls, so the section of the Via Aurelia leading to the city gates became lined with sarcophagi. This was such a popular burial ground with rich citizens that bodies arrived from all over Europe; and the sarcophagi were stacked three high in places. Eventually, the Alyscamps, or the Elysian Fields, covered hundreds of hectares. Today, all that remains is a long, tree-shaded esplanade lined with rows of tombs that capture a sense of the Alyscamps' ancient calm repose. This walk, with its romantic, dappled light, has caught the interest of generations of artists, including Van Gogh and Gauguin.

When to Go From May to September Arles is warm and dry. During the mid-September Days of Historic Patrimony, many ancient sites open to visitors. The rice festival, Les Prémices du Riz, is also in September.

Planning The Alyscamps is a ten-minute walk south from the center of Arles, an ideal town to explore on foot. A week will give you time to see the many Roman and medieval sites and explore the Camargue region. The cemetery's old pathways of uneven rocks call for sensible footwear.

Website www.tourisme.ville-arles.fr

IRELAND

Newgrange

For sheer ancient mystery this giant, almost superterrestrial megalithic mound is hard to beat.

The 5,300-year-old Newgrange, one of the oldest structures in the world, is a massive egg-shaped mound 40 feet (12 meters) high and 250 feet (76 meters) across, and you'd swear there's a flying saucer buried beneath the grass. Instead, the interior is a huge stone cave with a tomblike chamber. Archaeologists believe Newgrange was a burial site for pagan rulers. Surrounded by curbstones with mysterious spiral designs—said to represent life, death, and eternity or the sun—Newgrange was also a holy place for religious rituals. The foremost of these was during winter solstice; for 17 minutes at dawn every December 21, a narrow beam of sunlight enters a hole in the huge edifice and creeps like a spotlight across the chamber floor to the end of the 62-foot (19 meter) long passageway, sending shivers up the spines of those lucky enough to view it. As the light penetrates the darkness, visitors feel a sense of communion with those who watched and waited five millennia ago to observe the same phenomenon. But you don't have to be there for winter solstice, nor are you likely to be able to, as entry is by lottery. Tours includes a solstice reenactment, however. No matter when you visit, as you enter the eerily silent cave, you'll instantly feel its power.

When to Go Newgrange is open year-round save December 24 to 27. Places are limited to 700 people a day in high season. Arrive early, especially in summer, since tours sell on a first-come, first-served basis.

Planning A visit to Newgrange begins with the exhibition at the visitor center, with a replica of the chamber. Allow an hour each for Newgrange and the exhibition and an extra hour if you want to visit the nearby tomb site of Knowth, too. Entry to Newgrange is by guided tour only. Tours begin at the Brú na Bóinne visitor center in Donore, County Meath, from which buses take visitors to the site in groups. To experience the winter solstice from inside Newgrange, enter a lottery at the interpretive center. Each year 100 winners are split into groups of five, and taken in on one morning from December 19 to 23.

Websites www.newgrange.com, www.heritageireland.ie

EUROPE

HIGHLIGHTS

■ Carved with intriguing spiral designs, 97 large **curbstones** decorate the exterior of the tomb. Scholars think they were recycled from an earlier burial place. Don't miss the especially impressive Threshold Stone (Entrance Stone), Curbstone 52 (opposite the entrance on the northwest side), and Curbstone 67 (on the northeast side).

■ When you enter, watch out for the **"roof box,"** which lets in the sunlight on the winter solstice. Once inside, gaze at the 20-ft (6 m) **corbeled roof** that has remained essentially intact and waterproof for more than 5,300 years.

■ In County Meath, 37 **satellite tombs** form the Brú na Bóinne complex. Two other nearby tomb sites, Knowth and Dowth, are both as old as Newgrange.

Despite its futuristic appearance, this mound dates from around 3200 B.C.

EGYPT

Valley of the Kings

Although their eventual occupants intended them as secret graves, the underground chambers in the Valley of the Kings now rank among the world's best-known burial sites.

Having learned that the monumental pyramids of older generations attracted tomb robbers, the pharaohs of the New Kingdom (circa 1539 to 1078 B.C.) determined that their burial places should be secret, hidden beneath tons of soil and scree on the edge of the desert. Foremost among these covert necropoli was the Valley of the Kings, at the base of a pyramid-shaped peak that takes on a golden glow at sunrise. Many of the ancient world's most formidable rulers—including Ramses the Great and Tutmosis II—were buried beneath the valley in elaborate underground chambers. They took with them everything considered necessary for the afterlife, including food, clothing, and furniture, and mystical statuettes called *ushabti*—small figurines believed to spring to life in the ancient Egyptian underworld to labor for Osiris, the god of the dead, in place of the deceased. Despite best-laid plans, robbers plundered most of the royal tombs, perhaps not long after the original funerals. It wasn't until 1922, when British archaeologist Howard Carter discovered the boy-king Tutankhamun's tomb, that the modern world came to realize the artistic and mystical significance of the Valley of the Kings. And it continues as an active place of archaeological discovery and scientific research into ancient Egyptian life, with new discoveries each year.

When to Go Avoid the Valley of the Kings in summer (June to September), when daytime temperatures often soar above 100°F (38°C). Winters can be chilly after dark, but the days are warm.

Planning Sixteen of the tombs are open to visitors, although not always all at the same time. The valley is on the west side of the Nile, opposite Luxor, and linked to it by regular ferry service. At the ferry port on the west bank, taxis, donkeys, and guides are available. Or you can book a tour in Luxor. You can rent a bicycle in Luxor and take it across on the ferry. Entry tickets to the valley cover three tombs of your choice; you need a separate ticket for Tutankhamun's tomb. Most organized tours cover the valley and the other west-bank sites, such as the Temple of Hatshepsut and the tombs of the nobles, in a day, but two days are better. Allow an extra day to include the temples of Luxor and Karnak on the east bank.

Websites www.thebanmappingproject.com, www.valleyofthekings.org, www.egypt.travel

HIGHLIGHTS

■ King Tutankhamun's tomb still contains Its solid stone outer sarcophagus, as well as the pharaoh's **mummy.** Since 2007, this has been on display in a climate-controlled glass case inside an anteroom.

■ The corridors and halls of the tomb of **Ramses III** bear painted scenes from the *Book of the Dead* and the *Litany of Ra*. Their subjects are as varied as the pharaoh's armory, boats on the Nile, and two blind harpists.

■ Up a narrow ravine, one of the valley's most secluded tombs, that of Seti I, also has the **most unusual decoration.** Its artists tinted some of the walls yellow to imitate papyrus and covered the ceilings in yellow stars set against a deep-blue night sky. The vestibule bears images of 741 ancient divinities, while the oval burial chamber resembles a huge scroll imprinted with the *Book of Amduat*. Until the discovery of Tut's tomb, Seti's was the valley's prize draw—the longest, deepest, and most richly adorned tomb of the entire necropolis. The paint seems as fresh as the day it was applied.

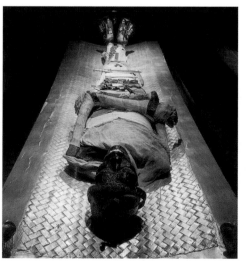

Opposite: More than 60 royal notables were buried in a wadi in the Valley of the Kings behind a row of hills that flank the River Nile's west bank. Above left: This decoration in King Horemheb's tomb depicts the goddess Hathor. Above right: Largely insignificant in life, Tutankhamun became feted in death as his tomb is so far the only one found intact.

10 Retreats

Of all the sacred places on the planet, those within ourselves can be the hardest to reach. Daily life, with all its distractions, impedes the habit of reflection. This is nothing new. Sages and saints have always left the material world behind to seek out tranquil places where they could meditate, refresh their spiritual energies, and listen to their gods or their own hearts. Religious communities throughout the world welcome seekers after truth—or simply silence. Their locations are part of the magic and some defy all expectations. Buddhist retreats, for instance, are found not only in Asia but on the red earth of Australia and in windswept Nova Scotia. Hospitable Christian communities perch on hills in Italy and France, or float alluringly offshore on the tiny islands of Iona and Caldey. Some places avoid denominational connections—such as Scotland's Findhorn Community, an eclectic, holistic retreat for all shades of New-Age belief.

A voluptuous statue of the Hindu god Vishnu graces the holy Indian city of Rishikesh, which offers many paths to spiritual awareness, from spaces beside the sacred Ganges River in which to meditate to classes in yoga.

Beside the crystalline sea, a moose grazes in the peaceful surroundings of Gampo Abbey.

CANADA

GAMPO ABBEY

Practicing Buddhists experience monastic life amid the dramatic wilderness highlands of Cape Breton Island, Nova Scotia.

An immaculate farmhouse and barn stand in a soft green meadow high above the endless deep blue waters of the Gulf of St. Lawrence. Here maroon-robed monks and nuns lead a contemplative communal life of study, meditation, and teaching, following a western-style Tibetan Buddhist practice. Life at Gampo Abbey is structured around periods of intense activity, ritual, and quiet meditation. Silence reigns from mid-evening until noon, occasionally broken by ringing gongs, sharp clackers, and the spellbinding hypnotic hum of Tibetan singing bowls. Most spiritual activity takes place in the Shrine Room, with its saffron-robed golden statue of Buddha, where residents spend mornings and evenings engaged in meditation practices and periods of rhythmic chanting. They dedicate their afternoons to the daily work of the abbey.

When to Go Public tours and programs are available during the summer months, while monastic opportunities requiring a six-month or longer commitment are available throughout the year.

Planning From June 15 through September 15, tours of the abbey are available to the public on weekdays at 1:30 p.m. During July and August, 7- to 14-day retreats are available for laypersons. Personal retreats, work-study, and monastic stays are available all year. Gampo Abbey is located near the village of Pleasant Bay, along the Cabot Trail, a 6.5-hour drive from Halifax International Airport. Bring Buddhist robes or appropriate clothing, slippers for indoor use, and be prepared for cold, windy, and wet weather most times of the year. Summers can be hot, so include a bathing suit and light clothing as well.

Websites www.gampoabbey.org, novascotia.com

HIGHLIGHTS

■ Walk around the **Stupa of Enlightenment**, which contains relics of the Vidyadhara Chogyam Trungpa Rinpoche, who founded Gampo Abbey in 1984. It is topped by a bronze sculpture of Gampopa, the 12th-century founder of the Kagyu lineage of Tibetan Buddhism, after whom the abbey is named. The stupa is inscribed with the **59 slogans of Buddhist teachings** on wisdom, kindness, and compassion.

■ Stroll through meadows filled with **flowers and wildlife**. Here foxes scamper about and moose graze near the edge of the sea. You can spot whales swimming offshore and eagles soaring overhead. Trails lead through the woods, down to the beach, or across the fields to a viewpoint high above the sea.

■ Join a **whale-watch tour** or rent a boat in the nearby village of Pleasant Bay: an exhilarating way to see the abbey and coast of Cape Breton.

NORTH AMERICA

WEST VIRGINIA

Bhavana Society

In the tranquil woods of West Virginia, meditation practices are based on the earliest surviving teachings of Buddha.

Flowing robes in hues of gold and burnt orange enfold monks and nuns sitting as peacefully and silently as the golden Buddha on the candlelit pedestal at the front of the long meditation hall. The walls and soaring arched ceiling glow with the warmth of natural wood, and the windows on either side of the Buddha offer views out into the green woodlands of the Bhavana Society forest monastery and retreat center. Here the community practices *vipassana* (insight) meditation in the Theravada Buddhist tradition, alternating sitting meditation with walking meditation. Many choose to meditate outdoors in a clearing in the sun-dappled woods, where birdsong and breezes aid the attainment of a peaceful state of mind. Grass- and fern-lined paths crisscross the shady woodlands, where sienna-colored buildings, dormitories, and *kuti* (meditation cabins) stand isolated from each other. Most retreats have a unique theme and include a daily practice of six to eight hours of meditation. The days pass quickly, and in the fading light of the evening, the flickering glow of oil lamps softly illuminates the interior of the simple kuti as retreat participants prepare for the peaceful night.

When to Go The monastery and retreat center are open all year, offering scheduled retreats and short-term stays for lay visitors. Residencies, or personal intensive meditation retreats, are available for those who already have a strong background in Buddhism; they last several weeks to a year or more.

Planning Organized on a variety of themes, public retreats vary in length from two to nine days. The monastery and retreat center are located on 42 forested acres (17 hectares) in West Virginia near the town of High View, which is one hour from Dulles International Airport and two hours from Washington, D.C. Pack comfortable but modest clothing, a flashlight, and alarm clock. Do not bring secular reading material, musical instruments, or radios. Retreats are offered in exchange for *dana*, or money given freely from the heart, without guidelines. The monastery survives entirely on donations, so be generous.

Websites www.bhavanasociety.org, www.wvtourism.com

HIGHLIGHTS

■ People on retreat participate in the society's community by helping with cleaning or food preparation, often gaining **insights into Buddhism** that go beyond textual teachings.

■ Breakfast and lunch are hearty vegetarian meals served in the simple dining hall and are accompanied by silence to encourage **mindful eating.** Dinner is replaced by a yoga session to promote moderation.

■ Just outside the main building complex, the **lily pond with a statue of Buddha** is a quiet place for reflection.

■ Take a long walk through the **beautiful woods** with a monk, or by yourself, and watch for wild deer.

At the Bhavana Society, meditation methods are taught according to the original precepts of Buddha, whose "middle path" is said to lead to peace of mind and wisdom.

People come on retreat to Harbin for the rustic peace, healthful hot springs, and a unifying spiritual experience.

CALIFORNIA

HARBIN HOT SPRINGS

Local Miwok people were the first to attribute healing powers
to these secluded springs in the foothills of northern California.

The Heart Consciousness Church acquired Harbin in 1972, transforming the 1960s' hippie commune into a nonprofit retreat and workshop center with an emphasis on New-Age themes such as holistic healing and universal spirituality. Eclectic if nothing else, the springs draw a mixed bag of leftover flower children, Tantric devotees, would-be Buddhists, nudists, druids, and others searching for alternative enlightenment. Fed by seven different sources, the clothing-optional springs are the main attraction. But there are plenty of other diversions: hot stone massage and *watsu* (water shiatsu), yoga and meditation sessions, dances and film shows, shamanic circles and Kirtan chanting, Native American sweat lodges and ancient Sufi study, and a serene early morning session called "Just Sitting." The 1,600-acre (647 hectare) spread also boasts several good hiking trails to secluded spots in the surrounding oak forest.

When to Go May to October is best, with longer, warmer days. Most guests book for two nights, with rooms at a premium on weekends. Week-long stays are also popular, and anyone can apply to the residency program. Your visit can coincide with local events such as the Clear Lake Catfish Derby in May.

Planning Harbin is in Lake County, CA. Accommodations include dormitories, motel rooms, cottages, the funky Harbin Domes (private rooms on the mountainside), and a creekside campsite where you can pitch your own tent. Guests can purchase meals at the Stonefront Restaurant and several cafés, or pick up their own organic produce and other edibles at the Harbin Market. All guests have kitchen privileges.

Websites www.harbin.org, www.lakecounty.com

HIGHLIGHTS

■ Harbin's **five naturally heated water features** include a large outdoor recreational pool with swim lanes, a tree-shaded warm pool around 95°F (35°C), and an indoor hot pool that hovers around 113°F (45°C). There's also a refreshing cold-water plunge and a "secret" waterfall at the end of a trail.

■ Regular **educational offerings** include massage courses and Tantric seminars, as well as love, intimacy, and sexuality workshops.

■ Sansang—an ongoing series of **lectures and films** led by prominent New-Age teachers, experts, and gurus from around the globe—takes its name from the Sanskrit term for "being together in truth."

■ The **largest freshwater lake** completely within California, Clear Lake offers sailing, swimming, kayaking, fishing, and motorized water sports, including paragliding and jet-skiing.

NORTH AMERICA

JAPAN

BEPPU ONSEN

An ancient geothermal "hell on earth" on Japan's southernmost island helps relax the stressed modern mind and body.

ASIA

Clouds of steam billow up from volcanic bathing *onsen* (springs) and from bubbling pools and waterspouts, or *jigoku* (hells)—which are for viewing, not using. A sulfurous odor permeates the air, a constant reminder of the geothermal activity that created these 3,800 hot springs, geysers, and fumaroles. Sandwiched between the sea and mountains on the northeast coast of Kyushu, they were created during the eruption of Tsurumi in A.D. 867. Volcanic minerals brilliantly color the pools, where temperatures reach 122–210°F (50–98.9°C). Named after the *sutras* (sayings) that characterize the Buddhist conception of hell, *jigokumeguri* (or "hell pilgrimages") have been made to Beppu since the Edo Period in the 17th century because of the supposed curative properties of the volcanic minerals. Hot springs and thermal baths envelop each visitor, relaxing the body, mind, and spirit. In spring, cherry blossoms dot the landscape in the hills above Beppu, where hidden stone-lined *rotenburo* (open-air hot springs) offer less crowded bathing in their milky-white waters.

When to Go It is best to visit in March to May (spring) and September to November (fall). The jigoku are open from 8 a.m. to 5 p.m. daily.

Planning Arrive at Beppu by train, bus, or plane–there is a nearby domestic airport. Many hotels double as spas. The "hells" can be visited in one day, but allow three to four days to experience all the thermal treatments. All onsen involve naked bathing, so if you prefer to wear a bathing suit look for a private or family onsen. Purchase the Kamenoi Mini Free passes to use the buses for a day and a combined ticket for the jigoku. The Tourist Information Office is open from 9 a.m. to 5 p.m.

Website www.japan-guide.com

HIGHLIGHTS

■ **Enjoy being buried** under piles of steaming, jet-black volcanic sand at the Takegawara Onsen, and don't miss a dip in a hot spring.

■ Wallow in the ooze of a *doroyu*, or **hot mud bath**, and let your body absorb the natural volcanic minerals.

■ Lie on a bed of herbs and perfumed iris that covers the floor of a **steam bath** (*mushiyu*), heated by a hot spring from below.

■ Be sure to visit some of the "hells" for their **spectacular colors**, including cobalt blue and blood red.

Shaded by umbrellas, participants in a sand bath wear cotton kimonos and lie buried up to their necks in hot, wet sand for 15 minutes.

JAPAN

KOYA-SAN

Sample monastic life by spending a night in a mountaintop temple dedicated to the Japanese sect of Shingon Buddhism.

In A.D. 816, the emperor of Japan gave the monk Kobo Daishi permission to build a monastic complex atop 2,952-foot (900 meter) Koya-san, and the first temple was consecrated three years later. Kobo Daishi hereby established Shingon Buddhism, a form of the religion emphasizing ritual, symbolism, and Buddha's secret, or esoteric, teachings. The revered monk is also famous for diverse achievements from engineering to the invention of the twin Japanese phonetic alphabets. Since he was buried on Koya-san in A.D. 835, the pious and the powerful have competed to occupy adjacent plots, turning the mountaintop into a vast necropolis. By 1600, there were more than a thousand temples, of which only about 120 remain today; about 60 of these are *shukubo* (active temples that receive guests). The walk to Kobo Daishi's mausoleum, Okuno-in, the mountain's most sacred site, leads past temples and roadside shrines surrounded by topiaried pines. To reach his shrine you must hike uphill through an ocean of graves—the only sound you hear is the tinkling of bells attached to pilgrims' staves. In the main temple, the Toro-do, the orange robes and immaculate white socks of the monks glow in the soft light of innumerable candles. Two lanterns here are said to have burned continuously since the first visitors appeared more than a thousand years ago.

When to Go Avoid "Golden Week" at the end of April and beginning of May, the Obon Festival in August, and New Year—all are busy seasons for domestic travel. Summers are hot and humid, so spring and fall are best for those planning to walk up to the cooler mountaintop.

Planning Stay for at least one night. An early afternoon arrival and departure after lunch the next day allow you to see the main shrine, museum, and several temples. Travel to Koya-san by train from Osaka, and then reach the top by funicular, which takes five minutes, or a steep climb on foot of about 50 minutes. Shukubo can be very popular, so book well in advance. Although shukubo are closed in the daytime, rarely allowing visitors in before 4 p.m., a polite tap at the gate and a whispered or gestured request will usually gain you permission to leave your baggage while you explore.

Websites www.jnto.go.jp, www.japaneseguesthouses.com/db/mount_koya

HIGHLIGHTS

■ Visitors are welcome to attend the early morning rites in the temples to watch a **Shingon ceremony** in which the abbot spectacularly battles a flame with wild strokes of a sword. The prayer halls are beautifully decorated and perfumed with incense. The hypnotic chanting of the monks creates its own sacred aura.

■ The **tranquil and tasteful temple surroundings** create a perfect environment for meditation. Take the opportunity to follow *zazen*, **Zen Buddhist meditation** offered by some of the temples.

■ The vegetarian *shojin ryori* dinner, especially the rich and creamy *goma* (sesame) tofu, is prepared to the highest standards by the monks using an 1,100-year-old secret recipe. Shojin ryori, or **"ascetic cooking,"** was introduced from China along with Buddhism, and its pursuit forms part of Sino-Japanese religious practice.

■ Wandering among more than **2,000 shrines and stupas** beneath forests of ancient, lichen-covered pines allows you to breathe in the atmosphere of this serene mountain retreat.

Opposite: The huge Kongobu-ji Temple is the headquarters of Shingon Buddhism in Japan and has the country's largest rock garden. Above left: The Daito Pagoda represents the central point, geographically, of both Koya-san and Japan. Above right: The gorgeous gardens of Eireiden Temple shimmer with colored foliage.

EIHEI-JI

Eihei-ji—meaning the "Temple of Eternal Peace"—is a mountain sanctuary with a major influence on Zen Buddhism.

ASIA

As the deep resonance of the bronze *daibonsh* (bell) reverberates along the covered walkways of Eihei-ji, black-robed monks scuttle along polished wooden floors to attend *zazen* (meditation). Mountain streams wind their way through the inner courtyards and temple gardens of more than 70 monastery buildings arranged in the symbolic form of Buddha, with the main teaching temple as the head and a statue of Buddha as the heart. A chorus of chants flows through the temple as the sutras are recited to the beat of a large wooden drum. Eihei-ji is a testament to ancient Japanese architecture, which aimed to enhance the unity of man and nature. Nestled among the 600-year-old cypress trees, it was established by the Zen master Eihei Dogen, who brought Soto Zen Buddhism from China in 1244. This is the principal training monastery for more than 150 monks and novices, who reside at the temple for two years on their pathway to priesthood, following the daily tasks of *samu* (cleaning) and zazen, and attending services and ceremonies. Men may participate in the retreats; they follow the monastic timetable of meditation, daily services, and work fueled by a simple diet.

When to Go April to September, when the weather is warmer. The monastery is open from 5 a.m. to 5 p.m. daily for visits. For a few days each month, it allows lay visitors (men only) to attend meditation training.

Planning Allow one to two hours to look around the monastery, one to four days to experience the Soto Zen monastic way of life. Take the train from Kyoto to Fukui City and change to another train or a bus for Eiheiji-Guchi. There is a small admission fee to the monastery. If you plan to stay, book at least a month in advance. To attend the sanzensha (three-night meditation training), you must be proficient in zazen and prepared for the rigorous monastic routine.

Websites www.sotozen-net.or.jp/kokusai/list/eiheiji.htm, www.japan-guide.com

HIGHLIGHTS

■ Attend the *sanrosha* **meditation training** for two days and one night or the *sanzensha* that lasts for four days and three nights.

■ Observe the **ritual of bell ringing.** A novice priest kneels down to pray between each strike of the bronze monastery bell when it is rung to announce zazen (four times a day) and on other ceremonial occasions.

■ Admire the huge reception room's **paneled ceiling**, painted with fish, birds, mountains, and flowers by different artists in the 1930s.

■ Look for the **half-dipper bridge** as you approach the monastery. It's where Eihei Dogen always returned half of the water he scooped out of the stream.

The temple complex of Eihei-ji is sheltered by a species of giant, soaring cypress known as *sugi*, which is traditionally associated with shrines and holy places.

Inside the Main Temple, or Hall of the Great Hero, sit the golden Buddhas of the past (left), present (center, with two attendants), and future (right).

CHINA

Po Lin Monastery

On the largest of Hong Kong's outlying islands, the "Precious Lotus" monastery offers a spiritual tour in a lofty landscape.

As the sun sets over Lantau Island, the roofs of Po Lin glow orange and gold on the lush verdant slopes below the peaks. In this tranquil spot, three Zen masters built the first retreat over a century ago. Po Lin has since grown into one of Asia's most sacred places. Up on the hill, the Big Buddha—at 112 feet (34 meters) the largest seated outdoor Buddha in the world—watches over pagodas and temples, his figure radiating calm and compassion, gentleness and strength, from his position on a giant lotus. Pilgrims, smaller than one of the statue's fingers, climb 268 steps to walk around the base and lay offerings at the Buddha's feet. His pedestal is a three-level circular exhibition hall—stepping through a lotus petal, you set eyes on paintings of the master's life. A large bell, engraved with Buddhist figures and prayers, rings 108 times a day for the eradication of 108 vexations (personal distractions). Meanwhile, in the main complex, devotees make their way to the Welto Temple, a web of winding corridors and upturned eaves, and the Hall of the Great Hero, the heart of the monastery, housing the three Buddhas of the past, present, and future. Sometimes, through the fragrant clouds of incense, you catch a glimpse of nuns or monks heading for private prayers.

When to Go Visit in winter, when clear weather is more likely, though not guaranteed.

Planning Allow a day, or stay overnight at the nearby youth hostel to see the sunrise on Lantau Peak, 3,064 ft (934 m) high. Arrive at Tung Chung on Lantau Island by train, and follow the signs for the Skyrail. Take the cable car (or bus) to Ngong Ping village—a short walk to the monastery—then walk down if you wish. However, the trek is long and can be treacherous in changeable weather, as on Lantau Peak itself. Po Lin is popular, so if you are looking for peace, head for the smaller temples or linger at the end of the day. There are restaurants at Ngong Ping, or you can order the vegetarian lunch in the monastery. Meal tickets are on sale below the Big Buddha and include the entrance fee to the exhibition hall.

Websites www.plm.org.hk/blcs/en, www.np360.com.hk

HIGHLIGHTS

■ In good weather, the 25-minute cable-car ride from Tung Chung offers **unrivaled views of Hong Kong**.

■ Also known as the Tian Tan Buddha, the **Big Buddha** sits on a base modeled on the circular, three-tiered Altar of Heaven at the Temple of Heaven (Tian Tan) in Beijing. Here the Chinese emperor came every year to worship heaven and pray for a good harvest.

■ The 38 columns of the **Wisdom Path** are inscribed with the ancient "Heart Sutra," the prayer widely invoked by Buddhists, Taoists, and Confucians. The last column is blank to symbolize "emptiness," the road to harmony. The **beautiful trail** continues through the woodland and along the streams of Lantau Peak. Or stroll around the gardens and a small tea plantation.

ASIA

PUTUOSHAN ISLAND

With a temple at every turn, this tiny island in the Yangtze River
Delta has been a Buddhist sanctuary since the tenth century.

ASIA

The imposing golden statue of Guanyin (the Goddess of Mercy) stands 108 feet (33 meters) tall, a ship's wheel in one hand, overlooking the still waters of the harbor, guiding vessels laden with worshipers toward her island. In A.D. 916, a ship carrying a Japanese monk was caught in treacherous seas nearby and he prayed to Guanyin for deliverance. The seas calmed and in thanks he enshrined his statue of the goddess in a fisherman's house that later became the Bukenqu Guanyin Temple. Crowned by Mount Putuo, the fourth most sacred Buddhist mountain in China, the island, only 4.8 square miles (12.5 square kilometers), is dotted with more than 300 temples, monasteries, and convents nestling among forests of plane trees. The fragrance of incense from giant burners at the temple doors floats across the tree canopy, accompanied by the chanting of prayers, the ringing of bells, and the deep beat of temple drums guiding pilgrims to houses of worship. In the mountain forests and along serene pathways, orange-robed monks and black-clad nuns kowtow (touch their forehead to the ground) alongside devout worshipers, once for every three steps in their pilgrimage.

When to Go April to June and September to November, when the weather is cooler. The busiest times are the festivals of Guanyin's birth (February 19), day of enlightenment (June 19), and achievement of nirvana (September 19). Allow three to four days, plus one to see the temples on the tiny island of Luojia Shan.

Planning Ferries go to Putuoshan from Ningbo or Shanghai. Minibuses link the main temples but don't always stop near them; walking is the best way to visit the more remote areas. Monasteries charge an entrance fee. Accommodations are usually easy to find, but reserve ahead during festival times.

Websites www.tour-beijing.com, www.chinadirect-travel.co.uk

HIGHLIGHTS

■ Join in **early-morning prayers and chants** at the Puji Temple at the heart of the island. Entrance is only by a side door, as Emperor Zhuang was once mistaken for a peasant and refused entry by the main door. He ordered it to be closed thereafter.

■ Visit **Fanyin Cave** (Cave of Buddhist Sound). Monks claim to have visions of Guanyin when praying here, and in the past some threw themselves into the waves (and to their death) to seek nirvana.

■ Take the gondola to the summit of Foding Hill and visit Huiji Temple to see its collection of **ancient brick carvings** of Guanyin. Walk back down the 1,060 stone steps.

The Purple Bamboo Forest garden is a Buddhist study center on the island.

The monks' *kutis*, or meditation huts, are simply made and command open views in all directions.

AUSTRALIA

BODHI TREE FOREST MONASTERY

In the rolling landscape of New South Wales, this monastery and retreat center opens its doors to all practitioners of Buddhism.

From the tall flagpole at the edge of the wooden balcony, a warm humid breeze ripples the striped flag colored to represent the hues of the aura surrounding Buddha after his enlightenment. On 95 acres (38 hectares) in a beautiful area of northern New South Wales that used to be known as the Big Scrub, the center was established in 2005 by Venerable Pannyavaro Thera. While devoted to Theravada Buddhism, the monastery is a nonsectarian community for monks, nuns, and lay yogis of all traditions of Buddhism. The buildings are corrugated iron shelters painted blue, in part or entirely, to represent the purity of turquoise, the Buddhist symbol for the sea and sky believed to enable limitless heights of spiritual ascension. At the heart of the monastery a statue of a Borobudur Buddha in meditation sits serenely under the sacred Bodhi tree, where inspiring views unfold of red earth and tree-lined valleys.

When to Go Anytime—temperatures are mild to warm year-round.

Planning Lismore is the closest town to the Bodhi Tree Forest Monastery and Retreat Centre. The monastery relies on donations, especially those given as payment for meditation retreats, which may last for days, weeks, or months. (The practice of generosity is the first step in characterizing the Buddha's teaching.) There are three lay hermitage areas in a wooded valley for lay yogis to practice meditation. Monks are available for guidance, and people stay in small meditation huts, or kutis, each with its own walking meditation area.

Websites www.visitlismore.com.au, www.buddhanet.org

HIGHLIGHTS

■ Attend a **meditation retreat**, available for weekends, ten-day sessions, and also for longer periods. *Vipassana* (the deep interconnection between body and mind) and *metta bhavana* (unconditional and unattached loving kindness) meditation courses are held in the new meditation hall, while accommodations are in the new dormitory.

■ Dedicated to replanting the landscape, the monastery has planted more than **1,500 rain-forest trees** in the valleys and along the creeks.

■ Visit **Boatharbour Reserve** east of Lismore town—all that remains of the original 185,329 acres (75,000 hectares) of the lowland subtropical forest that was felled after European settlement of the area from 1843.

AUSTRALIA AND OCEANIA

BHUTAN

TAKTSANG

One of the most remote monastery locations in the world, this sacred site commemorates the arrival of Buddhism in the tiny Himalayan kingdom.

Poised on a ledge 2,625 feet (800 meters) above the Paro Valley in Bhutan, Taktsang, or the Tiger's Lair, seems closer to the sky than the ground, and quite inaccessible to earthbound mortals. But it was here that, according to legend, the Indian saint Guru Rinpoche flew on the back of a tigress in the eighth century. After prolonged meditation in a cave, he overcame obstructive demons and converted the valley to Buddhism, an event commemorated by the monastery. This makes it the holiest site in Bhutan and one where saints and yogis are believed to have achieved enlightenment. Today, pilgrims follow in their footsteps, climbing through blue pines and rhododendrons, past Buddhist flags, prayer wheels, and makeshift stalls selling temple bells and skulls for ritual offerings. Temples are scattered all over the hills, where cobwebs of lichen hang from the trees and mysterious caves and rocks line the path. Beyond the viewpoint garlanded in flags, the trail plunges straight down to a bridge, where a 197-foot (60 meter) waterfall cascades into a sacred pool. After the final climb, the main sanctuary greets you with bright paintings on the walls. Here you will find Guru Rinpoche's meditation cave, open once a year. The air is perfumed with incense and butter lamps and the chanting of monks echoes all around. In a lonely retreat at the very top of the ledge, monks meditate in solitude for up to seven years.

When to Go Spring, fall, or winter if you don't mind the cold.

Planning The best way to reach Paro is by air. Independent travel is not allowed in Bhutan, so book a custom package, which includes a guide who will take care of all arrangements. Accommodations range from comfortable hotels to camping in remote areas. Allow one day for this trip, which may be done on foot or horseback. Climb slowly, especially if you have just arrived, to avoid altitude problems, and be prepared for changeable weather. It takes about 2.5 hours to climb to the monastery. Photography is not allowed inside the sanctuary. Respect local sensitivities and leave a small donation in every temple.

Website www.bluepoppybhutan.com

ASIA

HIGHLIGHTS

■ As you climb, the **dizzying panorama** of the mountains and valley is coupled with a sense of peace in the forest—only the sound of tumbling water and the bells of ponies tinkling far below interrupt the stillness.

■ Beyond the lodge, see the **cave temple** where a former head of the monastery was born. It's awash with offerings and prayer flags. Tiny clay urns shaped like stupas are placed along the way at auspicious points; they contain human ashes.

■ Your guide will point out the **footprint of Guru Rinpoche** on a sacred rock. In the sanctuary, find the lucky rock where, if you close your eyes and place your thumb in the hole, it's said your wish will come true.

■ The **ruins of Drukgyel Dzong** (Bhutan Victory Fortress) lie north of Taktsang. Built in 1649, this *dzong* (fortified monastery) was a defense against Tibetan invasions. On a clear day, you can see Mount Jumolhari.

■ Enjoy the **log fire and hot food** in the lodge on the way down, but be sure to order your food on the way up.

Oposite: The fragile-looking monastery on the sheerest of foundations acts as a beacon for the devout and for seekers of beauty and tranquillity. Above left: Prayer flags are planted nearby to send uplifting spiritual vibrations across the land as the wind blows. Above right: A monk follows the monastery trail high above the valley.

Ten Mountain Monasteries

Religious orders have long sought the peace of mountaintop retreats, which lie far above earthly bustle and closer to the gods.

❶ Zen Mountain Monastery, New York

Lying in a forest preserve high up in the Catskill Mountains, this striking four-story monastery of bluestone and oak is the home of the Mountains and Rivers Order of Zen Buddhists. It offers weekend or longer residential retreats for those wishing to deepen their practice in tranquil surroundings.

Planning The Zen Mountain Monastery also offers tours of the grounds on select Sundays. It lies about 2.5 hours by car or 3 hours by bus from New York City. www.mro.org

❷ Tashilhunpo Monastery, Shigatse, China/Tibet

Founded in 1447 by Gendun Drup, the First Dalai Lama, the Tashilhunpo Monastery—its name means Heap of Glory—has been the seat of the Panchen Lama for hundreds of years. The monks welcome visitors, who gaze in awe at the 86-ft (26 m) gilded Maitreya Buddha adorned with diamonds, pearls, amber, corals, and other precious jewels.

Planning Open to visitors daily, the monastery is on the western side of the city of Shigatse and can be reached by foot or pedicab. www.travelchinaguide.com

❸ Ladakh Monasteries, India

Rich in religious life and heritage, the Buddhist monasteries, or *gompas*, of Ladakh perch perilously on rocky outcrops and cling to craggy mountainsides. Each is different: Hemis is the largest and holds a colorful festival every summer, while Thiksey is famous for its vast art collection.

Planning The different gompas have varying opening hours and entry fees. www.lehladakhindia.com

❹ Kopan Monastery, Nepal

Kopan Hill soars high above the rice paddies on the outskirts of Kathmandu, and here, beside the iconic Bodhi tree, children as young as seven flock from the Himalayan kingdoms to study the precepts of Buddhism. Western visitors, too, come to learn from the spiritual example of the monastery's 360 resident monks.

Planning Kopan Monastery is about 9 miles (15 km) from Kathmandu. It offers ten-day courses or longer retreats. www.kopan-monastery.com

❺ Sinaia Monastery, Romania

Prince Mihai Cantacuzino founded this Orthodox monastery in 1690 after a pilgrimage to Mount Sinai; its bricks are said to incorporate stone from the Holy Land. Today, it is home to a group of elderly monks. It has a lovely location and a 19th-century church that is full of royal associations.

Planning Sinaia is in Prahova County, about 75 miles (120 km) from Bucharest. www.welcometoromania.ro

❻ Rila Monastery, Bulgaria

In the tenth century, the hermit John of Rila founded the imposing Orthodox Rila Monastery in the valley of the Rilska River. It's now famed for its elegant cloisters and impressive murals. The hermit's relics are still here, exhibited in the church that was built by his followers.

Planning Visit the monastery museum and take a look at the intricately carved Raphael's Cross. www.bulgarianmonastery.com

❼ Metéora Monasteries, Greece

Monks first took refuge on these clifftops from an invading Turkish army in A.D. 935 and built 24 monasteries in the centuries that followed. All the building materials had to be carried on their backs or winched up in baskets. Today, you can climb a trail or ride up in a cable car to visit the six surviving Greek Orthodox monasteries. Great Metéoron Monastery is the largest, highest, and best preserved.

Planning Visit in spring or fall to avoid the baking heat of summer. The nearest large town is Thessaloniki, which can be reached by train from Athens. Five of the monasteries are open to visitors, but only three are still in use. www.greecetravel.com, www.gnto.gr

❽ Andechs Monastery, Germany

On the holy mountain above Bavaria's Lake Ammersee sits the Benedictine Andechs Monastery, where monks have been brewing beer since the Middle Ages. Today, the brewery is a full-fledged commercial business with a *Bräustüberl* (brewery pub) and restaurant that serves up Bavarian specialties.

Planning Guided tours of the monastery, brewery, and the church are available, and the public is welcome to attend services. The restaurant is open from 10 a.m. to 11 p.m. www.andechs.de

❾ Great St. Bernard Hospice, Switzerland

For almost a thousand years, monks have lived at the hospice at Great St. Bernard Pass on the Swiss-Italian border, once the only north-south route through Europe for hundreds of miles. Its Augustinian friars became famous for their ministrations to travelers—their rescue missions were aided by St. Bernard dogs.

Planning The hospice is above the town of Martigny. It's still a functioning religious community and also offers accommodations. www.myswitzerland.com

❿ Monastery of San Juan de la Peña, Spain

San Juan de la Peña, or St. John of the Rock, is a medieval gem, carved dramatically into a cliff face overlooking the Pyrenees in Spain's Huesca province. As the Moorish invaders advanced north from Africa during the Middle Ages, it is said that the Holy Grail was sent here for safekeeping. Today, however, it's the Benedictine monastery's 12th-century Romanesque cloister, engraved with biblical scenes, that attracts visitors.

Planning Open to visitors year-round, the monastery is situated near the town of Jaca. www.monasteriosanjuan.com

Metéora means to "hang in midair," and Agia Triada (Holy Trinity) monastery lives up to the name. It is reached by 139 steps carved into the rock.

BOUDHANATH

One of the most important centers of Tibetan Buddhism, this great stupa is named after the path to enlightenment, or *Bodhi*.

ASIA

In the late afternoon in Kathmandu, the Tibetans of Boudhanath slip out of their homes, shuffling quietly through dusty alleyways toward the white stupa festooned in prayer flags. Old folk hobbling on bamboo staffs, mothers with babies on their backs, teenagers, and men—all in the colorful procession walk around the dome seven times, chanting mantras and spinning prayer wheels, or prostrate themselves on the cobbles. Red-robed monks sit in meditation, clutching prayer beads and alms bowls, under the eyes of Buddha, who stares out from all four sides of the stupa. In clear weather, the snowy peaks of the Himalaya, the mysterious abode of the gods, can be seen on the horizon. Shaped like a mandala to represent the Buddhist cosmos, and symbolizing the five elements of earth, water, fire, air, and ether, Nepal's largest stupa dates back to the 14th century, though for many believers its true origins are based in more ancient times. Either way, Buddhists have long worshiped on this site which, after 1959, grew into a major center of Tibetan Buddhism for refugees and Nepalese alike. Monasteries, temples, and shrines are scattered in the nearby lanes all the way to the hilltop monastery of Kopan, the perfect place to explore your own path to nirvana.

When to Go Any time except during the summer monsoon. Arrive early or stay late to avoid the tourist groups heading for Boudhanath during the day.

Planning The Boudhanath district is on the eastern edge of Kathmandu. The easiest way to get there is by taxi. Be discreet if you wish to take photographs during prayers, and save a little time to browse the Tibetan stalls, full of local crafts and religious artifacts. Allow a day for a visit, longer if you are seeking a spiritual experience. There is a wide choice of accommodations and transportation, although buses are probably best avoided. During periods of unrest, check on the security situation before traveling.

Websites www.go2kathmandu.com, www.travel-himalayas.com

HIGHLIGHTS

■ Visit at dawn or dusk to **witness local devotions**, which you are welcome to join. Sit on a rooftop café terrace for beautiful views of the stupa and the golden roofs of the monasteries.

■ After the monsoon—in July to August—monks hold a **"rains retreat,"** with teaching, meditation, and prayer.

■ Join in the **Tibetan New Year celebrations**, or Losar, usually around the February full moon, when monks perform special rites, blowing long copper horns and throwing handfuls of roasted barley in the air. Devotees from all over Nepal and beyond attend, many of them draped in traditional clothes adorned with chunky turquoise and coral.

A Buddhist monk pauses at the base of the stupa, on the uppermost of three platforms that symbolizes earth. The two circular plinths under the stupa represent water.

FRANCE

TAIZÉ

Reconciliation, trust, and simplicity reign in this community, where different spiritual traditions come together in a village in Burgundy.

EUROPE

Repeated to the simplest of melodies, the renowned Taizé chants create their own temple of sound. Gathered in the community's Church of Reconciliation, hundreds of people, mostly young, participate in the pared-down liturgy as part of their week-long retreat. They come from many countries and so the morning, midday, and evening prayers form a kind of common ground. This internationalist approach was the life's work of Swiss-born Brother Roger (Roger Schütz, son of a Protestant pastor), who first came to the tiny hilltop village of Taizé in 1940. It lay just outside the zone under Nazi occupation, and he spent the next two years helping Jews escape into Switzerland. Breaking down differences became his mission, and in 1944 he founded the ecumenical monastic community of Taizé, which has both Roman Catholic and Protestant members. Brother Roger continued as prior until 2005, when he was fatally stabbed, at the age of 90, by a young woman suffering from schizophrenia. The community continues to provide refreshing human and spiritual encounters, however, which sustain participants on their return to everyday life.

When to Go Anybody can join in the communal prayers at any time of year. Retreats run from Sunday to Sunday. Young people aged 15 to 29 can go throughout the year, those aged 30 or over from March to October only. You need to book in advance.

Planning Arrive in Taizé by car on the A6 autoroute, or by train from Paris to Mâcon Loché, from where there is bus service to the village. Either bring a tent or reserve a place in one of the dormitories–at quiet times of the year, you may be able to get a room in one of the community's guesthouses. Although this is one of the world's most famous wine and food regions, meals at the retreat are basic. The monks will expect you to help with cleaning, including the restrooms. Hot showers are available for only an hour or two each day–if you miss the time slot, it will be a bracing splash under cold water.

Website www.taize.fr

HIGHLIGHTS

■ You can join talks by one of the members of the community, as well as **discussion groups** to air the issues they raise. Usually, the members of each group have some grasp of a common language.

■ There are plenty of **opportunities for walking** in the beautiful countryside of southern Burgundy. In the evenings people gather with their guitars and other instruments to sing and play popular songs and the folk music of their own countries.

■ If you have time and transportation, allow a few days before or after the retreat to **explore the region.** Its sights include Cluny, the historic town of Tournus, and, of course, the vineyards of the Mâconnais.

In the huge, candle-lit Church of Reconciliation, rows of white-robed Taizé brothers join in evening prayers.

FRANCE

St.-Honorat

Just off the French Riviera, a Cistercian community tends its island home and shares this miniature paradise with visitors seeking balm for the soul.

As the small passenger ferry approaches tiny St.-Honorat—one of a group of islands together known as the Isles de Lérins—the azure waters and warm sea breezes wash away the bustle of Cannes. The island is named for St. Honoratus, who sought solitude and hermitage here; his disciples soon joined him and they established an active monastery by A.D. 427. As you step off the boat onto the small jetty, the sound of cicadas assails you. And it follows you along the shaded sandy pathways toward the southern shore where the monastery lies. The scent of eucalyptus and pine fills the air and the path skirts the ruins of some of France's oldest chapels, dating to the 5th century. You may encounter monks in white cassocks, the island's only residents, who tend the vineyards and lavender fields that carpet the interior. A fortification was built in the 11th century to protect the monastery from repeated raids. In 1859, the bishop of Fréjus bought the island, hoping to revive the monastery after its secularization during the Revolution. The present monastery of the Cistercians of Sénanque dates from ten years later and encloses the original cloister, chapter hall, and refectory. The brothers carry on the spirit of the first Christian community, living, sharing, working, and praying together—and offer visitors the chance to experience this from time to time.

When to Go Visit in April to May and September to October, when the weather is good but it should be quiet. St.-Honorat is open to the public each Tuesday during summer for a day of prayer and reflection.

Planning Allow a day to cover the island's ancient chapels and castles, attend a service, and explore the terrain. Cannes' new ferry terminal is at the far southwest corner of its harbor. Ferries run hourly (except during the sacred French lunch period, from about noon to 2 p.m), and the last one back is at 6 p.m. (5 p.m. in winter). Bring food and plenty of water on a hot day. Wear your bathing suit under your clothes as there are no official places to change, and wear respectable dress throughout the island. Avoid speaking in the monastery and remember that some monks have taken a vow of silence. Book a retreat at least two months in advance: info@abbayedelerins.com.

Website www.cannes-ilesdelerins.com

HIGHLIGHTS

■ Visitors are welcome to attend **any of the seven services** (Vigils, Lauds, Third, Sext, None, Vespers, and Compline) held each day in the Abbey Church (Église Abbatiale de Lérins).

■ Men can take the chance to follow **the monastic way of life**, working, praying, studying, and eating with the monks, who are of various backgrounds. The monastery can host up to 30 visitors at a time. In summer there are special days of reflection on Christian themes.

■ The gift shop sells the **award-winning St. Sauveur wine** and liqueurs, as well as pure lavender oils and honey, all made by the monks. They also run events such as Liqueur Spring (*Printemps des Liqueurs*), where you can taste and buy.

■ Discover **hidden rocky coves** and the most idyllic swimming in the blue Mediterranean Sea.

■ Visit the sister **island of Ste.-Marguerite**. It was here, in the Fort Royal, that the Man in the Iron Mask was incarcerated.

Opposite: The palm-shaded abbey now houses about 25 monks. The main buildings date from the 19th century, but the cloister (above left) is about a thousand years older. Above right: Vulnerable to pirates and other seaborne invaders, the monastery was protected by a fort, cannons on the chapel roofs—still visible—and a system of signaling with fires.

FINDHORN

A pioneering community, established more than 20 years ago,
lives truly as friends of the Earth—and each other.

Near northeast Scotland's secluded Findhorn Bay, this celebrated rural community outside a former fishing village has great physical beauty—but its spiritual quality is what draws visitors from around the world. The Findhorn Community follows the principles of "attunement to the sacred, inner listening, respect for the interconnection of all life, service to the planet, and personal sharing." It now covers several sites, from a college at former hotel Cluny Park to an eco-village—which includes a house fashioned from a huge whisky cask. Findhorn came about in the early 1960s, when Eileen and Peter Caddy and their friend and colleague Dorothy Maclean, who had been running the Cluny Park and another hotel nearby, were laid off and had nothing to live on save the garden plot near their small trailer home. When their first fruits and vegetables failed in the sandy soil, Eileen, a devotee of unorthodox spirituality, began praying to the plants' "devas" (spiritual essences) and soon grew cabbages weighing up to 40 pounds (18 kilograms). Whether that tale is apocryphal or not, the gardens' fecundity and the inhabitants' fellowship have made Findhorn a center for holistic living and enhanced consciousness—as well as a place of human habitation with one of the world's smallest measurable carbon footprints.

When to Go "Experience Weeks" (prerequisites for other workshops and courses) take place year-round. There are visitor tours from April through November.

Planning The time you need to visit Findorn depends on your purpose. To see the eco-village, a day trip will do; but if you want to absorb the spirituality, try an Experience Week or a taste of community living on the Isle of Erraid. At Traigh Bhan on Iona, summer retreat weeks are available from July to September.

Website www.findhorn.org

EUROPE

HIGHLIGHTS

■ Findhorn's **eco-village** is famed for its "living machine," a greenhouse-based system of plant filtration that takes the cooperative's sewage and turns it into water, considered safe by European swimming standards.

■ The community owns the **Isle of Erraid** and **Traigh Bhan**, a retreat house on the Isle of Iona. Both offer visitors different, quieter ways to experience the Findhorn way.

■ Conferences on **planetary issues** take place regularly with speakers from the community and thinkers and practitioners from around the world. Findhorn also runs courses on holism and environmentally friendly design.

Using a simple wooden construction of locally grown timber, residents at Findhorn build their own cabins, in a model of all-round eco-friendly design.

The long-derelict abbey church was restored in the 20th century and has regular services open to the public.

SCOTLAND

Iona

Barren, windswept, and remote, this tiny Hebridean island holds a special place in the hearts of devout Christians.

t was on this unprepossessing patch of peat bog, heather, and bare rock that, in A.D. 563, an Irish princeling turned monk founded Scotland's first Christian mission. Columba came to Iona with just 12 companions and set about converting the Picts and Scots and eventually spread the gospel as far south as Northumberland in England. The island gradually became a magnet for pilgrims from all over the newly Christianized world of northern Europe. From the ninth to eleventh centuries, six Scottish kings were buried in the abbey's graveyard, and a forest of intricately carved stone crosses grew up around them. But the island's fame and riches had already begun to attract less peaceful visitors. Vikings first plundered Iona in A.D. 794, carrying off its sacred treasures. After half a century of such raids, the monks abandoned the abbey; it remained deserted until, in 1203, it was resettled by Benedictine nuns. The convent flourished until the Reformation (1560), when all but three of its Celtic crosses were toppled or smashed. The nunnery still lies in ruins, but St. Mary's Abbey survives as the finest example of medieval church architecture in the Hebrides. Iona remained almost deserted until 1938, when the Reverend George MacLeod founded the ecumenical Iona Community, which now has three residential centers on Iona and neighboring Mull, giving Christians of every persuasion, an opportunity to live and work together.

When to Go Visit from April through October for the mildest weather.

Planning The ferry from Fionnphort on Mull to Iona takes ten minutes. CalMac ferries to Mull operate from Oban, Ardnamurchan, and Lochaline on the mainland. Only residents may drive on Iona, but you can rent bicycles at the harbor. Accommodations include the Argyll Hotel, built in 1868, which also has the island's best restaurant, using mainly organic produce; and the St. Columba Hotel, with sweeping views across to Mull. The charter vessel M.V. *Volante* leaves the ferry pier at 2 p.m. for trips around the coast, which take around 90 minutes.

Websites www.historic-scotland.gov.uk, www.visitscotland.com, www.calmac.co.uk

HIGHLIGHTS

■ The restored abbey retains its tranquil atmosphere and houses a superb collection of **medieval and religious carved stones**.

■ Iona offers a fascinating **dip into history.** Monarchs buried on Iona include Macbeth (MacBeata), the Pictish-Scots king and model for Shakespeare's murderous antihero.

■ The island's coasts have extraordinarily beautiful, almost **deserted white sand beaches** that are perfect for beachcombing. Look out for green sea-polished pebbles of famous Iona marble.

■ There are **sightseeing trips** around Iona's wild coast, with the chance to see seals, dolphins, puffins, and other seabirds, and even minke whales and basking sharks.

EUROPE

Although Lindisfarne Priory in A.D. 635 was a center of Anglo-Saxon Christianity, the current ruins are Norman, dating from the 11th century.

ENGLAND

Lindisfarne Holy Island

This tidal island off the north coast of England was an early outpost of Christian mission. Many find its stillness a pick-me-up for the soul.

From Lindisfarne, also called Holy Island, the view changes with the tide. At low water, a modern paved causeway runs from the coast of Northumberland across the North Sea to the isle, while during high tide the causeway vanishes to leave a waterbound outpost. From the mainland, two landmarks herald the presence of Lindisfarne: its rugged fort atop a high knoll and the arched bridge of its ruined priory. Once across, visitors can follow the island's worn paths in the footsteps left by two of Christianity's holiest men. An Irish-born monk, St. Aidan, arrived here in A.D. 635 as a missionary from a monastery on the Scottish isle of Iona, charged with bringing Christianity to those English who continued to practice paganism. Ever since, Lindisfarne has signified serene spirituality, gaining in the 11th century the name Holy Island. The wooden monastery Aidan and his 12 brethren created no longer exists. The ruins one can see today are those of the abbey built after the Synod of Whitby, when the monks, under St. Cuthbert, began answering to mainland ecclesiastical authority in 664. More than a century of peaceful monastic life ended with the beginning of Viking raids in 793. The monks left for good in 875, although a later community lived here from the 11th century to 1537, when Henry VIII dissolved England's monasteries.

When to Go Late spring is ideal, when England's border-country flora is in full bloom.

Planning Consult tide tables, particularly if you're planning to drive. Allow at least two days—one for Holy Island itself and one for the wild but beautiful Northumbrian coast so that you can understand the early challenges monks faced. St. Cuthbert's Centre on Lindisfarne has a bothy, or hut, where visitors can stay on an "individually guided retreat." It also runs "organized retreats."

Websites www.holy-island.info, www.lindisfarne.org.uk

HIGHLIGHTS

■ The **Lindisfarne Gospels** are among Britain's best-preserved illuminated manuscripts. The isle's monks created them around A.D. 715, in honor of St. Cuthbert. The British Museum holds the original, but the Lindisfarne Centre has a replica.

■ Enjoy a **quiet day** on the island, perhaps based at the Anglican Church of St. Mary the Virgin, a focus for all Christian pilgrims.

■ Lindisfarne produces **fortified wine** and **mead**, sold at the village winery.

■ **Lindisfarne Castle** was built in 1515 with stones from the ancient priory. In 1901 a new owner hired Sir Edward Lutyens to refit the castle in the Arts and Crafts style and Gertrude Jekyll to lay out the gardens.

EUROPE

WALES

CALDEY ISLAND

First settled by monks in the sixth century, the island is renowned for its rugged beauty and ancient spirituality.

EUROPE

The boat that has carried you 3 miles (4.8 kilometers) across Caldey Sound bumps against the slipway in the island's Priory Bay. As you scramble ashore, the abbey's guestmaster—the monk who looks after you—stands in white robes, ready to lead you up the hill to St. Philomena's Retreat House, your home for the next few days. That short sea journey is like a detour from ordinary life—you have stepped aside from the world, perhaps in order to understand it better. This isle off the southern coast of Wales belongs to Trappist monks, formally called Cistercians of the Strict Observance. They are not vowed to silence, as many assume, but encouraged to shun unnecessary talk. Just 1.5 miles (2.4 kilometers) long, Caldey is like a tiny self-contained universe, particularly after the final boat has returned the last day-trippers to mainland Tenby. Caldey provides all the natural beauty you could hope for—sea cliffs, wild heathland, sandy beaches, and abundant wildlife, including seals, cormorants, and puffins. Your fellow retreatants are almost invariably entertaining folk—and the ban on unnecessary talk definitely doesn't extend to St. Philomena's. Optional abbey services aside, the retreat is unstructured, yet many guests find it a fine way to put life into perspective.

When to Go Visit from Easter to the end of October. No boats serve Caldey on Sundays, Good Friday, and some Saturdays. Abbey services start with Vigils at 3:30 a.m. and end with Compline at 7:35 p.m.

Planning Weather permitting, the day's first boat usually leaves Tenby around 10:30 a.m. and the last departs Caldey before dusk. For up-to-date information, call +44 (0)1834 844453. Accommodations at St. Philomena's include full board; you make your own bed and help wash up after meals. To book, write to the abbey's guestmaster by mail, enclosing a self-addressed, stamped envelope. Easter retreats fill up quickly—reserve well in advance. There are no fixed fees—you donate according to your means.

Website www.caldey-island.co.uk

HIGHLIGHTS

■ Across a small valley from the retreat house, the **abbey** showcases the early 20th-century Arts and Crafts style. Past islanders left the **Caldey Stone** (inscribed in both ancient Celtic and Latin scripts), the 12th-century **St. Illtyd's Church**, the **Old Priory**, and a clifftop **lighthouse**.

■ **Chat to the monks.** Many had interesting secular careers. They'll gladly talk and give advice if asked.

■ Here as elsewhere, Trappists make goods to sell. The quirky post office sells **abbey toiletries.**

■ Enjoy a summer swim from **Priory Bay's sandy beach.** If you're ready for a little rock climbing, ask someone to guide you to Caldey's impressive **sea caves.**

The Cistercians arrived on Caldey in 1929, but they continue a monastic tradition started by Celtic monks in the sixth century.

IRELAND

SKELLIG MICHAEL

Its sixth-century founders believed seclusion was the best way to union with God, and this exceptionally remote outpost of Christianity still acts as a beacon to pilgrims.

A secluded monastery squats atop a rounded peak on uninhabited Skellig Michael, a conical rocky outcrop about 8 miles (13 kilometers) off the southwest coast of Ireland. Accessible only by a grueling climb up 640 stone steps, the monastic outpost was home to an order of early Irish Christians from around the sixth century until the twelfth, when they abandoned the 44-acre (18 hectare) island for Ballinskelligs Priory on the mainland. The monks, most likely never numbering more than a dozen, constructed six corbeled stone beehive huts, known as *clocháin* (singular *clochán*), on a sheltered terrace on the summit of a 607-foot (185 meter) peak. Nearby lies a tiny cemetery, its graves marked by stones—the vestiges of crude crosses—and the Oratory Terrace with a large Celtic cross and two places of worship, including the Church of St. Michael. Isolation brought ingenuity, with the island's inhabitants developing a sophisticated system to divert rainwater off the rock face into cisterns. On the nearly vertical slope of the 715-foot (218 meter) high South Peak, beyond a small grassy valley known as Christ's Saddle, are the ruins of an ancient hermitage. Although built to accommodate only a single cloistered monk, it also served as a hiding place when the monastery came under attack by marauding Vikings in the ninth century.

When to Go Boat trips are scheduled only from April to September, weather permitting. To see the puffins that nest on Skellig Michael, visit before early June when they migrate off the island.

Planning Allow five hours, which includes the boat trip and about three hours on the island. Boats leave between 10 and 11 a.m. from Valentia Island for the 50-minute trip, subject to weather and sea conditions. Dress in layers, and bring lunch and water as the island has no facilities. The two-hour Skellig Experience Sea Cruise allows visitors to view the islands and marine life, including dolphins and gray seals, without landing. Purchase a combination ticket for the exhibits and cruise at the Skellig Experience Heritage Centre.

Website www.skelligexperience.com

EUROPE

HIGHLIGHTS

■ Examine the island's **ancient stone architecture**, including the sleeping huts constructed entirely of native stone without the use of mortar.

■ Skellig Michael and neighboring Little Skellig are premier **birding** areas for observing kittiwakes, northern gannets, guillemots, razorbills, and Atlantic puffins.

■ Visit the **Skellig Experience Centre** on Valentia Island, open April through November, to learn about the history, wildlife, undersea life, and lighthouses of the two Skelligs. Their names derive from the Irish *sceilig*, or rock.

Opposite: The smaller of the Skellig islands, Little Skellig, in the background, is home to the world's second largest northern gannet colony. The island is closed to the public. Above left: Thousands of Atlantic puffins nest on Skellig Michael. Above right: Stone huts, or clocháin, overlook the simple graves of Skellig Michael's cemetery.

At sunrise the ruins of the old city of Siwa offer fine views over the mosque and the whole oasis.

EGYPT

Siwa Oasis

History meets legend in this desert fastness, watered by healing springs, where you can relax into the peaceable Berber way of life.

After crossing the Great Sand Sea near the Libyan border, the old caravan route between the Libyan Coast and the Nile Valley dives steeply into the basin of Siwa oasis, 65 feet (20 meters) below sea level. The ancient Egyptians knew the oasis as Sekht-am (Palm Land), and today sand and rocky outcrops vie for attention with a mosaic of date palms and irrigated fields. Crystal-clear lakes, fed by almost 200 springs, have allowed continuous habitation here since 10,000 B.C. The oasis was a vital halt on the caravan route, giving rise to the ancient fortified settlement of Shali Ghali, whose ruins still overlook the town of Siwa, a grid of lowrise sandcastles and dusty streets full of donkey carts conveying chattering Berbers. On a nearby hill stand the crumbling walls of the Temple of Amun, whose famous oracle, it is said, was in demand from pharaohs and Greek heroes alike. After Alexander the Great visited it, he declared himself the son of Zeus Amun, legitimizing his claim to Egypt and other lands he had conquered.

When to Go Visit from March to May and September to November, when the weather is mildest.

Planning Siwa lies 350 miles (560 km) west of Cairo and takes ten hours by bus. Alternatively, it is seven hours by road from Alexandria. Allow four or five days to visit all the sites and absorb the Siwan way of life. Dress conservatively and respect local customs. Wear clothing that will amply cover you if you swim—many swim fully clothed. Get around the town by donkey cart or rent a bike. Accommodations range from small hotels to luxurious lodges. Safaris into the desert can include overnight stays under the stars.

Websites www.somewheredifferent.com, www.touregypt.net

HIGHLIGHTS

■ Cool off in the **natural springs** at Fatnas, which are 2,300 ft (700 m) deep, on the edge of Birkat Zaitun, or Olive Lake, the largest of the area's salty lakes. Also try the unspoiled Ain Qurayshat and Abu Shuruf springs, 19 miles (30 km) east of Siwa.

■ Watch the sun set from the top of a sand dune and witness the **multitude of stars** gradually appearing as night envelops the desert.

■ Be buried up to your neck in the **warm mud baths** at Gebel Dakrur—which are claimed to help rheumatism—and take a midnight dip in the nearby **hot springs**.

■ Visit the **rock-cut tombs** of Gebel al Mawta (Mountain of the Dead), north of the city, decorated with wall paintings and still containing human bones; the ruins of the Temple of Umm Bida; and the Roman tombs of Al Zeitum.

AFRICA

ETHIOPIA

DEBRE ZION MONASTERY

A moment of early Christian history is preserved on an island monastery, where every visitor can make the experience their own.

In a shallow bay on Lake Ziway, donkeys and cows wander on the mudflats as children chatter and play. Here, on the crest of an acacia-covered promontory reaching into Lake Ziway, the Debre Zion Church on Tullo Gudo island lies isolated from the outside world. Though reconstructed, it has changed little in purpose and spirit. It was built around A.D. 800 to give temporary sanctuary to the Ark of the Covenant when Queen Judith, a tenth century non-Christian queen, threatened to seize it from Aksum, the ancient capital of Christian Ethiopia. So runs the story, one of many woven around the location and history of this holiest of objects. For four decades, more than 500 monks lived on Tullo Gudo and protected the ark, thought to hold the Ten Commandments, until it was safe to return it to Aksum. Today, the church still houses ancient manuscripts and parchment bibles, guarded by just three monks in black robes enveloped in white shammas. Inside, brightly colored icons adorn the walls leading to the curtained Holy of Holies. Time has remained in suspended animation for the island Lak'i (descendants of the Aksumites), but the curious and intrepid visitor will be warmly welcomed.

When to Go Visit in September to April to avoid the rainy season.

Planning A visa is needed to enter Ethiopia. Travel to Ziway, which is approximately 120 miles (193 km) southwest of Addis Ababa, and look for a boat to take you to Tullo Gudo. There is no ferry service to the island: it is a four-hour journey by reed boat or one hour by motor boat. Allow one full day to visit Tullo Gudo and Debre Zion (there are no hotels on the island). Pay great respect to the Lak'i and monks on the island as visitors are very rare. Remember to dress conservatively; you may have to take off your shoes when entering the church. In Ziway you can stay at a chalet at the Bekele Mola Hotel (it has hot-water showers) or at the Kasi Hotel (which only has cold water).

Websites www.ethiopianquadrants.com, www.timelessethiopia.com

AFRICA

HIGHLIGHTS

■ Lake Ziway has an abundance of **birdlife** along its extensive shores. Look out for the African snipe, black-winged stilt, and pied avocet.

■ Try some **traditional Ethiopian food**, which is served on a communal plate, with a cereal-based "pancake" topped with tasty meats and vegetables. Use only your right hand for eating, avoid touching your mouth, and take food only from your side of the plate.

■ If you are offered coffee (*buna*) notice the ritual of the **coffee ceremony**. It is polite to drink three cups of the strong sweet beverage. *Berekha*, the last one, is known as the blessing cup.

Precious parchment manuscripts are curated by the monks in this outpost of the Ethiopian church.

GLOSSARY

Italics indicate a separate entry.

Anasazi people Prehistoric Native American people active in the region where the modern states of Arizona, New Mexico, Colorado, and Utah meet. Ancestors of modern Pueblo people.

Anglican Church Protestant denomination within the Christian Church. Churches in the worldwide Anglican Communion have historical links with the Church of England or use a liturgy consonant with it. See also *Episcopal Church*.

Ark In a synagogue, a cabinet containing the *Torah* scrolls used in Jewish worship.

Ark of the Covenant Chest that in the biblical era contained sacred tablets (including the Ten Commandments) and was stored in the Holy of Holies within the ancient First Temple in Jerusalem; also the sacred shrine symbolizing the earthly dwelling place of God.

Ashkenazic Jews Jews whose ancestors and traditions originated among the medieval Jewish communities of Germany and eastern Europe. See also *Sephardic Jews*.

Assumption of the Virgin Mary The transporting of Mary, the mother of Jesus, to heaven at her death. In Roman Catholic theology, she was raised to heaven with body and soul united. Catholics celebrate the festival of the Assumption each year on August 15.

Aymara Native people of the Andes and Altiplano regions of South America, covering parts of Bolivia, Peru, Chile, and Argentina. Perhaps creators of Bolivia's advanced Tiwanaku (or Tiahuanaco) civilization (circa 1500–1200 B.C.), they were subjects first of the *Inca*, then of Spain.

Aztec Native people of Mexico, creators of a great empire in *Mesoamerica* (including parts of Central America) in the 14th–16th century. Spanish adventurer Hernán Cortés conquered the Aztecs in 1519–21.

Baal Fertility, sky, and storm god in the ancient Middle East and a patron deity for various ancient cities, including Tyre and Carthage. In biblical references, usually a local god worshiped in the form of a cult image.

Bahaism Religion founded in 19th-century Persia by the teacher Mirza Hoseyn 'Ali Nuri or Bahá'u'lláh (Arabic for "Glory of God"). The religion teaches humankind's spiritual unity.

Baptist Church Protestant denomination within the Christian Church. Believers promote the importance of adult rather than infant baptism (immersion in or washing with holy water as a symbol of rebirth as a Christian).

Basilica Originally a large public building in the era of ancient Rome, later the name of a large and significant church in the Roman Catholic and Greek Orthodox traditions.

Belfry The part of a tower or steeple containing bells, also known as a bell tower.

Benedictine Orders Communities of Christian monks and nuns who follow the Rule of St. Benedict, written by Benedict of Nursia (circa 480–circa 547) in Italy. The Benedictine Rule became the fundamental monastic code in western Europe: the day was devoted to prayer, sacred reading, and manual labor. Monasteries became centers of agriculture and learning.

Bishop Member of clergy in some Christian churches with authority to oversee priests. In Roman Catholic, Orthodox, and Anglican churches, a bishop ordains clergy and has authority over a diocese, an area with many congregations. See also *Cathedral*.

Bible Collected sacred writings of *Judaism* and *Christianity*; includes the Old and New Testaments.

Bod(d)hi In *Buddhism*, a person's *enlightenment* or "awakening" when he or she realizes the true nature of reality.

Bod(d)hisattva Enlightened existence. In *Mahayana Buddhism*, a being who could enter *nirvana* but chooses to be reborn to show others how to overcome suffering.

Bon Ancient indigenous spiritual tradition of Tibet, which may have influenced the development of *Tibetan Buddhism*. Elements of the early religion included shamanism and worship of divine kings and atmospheric deities; later Buddhist-influenced forms of Bon aim at ending suffering by attaining an enlightened state of unified consciousness called "rigpa". Around one in ten Tibetans still follow the Bon religion.

Book of the Dead Ancient Egyptian funerary text containing spells, sacred songs, and instructions to help a deceased individual in the afterlife. Often written on the walls of burial chambers and on papyri placed in burial chambers.

Bretons Indigenous Celtic people of Brittany in northwestern France.

Buddha Founder of *Buddhism*, ancient Indian spiritual teacher Siddhartha Gautama (circa 563–circa 483 B.C.). In some strands of Buddhism, a buddha is a person who has achieved *enlightenment*; also used to refer to a statue of a, or the, Buddha.

Buddhism Religious and philosophical tradition derived from teachings of the *Buddha*, according to whom the mind is all-important. Buddhists meditate to achieve a peaceful and lucid state of mind, believing that in this way they will be reborn after death at a higher level of being. Two main strands of Buddhism practiced widely in Asia are *Mahayana* and *Theravada*.

Caliph Successor to the *Prophet Muhammad* as civil and religious ruler of Muslims in the Islamic form of government called a caliphate.

Canonization In Roman Catholicism, the declaration of a deceased person as a *saint*. So-called because the person's name is entered in the canon (list of recognized saints).

Carillon Musical instrument with up to 47 bronze bells usually situated in the tower of a church or municipal building. Played from the main building with a keyboard and foot pedals; also played electronically.

Cathars or **Albigensians** Christian sect in southern France in the 11th–13th century. Forceful critics of priestly corruption, they were persecuted as heretics by the *Roman Catholic Church* in the Albigensian *Crusade* (1209–29). The Cathars continued fighting until 1255.

Cathedral Large Christian church that is the seat of (base for) a *bishop*.

Celts Ancient European peoples of pre-Roman times, speakers of Celtic languages.

Chancel Term used by Protestant Christians for the area around the altar for the use of clergy and choir. Roman Catholic and Orthodox Christians call this area the *sanctuary*.

Cherusci Germanic tribe who lived in the northern Rhine region in the 1st century B.C. to 1st century A.D.

Christ Pantocrator Christ in his guise as Almighty Ruler of All, or Ruler of the Universe, a popular image in Orthodox iconography. Pantocrator was the translation of the Hebrew title "El Shaddai" (God Almighty, all-sufficient) ascribed to Christ by early Christians.

Christianity Religion based on the life and teaching of Jesus of Nazareth (Jesus Christ), as recounted in the New Testament of the *Bible*. Christians believe Jesus to be the Son of God.

Cistercian Order Roman Catholic order of monks and nuns, established at Cîteaux Abbey, near Dijon, France, in 1098. The order returned to a literal obedience to the Rule of St. Benedict followed by the *Benedictine Orders*. Cistercians became very powerful in the *Roman Catholic Church* during the 12th century.

Cluniac Order Medieval Roman Catholic order of *Benedictine* monks, based at the Abbey of Cluny in eastern France, founded in 910 by Duke William of Aquitaine and a monk named Berno.

Codex Ancient or medieval bound manuscript book. The codex replaced the scroll.

Compline The last in the daily series of church services (offices), celebrated at the end of the working day. Also known as Night Prayer.

Confucianism Ancient Chinese political, moral, and religious system of thought based on the teachings of philosopher K'ung-fu-tzu, or Confucius (551–479 B.C.).

Congregational Church Protestant Christian denomination within which individual churches are self-governed by their congregations. Descended from 16th-century European Congregationalist churches: there were many Congregationalists among the Founding Fathers of the United States. Notable American colleges and universities such as Harvard, Yale, and Amherst were founded by Congregationalists.

Coptic Church Egypt's ancient Christian Church. It uses the Coptic language, which is descended from Ancient Egyptian.

Corpus Christi Christian festival celebrating the *Eucharist* or *Holy Communion*, in particular the identification of the bread or wafer used in the rite with the body of Christ (*corpus christi* in Latin). Celebrated on the Thursday, or sometimes the Sunday, after Trinity Sunday.

Crusades In general usage, a series of wars fought by western Christians against Muslim powers in the Middle East, 1095–1291. Crusades were also called against Muslims in Spain and Portugal, pagans in the Baltic area, and Christian heretics such as the *Cathars* in southern France and the Hussites in Bohemia.

Crypt Chamber or vault, often underground and beneath the floor of a church, used as a chapel or burial place.

Deacon In the Roman Catholic, Orthodox, and Anglican churches, the third level of ordained minister, beneath a *bishop* and *priest*. In some other Protestant churches, a deacon is a member of the laity (people who are not clergy) elected or appointed to take part in ministry.

Dravidian Native people of southern India; also refers to the languages they speak.

Easter The main festival of the Christian Church, celebrating Jesus Christ's Resurrection on the third day after he was crucified.

Ecumenical Adjective applied to movements or groups promoting the unity of the Christian Church.

Enlightenment In Indian religions, realization of the true nature of reality and experience. Also, an 18th-century intellectual movement advocating use of reason and promoting science.

Episcopal Church *Anglican Church* in the United States. The Scottish Episcopal Church is the Anglican Church in Scotland.

Eucharist Christian sacrament, also called *Holy Communion* by some Christians, commemorating Christ's last meal with his disciples before his crucifixion. For some Christians the Eucharist is the bread and wine received during the sacrament.

Franciscan Orders Roman Catholic religious orders that follow the rule established by St. Francis of Assisi in the 13th century.

Fresco Painting on fresh plaster on a wall or ceiling. Usually done with water-based pigments.

Gopuram Ornate tower standing at the entrance of an Indian temple, particularly in southern India. Also called "vimanam".

Gospels Any of four books of the New Testament that recount the life and teachings of Jesus Christ. The four Gospels are those of Matthew, Mark, Luke, and John; also the message about Christ, as in the Gospel of Judas.

Greek Orthodox Church Established church of Greece, part of the wider *Orthodox Church*. See also *Russian Orthodox Church*.

Hinduism Religious tradition with roots in ancient India. It has no founder or original teacher, and is often referred to as Sanatana Dharma (the Eternal Law). Some elements date back to the 6th millennium B.C.

Holy Communion Christian sacrament, also called the *Eucharist*, commemorating Christ's farewell meal—the Last Supper—with his disciples before his crucifixion. Centers on the blessing and sharing of bread (or wafers) and wine. When Jesus broke the bread, he said, "This is my body," and when he passed the wine, "This is my blood. Do this in remembrance of me."

Iconostasis In churches of Eastern Orthodox Christianity, an icon stand dividing the nave from the *sanctuary*.

Imam Leader of prayers in a mosque. In *Shiite Islam*, imams are also leaders of the religious community, believed to be divinely appointed.

Inca Native people of Peru who established an empire in the region in the 15th century.

Inquisition Tribunal established by the *Roman Catholic Church* to root out and suppress heresy.

Islam Religion based on the teachings of the sixth-century Arab *Prophet Muhammad*. Islam means "submission" and the religion calls for submission to the will of Allah (the Arabic term for God).

Jainism Religious tradition originating in ancient India, with roots at least as far back as the teacher Vardhamana or Mahavira ("Great Hero") in the 6th century B.C. Jains strive to practice "ahimsa" (avoiding injury to all living creatures).

Jesuit Member of the Roman Catholic religious order of the Society of Jesus. Jesuits are particularly known for educational work.

Judaism Religion of the Jewish people, with roots as far back as circa 2000 B.C. They believe in the one transcendent God, creator of all things, who revealed himself to Abraham, Moses, and the prophets. Religious practice follows the *Torah*, *Talmud*, and rabbinic traditions.

Koran or **Qur'an** The holy book of *Islam*. Muslims believe that the archangel Gabriel revealed the Koran to the *Prophet Muhammad*.

Kush Ancient civilization in Nile River valley (in what is now northern Sudan). At its height in the 3rd millennium B.C.

Last Judgment In Christian belief, Jesus Christ's judgment at the end of the world of all humans according to their earthly lives. A very popular subject for Christian religious art.

Liturgy Rituals of public worship, usually the words of a church service such as *Mass*.

Lutheranism Branch of Protestant *Christianity* descended from the teachings of German religious reformer Martin Luther (1483–1546). See also *Protestantism*.

Mahabharata Epic of Indian Sanskrit literature, composed circa 300 B.C.–circa A.D. 400 and, with nearly 100,000 couplets, the world's longest poem. It contains the Bhagavad Gita (Song of the Lord), one of *Hinduism*'s most sacred texts.

Mahayana Buddhism One of two influential strands of *Buddhism*, practiced in Japan, China, Tibet, Vietnam, and Korea. Mahayana Buddhists see the Buddhist's highest goal as becoming a *bodhisattva*. See also *bodhi*.

Mandala A symbolic representation of the universe, used for focusing attention and spiritual instruction, especially in *Hinduism* and *Buddhism*.

Mantra or **mantram** A spiritually charged word or phrase used to concentrate the attention in spiritual practices, especially in *Hinduism*, *Buddhism*, *Jainism*, and *Sikhism*.

Mass Celebration of the *Eucharist*, principally in the *Roman Catholic Church*. The Latin Mass is a traditional form celebrated prior to modernization in the 1960s. High Mass is the celebration of a traditional Latin Mass with incense and music, by a *priest*, *deacon*, and subdeacon; Low Mass is celebrated by a priest alone without music or incense. A Requiem Mass is a funeral mass.

Maya Native American civilization in *Mesoamerica*, at its height in circa 250–900 A.D.; or, in Indian religions, the divine creative power or the "illusion" of an individual's separateness from the created universe that prevents humans seeing reality as a divine unified whole.

Medicine wheels or **sacred hoops** An alignment of stones laid on the ground by Native Americans.

Mesoamerica Historical region in Middle America (including areas of Mexico, Guatemala, Honduras, Nicaragua, and Costa Rica) settled by Native American peoples in circa 12,000 B.C.–A.D. 1521. Culture of this region and period.

Methodism Branch of Protestant *Christianity*, its system and practices initiated by English preacher John Wesley (1703–91).

Mihrab Niche in wall of mosque indicating the direction of the Islamic holy city Mecca, which Muslims should face when praying.

Minaret Distinctive feature of a mosque, a tall, slender tower, usually freestanding, from which the faithful are called to prayer.

Minbar Pulpit in a mosque, from where an *imam* (prayer leader) gives his sermons.

Monstrance Vessel used to display the consecrated Host (sacramental bread) to the congregation in Roman Catholic and Anglican churches.

Muezzin Person who calls Muslims to their five daily prayers from the *minaret* of a mosque.

Native American religions Religious ceremonies and spiritual practices of Native American peoples, many centered on honoring the natural world.

Nirvana In *Buddhism* and *Jainism*, attainment of *enlightenment* and release from suffering and the cycle of reincarnation. The word means "blowing out" in the ancient Indian language Sanskrit.

Oculus Architectural feature: either a small, round or oval window, or a circular opening at the apex of a dome.

Orthodox Church Second largest Christian church (after Roman Catholicism). Disagreements over beliefs and rituals led to a split from the *Roman Catholic Church* in 1054. Includes the *Russian Orthodox Church*, *Greek Orthodox Church*, and others.

Orthodox Judaism Branch of Jewish faith that adheres to the Law of Moses as found in the *Torah* and expounded in the *Talmud* and other texts.

Patriarch A *bishop* in the *Orthodox Church*.

Pentecost Also known as Whitsunday, Christian festival celebrated 50 days after Jesus' death when the Holy Spirit descended on the Apostles, as described in the Acts of the Apostles in the New Testament of the *Bible*. It corresponds to the Jewish festival of Shavuot.

Pope The *bishop* of Rome, and spiritual leader and head of the *Roman Catholic Church*; believed to be the successor of St. Peter.

Prayer wheel In *Tibetan Buddhism* a small wheel marked with prayers and *mantra*. Spinning the wheel, for example in the wind, is said to be as effective as reciting the prayers.

Priest Person with authority to perform religious rituals. In Roman Catholic, Orthodox, and Anglican Christianity, the second level of ordained minister, beneath a *bishop* and above a *deacon*.

Prophet Muhammad Arab founder of *Islam*, lived circa 570–632. Believed by Muslims to be the Messenger and Prophet of Allah (God).

Protestantism Broadly speaking, any Christian faith not of the *Roman Catholic Church* or *Orthodox Church*; includes, among others, the Anglican, Calvinist, Lutheran, Methodist, and Baptist faiths.

Pulpit A small raised platform, often enclosed with very ornate carving and set against a pillar, from which the sermon is delivered in a church or *cathedral* during a Christian service.

Psalter Book containing the biblical Psalms and often other sacred material. Many medieval psalters were made as illuminated manuscripts.

Pueblo people Native American people from what is now the southwestern United States.

Quechua people Native American people from the Andean highlands in South America. They were subjugated by the *Inca*. Quechua also describes the languages of the region.

Ramayana Ancient Indian Sanskrit epic poem, composed circa 200 B.C.–circa A.D. 200. Recounts story of Prince Rama, believed to be a form of the Hindu god Vishnu, and is viewed as scripture.

Rastafari Religious and political movement followed predominantly by groups in the black population of Jamaica and other countries. Rastafarians (or Rastas) revere Ethiopian Emperor Haile Selassie I (1892-1975) as an incarnation of God. The term Rastafari is preferred to Rastafarianism by its followers.

Reformation Revolution in European religion in the 16th century, centered on calls for reform of the *Roman Catholic Church*. Led to the emergence of Protestant Christianity.

Relics Bodily remains of a *saint* or objects that have been used by a saint. A reliquary is an often splendid container used to hold a relic.

Rinzai school Tradition in Japanese *Zen Buddhism* that emphasizes sudden awakening to *enlightenment*. Founded in China in the 9th century and established in Japan in the 12th century.

Roman Catholic Church World's largest Christian church. Members accept the *Pope* in Vatican City as the highest earthly authority.

Russian Orthodox Church Russian-based branch of the *Orthodox Church*.

Saint Individual of exemplary conduct, often a worker of miracles. Usually deceased, may be biblical, historical, or mythical. Some Christians believe saints have power to answer prayers. Saints are revered in *Hinduism* and other religious traditions as well as in *Christianity*.

Sanctuary Consecrated area around the altar in the Roman Catholic and Orthodox churches. See also *Chancel*.

Sephardic Jews Jews whose ancestors and traditions originated in the Iberian peninsula (modern Spain and Portugal) and North Africa. See also *Ashkenazic Jews*.

Shiite Islam Minority branch of *Islam*, also known as Shia. Shiites believe that the *Prophet Muhammad*'s son-in-law Ali was his rightful successor and reject the authority of the first four caliphs or successors to the Prophet. Shiites developed their own distinctive religious traditions, with an *imam* leading the community. Around 15 percent of Muslims worldwide are Shiites. See also *Sunni Islam*.

Shingon Buddhism Branch of Japanese *Buddhism*, introduced from China in the 9th century by the monk Kobo Daishi. Emphasizes use of gesture, mystical words, and meditation to access the essence of the teachings of the *Buddha*.

Shinto or **Shintoism** Indigenous religion of Japan, often called "The Way of the Gods." Centered on worship of kami (spirits).

Shrine A place for devotion, or sacred place containing a reliquary or a tomb.

Sikhism Religion derived from the teachings of Guru Nanak Dev (1469–1539) and his nine successors. Sikhs seek salvation through living a virtuous life and meditation on the name of God. The religion's holy book is the Adi Granth.

Stupa In Buddhist countries, a mound containing the relics of a *Buddha* or *saint*. A stupa is a *mandala* as well as a reliquary—devotees trace their steps around the mound in a religiously significant symbolic pattern.

Sunni Islam Mainstream branch of *Islam*. Sunni Muslims accept the authority of the first four caliphs (successors to the *Prophet Muhammad*). Around 85 percent of Muslims worldwide are Sunni. See also *Shiite Islam*.

Synod Church council gathered to rule on doctrine or administration.

Synoptic Gospels The first three of the four Gospels in the New Testament of the *Bible*, those of Matthew, Mark, and Luke, which recount the life and teachings of Jesus Christ and are very similar in content and structure. The fourth New Testament Gospel, that of John, differs in that it gives a variant chronology of Jesus' life, presents him as Christ the exalted Lord from the very beginning, and includes personal, meditative discourses on different themes.

Talmud Written record of the oral traditions and law of *Judaism* that complements the *Torah*. The Talmud comprises the Mishnah (circa A.D. 200) and the Gemara (circa A.D. 500). They contain commentaries, explanations, and debates on many aspects of Jewish life and belief.

Taoism or **Daoism** Ancient Chinese religious and philosophical tradition. A key text is the Tao Te Ching, traditionally written in the 6th century B.C. by the sage Lao Tzu.

Ten Commandments Religious imperatives listed in the books of Exodus and Deuteronomy in the Old Testament of the *Bible*, recognized by both Jews and Christians.

Tendai Buddhism Japanese school of *Mahayana Buddhism*, imported from China in the 8th century A.D. Adapts *Buddhism* to *Shintoism* and Japanese culture.

Theravada Buddhism Strand of *Buddhism* dominant in Cambodia, Thailand, Sri Lanka, and Myanmar (Burma). Theravada Buddhists see the highest goal as becoming an arhat (*saint*) and entering *nirvana*.

Tibetan Buddhism Strand of *Buddhism* dominant in Tibet, and in the Himalaya. It is a branch of *Mahayana Buddhism*.

Toltec People of central Mexico, revered by the *Aztecs* as ancestors, who ranged over central Mexico from the 10th to the 12th century.

Torah First five books of the Hebrew *Bible*: Genesis, Exodus, Leviticus, Numbers, and Deuteronomy. Jews believe them to be the Word of God. Also known as the Pentateuch.

Transfiguration Transformation of Jesus Christ described in the *Synoptic Gospels* (Matthew, Mark, and Luke). On a high mountain Jesus became radiant with light, spoke with the prophets Moses and Elijah, and was addressed as "Son" by God.

Trappists Branch of the *Cistercian Order*, officially called the Order of Cistercians of the Strict Observance. The familiar name derived from the Abbey of La Trappe in Normandy, France, where the order was founded in 1664. Trappists are monks; nuns are called Trappistines. The austere, reformed Rule (monastic code of behavior) that they follow includes a vow of silence.

Trinity Sunday Celebration of the Christian doctrine of God as Father, Son, and Holy Spirit. Celebrated in western Christian churches on the first Sunday after Pentecost, and in eastern churches on Pentecost Sunday.

Universalism Religious outlook holding that all creatures have a connection to God; sometimes the conviction that all religions are of equal standing. In Christian theology, the belief that all creatures will be reconciled to God through the life and actions of Jesus Christ.

Vespers Service of early evening prayers in Christian churches, the sixth of seven appointed hours for prayer.

Vigils Nighttime service of prayer, particularly observed in ancient *Christianity*; now often recited at daybreak with the next service, lauds.

Virgin Mary The mother of Jesus Christ, believed by most Christians to have been a virgin despite having conceived and given birth to Jesus.

Yogi In Indian religions, a person who practices meditation and spiritual disciplines.

Zen Buddhism Branch of *Mahayana Buddhism* practiced in Japan and marked by its stress on maintaining mindfulness (full consciousness) of the present, and on acting with spontaneity.

Zoroastrianism Major ancient religion established by Iranian prophet Zoroaster in the 6th century B.C., centered on the worship of one God, Ahura Mazda ("Wise Lord"). Probably the first monotheistic religion, and may have influenced the later religions of *Judaism*, *Christianity*, and *Islam*. Zoroastrianism survives in modern Iran and India. There are around 200,000 Zoroastrians worldwide. In India they are called Parsis.

ENTRIES BY RELIGION

INDEX

Acknowledgments

Authors

Jill Anderson
Lisa Armstrong
Steven Baker
Eleanor Berman
Monica Bhide
Hannah Bowen
Mary Frances Budzik
Kim Burstein
Riazat Butt
Karryn Cartelle
Marolyn Charpentier
Kathy Chin Leong
Helen Douglas-Cooper
Denise Dube
William Dupont
Polly Evans
Kay Fernandez
Mary Frances Budzik
Paul Franklin
Ellen Galford
Robin Gauldie
Dan Gilpin
Margie Goldsmith
Ruth Ellen Gruber
Lisa Halvorsen
Solange Hando
John Haywood
Randy B. Hecht
Tom Jackson
Laura Kearney
Andrew Kerr-Jarrett
Judy Kirkwood
Tom Le Bas
Susan McKee
Anne McKenna
Antony Mason
Nancy Mikula
Peter Neville-Hadley
Theresa Pasqual
Bethanne Patrick
Zoe Ross
Richard Rubin
Sathya Saran
Amy Smith
Peter Sommers
David St Vincent
Linda Tagliaferro
Alex Talavera (translated by Randy B. Hecht)
Pat Tanumipaja
Jenny Waddell
Joby Williams
Joe Yogerst

Picture Credits

Abbreviations:
GI (Getty Images); LPI (Lonely Planet Images); RH (Robert Harding).

1 Left to right: Anwar Hussein/EMPICS Entertainment/PA Photos; Andre Jenny/Alamy; Jon Arnold Images/Photolibrary Group; Mike Norton/Shutterstock; joSon/GI; Jon Arnold Images/Photolibrary Group. **2-3** Hoberman Collection/Corbis. **4** Chung Sung-Jun/GI. **5** David Carriere/Photolibrary Group (1); Nevada Wier/Corbis (2); Schmid Reinhard/4Corners (3); Steve Vidler/Photolibrary Group (4); Francesco Venturi/Corbis (5); Michael Freeman/Corbis (6); Zainal Abd Halim/Corbis (7); Nevada Wier/Corbis (8); Rob Bourdreau/GI (9); © Paul Beinssen/LPI (10). **6** Ahmad Al-Rubaye/GI. **8-9** Index Stock Imagery/Photolibrary Group. **10** WorldFoto/Alamy. **11** Bill Ross/Corbis. **12** Tim Harris/GI. **13** George H. H. Huey/Corbis, L; Buddy Mays/Corbis,R. **14** David Muench/Corbis. **15** Chris Rodenberg Photography/Shutterstock. **16** Alaska Stock Images/Photolibrary Group. **17** Tim Heacox/GI. **19** Gallo Images/Corbis. **20** Larry Neubauer/Corbis. **21** Carolyn Brown/GI. **22** F1 Online/Alamy. **23** Joe Blit/Shutterstock. **25** Al Rod/Corbis. **26** Sam Stearman. **27** Lowell Georgia/Corbis. **28** The Travel Library/Rex Features. **29** Australian Only/Paul Nevin/Photolibrary Group. **30** Kazuyoshi Nomachi/Corbis. **31** Kazuyoshi Nomachi/Corbis, L; Edward North/Alamy, R. **32** John Carnemolla/Australian Picture/Corbis. **33** Larry Williams/zefa/Corbis. **34** Tomas del Amo / Alamy. **35** © David Wall/LPI, L; © Michael Gebicki/LPI, R. **36** Fred Bruemmer / Still Pictures. **37** Jon Arnold Images / Alamy. **38** Vanni Archive/Corbis. **39** Reza Webistan/Corbis. **41** Hiroshi Ichikawa/Shutterstock. **42** Fridmar Damm/zefa/Corbis. **43** imagebroker/Alamy. **44-45** Nevada Wier/Corbis. **46** © Jim Wark/LPI. **47** Yann Arthus Bertrand/Corbis. **48** Gordon Galbraith/Shutterstock. **49** Pacific Stock/Photolibrary Group. **50** JTB Photo/Photolibrary Group. **51** Colman Lerner Gerado/Shutterstock, L; World Pictures/Alamy,R. **52** Michael Zysman/Shutterstock. **53** N.J.Saunders/Werner Forman Archive. **55** Anders Blomqvist/Photolibrary Group. **56** Jarno Gonzalez Zarraonandia/Shutterstock. **57** JTB Photo/Photolibrary Group. **58** Yann Arthus-Bertrand/Corbis. **59** Douglas Peebles/Corbis. **60** F1 Online/Photolibrary Group. **61** Jose Alberto Tejo/Shutterstock. **62** Colin Brynn/RH. **63** Vladimir Sidoropolev. **64** Index Stock Imagery/Photolibrary Group. **65** Charles Bowman/RH. **66** Jon Arnold Images/Photolibrary Group. **67** Lindsay Hebberd/Corbis, L; Mauritius/Die Bildagentur/Photolibrary Group, R. **68** Photononstop/Photolibrary Group. **69** Ken Gillham/RH. **70** © Patrick Syder/LPI. **71** Hans Georg Roth/Corbis. **72** Taxi/Vincenzo Lombardo/GI. **73** Sergio Pitamitz/Corbis. **74** Laura Frenkel/Shutterstock. **75** Fridmar Damm/zefa/Corbis. **76** Patrick Dieudonne/RH. **77** Skyscan/Corbis. **79** JTB Photo/Photolibrary Group. **80** Adam Woolfitt/RH. **81** Jane O'Callaghan/RH. **82** Michael Freeman/Corbis. **83** McPhoto/Still Pictures. **84-85** SIME/Schmid Reinhard/4Corners. **86** Philip Scalia/Alamy. **87** JTB Photo/Photolibrary Group. **89** © The Board of Trinity College, Dublin, Ireland/The Bridgeman Art Library. **90** Panorama Media (Beijing)/Photolibrary Group. **91** Dinodia/Art Directors. **92** Rob Howard/Corbis. **93** Craig Lovell/Corbis, L; Steve Allen Travel Photograph/Alamy, R. **94** Pep Roi/Alamy. **95** AP Photo/PA Photos. **96** SIME/Grafenhain Gunter/4Corners. **97** Kim Berstein. **99** Suzanne Held/akg-images, London. **100** E Simanor/Robert Harding/Corbis. **101** Alvaro Barrientos/AP/PA Photos. **102** Photographer's Choice/Sylvain Grandadam/GI. **103** Sandro Vannini/Corbis. **104** AMR NABIL/AP/PA Photos. **105** Andrew Holt/Alamy. **106** Israel Images/Alamy. **107** © Peter Ptschelinzew/LPI. **109** De Agostini/GI. **110** Yann Arthus Bertrand/Corbis. **111** akg-images, London. **112-113** Steve Vidler/Imagestate/Photolibrary Group. **114** Vladimir Korostyshevkiy/Shutterstock. **115** Anthony Cassidy/Photographer's Choice/GI. **116** Steve Vidler/Imagestate/Photolibrary Group. **117** Weibiao Hu/Panorama Stock/Photolibrary Group. **118** Radius Images/Photolibrary Group. **119** Photoshot, L; Christian Kober/RH, R. **120** Mustafiz Mamun/Majority World/Still Pictures. **121** © Chris Mellor/LPI. **122** JTB Photo/Photolibrary Group. **123** Hemis/Photolibrary Group. **124** © Richard I'Anson/LPI. **125** Luca Tettoni/Corbis, L; Lindsay Hebberd/Corbis, R. **127** Christophe Boisvieux/Corbis. **128** JTB Photo/Photolibrary Group. **129** AP Photo/Burhan Ozbilici/PA Photos. **130** Gianni Dagli Orti/The Art Archive. **131** Joseph Calev/Shutterstock. **132** Ruth Ellen Gruber. **133** Arcangel Images/Marco Scataglini/Photolibrary Group. **134** Travel Library/RH. **135** Richard Wadey/Alamy, L; Sandro Vannini/Corbis, R. **136** De Richemond/Andia/Still Pictures. **137** AA World Travel Library/TopFoto. **138-139** Francesco Venturi/Corbis. **140** Bob Krist/Corbis. **141** Ethel Davies/RH. **143** Andre Jenny/ Alamy. **144** Catherine Karnow/Corbis. **145** Philippe Eranian/Corbis. **146** Peter Adams/Jon Arnold Images/Photolibrary Group. **147** Peter Adams/Jon Arnold Images/Photolibrary Group. **148** Tibor Bognar/Art Directors. **149** Christophe Boisvieux/Corbis. **150** JTB Photo/Photolibrary Group. **151** Lonely Planet Images / Martin Moos, L; Helene Rogers/Art Directors, R. **152** Axiom Photographic Agency/Mark Thomas/GI. **153** National Geographic/Paul Chesley/GI. **154** Wolfgang Kaehler/Corbis. **155** F1 Online/ URF/Photolibrary Group. **156** K M Chaudhry/AP/PA Photos. **157** Michele Falzone/Alamy, L; Ed Kashi/Corbis, R. **158** © Ryan Fox/LPI. **159** Ellen Rooney/RH. **160** Andrew McConnell / Alamy. **161** Authors Image/RH. **162** SIME/Da Ros Luca/4Corners. **163** Index Stock Imagery Michele Burgess/Photolibrary Group. **164** F1 Online/Colorvision/Photolibrary Group. **165** Jose Fuste Raga/Corbis. **166** Rex Allen / Alamy. **167** Photoshot. **168** Nathan Benn/Corbis. **169** © Richard Nebesky/LPI, L/R. **170** Melvyn Longhurst/Alamy. **171** © age fotostock/SuperStock. **173** Richard Ashworth/Robert Harding World Imagery/Corbis. **174** Thomas David Pinzer / Alamy. **175** Photoshot. **176** Jozsef Toth/Rex Features. **177** Guenter Rossenbach/zefa/Corbis. **179** Bernard O'Kane/Alamy. **180** Photoshot. **181** JTB Photo/Photolibrary Group. **182** CuboImages/RH. **183** Jon Arnold Images/Photolibrary Group. **185** Scrovegni Chapel Padua/Alfredo Dagli Orti/The Art Archive. **186** Photoshot. **187** Fred de Noyelle /Godong/Corbis, L; SIME/Baviera Guido/4Corners, R. **188** Photoshot. **189** SIME/Ripani Massimo/4Corners. **191** Sonia Halliday Photographs. **192** Craig Thomas/Index Stock Imagery/Photolibrary Group. **193** Photoshot. **194** Travel Library/RH. **195** SIME/Giovanni Simeone/4Corners. **196** Michael Nicholson/Corbis. **197** Photoshot, L; Liquid Light/Alamy, R. **198** Gavin Hellier/JAI/Corbis. **199** LEPETIT Christophe/Hemis/Photolibrary Group. **200-201** Michael Freeman/Corbis. **202** Franklin Viola/Photolibrary Group. **203** William S Kuta/Alamy. **204** Robert Harding/Photolibrary Group. **205** Robert Harding/Photolibrary group, L; Mireille Vautier, R. **206** Reuters/Corbis. **207** Tony Morrison/South American Pictures. **208** Everett Kennedy Brown/epa/Corbis. **209** Chris Rennie/ArkReligion.com. **210** © Krzysztof Dydynski/LPI. **211** Robert Preston/Alamy, L; Photoshot, R. **212** Indiapicture/Anand/Alamy. **213** Jeremy Bright/RH. **214** Bruno Morandi/Reportage/GI. **215** Bruno Norandi/Reportage/GI. **216** Christopher Rennie/RH. **217** Geoffrey Morgan/Alamy. **218** Michael Good/ArkReligion.com. **219** Robert Harding. **220** Gary Cook/RH. **221** Photoshot. **222** Cologne Cathedral, Germany/The Bridgeman Art Library. **223** Robert Harding/Yadid Levy/Photolibrary Group, L; Heiko Specht/VISUM/Still Pictures, R. **225** Daryl Benson/Photographer's Choice/GI. **226** Gianni Dagli Orti/The Art Archive. **227** San Francesco, Assisi, Italy, Giraudon/The Bridgeman Art Library. **228** Paul Raftery/Photolibrary Group. **229** Christophe Boisvieux/Corbis. **230** Reuters/Corbis. **232** Photoshot. **233** Tibor Bognar/ArkReligion.com. **234-235** Zainal Abd Halim/Reuters/Corbis. **236** Jonathan Blair/Corbis. **237** David Alan Harvey/National Geographic Image Collection. **238** Ricardo Siqueira/BrazilPhotos/Alamy. **239** Eliseo Fernandez/Reuters/Corbis. **240** Kazuyoshi Nomachi/Corbis. **241** Ira Block/National Geographic/GI, L; Kazuyoshi Nomachi/Corbis, R. **242** DAJ/GI. **243** JTB Photo/Photolibrary Group. **244** Travel Ink/GI. **245** Chinju/digipix/Alamy. **246** Pep Roig/Alamy. **247** Oriental Touch/RH, L; Hugh Sitton/GI, R. **248** SIME/Johanna Huber/4Corners. **249** Faleh Kheiber/Reuters/Corbis. **250** Arcangel Images/Tal Paz-Fridman/Photolibrary Group. **251** Gali Tibbon/AFP/GI. **252** Gali Tibbon/AFP/GI. **253** Das Fotoarchiv./Still Pictures. **255** Axiom Photographic Agency/Mark Thomas/GI. **256** Behrouz Mehri/AFP/GI. **257** Photoshot. **258** Ariadne Van Zandbergen/Alamy. **259** SIME/Johanna Huber/4Corners. **260** Gary Cook/RH. **261** Betermin/Andia/Still Pictures. **262** SIME/Giovanni Simeone/4Corners. **263** Anthony Pilling/Alamy, L; Funkytravel London/Paul Williams/Alamy,R. **264** Pascal Deloche/Godong/Corbis. **265** R H Productions/RH. **266-267** Nevada Wier/Corbis. **268** José Patricio/Acoma Pueblo. **269** © Emily Riddell/LPI. **270** AP Photo/Ramakanta Dey/PA Photos. **271** AP Photo/Colin Reid/PA Photos. **272** Jose Luis Jeronimo/AFP/GI. **273** Jose Luis Jeronimo/AFP/GI. **274** Jorge Silva/Reuters/Corbis. **275** Tony Morrison/South American Pictures. **276** Walter Hupiú/epa/Corbis. **277** John Lander/Alamy. **279** AP Photo/Silvia Izquierdo/PA Photos. **280** JTB Photo/Photolibrary Group. **281** Kazuhiro Nogi/AFP/GI. **282** Kim Kyung-Hoon/Reuters/Corbis. **283** Jay Directo/AFP/GI. **284** AP Photo/Wally Santana/PA Photos. **285** Ian Trower/Alamy, L; Pat Behnke/Alamy, R. **286** Ahmad Yusni/epa/Corbis. **287** Patrick Ward/Corbis. **288** Blaine Harrington III/Alamy. **289** The Image Bank/Philip Kramer/GI. **290** Superstock. **291** Raj Patidar/Reuters/Corbis,L; Radhika Chalasani/Corbis, R. **292** Jayanta Shaw/Reuters/Corbis. **293** Dinodia/Art Directors. **294** AP Photo/Ariel Schalit/PA Photos. **295** Anwar Hussein/EMPICS Entertainment/PA Photos. **296** Kevin Galvin/Alamy. **297** Susan Frost/Alamy, L; Michael Dalder/Reuters/Corbis, R. **298** Picture Contact/Alamy. **299** Apneaworld. **301** E Simanor/RH. **302** Photoshot. **303** Arturo Mari/Osservatore Romano/AFP/GI. **305** Vanderlei Almeida/AFP/GI. **306** Marco Di Lauro/GI. **307** SIME/Da Ros Luca/4Corners. **308** Photo by Haga Library/JTB Photo/Photolibrary Group. **309** Marco Di Lauro/GI. **310-311** Rob Boudreau/GI. **312** All Canada Photos/Alamy. **313** Larry Downing/Reuters/Corbis. **314** © Lee Foster/LPI. **315** Photoshot,R; Nigel Hudson Photography/Alamy, R. **316** Richard A. Cooke/Corbis. **317** David Muench/Corbis. **319** eStock/Pictures Colour Library. **320** Layne Kennedy/Corbis. **321** David Seawell/Corbis. **322** Odyssey/RH. **323** Martin Barlow/ArkReligion.com. **325** SIME/Ripani Massimo/4Corners. **326** JTB Photo/Photolibrary Group. **327** R H Productions/RH. **328** Tobor Bognar/ArkReligion.com. **329** Liu Xiaoyang/China Images/Alamy,L; James Nesterwitz, R. **330** Bob Krist/Corbis. **331** Colin Gibson/Ark Religion.com. **332** Dean Conger/Corbis. **333** Peter Adams/GI. **334** Boris Saktsier (b.1942).Korczak and the Ghetto's Children,1978. Cast bronze. Collection of the Yad Vashem Art Museum, Jerusalem. Gift of Mila Brenner and Ya'acov Meridor/Dave G. Houser/Corbis. **335** Nandor Glid (1924-1997). Memorial to the Victims of the Concentration and Extermination Camps, 1979. Cast bronze. Collection of the Yad Vashem Art Museum, Jerusalem. Gift of the artist. **336** Nordicphotos/Alamy. **337** Photoshot. **338** Momatiuk-Eastcott/Corbis. **339** Radim Beznoska/isifa/GI. **340** Ruth Ellen Gruber. **341** Steven Weinberg/National Geographic Image Collection **342** Alfredo Dagli Orti/The Art Archive. **343** Michel Setboun/Corbis. **344** Werner Forman Archive. **345** Peter Barritt/Alamy. **346** Araldo de Luca/Corbis. **347** Travel Library/RH. 348 Photoshot. **349** Clement Guillaume/The Bridgeman Art Library, L; Alan Copson/JAI/Corbis, R. **350** Jon Hicks/Corbis. **351** The Irish Image Collection/Corbis. **352** Ellen Rooney/RH. **353** Gianni Dagli Orti/The Art Archive, L; Pharaonic Village Cairo/Gianni Dagli Orti/The Art Archive, R. **354-355** © Paul Beinssen/LPI. **356** Courtesy of gampoabbey.org. **357** 2007 L.E.Halfpenny/Bhavana Society. **358** Harbin Hot Spring/Ann Prehn. **359** Koichi Kamoshida/GI. **360** Jon Arnold Images/Demetrio Carrasco/Photolibrary Group. **361** Tibor Bognar/ArkReligion.com, L; Jochen Schlenker/RH, R. **362** Photo by Haga Library/JTB Photo/ /Photolibrary Group. **363** © Holger Leue/LPI. **364** Dennis Cox/Alamy. **365** Shona and William Townend. **366** © Wes Walker/LPI. **367** Angelo Cavalli/RH, L; © Lindsay Brown/LPI, R. **369** Tibor Bognar/ArkReligion.com. **370** Don Smith/RH. **371** Christophe Boisvieux/Corbis. **372** Jon Arnold Images/Alamy. **373** PCL/Alamy, L; Olaf Meinhardt/transit/Still Pictures, R. **374** Wolfgang Kaehler/Corbis. **375** Buddy Mays/Corbis. **376** Vittoriano Rastelli/Corbis. **377** Christophe Boisvieux/Corbis. **378** Henri Gaud/CIRIC/ArkReligion.com. **379** Photononstop/Photolibrary Group, L; Photoshot, R. **380** Gideon Mendel/Corbis. **381** Geoff Renner/RH. **382** Peter Terry/ArkReligion. **383** Manor Photography/Alamy. **384** David Lomax/RH. **385** Biosphoto/Menghini Julien/Still Pictures, L; Patrick. Dieudonne/RH, R. **386** James McClean/Alamy. **387** Sean Sprague/Still Pictures.

Front Cover
Background Image: Paul Thompson Images/Alamy
Picture strip, left to right: Anwar Hussein/PA Photos; Andre Jenny/Alamy; Jon Arnold Images/Photolibrary Group; Mike Norton/Shutterstock; joSon/GI; Jon Arnold Images/Photolibrary Group.

Back Cover
Background Image: Paul Thompson Images/Alamy
Picture strip, left to right: Atlantide Phototravel/Massimo Borchi/Corbis; Das Fotoarchive/Still Pictures; Martin Harvey/Corbis; Daryl Benson/GI; Kim Kyung-Hoon/Corbis; salamanderman/Shutterstock.

Spine: Hiroshi Ichikawa/Shutterstock

Sacred Places of a Lifetime

Published by the National Geographic Society

John M. Fahey, Jr., President and Chief Executive Officer

Gilbert M. Grosvenor, Chairman of the Board

Tim T. Kelly, President, Global Media Group

John Q. Griffin, President, Publishing

Nina D. Hoffman, Executive Vice President; President,
Book Publishing Group

Prepared by the Book Division

Kevin Mulroy, Senior Vice President and Publisher

Leah Bendavid-Val, Director of Photography Publishing and
Illustrations

Marianne R. Koszorus, Director of Design

Barbara Brownell Grogan, Executive Editor

Elizabeth Newhouse, Director of Travel Publishing

Carl Mehler, Director of Maps

Lawrence M. Porges, Project Manager

Carol Farrar Norton, Design Consultant

Anne Marie Houppert, Karin Kinney, Mary Stephanos,
Contributors

Jennifer Thornton, Managing Editor

R. Gary Colbert, Production Director

Manufacturing and Quality Management

Christopher A. Liedel, Chief Financial Officer

Phillip L. Schlosser, Vice President

Chris Brown, Technical Director

Nicole Elliott, Manager

Monika D. Lynde, Manager

Rachel Faulise, Manager

Created by Toucan Books Ltd

Ellen Dupont, Editorial Director

Helen Douglas-Cooper, Senior Editor

Barbara Bonser, Jo Bourne, Hannah Bowen, Cecile Landau,
Alice Peebles, David St Vincent, Editors

Tom Pocklington, Editorial Assistant

Leah Germann, Designer

Christine Vincent, Picture Manager

Tam Church, Marian Pullen, Picture Researchers

Marion Dent, Proofreader

Michael Dent, Indexer

The information in this book has been carefully checked and is, to the best
of our knowledge, accurate as of press time. It's always advisable to call
ahead, however, as details are subject to change. The National Geographic
Society cannot be responsible for any changes, or for errors or omissions.

Founded in 1888, the National Geographic Society is
one of the largest nonprofit scientific and educational
organizations in the world. It reaches more than 285
million people worldwide each month through its
official journal, *National Geographic*, and its four
other magazines; the National Geographic Channel;
television documentaries; radio programs; films; books;
videos and DVDs; maps; and interactive media. National
Geographic has funded more than 8,000 scientific
research projects and supports an education program
combating geographic illiteracy.

For more information, please call
1-800-NGS LINE (647-5463)
or write to the following address:

National Geographic Society
1145 17th Street N.W.
Washington, D.C. 20036-4688 U.S.A.

Visit us online at
www.nationalgeographic.com/books

For information about special discounts for bulk purchases,
please contact National Geographic Books Special Sales:
ngspecsales@ngs.org

For rights or permissions inquiries,
please contact National Geographic Books
Subsidiary Rights: ngbookrights@ngs.org

LIBRARY OF CONGRESS CATALOGING-IN-PUBLICATION DATA

Sacred places of a lifetime : 500 of the world's most peaceful and powerful
destinations / introduction by Keith Bellows.
    p. cm.
  Includes index.
  ISBN 978-1-4262-0336-7 (hardcover)
  1. Sacred space.
  BL580.S235 2008
  203'.5--dc22

                                    2008021396
Printed in China